La Chulla Vida

Gender and Globalization
Susan S. Wadley, *Series Editor*

Syracuse University Press is pleased to announce the inauguration of a new series, Gender and Globalization, with Susan S. Wadley, Ford Maxwell Professor of South Asian Studies, Maxwell School of Citizenship and Public Affairs, Syracuse University, as its editor. This series aims to create a greater awareness of the gendered nature of economic, political, social, and cultural processes associated with globalization, in particular the increasing flow of capital, labor, and information across national boundaries. Books in Gender and Globalization will examine not only formal, state-based mechanisms such as law where injustices associated with globalization processes have been addressed but also the informal, everyday means deployed by men and women to cope with, accommodate, redress, and resist the changed lifestyles and injustices associated with globalization.

All persons interested in submitting manuscripts-in-progress, book proposals for monographs, edited volumes, or text-oriented manuscripts for this series should contact Professor Wadley at sswadley@maxwell.syr.edu or Mary Selden Evans, Executive Editor, Syracuse University Press, Syracuse N.Y. 13244 msevans@syr.edu.

La Chulla Vida

*Gender, Migration, and the Family in
Andean Ecuador and New York City*

Jason Pribilsky

Syracuse University Press

First Edition 2007

07   08   09   10   11   12   6   5   4   3   2   1

The paper used in this publication meets the minimum requirements
of American National Standard for Information Sciences—Permanence
of Paper for Printed Library Materials, ANSI. Z39.48–1984.∞™

For a listing of books published and distributed by Syracuse University Press,
visit our Web site at SyracuseUniversityPress.syr.edu.

ISBN-13: 978-0-8156-3119-4 (cloth); 978-0-8156-3145-3 (pbk.)
ISBN-10: 0-8156-3119-7 (cloth); 0-8156-3145-6 (pbk.)

Library of Congress Cataloging-in-Publication Data

Pribilsky, Jason.
   La chulla vida : gender, migration, and
the family in Andean Ecuador and New York City /
Jason Pribilsky. — 1st ed.
      p. cm. — (Gender and globalization)
   Includes bibliographical references and index.
   ISBN 978-0-8156-3119-4 (hardcover : alk. paper)
   ISBN 978-0-8156-3145-3 (pbk. : alk. paper)
   1. Ecuadorian Americans—New York (State)—
New York—Social conditions. 2. Ecuadorian
Americans—New York (State)—New York—
Economic conditions. 3. Ecuadorians—Migrations.
4. Azuay Region (Ecuador)—Social conditions.
5. Sex role—Ecuador—Azuay Region. 6. Family—
Ecuador—Azuay Region. 7. New York (N.Y.)—
Social conditions. 8. Sex role—New York (State)—
New York. 9. Family—New York (State)—New York.
10. Transnationalism. I. Title.

F128.9.E28P75 2007
305.897'086624—dc22   2007014598

Manufactured in the United States of America

 *For Suzanne*

Jason Pribilsky is assistant professor of anthropology at Whitman College in Washington State.

Contents

Illustrations

ix

Figures, Tables, and Maps

Preface

This book is about transnational labor migration, gendered identities, and the remaking of families in the Ecuadorian Andes and New York City. It is an ethnographic account of the ways young men and women in these two locales—intimately connected through globalization—have ordered their lives toward the priorities of living a transnational existence. At the same time, it also conforms to the standards of a typical village study, looking at the effects of gender, generation, and new forms of wealth in a single Andean community.

For many of the people whose lives it chronicles, however, it is simply the story of *la chulla vida*: "Así es la chulla vida" (It's just the *chulla vida*). Over the course of fieldwork in rural villages of highland Ecuador, as well as in Queens, New York, how many times and in how many places did I encounter this phrase? Capping villagers' stories of barely making ends meet and the necessities of migration? In newspaper quotes? In the spray-painted graffiti that covers the stuccoed exteriors of buildings in Cuenca's colonial center? Scribbled on a note sent by a migrant in New York to his family in Ecuador? The translation of the expression is deceptively simple. The phrase is often used to capture the sense of "That is how life is," or perhaps "You have only one life to live," or even "There is only one life to leave." Such translations, although correct, just begin to capture the phrase's rich meaning.

Chulla, or more precisely *shuj lla*, is a Quichua word that has crept its way into the local register of Azuayo-Cañari Spanish.[1] For nonindigenous

---

1. The name *Quichua* refers to the Ecuadorian registers of the language Quechua spoken throughout the southern Peruvian and Bolivian Andes. In the highland region of Azuay

people, *chulla* is frequently defined as *sin par*, "without a pair," as in the examples *chulla guante* (one glove) or *chulla media* (one sock). Within an indigenous context, the meaning is further changed. Although Quichua speakers define *shuj lla* in a similar way to non-Quichua speakers, the phrase speaks as much to an altered worldview as it does to an individual life. In a uniquely Andean worldview and cosmovision ordered by balance and dualisms—between high *(hanan)* and low *(urin)*, between man *(cari)* and woman *(warmi)*—*chulla* connotes not simply something missing, but also something profoundly out of balance.[2]

"Implicit social knowledge," anthropologist Roger Lancaster explains in *Life Is Hard*, his ethnography of poverty and gender in post-Sandanista Nicaragua, "often takes the form of a proverb or maxim" (1992, xv). More maxim than proverb, "así es la chulla vida," like "la vida es dura" that peppers Nicaraguan speech, similarly serves "as a reliable index of the time" and "a strategy for linking the particular to the general, the personal to the social" (xv). Indeed, as I often witnessed, when people would speak of *la chulla vida*, they tacked between the individual and collective experiences of life. The implicit social knowledge behind *la chulla vida* was revealed to me in a variety of surprising ways during my fieldwork. Throughout months of economic and political instability in Ecuador, punctuated by strikes and protests and near hyperinflation, people spoke of the hardships they had

---

province and the southern portion of Cañar province, only a handful of communities speak Quichua as their primary language. Knapp estimates that by 1950 less than 50 percent of the rural population of the Azuayo-Cañari region spoke Quichua (1987, 44–45). Today, the local Spanish reflects a colorful melding of Quichua and Spanish words. See Encalada Vazquez 1990 and Cordero de Espinosa 1999 for examples of the *mestizaje* (or what Frank Salomon [2004] calls "Hispano-Quechuaism") of regional Quichua speech.

2. Readers familiar with Ecuadorian literature will no doubt identify a rather different usage of *chulla*. Celebrated writer Jorge Icaza developed the character "La Chulla Romero" in his 1958 novel *La Chulla Romero y Flores* based on the caricature "La Chulla Quiteño." In the embodiment of Romero, Icaza described the triumphs and follies of a mostly mestizo middle class determined to climb the social ladder through their imitation of upper-class mores (see Sackett 1988). With respect to a person, *chulla* refers to one who attempts to be something he or she is not. In urban Ecuador, *chulla* can also be used pejoratively to describe a woman considered "easy" and promiscuous.

to endure—the belt tightening and meal skipping—as *la chulla vida*. There was simply no choice in the matter. I also encountered the expression *la chulla vida* in less-obvious places. A bus driver who parked his mammoth vehicle near my first apartment in Cuenca had a friend carefully paint the expression across the hood of the bus. One day when I asked him about the phrase, he grew animated. "When you drive these roads, you don't know what to expect. That's *la chulla vida*."[3] His hands snaked through the air, conjuring the image of his bus making hairpin turns along the thin strips of Andean highways until it dipped down, as if off a cliff. It was rumored that Ecuador had the highest reported number of automobile accidents in the world per capita; I felt I knew what he meant.

But up against the pessimistic and at times fatalistic usages of the phrase, others I encountered spoke of the *chulla vida* in more celebratory terms. Young men I knew who left for the United States and migrants already there sometimes expressed *la chulla vida* to me as the journey they were on—as an adventure. It is the only life one *should* live. Because of the various ways people saturated the maxim with contradictory meaning, placing it at the end of tragic stories or using it to celebrate someone's amazing luck, I was struck by how the phrase so closely mirrored social science discussions of the interplay between "structure" (the external forces that shape and impinge upon individual action) and "agency" (the human ability to act).[4] Depending on context and speaker, *la chulla vida* captured either a life without options or one guided only by individual actions. In the following pages, I explore the ways Ecuadorians I knew thought about their *chulla vida* and in particular how they went about composing a life that was full of both possibility and constraint.

3. All translations of Spanish-language spoken and written materials are mine unless otherwise indicated in citations.

4. For discussions of structure and agency in anthropological and social science writing, see reviews by Ahearn 2001 and Ortner 1984.

Acknowledgments

It is a pleasure to be able to extend my gratitude, thanks, and admiration to the many people and institutions that have helped to see this book inch its way to completion. My deepest obligation is to those families in and around the village of Jatundeleg and their relatives who live clandestinely in the United States. I promised not to mention people by name, so I can only send a genuine *dioslipagui* to everyone who gave me the gift of their time and the honesty of their experiences. For those migrants in New York who welcomed me into their homes and shared with me their powerful stories without being completely sure of the safety of their actions, I owe an enormous debt. To my *compadres* and their children back in the Andes, I hope for better times and a world where the dangerous choice of migration is not the only pathway to a life of dignity.

My interests in anthropology were first piqued as a somewhat reckless college student bopping from institution to institution in the Pacific Northwest—from an introductory course at a community college in Spokane, Washington, to the University of Montana, to Reed College, and eventually to Whitman College, where I would also return many years later as an assistant professor. Many thanks to Jerry O'Neal, Katherine M. Weist, George Castile, and Vassos Argyrou, as well as to other early influences whose names I have forgotten but whose insights in the manifold powers of anthropology I have not. The early ideas for this book reflect the shaping of a number of minds. First, as a dissertation, *La Chulla Vida* has benefited immensely from the intellectual and professional mentoring I received at Syracuse University and especially among the faculty of the Department of Anthropology. Hans Buechler, through his own love of fieldwork and puzzles of culture, inspired me to do research in the Andes. I continue to learn from his example in his tireless commitment to ethnographic field-work. It is no exaggeration to say that I would not have completed graduate school (or at least in a timely fashion) without the unflagging support of Susan Wadley. Although we pursue research in completely different parts of the world and often on different topics, Sue has always shown an active interest in my work—improving it, questioning it, and forever promoting it. She helped me believe in the unwieldy manuscript before me in the dark hours of writing, even when I did not. Other members of the Syracuse University's Department of Anthropology and of the Maxwell School of Citizenship and Public Affairs also helped me in different stages of this project, and it is honor to thank them here: Deborah Pellow, John Burdick, Robert A. Rubinstein, Micheal Freedman, Karin Rosemblatt, Bill Mangin, and David Richardson. Also, I must extend my appreciation to Kristina Ashley for all her administrative help (especially from afar).

I have been fortunate to have great friends and colleagues to learn from over the years. Derek Jentzsch has been a tireless supporter of me and my ideas for way too long, even when I didn't make sense. He offered a shoulder to cry on, a soundboard for crazy thoughts, and reminders of the insanely political nature of human life. In graduate school, Gregory Feldman, Mark Hauser, John Karam, Kalyani Menon, Suzanne Morrissey, Keri Olsen, Brian Selmeski, and Valerie Singer formed a special cohort, making anthropology real outside of the classroom. I will especially for-ever cherish Brian Selmeski's intellectual wit and our early days trudging up to the "puna" of Hans Buechler's office on the top floor of Syracuse's Maxwell School to discuss all things Andean. Ann Miles, another Syracuse alum and fellow Andeanist, has been a trusted *compañera* whose honest and sincere advice on everything from publishing to parenting will prob-ably never be repaid. Brad Jokisch deserves special notice for showing me the ropes of doing field research in the Ecuadorian campo. A very special thanks and appreciation are also in order for Mary Weismantel, whose work I envy and whose support of young scholars is emblematic of what academia should be. I am also grateful for the many conversations (some over e-mail) and research support I have received from Rudi Colloredo-Mansfeld, Janet Finn, Nancy Foner, Judy Blankenship, Christine Gailey, Don McVicker, Louis Corsino, Linda Belote, Barbara Grünenfelder Elliker,

Lynn Hirschkind, Lauris McKee, Lynn Meisch, the late John Murra, Roger Rouse, and Caroline Brettell.

My fieldwork in Ecuador and New York was funded by a Fulbright Grant, the Graduate School of Syracuse University, and the Maxwell School of Public Affairs and Citizenship. A small grant to carry out survey research (awarded to Suzanne Morrissey) also helped further along my work. Numerous teaching assistantships, adjunct classes, and consultancies helped to fund my stints of research in New York. In Ecuador, the Fulbright Commission provided more than just funding. I am especially grateful to Susana Cabeza de Vaca and Susana Chiriboga. Their graciousness and friendly faces made for a smooth fieldwork experience.

Ecuador has been like a second home for more than ten years, and I have accrued many debts there as well as many wonderful friends. My connection to the villages of Jatundeleg, Ayaloma, and Shullín would not have been possible without the unfettered generosity of Dr. Jaime Chavez and his work for the Seguro Campesino, a rural health program. His relationship with villagers was both a model of and a model for my own interactions in village life. Jaime opened up his clinic and its files to me, and I thank his staff for putting up with my frequent requests and questions. He also has one of the warmest hearts in all of Latin America. In Déleg and surrounding areas, I am also indebted to Padre Elisio Cabrera, Blanca Toledo, Dr. Emanuel Flores, and the staff of the Déleg high school and elementary school. María Eugenia Rojas helped with interviews and focus groups in the beginning of my research.

Cuenca has long been my "base camp" for research in the *campo*. Since 1995, when I was employed as an English-as-a-second-language teacher, the Centro de Estudios Interamericanos has been research home. I thank Steve Wille and his staff, especially Janett Orellana, for all their help. Also in Cuenca, I thank Ana Cordero and the staff of the Pájara Pinta, Dr. Hernán Urgílez of SOLSIDA, and Pablo Torres, president of El Movimiento de Defensa de los Migrantes del Azuay (MODEMI). The staff of the libraries of the Universidad de Cuenca, the Universidad de Azuay, the Casa de la Cultura, and SENDAS provided me with various pieces of documentation and secondary sources. Pedro Alvarado, a help to many greenhorn gringos in Cuenca, has been a trusted friend and someone I could always count on for a place to stay and a warm meal each time I returned to the city. Esha Clearfield and Paul Goldstein were good friends in the field and fellow Fulbrighters.

In Queens and in New York City more generally, I received research help from Our Lady of Sorrows in Corona, Ciudadanos Conscientes de Queens, the Corona Department of Health, the New York City Task Force on Immigrant Health, and the Rockland County Department of Health. Dr. Germaine Jacquette deserves special credit for helping me find the relevancy of my work in the important services she provides for Ecuadorian migrants. I value her intellectual curiosity, warm heart, and interest in anthropology. During the phase of data analysis, Dustin Brown put his skills to work to crunch my survey data.

A number of individuals, many of whom I will unfortunately never even meet, have also helped in the process of producing this book. I wish to acknowledge their contributions, but the ultimate responsibilities for the contents of this work are mine alone. Mary Weismantel, Michael Freedman, and Susan Wadley read the entire manuscript, offering numerous suggestions to sharpen my ideas and improve the writing. At Syracuse University Press, Mary Seldan Evans and her staff provided this rookie book writer with solid support and encouragement. Joseph Stoll provided cartographic services.

Attending to the final stages of this book would not have been so smooth without the support and friendship of my colleagues at Whitman College. In the Department of Anthropology, Charles F. McKhann and Gary Rollefson have been the best colleagues one could hope for. I also wish to acknowledge the support I have received from the Dean of Faculty's Office and the Office of the President, as well as the Aid to Scholarly Development fund that has allowed me to pursue fieldwork alongside my teaching duties.

Finally, it is only right that the people who have had to endure the long gestation of this book, including the attendant promises of its arrival, the reading and re-reading out loud, and the many excuses—should receive my greatest thanks. First, I owe much credit to my parents, Karen and Wilber Pribilsky, who supported my crazy decision to become an anthropologist, even at times when they did not know what that meant. I thank them for their trust in me. Suzanne Morrissey, who in the middle of my graduate school experience became my wife, knows my research well, perhaps too well. She has been so many things over the years since we first met sharing a windowless basement office in the "grad bays" of Syracuse University: fellow student, counselor, wife, coparent, and friend. Much of this research is also hers in so many ways, and I hope I have been honest in its presentation. She spent wonderful months with me "high in the remote Andes," as she liked to describe over e-mail to friends back home, while I wrestled with the frustrations of fieldwork. She kept me centered in the process. The gifts she continues to give me are too numerous to document here. All I can say is that I hope I have given at least a fraction of the support and love that I continue to receive from her.

In the Andes, *un matrimonio* (a married couple) is not considered a household. Indeed, it is generally understood that no household should ever be without children. In my case, marriage brought an "insta-family," a stepdaughter, Madelaine. She gets a big "thank you" for sharing her mother with me and an apology for having to endure a household where two dissertations vied for her time. In October 2000, the birth of my son, Jacob, graced my life just as I had just finished writing the first draft of my thoughts on Ecuadorian fatherhood. With so much love in the house, future drafts would never be the same, and I have Jacobo to credit for that.

La Chulla Vida

1

Introduction

"¡Mira, mira, este es mi Miguelito!" (Look, look, this is my little Miguel!), Carmela Quispe shouted, pointing at the television screen. Indeed, her husband appeared much the way she had described him to me during our many conversations sitting on the stoop of her *tienda* (store) in Jatundeleg[1] in Ecuador's south-central Andes. Miguel Pomaguiza's frame was small, like most Ecuadorians, though a clearer sense of his size was lost in the folds of his baggy jeans and ill-fitting black nylon athletic jacket with "Chicago Bulls" emblazoned down one sleeve. Although he seemed upbeat and healthy, in comparison to his image in their wedding portrait that hung high on a cracked cement wall of the family's living room, he looked thin and tired through the eyes.

The scene was lower Manhattan and the season distinctly fall. Battling sudden gusts of wind, Miguel was making his way up a wide avenue, cars and yellow taxicabs whizzing past in the background. Every few minutes he would stop and point upwards toward the awesome skyscrapers that flanked the street. Aware of his audience back home, his face burst with the exaggerated expressions of a mime struck by the enormity of the buildings before him. Carmela's children, Valentino and Jennifer, sat cross-legged on the dusty wood floor, their eyes glued to the television, laughing at their father's antics and ogling the cityscape before them.

---

1. *Jatundeleg, Shullín,* and *Ayaloma* are pseudonyms. The name of Jatundeleg's "county seat," *Déleg,* has not been changed because it occupies a unique place in the local history of migration. All other place-names mentioned are real, except where I indicate otherwise. All personal names are fictitious (see the appendix), yet the pseudonyms I employ are common names that one might expect to encounter in the south-central highlands.

1

Together we followed the camera off the busy street and through the front doors of an Italian restaurant. The camera whisked through an empty dining room of neatly arranged tables, each with a red-checkered tablecloth and elaborately folded napkins. Through a pair of swinging doors the camera headed into the restaurant's kitchen, where two other dark-skinned men, perhaps also Ecuadorians, were furiously chopping vegetables. From behind an imposing industrial dishwashing machine another man waved to the camera. Miguel had just taken his family to work.

The screen blackened, then opened up to a scene of people dancing, singing, and passing around small cups of alcohol. Wading through a huddle of gyrating bodies, the camera seized on a group of men sandwiched together on a mattress that served as a makeshift couch. One of those seated, a young-looking man no older than Miguel—perhaps twenty-six or twenty-seven—addressed the camera in a heavy accent: "Hell—o. Welcome to New York. How you d-o-o-o-ing today?" The others on the mattress burst into laughter. In unison, Valentino and Jennifer shouted, "¡Tío Antonio!" Carmela, noticing the puzzled look on my face, quickly followed up the children's exclamation: "That is my older brother, Antonio. His wife is Gloria. ¿Le conoce usted? [Do you know her?]"

"I believe so," I said.

"Antonio traveled with Miguel the first time he went to the United States. They were like brothers."

"Has Antonio returned to Jatundeleg?" I asked.

Carmela's demeanor quickly turned somber. She shook her head no and rolled her eyes.

The video ended with Miguel alone, on the mattress, the camera positioned steadily in front of him. He spoke directly to his kids: "Buenas noches mis ñaños [Good night, my little children]. . . . I hope to get home real soon. I think about you a lot and wish we could play together. I love you. I hope school is going well. Always help your mother with the fields and the animals. I can't wait to be home to see you . . . I love you." The expression in Miguel's voice as he said good night to his children forced a number of questions into my mind: In what ways had the migration of so many men to the United States affected family life in the Ecuadorian highlands? In particular, how had migration reorganized the meaning of and perhaps intensified the importance of family? In that process, how had both men's and women's identities been shaped by the priorities of transnational migration, and how were these identities influenced by long-standing gender ideologies and practices of the Andean region? How and to what degree did men maintain relationships with their children from abroad?

Five minutes later the video ended, and another set of questions came up: "Are all the buildings so tall in New York?" asked Valentino. "Does everyone own a car there?" Jennifer followed. Some questions were more serious: "Do you think my father is safe?" "Aren't there a lot of thieves [*ladrones*] in New York who prey on migrants that can't speak English?"

The evening video showing had captured Carmela and her family in a moment of joy as they laughed and showed affection for one another. They even forgot, if only for a short while, that they had invited the anthropologist to be a voyeur at one of their increasingly important family rituals—watching the videos, reading the letters, and opening the small gift packages Miguel would periodically send home. Although my presence bordered on the inappropriate by highland standards of etiquette—a woman unaccompanied by her husband allowing a strange man into the inner reaches of her home (as opposed to the outside patio, where we usually talked) —Carmela was visibly anxious to display the fruits of her husband's labor. Their house, neither the newest nor the largest to have gone up in Jatundeleg in recent years, revealed signs of upkeep and improvement that only remittances from abroad could make possible. Likewise, Valentino and Jennifer were always smartly dressed in the fashions their father had purchased for them in Queens. In addition to the television and VCR used to watch Miguel's video, a stereo system in their living room, adorned with plastic flowers and the small figurines *(capios)* customarily handed out at baptisms and first communions, appeared like an altar to the migrating life rather than merely a symbol of its success.

However, beyond the commodity emblems of a migrant household's success, many villagers like Carmela could recount stories of Jatundeleg's *nueva generación* (new generation) that revealed the hardships of migration and its toll on families. Gloria's story was similar to many that I heard. Her husband, Antonio, had left for the United States when Gloria was pregnant with their first child. Antonio initially expressed excitement about having a child and called regularly. A year later, however, just a few short months after the birth of their son, the calls stopped coming and soon thereafter the remittances, too. Through Miguel, Gloria learned that Antonio had begun seeing a Puerto Rican woman with whom he worked in a Queens clothing factory. The news left Gloria devastated and paralyzed for days in a depressive state of *pena*.[2] "For weeks, she couldn't hold the baby," Carmela elaborated. As a single woman with a child and without her own land to work, Gloria was forced to move back into her parents' home and help in their fields as she had done as a child. Antonio also left behind more than $5,000[3] in debt he owed to a loan shark who had funded his undocumented entry into the United States. With such realities, few of the wives I met in Jatundeleg could watch their husbands leave without experiencing a nagging feeling they would never come back.

In the face of adversity, Carmela considered herself and her children to be truly blessed by God that migration had afforded them the ability to improve *(mejorar)* their living conditions beyond the monotony and instability of agricultural poverty. By anyone's calculation, Miguel's migration incurred emotional, social, and financial risks for the entire family. Yet after a profitable month of work in New York, Carmela could hope to receive between $200 and $300 from Miguel. Challenging the odds, Carmela credited more than faith alone. With so many men gone to the United States, she informed me, to maintain families and make migration work, "Las familias tuvieron que cambiar" (Families had to change). During one of our interviews, she, like other villagers of her generation, wanted me to see specifically how families had "become modern," how they had adopted new practices and outlooks, and the ways migration fit into this puzzle:

> Before, we had little choice in the matter of marriage, and then once you were married there seemed even less choice. Women before were used by their husbands and did what they said. Husbands, though, could do anything or they could do nothing. Money was always an issue. When we had it, so much went to the man—for his vices [*para sus vicios*]. The

2. See Tousignant 1984 for a discussion of the depression-like disorder called *pena*.
3. All dollar amounts given in the book are U.S. dollars unless otherwise noted.

children had nothing. Thank God you had your children and your own family to escape to.[...] Those were the *ñaupa tiempos* [olden times]. With the men who leave to the United States, it is different, better. Yes, we are alone and we are sad, but Miguel is different. Many women whose husbands are gone say it is different. They [the men] are away, but they are still here. Money is still an issue, but it's better. Yes, families are moving forward [*adelantando*].

This book chronicles the experiences of young Andean families like Miguel and Carmela's whose lives extended between the Ecuadorian highlands and the United States as I participated in them during different periods of fieldwork between 1997 and 2001, both in rural villages of Ecuador's Azuayo-Cañari region[4] and in the immigrant neighborhoods of New York City. At the center of this work are the questions I first pondered that evening in Carmela's home concerning the creative ways people continue to "move forward" with their families despite the spatial and temporal challenges of migration and the centrality of gender to these changes. More than just economic changes within Azuayo-Cañari households have been catalyzed by the emergence of transnational migration strategies through which rural peoples cope with cycles of poverty that have chronically afflicted this part of the Andes for centuries. As families trade an economy based on a mix of agricultural and artisan production for one driven by remittances, significant changes have occurred in the relationships between people within families—between spouses as well as between parents and children; in relationships *between* families; in the meanings of marriage; and ultimately resulting in new meanings of "family." This work looks at these new definitions and at the social actors that enact them.

Although I seek to describe a particular livelihood holistically—documenting the effects of migration on both those who leave and those who stay behind, as well as on key institutions of Andean society—I center my inquiry on men's lives as migrants, drawing attention to the gendered meanings and practices they bring to their mobility and the implications

4. A description of Jatundeleg and a map of the Azuayo-Cañari region are provided in chapter 2.

of these processes for familial and social relationships in transnational contexts. At one level, this focus reflects the greater access I had to men's experiences than I had to women's during my fieldwork. More important, though, it derives from a decision, both empirical and theoretical, to look seriously at migration within a life-course perspective that seeks to account for male migrants' maturation from teenage boys to men, but also for their often ambivalent though frequent transition into the roles of husbands and fathers. Early in my fieldwork, I was struck by the results of a household census I conducted in Jatundeleg that exposed a simple fact: women migrants were few in numbers, but out-migration was substantially draining Azuayo-Cañari villages of men between the ages of eighteen and twenty-five, at a time when their adult lives seemed to be just beginning. Of the 193 male migrants recorded in my census, 100 (51 percent) were between the ages of fifteen and twenty-five. Like Miguel Pomaguiza, more than half (52 percent) left as husbands and some as new or expectant fathers.[5] These data were a reminder that although migration takes place in space, it also takes place in time.

By bringing into parallel focus men's public life as labor migrants and their private lives as husbands and fathers, this work explores various ways gender identities shape men's migration experiences. When young men from rural villages of the Andean highlands come to the United States as undocumented migrants, they find the changes they experience to be neither clear-cut nor overwhelmingly positive. They go from stable, if not somewhat fixed, identities as villagers, citizens, husbands, fathers, sons, and brothers to ambiguous subject positions as second-class citizens, "illegal aliens," and disciplined wage laborers. Migrants I knew thus struggled to piece together elements of their past lives with their new ones in an attempt to order their experiences into a logical and meaningful existence. Because the urban milieu in which they found themselves offered few resources to reconstruct their previous identities as farmers or village leaders, for instance, they latched on to the idioms of family and

---

5. Other researchers have reported a similar pattern in their data. See, for example, Borrero and Vega Ugalde 1995; Carpio Benalcázar 1992; Consejo Nacional and Universidad de Azuay 1995; Kyle 2000.

in particular to the roles of husband and father as enduring and powerful resources for keeping people together, for articulating a sense of who they are, and for making their lives meaningful. The dramas I document here speak to the ways in which migration of Ecuadorians to the United States has fundamentally altered life in the Andes.

Andean Migration to the United States

The outflow of Ecuadorians to the United States constitutes one of the most significant migrant streams linking the North and South American continents. Adjusting for survey error and undercounting, results of the 2000 U.S. census suggest that there are nearly 600,000 Ecuadorians in the United States, making them the nation's eighth largest Hispanic/Latino group (Jokisch and Kyle 2005, 57; Logan 2001).[6] The majority of these migrants,[7] roughly 70 percent, is clustered in the New York City metropolitan area (U.S. Bureau of the Census 2000).

In the early 1970s, modest numbers of Ecuadorians began entering the United States on tourist and work visas (Carpio Benalcázar 1992; Preston 1974). Many of these early migrants fit the profile of what researchers term *target earners* (migrants with specific short-term economic goals) because they intended to return to Ecuador one or two years after overstaying their visas and working illegally (Piore 1979). With passage of the Immigration Reform and Control Act (IRCA) in 1986, which conferred legal status to thousands of undocumented migrants (as well as the same possibility for their families back home), the number of Ecuadorians receiving citizenship between 1961 and 1995 swelled to more than 180,000 (Immigration and Naturalization Service 1992, 72; 1997). Many migrants who had intended to return to Ecuador once their economic goals had been met instead set down permanent roots in the United States.

---

6. The 2000 U.S. census officially enumerated 257,760 persons with Ecuadorian ancestry living in the country (U.S. Bureau of the Census 2000).

7. I employ the terms *migrant* and *migration* rather than *immigrant* and *immigration* throughout this text to stress the transitory situation for Ecuadorians in the United States.

Out-migration began to accelerate significantly in the early 1990s, and Ecuadorians joined other so-termed "New Latinos" from Central and South America (e.g., Columbia, El Salvador, Guatemala, and Peru) as a major portion of the "third wave" of U.S. immigration (Logan 2001; Portes and Rumbaut 1996). Corrected estimates of the 2000 census reveal a 99 percent increase in the number of Ecuadorians entering the United States in the past decade, from 199,477 in 1990 to 396,400 in 2000 (Logan 2001, 6). If, as an aggregate, "an outstanding characteristic of New Latinos is their diversity" (Logan 2001, 7), Ecuadorians can be distinguished from other migrant groups by two principal characteristics: a disproportionately large group with undocumented status and a clustering of poor peasants with limited resources from the Azuayo-Cañari region.[8]

During the 1980s and early 1990s, widespread poverty and the lack of economic opportunities to escape it "pushed" thousands of individuals out of Azuay and Cañar provinces and into low-paying, low-skilled work in the burgeoning service and manufacturing sectors of the New York City economy. Latin America's "Lost Decade" of the 1980s, characterized by a massive decline in revenues, mounting national debt, and debilitating austerity measures,[9] translated into the contraction of incomes and wages at a rate of 7.6 percent annually, driving such "luxuries" as cooking gas, cooking oil, and sugar out of reach for the majority of rural households (Larrea 1998; Weiss 1997). Little had changed by 1995 when Miguel Pomaguiza left Jatundeleg. In Ecuador's countryside, 73.2 percent of households subsisted below the official poverty line (Larrea 1998). By the close of the 1990s, Ecuador was heading into its worst economic crisis of the century. Fueled by a national banking scandal, massive infrastructure

8. By the mid-1990s, the New York City Department of City Planning (1999) was reporting that Ecuadorians had become the largest undocumented group of Latinos in the city's metropolitan region, edging out the city's massive Dominican population for that dubious distinction. Seventy percent of Ecuadorians in the United States are believed to have originated from the south-central highlands, making it perhaps the single largest migrant-sending region in South America (Jokisch 2000, 2).

9. Under the austerity measures, public expenditure as a proportion of GDP fell from 20.5 percent in 1982 to 11 percent in 1992, with significant deterioration in social services, including education and health (Larrea 1998, 188–89).

expenditures as a result of the 1997–98 El Niño, and a precipitous drop in petroleum revenues, gross domestic product (GDP) shrank by 7.3 percent, inflation rose to 60 percent, and the national currency, the sucre, began a downward path of endless devaluation, which would eventually lead to a complete "dollarization" of the economy by March 2000 (Gerlach 2003; International Monetary Fund 2000, 23; North 1999; Vizuete 2000).[10] With diminished opportunities, rural families not already cushioned by dollar remittances looked for ways to get to the United States and other destinations, including Spain, which caused a massive wave of new out-migration.[11] Sending dollars from abroad became a central economic strategy for Azuayo-Cañari families, in some cases becoming the sole income of rural households, following right behind petroleum in contributions to gross national income. In 2000, Ecuador's Central Bank estimated that $1.25 billion flowed into the country; an estimated 80 percent of these remittances flowed directly into rural households in Azuay and Cañar ("Los réditos escondidos" 2001, 7).

It is no exaggeration to state that there is scarcely a household in the Azuayo-Cañari region at the start of the twenty-first century that has not been affected by the massive exodus to the United States. Distinct from twenty years ago, however, patterns of permanent settlement characteristic of earlier waves of migration have largely given way to what scholars have described as strategies of transmigration, a cluster of processes by which migrants "forge and sustain simultaneous multi-stranded social relations that link together their societies of origin and settlement" (Glick Schiller, Basch, and Szanton Blanc 1995, 48; see also Guarnizo 1997; Guarnizo and Smith 1998; Kearney 1995; Mahler 1998; Portes, Guarzino, and Landolt

10. In 1999, the sucre was devalued by 152 percent (International Monetary Fund 2000, 23).

11. Out-migration from Ecuador beginning in 1999 can be described as nothing short of a "panic to leave" (Jokisch and Pribilsky 2002). A total of 504,203 Ecuadorians departed Ecuador legally in 2000. Provincial government offices became inundated with passport requests and in mid-1999 temporarily suspended their issuance, only to begin issuing them again months later with new exorbitant fees aimed at thwarting emigration. Ecuadorian emigration to Spain alone jumped from 11,000 people in 1997 to nearly 125,000 by 2000 (Jokisch and Pribilsky 2002, 76).

1999; Rouse 1989, 1991). For Ecuadorians, short-term "target-earning" goals have given way to long-term employment schemes and to the reality that migration is a permanent way of life that blends together migrant-sending and migrant-receiving communities into a single social field. However, more than simply the "continuous circulation of people, money, goods, and information" (Rouse 1991, 14), transmigration as practiced by Azuayo-Cañari families is a strategy to negotiate the insecurities of the global economy. As economic opportunities have eroded in both the "sending" areas of the Ecuadorian highlands and the receiving areas of the United States, and as immigration policies become tightened, migrant households struggle with the inability to secure a full livelihood in either locale. By keeping multiple options open, families somewhat unwittingly create transnational households within transnational communities.

Migration and I ♥ NY Modernity

At one level, the fact that poor Andean peasants must seek temporary low-wage work thousands of miles away from their homes in order to develop and sustain households in the rural Andes raises a series of questions about long-standing and ever-growing inequalities of wealth and privilege between the South and the North, underdeveloped and developed countries, Latin America and the United States. Although theories of migration that focus on "push and pull" factors have been widely criticized as being ahistorical and too individualistic in scope (Brettell 2000; Castles and Miller 1993:19–21), there is little to dispute the incredible material magnetism powering migration—the hunger, the land scarcity, and the racism that permeate Ecuadorian society, on one side, and the demand of a multitude of low-paying service jobs in "global cities" such as New York, on the other. Still, for many young men and women in Jatundeleg, both married and unmarried, the drama of migration represents much more than the exploitation of yet another group of global lumpen proletariat. For those who leave, as well as for those who stay behind to manage emerging transnational households, the promise of migration equally entails the powerful sway of seductive narratives of modernity and progress that reach across the Andean landscape through television and other media, as well as overwhelmingly through the social, cultural, and economic influences of migrants abroad and those who have returned.

As I explore in the coming chapters, for male youth on their way to adulthood, migration decisions encompass more than just economic concerns. Coming of age in a community long defined by the priorities of migration, young men find that the pathways to proper manhood almost always detour to include temporary stopovers in the United States. Whether young men wish to migrate or not, they clearly understand how the very prerequisites of manhood in the rural Andes—land ownership, marriage, and the establishment of autonomous households—have become almost impossible to acquire without the kinds of economic and social capital migration provides. Equally influential are the subtle ways in which the actions of migrant households who have put remittances to use in the countryside have forced all village households to confront long-standing paternalistic and racist discourses about the marginal status of rural places and peoples. As I discuss in chapters 2 and 3, although migration, at one level, has allowed rural households to combat negative representations of rural peoples by urban elites, it has also inadvertently redefined local definitions of wealth and status. Status, I argue, has become less tied to agricultural wealth and reciprocal labor and more intimately connected with family status, new homes, and the provision of children. In the process, even relatively well-off village households have come to recognize the benefits of migration, though less as a means to escape poverty and more as a means to make claims of personal status.

Migration is, for many rural youth, as much about the acquisition of dollars as it is about a chance to adopt *iony* (pronounced "I-OH-Knee") ways. *Iony,* a local expression derived from the popular bumper sticker "I ♥ New York," describes, at one level, North American styles of speech, fashion, and attitude adopted by return migrants. The full meaning, though, includes much more than the consumption of foreign culture. When, for instance, wives of migrants, such as Carmela, spoke to me about Jatundeleg families moving ahead *(salir adelante)* and about improving their lives *(mejorar)* in distinction to the *ñaupa tiempos,* their words reflected a vision and ordering of the world based on a perceived rupture from the past.

Whereas villagers in Jatundeleg and migrants in New York would be most inclined to speak of *iony* fashion *(moda), iony* styles *(estilos),* and *iony* ways, throughout the chapters that follow I intentionally link *iony* with the experience of "modernity" as it is currently explored ethnographically by anthropologists working in diverse parts of the globe. In the past decade, anthropological interest in "modernity" has shifted considerably, away from a paradigmatic statement focused on universal notions of "progress," "evolution," and "development" as built upon ideas of Western Enlightenment and modernization theory (e.g., Rostow 1960) and toward an acknowledgment of the varied and often contradictory experiences of peoples and cultures around the world. Current interests emphasize the plural or "vernacular" production of modernities in various, mostly non-Western settings to emphasis how, while the conduits of modernity are often global and universally shared—including television, global communications, consumer goods, and migration—the resulting processes are everywhere quite different and reflect the importance of local history and culture.[12] As historian Barbara Cooper suggests, "We must ask ourselves whether there are modernities . . . outside of global phenomena and postcolonial histories but that engage different understandings of wealth, personhood and the public sphere that are commonly taken for granted" (2001, 94). In other words, although dominant and pervasive models of modernity certainly exist at the global level, local peoples' agency to engage these processes creatively and to rework them to fit particular realities and cultural contexts produces alternative ideas and practices of what it means to be modern.

In linking the concept of *iony* with modernity approached from this perspective, I hope to stress the ways Jatundeleg youth themselves encounter discourses of modernity and appropriate them to fit a particular Andean reality. However, as is always the case with systems of ideology, discrepancies unfold between the ideal depictions of modernity and the

12. The literature on this subject is enormous. For foundational works, see Appadurai 1996; Berman 1982; Breckenridge 1995; Comaroff and Comaroff 1993. For a specific Latin American perspective, see García Canclini 1996. Useful compendiums of ethnographic case studies include Breckenridge 1995 and Hodgson 2001b.

lived experience. To be sure, in addition to presenting powerful ideas of adventure and sophistication, *iony* modernity is viewed like so many Horatio Alger stories, promising modern rewards in exchange for hard work. To the contrary, as we shall see in chapters 5 and 6, entry into the world of undocumented labor and the priorities of transnational remittances often reveal a different kind of modernity for most migrants. Rather than unlimited choices, the *iony* life abroad offers few options, requiring instead that migrants perform a balancing act that is difficult to master. As migrants learn to juggle their obligations to generate remittances with their desires for *iony* adventure, their experiences reveal that the contradictions and tensions they face are not only economic, but gendered as well.

An Ethnography of Men and Migration

Throughout this work, I foreground the importance of gender as a key way to understand how migration has contributed to the remaking of Andean families and identities in highland Ecuador and New York City. I understand gender not as a rigid accounting of masculinity and femininity, but rather as culturally understood and learned ways through which people organize their life experiences. Although always contested, flexible, and mutable, gender roles and ideologies can also be deeply ingrained and resistant to change. Simultaneously, categories of gender are produced and transformed through social relations of power, between men and women, and *among* men and women as well (see, e.g., di Leonardo 1991; Gutmann 1997b; Lamphere, Ragoné, and Zavella 1997).

Over the past three decades, the study of gender has moved to the forefront of anthropological research. Early scholarly inquiry, under the catchall of "the anthropology of women," drew upon the pioneering work of Margaret Mead (1935) and others to wrestle the discipline from its androcentric focus and bring the experiences of women to the center of ethnographic inquiry (Reiter 1975b; Rosaldo and Lamphere 1974). Less concerned with generating theories of gender, these early studies filled an urgent need to reexamine naturalistic assumptions about the asymmetry of "women's roles" and "men's roles" by exploring the variety of women's experiences across cultures and throughout history (Leacock 1980). Since the 1980s, anthropological interest in gender has grown tremendously, with an emphasis placed on the cultural construction of men's and women's roles (see, e.g., di Leonardo 1991; di Leonardo and Lancaster 1997; Ong 1991; Ortner and Whitehead 1981).

Efforts to bring a gendered perspective to the study of migration have followed a parallel history. Up until the early 1970s, women remained largely absent from migration studies, despite the empirical fact of their mobility for centuries.[13] The lack of attention paid to women as migrants lay in powerful stereotypes of "risk-taking men" who ventured from home and of conservative women who were charged with maintaining households and upholding community tradition (Pessar 1999). As June Nash notes of this period, "Whether investigators were influenced by neo-classical, Marxist, dependency or developmentalist paradigms, they tended to stop short of an analysis of women's condition in any but the most stereotyped roles in the family and biological reproduction" (1986, 3, quoted in Pessar 1999, 578). Despite such obstacles, a handful of important studies gained the attention of the scholarly community (see, e.g., J. Buechler 1976a, 1976b; Morokvasic 1984). These early researchers examined, among other issues, the adjustment of female migrants to life in urban settings (Foner 1978); gendered patterns in labor recruitment (Fernández-Kelly 1983; Safa 1981; Sassen 1984); and women's roles in upholding and transforming households and kinship relations (e.g., Pessar 1986).

In the shift away from an "anthropology of women" to a more inclusive anthropology of gender, a number of theoretically minded scholars questioned the scope of previous feminist efforts to bring women into the fold of migration studies. Arguing that too few attempts actually had gone beyond merely "adding women" to the mix, they paid greater attention to exploring men's and women's relations in migration (Alicea 1997; Fernández-Kelly and García 1990; Gailey 1992; Grasmuck and Pessar 1991; Hirsch 2003; Hondagneu-Sotelo 1994; Kibria 1993). In particular, researchers began to look at ways in which transnational migration and the global flows of commodities offer new avenues for gendered identities as goods,

13. See, e.g., Diner 1982 and Gabaccia 1994.

ideas, and wealth pour into new areas and are manipulated by new forms of global labor. Ethnographic research on this topic has focused most specifically on women's experiences along the global assembly line broadly defined (see, e.g., Fernández-Kelly 1983; Freeman 2000; Mills 1999; Ong 1987) and within the ranks of domestic service (see, e.g., Gamburd 2000; Hondagneu-Sotelo 2001; Parreñas 2001).

Taken together, this impressive corpus of literature deepens our understandings of the various ways gender organizes, shapes, and defines women's experiences and patterns of migration. The same, however, cannot be said for our understanding of male migrants. Ironically, whereas men have been the dominant focus of generations of migration research, men's lives, or what Matthew Gutmann refers to as "men in their roles as *men*," have not (1997b, 385, original emphasis). In a recent review of migration literature, for example, Willis and Yeoh list among the areas of study requiring further research "a much greater explicit recognition of men's migration experiences and the social construction of masculinities" (2000, xx).[14] In short, the study of men's experiences in migration has fallen ill to what anthropologist David Gilmore calls the "taken-for-granted syndrome" in much of social science writing about men (1990, 1–2).

Nevertheless, if most studies on migration have taken men's gendered experiences for granted, they have done so in remarkably patterned ways. Research dating from the 1970s and 1980s operated largely under an assumption that male migrants either altogether lack a clearly defined gender that influences their migration activities or else subsume this identity in their economic pursuits. *Birds of Passage,* political scientist Michael Piore's influential work on Latin American and European target-earner migrants, exemplifies this point. For Piore, when men migrate, they sever identity commitments, including gender, for the sake of material gain:

> The temporary character of the migration flow appears to create a sharp distinction between work, on the one hand, and the social identity of the worker, on the other. The individual's social identity is located in the place

14. This point has also been mentioned in other reviews by Hondagneu-Sotelo (1999); Hondagneu-Sotelo and Cranford (1999); Nash (1999); and Pessar (1998, 1999).

of origin, the home community. The migration to the industrial community and the work performed there is purely instrumental: a means to
gather income, income that can be taken back to his or her community
and used to fulfill or enhance his or her role within *that* social structure.
From the perspective of the migrant, the work is essentially asocial: It
is purely a means to an end. In this sense, the migrant is initially a true
economic man, probably the closest thing in real life to the *Homo eco-
nomicus* of economic theory. (1979, 54, original emphasis)

The conviction that migration separates "social identity" from "work identity" runs awkwardly against the grain of much recent scholarship linking
men's identities with work cultures (cf. Finn 1998; Glickman 1997). However, Piore's point is not that migration offers no avenues for masculine
expression, but instead that men choose to suppress their identities in order to maximize their returns. Gender identity, then, operates like a faucet
that can be turned on and off. According to Piore, when taking jobs that
are viewed as women's work, such as cleaning, men put on hold their "self
perceptions [because they are] working totally and exclusively for money"
(1979, 54–55). Like others who wrote about genderless male migrants at
the time (see, e.g., Berger and Mohr 1975; Bodnar, Simon, and Weber
1982), Piore described migrants who, in order to get ahead, consciously
check their gender identities at the borders they are crossing.

In the 1990s, greater anthropological attention paid to the subject of
masculinities brought male gender identities to the forefront of the social
sciences. Ethnographic work on Latin America, in particular, highlighted
the discipline's increasing exploration of men's identities (see, e.g., Gutmann 1996, 2003; Kulick 1993; Lancaster 1992), yet Andean men and masculinities remained largely outside of this development.[15] With compelling

15. Exceptions in the Andean literature include studies of subjects as varied as the
political currency of masculinity in comics in Guayaquil (Andrade 2000) and the symbolic construction of masculinity in fiestas (Weismantel 1997a). Two important volumes in
Spanish, *Masculinidades en Ecuador* (Andrade and Herrera 2001) and *Estudios de género*
(Herrera 2001) have begun to turn the tide. For general introductions to this literature,
consult Connell 1996; Cornwall and Lindisfarne 1994; Gutmann 1997b; and Moser 1991.
Noteworthy ethnographies include Carrier 1990; Heald 1999; Herdt 1994; Hodgson 2001a;

ethnographic portraits of men's lives, migrant researchers could no longer continue depicting genderless male migrants or assume that men suppress their gendered identities in their efforts to be successful. Instead, this new research seemed to indicate that the opposite was true: rather than suppress masculinity, migration was shown to exacerbate it and often with negative consequences. Much of this work built off the approach pioneered by anthropologist David Gilmore (1990), which suggests that masculine identity is most profitably studied when it is seen as something men must earn—what Gilmore calls "manhood in the making." Similarly, others have described how men form identities through the constant negotiation of "hegemonic masculinities," historically and culturally constructed models of masculinity that they must confront and define themselves against (Carrigan, Connell, and Lee 1987; Connell 1996). Ideas of "manhood in the making" and hegemonic masculinities share a tendency to characterize men's identities as fragile, provisional, and easily discredited, with "hypermasculine" behavior taken to be the only resource men have at their disposal to reclaim masculinity.

Within studies of migration, masculinity is often depicted as a dormant force or a latent machismo that arises during tensions when men face checks and challenges to their premigration masculine identities. A number of studies looking at migrant families in receiving societies consistently find that women's status vis-à-vis men improves in migration, an outcome leading to women's greater desire to settle in the new location (Chavez 1991; Georges 1990; Hagan 1994). In contrast, men's status frequently declines in migration, and ethnographers have worked to identify a variety of resultant "hypermasculine" behaviors that ultimately disrupt the migrant household, such as domestic violence, increased alcohol consumption, careless and excessive spending, and restrictions placed on women's mobility (Abdulrahim 1993; Gamburd 2000; Grasmuck and Pessar 1991; Hitchcox 1993; Hondagneu-Sotelo 1994). A small number of studies have also looked at the reorientation of masculinity in migration contexts where women are absent. Jane Margold's (1995) innovative study of Filipino

Peletz 1996; and Vale de Almeida 1996. Sweetman (1997) has edited a useful set of essays on masculinity written from a gender and development perspective.

peasant men who migrate to wealthy Arab Persian Gulf states found that overseas factory labor worked to "disassemble" men's sense of themselves. She explores how factory work and discipline construct men into "dogs," "tools," and "slaves," characterizations that eventually make their reentry into their home societies humiliating situations experienced as failures of masculinity. If work conditions whittle away at men's sense of manhood, men have also been shown to resist unfavorable conditions by drawing upon "traditional" masculine themes. Manuel Peña (1991) demonstrates how Mexican immigrant workers in the agricultural fields of California give voice to their economic insecurity and their need to "prove that we are men" through the telling of *charritas coloradas,* crude sex- and violence-charged jokes that objectify women. Dunbar Moodie (1994) explains how men in a South African mining context create elaborate gendered hierarchies in all male settings. In the absence of women, young men become the "wives" of older men and perform traditionally female duties such as beer making and sewing. In exchange, "real" men are expected to reciprocate with gifts and money.

Although the richness of the ethnographic examples from the Philippines, the agricultural fields of California, and the South African mines discourages comparison, the cases highlighted do point to ways in which masculinity is overwhelmingly equated with power—with its exercise, loss, and reassertion through compensating ("hypermasculine") behaviors. Ethnographers, however, have tended to present such incidences as representative of the whole of masculinity and to present men's identities and their performance as episodic—captured in the moments where men forcefully exert their sense of manhood. Of course we should not overlook those instances where men react forcefully or violently in response to uncomfortable positions in which their migration places them, but I take the position that such examples need to be accompanied by examinations of the subtle ways that men work and rework masculine identities in the context of migration. This latter approach opens up a new set of questions for unlocking the relationship of gender and migration. For instance, what is the nature of men's identities when they are not feeling threatened? What are men like in their roles as husbands, fathers, and friends when they do not feel a loss in status? Also, what other forces lie beyond feelings of inadequacy that guide men's sense of their masculine selves and shape their identities? As the following chapters explore, when men migrate, they do not merely enact established masculine identities; they also produce new identities in response to new situations as well as to the changing positions and identities of women back in Ecuador.

Rethinking the Cultural Commitment to Family:
Ecuadorian Transnational Households

Throughout this work, I follow men, as it were, along parallel journeys of coming to the United States and coming of age, but I also pay considerable attention to the ways migration reconfigures local definitions of family and household in the Ecuadorian Andes.[16] Within the social sciences, the concept of the "household" has served as a privileged site of observation positioned at the nexus of macrolevel and microlevel social processes (Netting, Wilk, and Arnould 1984; Smith, Wallerstein, and Evers 1984; Wilk 1989). Migration scholars writing in the 1970s and 1980s from a Marxist perspective used the household model to explore complex relationships between political economic factors, such as labor importing and exporting, and individual decision making (Dinerman 1982; Pessar 1982; Rothenberg 1977; Weist 1973). Other researchers, drawing on anthropology's interest in social network analysis, examined the household's role in strategies of adaptation and settlement that accompany migration. Following Lomnitz's (1977) pioneering work in Mexico City, researchers treated the household as the basic unit of production and consumption among rural-urban migrants (J. Buechler 1976a; Lamphere, Silva, and Sousa 1980; Stack 1974).

But as much as anthropologists have romanced the household concept, the relationship has remained a tortured one. Critics attuned to issues of methodology have argued that aside from the Western ethnocentric biases that lie behind many definitions of "the household" (Guyer 1988), these definitions often conflate the idea of a household as a useful way to

16. My subheading purposely draws from Gerald Creed's (2000) excellent review of research on "family values" and the "cultural commitment to the family."

enumerate groups of people (as in the case of a census) with the idea of a household as a social and economic group (Bender 1967; Wilk 1989; Wilk and Miller 1997).

These concerns notwithstanding, perhaps the greatest challenge to the use of the household model in migration studies has surfaced from within feminist scholarship. Less concerned with questions of the form, feminist scholars have challenged the notion that migrant households are organized largely on the basis of reciprocity, consensus, and altruism (Benería and Roldán 1987; Dwyer and Bruce 1988; Guyer 1989; Rapp [Reiter] 1979). Although solidarity may direct some household action, individual household members are just as likely to act in ways that are informed by power hierarchies structured along the lines of gender and generation (Grasmuck and Pessar 1991; Wolf 1991). Ethnographic research, such as Diane Wolf's (1992) work on the tensions that arise when newfound autonomy clashes with family obligation as young Javanese women migrate to factory jobs, serves to underscore the point that households are not necessarily driven by an overarching moral economy. As Wolf reminds scholars, "Households do not strategize; people do [and] researchers need to uncover who is strategizing (e.g., mothers, fathers, both parents together, individual children or same-sex children)" (1991, 39).

I was well aware of these critiques when I initiated fieldwork in Jatundeleg. Indeed, I proceeded with the idea that the household concept would prove useful and perhaps indispensable when I carried out a village census, but that further training of the analytical lens at the domestic unit would ultimately obscure more than it would illuminate. All clues pointing to the way that migration was reorienting Ecuadorian life indicated that it was not solidifying the family. Headlines in Cuenca's newspapers, like one that read "Migration Is the Equivalent of the Disintegration of the Family" ("Migración equivale" 1998), boldly conveyed the idea that family and migration did not mix. Yet, as my access to families in Jatundeleg increasingly landed me in the private areas of local homes (the living rooms and kitchens) and in the places where family life is made public—at children's fiestas, weddings, and schools—I was forced to confront a nagging question: Were families really areas of disintegration, or were they instead sites of integration where people could remake conceptions of themselves, their community, and the idea of family itself in the face of changes accelerated by migration? Migration in Ecuador, and perhaps in all contexts, surely places strains on families, taxing the emotional and financial resources of all household members. As the voices of Jatundeleg women and children attest in this work, abandonment by migrant husbands and fathers was a constant worry (and a not infrequent reality) in village life. However, despite these challenges and perhaps reinforced by them, the value and meanings of family *(la familia)* had strengthened with migration.

Previous research on households and migration has proven unsatisfactory for the purposes of framing this study, if for no other reason than that most approaches do not address the question of cultural commitments to family. Why, if family life is reduced to individual motives and personal self-interest, as much household research contends, do people continue to remain committed to the idea? Why do people, for instance, direct so much of their conspicuous consumption into an institution fraught with so much contradiction? The literature on migration and households, as it stands, is largely straight-jacketed. In addressing this problem, it asks little more than either-or questions: Does the cultural value placed on domestic life demonstrate that households work as collective units driven by solidarity and ultimately suppress individual desires? Or is it the case that "family values" mask the realities of inequality, patriarchy, and selfishness that characterize all households? In either case, the path of analysis is forked, predicated on the assumption that households are ultimately driven by economic concerns. Family commitments, if expressed at all, are viewed either as an afterthought—as a by-product of solidarity—or as calculating productions of duplicity by individual actors who are trying to maximize their position within the household.

I recognize that the value of family begins with its everyday economic significance, but argue that it does not stop there. Greater attention must be paid to the ways family relations and expectations influence people's choices within the migration context. To this end, I conceptualize the family to be more than simply aggregations of people bound together through relations of blood, kinship, and the exchange of goods and services. The standard emphasis on families as functional, economic units that structure productive, consumptive, and reproductive activities must be equally complemented with an evaluation of the values that ultimately make the idea of family a symbolic refuge and a repository of cultural meaning—indeed, as something "good to think," in anthropological parlance. In this blending of perspectives, an approach emerges that acknowledges that the economic function of families can be, and often is, dictated by the cultural commitments people bring to domestic activities.

In this work, I channel these general points into two rather different theoretical trajectories. The first trajectory I draw from is John Gillis's magisterial history of American holidays and family rituals, *A World of Their Own Making* (1997). Gillis's work is particularly useful in its attempt to answer the question of why families retain their ideological value when in practice they do not exhibit the solidarity and unity often associated with family life. Gilles argues that in modern American society the family has come to do the symbolic work once carried out by religious and communal institutions, namely that of "representing ourselves to ourselves as we would like to think we are" (1997, xv). Similar to the position taken by Collier, Rosaldo, and Yanagisako (1992) two decades ago (originally published in 1982), Gilles contends that families serve as symbolic and ideological buffers defined in opposition to the outside forces of state and market. Mediating "the tensions and contradictions built into a political and economic system based on the values of competition [and] finding no other location for such values as cooperation, enduring loyalty, and moral consideration," people map these principles onto families themselves (1997, xvi). For Gilles, this situation manifests itself in the development of two families that ultimately contradict one another: one that people live *with* and another they live *by*. The former is characterized by individual family members' divisive self-interests, the latter by the myths, images, and rituals that give the concept its ideological value. The goal for ethnography is to capture the relationship between the two.

Of course, although the processes of change in Jatundeleg are distinct from those in the modern American society that Gilles describes, the mass migration of Andean men to the United States and the counterflows of remittances and commodities clearly place strains on social relations, often to the point where some community institutions, such as reciprocal labor parties and the working of communal land, have ceased to define the moral character of village life. As I address in chapter 3, the increased importance of the representation of family in village discourse has grown in significance precisely while other kinds of bonds between community members have waned. In Gillis's terms, transnational households can be seen as sites of contradiction where the tensions between the families people live *with* and the families they live *by* stand oddly juxtaposed. In this situation, the families that migrant households live *by*—defined in part by the practices of commodity consumption rooted in domestic activities—take on important meanings, not only as a way to smooth the edges of the complex realities of migration, but also as part of the process of redefining the idea of family itself.

How have household and family become the central arenas for demonstrating modernity in Azuayo-Cañari migrant communities? When so many aspects of family life play out in a transnational social field, how do people reconnect their households to particular localities and local realities? Moreover, why do strong commitments to particular locales and places endure when social relations, work relations, and identity have become unhinged from local contexts? To answer these questions, I also turn to the work of Arjun Appadurai (1996), specifically his writing on "the production of locality." At the outset, Appadurai's work serves as a reminder that all societies, past and present, grapple with how to articulate a place of locality—a sense of place, home, and territory—in their self-definitions as individuals, families, and communities. Looking over the social fields that have been the stock-in-trade of anthropology, we find this claim to be true: from rites of passage that produce "local subjects . . . who properly belong to a situated community of kin, neighbors, friends or enemies . . . to the organization of paths and passages, the making or remaking of fields and gardens, the mapping and negotiation of transhuman spaces and hunter-gatherer terrains . . . [that are] the incessant, humdrum preoccupation of many small communities" (Appadurai 1996, 179–80).

Although locality is most obviously inscribed in space, it is also relational and contextual. For example, the replanting of a field after years of leaving it fallow can be understood as the reclamation of unused space, but it may also signify past relations—what was planted before, who worked the land, what relationships were formed around that work.

In the current moment when flows of people, commodities, and ideas circulate through the global economy at a rapid pace and an unprecedented scale, the task of documenting the production of locality has grown considerably thornier than in the days of classic village ethnography fifty years ago, particularly in "a world that has become deterritorialized, diasporic, and transnational" (Appadurai 1996, 188). "This is a world," Appadurai writes, "where electronic media are transforming the relationships between information and mediation, and where nation-states are struggling to retain control over their populations in the face of a host of subnational and transnational movements and organizations" (189). In the midst of movement, as Appadurai argues, place matters, and cultural commitments to specific locales remain fundamental to the human project: "The production of locality, though problematic, is central to social life" (182). Appadurai's discussion of the production of locality is germane to the discussion that follows here because it confers a kind of universality to what is otherwise a very peculiar feature of many situations of transnational migration—namely, that migrant people, often young people, choose to root themselves in their home societies despite the lack of opportunities there that drove them to migrate in the first place.

Fieldwork and Methodology: From Jatundeleg to New York

Jatundeleg

Ethnographic fieldwork often develops in moments of what Daphne Berdahl labels "structured serendipity" (1999, 14). Indeed, for all my systematic research efforts, it was often a good dose of luck and positioning (being at the right place at the right time) that saw different phases of my project to fruition. At the start of my research in Ecuador in 1997, I did not intend to focus on the themes of gender, family life, parenthood, and modernity that now frame this work, nor did I conceive of my project as extending much beyond a traditional community study. My training and interests were in medical anthropology, and I was looking for a project positioned at the intersection of health and migration. As I would come to report later (Pribilsky 1999, 2001a), health problems connected to transmigration resided in an import/export pattern of infectious disease: Ecuadorian migrants were entering the United States with latent tuberculosis, and HIV-infected returnees were contributing to a worrisome emerging rural AIDS epidemic. I settled on a project to look at emerging HIV/AIDS in the highlands.

To my delight, the project generated enough attention among Ecuadorian scholars and public-health officials to allow me to secure funding, to access epidemiologic data, and to be introduced to possible communities for study. One of those introductions drew my attention to Jatundeleg. Officials in the provincial Ministry of Health suggested that if I wanted to study AIDS and migration, the place to go was Déleg, a *cantón* (similar to a U.S. county) in southern Cañar province known to have the highest rates of HIV infection and confirmed AIDS deaths in the triprovincial area (Azuay, Cañar, and Morona Santiago to the east).[17] It made sense. Déleg was widely considered the oldest migrant-sending community in the Azuayo-Cañari region, with a large number of returnees. Many who had left Déleg in the late 1960s and 1970s received permanent residency in the United States and could pass easily between both countries, thus increasing the potential for HIV to follow in the paths of traffic. Although I did not appreciate it at the time, this long-established migration history would prove beneficial for the type of study I would eventually execute. In particular, many of the early processes of migration just developing in other communities in the region could be glimpsed in their advanced stages in Déleg and in Jatundeleg in particular. For more than a decade, numerous households had become completely enmeshed in the migrant economy, with families already strongly tied to a transnational existence. This long-established migration would also assist me when I extended my research to Queens, New York, by linking me to tight social networks connecting the two locales.

My formal introduction to Jatundeleg was facilitated by a Cuencan physician who worked for Seguro Campesino, a nationwide social-security-funded rural health program, and whom I met through contacts at a Cuencan nongovernmental organization (NGO). Fourteen years of service

17. Formal interview with Dr. Roberto Yajamín, director of the National AIDS Control and Prevention Program, Ministry of Public Health, Quito, Mar. 15, 1999.

in Jatundeleg had made the doctor a trusted friend of the community, dissolving the regular suspicions villagers had of "city folk." I passed many of my first days of fieldwork chatting with villagers in the clinic's waiting room, observing doctor-patient interactions, and visiting friends the doctor had in the community. Making house calls with the doctor to the village's bed-ridden patients proved to be an instantaneous way to develop rapport with residents, many of whom may not have participated in my study otherwise. After two months of visiting Jatundeleg three days a week with the doctor, I found a modest house in the center of town to rent. Jatundeleg would be home for the next eleven months.

Despite the ease I experienced in settling into Jatundeleg, villages in and around the *cantón* Déleg were not easy places for researchers to gain access. Beginning in the late 1980s, as news about the effects of migration in the countryside of Azuay and Cañar found its way into the national media, urban researchers and journalists found their way into rural villages. By the late 1990s, Cuencan editorialist Andrés Abad had derisively identified a "limitless" industry of *"migrantólogos"* (migration-ologists) producing quasi-ethnographic studies on migration in the south-central highlands (1997, 2). In particular, numerous students in the Development Anthropology Program at the Universidad de Azuay wrote theses on local migration topics (see, e.g., Cajamarca 1991; Carpio Benalcázar 1992; Cueva Malo 1991; Sempértegui 1991). For the most part, relations between researchers and communities were positive and amicable, but animosities soon developed when local researchers turned over data to journalists, who in turn produced "exposés" about migrant village life. In my case, however, villagers were less concerned with the ties I might possibly have with journalists and more with possible connections to U.S. immigration control. Although I escaped suspicion of being a CIA agent, a rumor circulated that I had ties with the U.S. Immigration and Naturalization Service (INS)—colloquially referred to as *la migra*—and that the information I was gathering could potentially endanger loved ones living abroad illegally. To quell people's fears, I went to great lengths to appear deliberately "unofficial." For instance, I rarely taped interviews during my initial meetings with study participants and avoided excessive note taking in public. In public forums, I snatched opportunities to speak about the progress of my research.

My status as an outsider from the United States, however, also at times helped ease and facilitate my relationships in the community. Because I was from New York (albeit upstate), villagers commonly assumed I possessed infinite wisdom about New York City and the literally dozens of boroughs and outlying towns where their relatives lived. Over many years, I have been called on to translate confusing green card information, carry mail and small packages back with me to the United States, cash checks, count and explain U.S. currency, and generally allay people's fear of crime, sickness, and the general immorality of American cities.

Over time, my status changed from that of outsider into *comunero,* or resident. At the start of my research, a neighbor family who looked after the church offered me the sanctuary's *convento*—a vacuous, filthy, and often cold building used to hold community meetings and confirmation classes—as a neutral space to carry out my interviews and focus groups. When my access to families increased, I was relieved to need the space no longer as they began to invite me into their homes. Formal interviews in the comfort of a living room or a smoke-filled kitchen gave way to informal meals and time spent exchanging stories and playing with children.

As should be evident from the theoretical and ethnographic issues already discussed, research questions about migration that sought cause and effect or that specifically addressed development (Have remittances had a positive or negative effect on society?) were not the central focus of my study. Many of the sophisticated comparative research designs employed in other migration studies thus proved inappropriate for my research. As gender roles and practices, family life, and the development of transnational households became central foci of my fieldwork, I began to see that a greater depth of research with a smaller number of migrating families would serve my purposes better than expanded sample sizes and comparisons. I utilized a "snowball" method that ultimately resulted in a balanced mix of migrating and nonmigrating households, in addition to a variety of household types. The snowball approach also served as an invaluable means to uncover natural networks between families (and between different villages) (cf. Cornelius 1982, 388–95).

The research I conducted in Jatundeleg and in its neighboring communities included three intertwined methodological approaches: a household census, semistructured interviews, and participant observation. The house-hold census of forty-five domestic units scattered throughout the commu-nity, carried out in the early months of my fieldwork in 1999, served as the bedrock of my research, providing answers to questions about house-hold size and composition as well as about the migration status of each individual in the household, income-earning strategies, and indicators of wealth. In addition to the survey, I generated a roster of every person in the village who had migrated (cf. Georges 1990, 23). Midway through my research, I also carried out a survey with students ($n = 137$) in the Déleg high school to learn about migrant household consumption patterns and students' opinions about migration. Over the course of my Jatundeleg fieldwork, I had conversations with women, children, and nonmigrating residents. However, the core of my study rests on forty-five interviews with young migrants, soon-to-be migrants, and young men hoping to migrate. A female research assistant conducted an additional seven interviews and assisted in or conducted eight focus groups of demographically distinct cohorts, including specific groups of adolescent girls and women.

Interviews and group conversations *(charlas)* were crucial to move my project beyond its narrow focus on AIDS and migration to issues that mat-tered most to people. Indeed, the death of returned migrants from AIDS was perhaps the most dramatic and symbolic of a number of changes re-lated to migration,[18] but it was by far not the most important. To be sure, as I began to hunt for patterns in my field notes, I noticed that more often than not my attempts to steer conversations toward the local meanings of SIDA and its relation to an emerging moral economy of migration often ended up in my filling the notebook pages with more quotidian aspects of family life in the village: the price of sending children to school, wor-ries over when a husband would call from the United States, the find-ing of a suitable marriage partner. With encouragement from villagers, I eventually charted a new course and honed down my interview guide to capture an understanding of four key aspects of migration and the re-making of families: (1) how men perceived changes in their relationships

18. During my stay in Jatundeleg, I attended the funerals of three migrants who had died of AIDS-related complications.

with their wives and children, and in what ways these perceptions altered how they understood their masculinity and their roles as husband and parent; (2) how couples viewed their commitments to their own parents and extended family as well the role they saw for their household vis-à-vis others in the community; (3) how local people viewed childhood and the place of children within the household, in the present as well as over time; and (4) how gender roles, parenting styles, and marital relations had changed over time. In order to develop an ethnographic portrait of the day-to-day context of experience in Jatundeleg and to determine the relationships between ideas and knowledge (as gathered through interviews and survey), on the one hand, and everyday practices, on the other, I acted as a constant participant-observer of daily life in the village. As it were, I often learned as much or more from my casual interactions as I did from formal interviews.

New York City

As my research interests in Jatundeleg shifted toward studying the ways men's identities were being transformed in the course of transnational migration, I grew convinced that it would be impossible to carry out a standard village ethnography. Conversations in the village with returned migrants about changing gender roles, relationships with spouses, and the centrality of money management and consumption in their lives, among other topics, invariably led to discussions of migrant life in New York City. Specifically, stories I collected from returned migrants about "fathering from abroad" and the adoption of patently feminine roles (i.e., washing their own clothes and cooking for themselves) left me interested, but skeptical. Reminded of the anthropological dictum that what people do and what they say they do are frequently two different things, I was compelled to want to investigate the former firsthand. Because of time and financial constraints, my research in New York was more focused and structured than my fieldwork in Ecuador. I made four separate trips to Queens, during the summers of 1999, 2000, and 2001, and in December 2000. Shorter follow-up research trips, in December 2001 and January–February 2002, to work with newly arrived migrants who had settled in suburban Rockland County northwest of Manhattan provided me with crucial information on wages and household budgets as well as the effects of the post-9/11 political climate.

My research in New York presented me with a different set of obstacles and considerations than those that existed in Jatundeleg. Undocumented migrants, because of their special circumstances, are not easily studied using traditional social science methodologies. Their need to remain clandestine and to protect their safety frequently thwarts the use of random sampling, structured interviews, and other common field methods.[19] When I began research in Queens, I worked from a list of phone numbers and addresses of migrants that I had collected from their families in Jatundeleg, Ayaloma, and Shullín. In addition, I relied heavily on social-service and public-health agencies that work with migrants, including New York University's Center for Immigrant Health and the Catholic Charities Brooklyn and Queens, to make initial contacts.

I complemented interviews with all possible participant-observation opportunities. A great deal of my participation included periodic attendance at public and community events that involved the men I knew: birthday parties, weekend excursions to parks and shopping areas, soccer and volleyball games, church events, and public-health forums. I also informally interviewed migrant day laborers *(esquineros)* who congregated each day looking for work. More so than in my research in Ecuador, spending time with undocumented migrants emphasized the fragility and distress of undocumented labor migration. I could pass entire days among villagers in Jatundeleg with the line between research and everyday life blurring, but migrants in New York could most often spare only an hour here or there to talk, often requiring that I interview them on their way to work or sometimes on the job.

The multisited fieldwork approach that I take here—now commonplace in many discussions of ethnographic research—aims to show how now more than ever events in New York City reverberate in the rural Andes

19. For useful discussions of methodological approaches to studying undocumented migrant and other "hidden" populations, consult Cornelius 1982; Mahler 1995, 26–30; Singer 1999; Stoller 1997.

and vice versa.[20] The bankruptcy of a single upscale restaurant in Manhattan can mean that multiple families will not see remittances for a month.[21] Although, for the moment, men are primarily the ones who move back and forth between sending and receiving points, entire rural households have become transnational, from wives whose economic contribution is largely to transfer dollars from remittance into consumption and investment to children who have lived their entire lives in the shadow of migration.

This study offers just one perspective through which to understand the richly complex lives of only one population of Ecuadorians. The experiences I relate here are not the celebratory ones presented by other scholars who have depicted transnational migrants as easily slipping across borders, recasting their identities, and altogether sidestepping nation-states that have for so long had them under thumb. Ecuadorian migrants' movements take place not in a "deterritorialized" context or in an imaginary "third space" (Bhabba 1990; Soja 1996). Rather, at a more experiential level, for families whose lives are increasingly hemmed in by the priorities and necessities of migration, borders remain real, exacting a price from both those who cross them and those who stay put. The costs of migration are high, and the triumphs remain a great deal more quotidian, ordinary, and partial.

Organization of the Book

This book unfolds in two parts intended to capture some of the narrative-like structure that human migrations often follow. The first part (chapters

20. On transnational and multisited research, see Hannerz 1998; Marcus 1995, 1998; and the collected essays in Gupta and Ferguson 1997.

21. Reverberations from the September 11, 2001, terrorist attacks upon the World Trade Center in New York City were felt throughout small villages of south-central Ecuador. The Windows on the World Restaurant located on the 106th floor of the Trade Center was well known among undocumented Ecuadorians as a safe place to work "without papers." Twelve of the forty-three restaurant employees killed on that day were employed with false Social Security numbers ("Labor: Unemployment" 2001); four of the workers were from the Azuayo-Cañari region. Soon after the attacks, family members of the victims appealed to the Catholic Diocese in Cañar province for help to recover the bodies and pay back the debts they owed.

2, 3, and 4) considers the historical and contemporary livelihoods of rural peoples of the Azuayo-Cañari region. The second part (chapters 5, 6, 7) is focused around men's experiences as undocumented migrants in New York City. However, because this story takes place in a transnational context, the ethnographic lens shifts between locales, treating the Andean highlands and New York City as a single stage on which the drama of migrant life plays out.

Chapter 2 presents a history of the economic and political development of the Azuayo-Cañari region and of the Ecuadorian Andes more generally. I trace the evolution of what I term *agri-artisan* households in the region and their increasing dependence on wage labor, handicraft production, seasonal circuit migration, and, finally, international migration.

Chapter 3 familiarizes the reader with the contemporary livelihoods of Jatundeleg villagers and their neighbors through an ethnographic description and analysis of key aspects of community life. In 1999 and 2000, many households linked to migration were shifting their economic base from agri-artisan production to a reliance on remittances sent from the United States. Central to this change was the commodification of agriculture and what locals referred to as the "dollarization of the cornfields." Tracing corn *(maíz)* as both a material and symbolic commodity through recent village history, I look at the impact of remittances on definitions of village wealth and status, community development projects, and everyday social relations. I stress how, as community bonds and the village's collective identity have waned with the consolidation of the local economy around individual transnational households, private family life has assumed a new importance in the making of status claims.

In chapter 4, I move away from the household level and address the particular experiences of rural youth to answer the following question: What is it like to come of age in a society at a moment when the values, traditions, and livelihood of that society are in a process of rapid change? I begin by looking at how village youth negotiate their way through an unstable state education system and an insecure employment market, all the while flirting with constant temptations to migrate. Traditionally, village youth sought autonomy through doing farm labor, marrying, and starting their own households while remaining in deference to parents through a set of ideals of respect *(considerándoles)*. However, as inheritance of land—the ultimate force binding parents and children—has waned, adult children have found that the basic costs of reaching adulthood have risen sharply in an economy radically transformed by remittances. Many male youths find the steps to proper manhood difficult to take without journeying to the United States, whether they wish to migrate or not. The latter half of this chapter looks at how young couples struggle to form autonomous family units through the constitution of "transnational households" dependent on and grounded in the priorities of U.S.–bound migration.

The second part shifts the focus of analysis from the Andean highlands to the urban landscape of New York City. In chapter 5, I explore the life experiences of young migrants, from the surreptitious and perilous journeys north to mundane workaday lives in the city. Although their status as undocumented migrants typically relegates them to the lowest-paid and least desirable jobs, migrants find value in the work they do. The men judge their employment foremost with respect to its ability to generate remittances, but other concerns also take center stage, including the ways employment fosters or impedes relationships between migrants as well as between employee and employer, the gendered nature of the work, and the extent to which work allows migrants to move outside the cloisters of U.S. immigrant life. Although men I knew occupied a wide variety of jobs, I concentrate my discussion on the experiences of migrants as day laborers *(esquineros)*, employees of Korean-owned grocery stores and garment factories, and restaurant workers.

At one level, land scarcity and a lack of economic opportunities drive migration to the United States, but migrants I met were equally motivated by their hopes and desires for *iony* modernity and adventure. However, in New York City, men's desires to achieve an *iony* lifestyle are highly attenuated by the priorities of saving money and generating remittances. Chapter 6 deepens the urban ethnography of Ecuadorian migrants by looking specifically at men's patterns of budgeting, saving money, and consuming commodities. The discipline men need to generate remittances demands that they confront long-standing relationships between proper masculinity and the uses of money in the Andes. Eschewing patently masculine forms of immediate consumption of such goods as alcohol and cigarettes requires these men to find new ways to balance consumption and gender identities.

Chapter 7 tacks between the Andean highlands and New York City in order to examine the form, quality, and experiences of transnational conjugal relationships. Building on the previous two chapters' exploration of the ways that migration-related changes for men are gendered transformations, I further explore how migration alters women's gender roles and identities in Jatundeleg. I ultimately address the ways in which couples separated by migration learn to "work in harmony" *(convivir)* with one another, despite the spatial and temporal boundaries created by migration. As many young couples come to realize, being successful in migration depends as much or more on wives' ability to work with husbands to orchestrate household affairs and to handle remittances as it does on husbands' hard labor in the United States. And finally, chapter 8 draws some conclusions based on the previous ethnographic chapters.

2

Historical Contexts

Economy, Migration, and the
Making of the Azuayo-Cañari Region

Jatundeleg and *Nuestro Folklórico*

The best vantage point to really see Jatundeleg, I was often told, was from atop Loma Lanzacay, an impressive hill above the village. Yet, in another respect, the hike up to the hill afforded a unique glimpse into the village's rich past. The spiraling dirt path passed by a number of dilapidated wattle-and-daub homes with brick red tile roofs and rolling pastures of grazing sheep and cattle. Some of the ailing structures served as storage sheds, littered with feed pots and frayed ropes used to tether animals. Villages referred to the highest portions of Lanzacay *(el cerro)* as *la comuna*, communal pasture land shared and looked after by all village families. Poor families relied on *la comuna* for cooking fuels: downed branches and thick grasses that they would bundle and transport on their backs to houses below. Many of the details of land ownership that once governed the use of the hills—the natural boundary markers and usufruct rights—had also faded into the past. Once-cultivated fields were now largely covered in *kikuyu*, a noxious Andean grass that gobbles up unattended lands. Down the sides of the Lanzacay's gentle slopes lived some of the community's poorest families in a series of humble domiciles, almost all of whom managed without piped water *(agua entubada)* and some without electricity.[1]

1. I have relied on my own household census and on village demographic and household economics data collected by Arízaga Rovalino and Daquilema Miranda (2001).

35

2.1. Traditional houses on the dirt road to Jatundeleg. Photograph by the author.

By contrast, on a flat plateau below the *cerro*, the center of Jatunde-leg appeared like a sprawling suburban housing development caught up in constant growth. Circling the settlement of houses stretched an uneven patchwork quilt of *maíz* fields, interrupted only by a crisscross grid of dirt roads and immature eucalyptus stands that dotted the perimeter of fields and roadways. Although the subtle beauty of deep green corn stalks and rusty-barked eucalyptus commanded attention, it was the garishly col-ored rooftops, fluorescent orangey red and aqua blue, that ultimately held one's stare. When I conducted research here in 1999 and 2000, Jatundeleg was awash in a construction boom. The village's most successful migrant families were using remittances to construct new houses based on North American design features. Built of brick and reinforced concrete, these two- and sometimes three-story structures were introducing novel ele-ments to the rural landscape. Homes with large windows, skylights, high ceilings, garages or carports, and intimidating fencing butted up against simple one- and two-room wattle-and-daub homes. This upsurge of only

2.2. Urbanization in Jatundeleg's *centro*. Photograph by the author.

partially constructed modern homes joined an already impressive number of domiciles in an orderly cluster on a citylike grid. Complementing this picture were the anchors of the village center (called the *centro*): the Seguro Campesino health clinic, an elementary school, a multiuse ball court, a small decorative park, and an imposing powder blue church, itself in the midst of a major reconstruction funded by migrant dollars. Power and phone lines connected houses, and a recently erected set of imposing streetlamps lined the main roadway. Just forty years earlier the village had been quite different. As one elderly resident told me, "The community used to be just a prairie, a wide-open space, where the *bayánes*[2] would grow. It was a favorite place for condors to congregate. It was the outskirts [*monte*], and everyone lived scattered around on the hillsides and on the *loma*. Now we have a modern town and people live in the center."

2. A *bayán* is a type of small tree indigenous to the Andes. Its branches are often used to make fences.

Approximately 177 households containing eight hundred people formed the community of Jatundeleg. In reality, it was difficult to tell where this village ended and the adjacent communities of Ayaloma and Shullín that hemmed Jatundeleg in from the east and west began. In many respects, Jatundeleg differed little from the many small communities (between five hundred and fifteen hundred people) that pepper the Azuayo-Cañari region and the handful I visited at the start my research. Regardless if households could count remittances from the United States or wages earned on the coastal plantations in their domestic budgets, most of them were subsistence farmers who worked extremely small plots of land *(minifundios)*. For as long as anyone could remember, households had to supplement their agricultural livelihoods with artisan production, temporary wage labor, and, more frequently now, long-term migration to the United States.

Located in south-central Ecuador, the Azuayo-Cañari region encompasses a major portion of the Andean highlands, linking together the modern provinces of Azuay and Cañar. (See map 2.1.) The region's cohesion is defined more by a common ethnicity and a shared economic and political history than by the placement of provincial boundaries. The region defies commonplace ethnic or racial classification in the trinity *indígena* (indigenous), mestizo (mixed blood), and *blanco* (white, considered of pure Spanish descent) so commonly employed in Ecuador.[3] Although rural peoples of the Azuayo-Cañari region are clearly distinguishable from nearby self-identified indigenous groups, the Cañari in northern Cañar province and the Saraguros in southern Loja province,[4] they are equally differentiated from the national culture of mestizos by their very borrowings of indigenous identity: peasant *pollera* skirts, felt and woven Panama hats, adherence to "traditional" medicine practices,

3. Ecuador also has a small (approximately 10 percent), though increasingly politically active, population of African descent. See Rahier 1998; Whitten and Quiroga 1995.

4. Indigenous identity in Ecuador is subtle and far from fixed. For the sake of convenience and clarity, I have adopted the determinants outlined by Meisch (1998, 11), including, most important, dress (clothing, hairstyle choices) and language (many but not all indigenous Ecuadorians speak Quichua, referred to as *runa shimi,* "people's language"). Indigenous communities in Ecuador also frequently self-identify as *runa* (meaning "person" or "human" in Quichua).

Map 2.1. Ecuador (Azuay and Cañar provinces).

and linguistic features that blend Spanish with a rich set of Quichua words and phrases as well as its "singsong" cadences (Brownrigg 1972, 107; Meisch 1998; Miles 1991; Weismantel 2001). Similar to other instances of intermediary ethnic identity in the Andes, Azuayo-Cañari peoples are frequently described, not altogether positively, as *cholos* (or *cholas*), a group of people defined by dress and lifestyle rather than by race.[5]

5. In many parts of the Andes, mestizos and *blancos* use the term *cholo* (often in the absence of the female referent *chola*) as an insult and racial slur. *Cholos* are described as

In practice, Azuayo-Cañari ethnicity is complicated by the fact that significant differences exist between how people define themselves and how they are defined by others, differences that are ultimately grounded in social rather than phenotypic criteria. To be sure, in the small expanse of the *cantón* Déleg, a wide variation of ethnic markers exists—ranging from *indígena* to *mestizo/a* to *cholo/a*—for both self-identification and the identification of others.[6] Despite such complexities, people in communities such as Jatundeleg nonetheless resoundingly retain a clear sense that in the recent past the region was "more indigenous." As Rosario Saldañes, one of the oldest residents of Ayaloma, who identified herself as a campesina, explained to me, "Somos indios [We are Indians], but we are leaving that now." Disuse of the Quichua language, in particular, represents for many the unraveling of this identity. Traditional dress styles have also changed (see Meisch 1998; Meisch, Miller, and Hirschkind 1998). Nearly all women older than forty in Jatundeleg continue to wear *pollera* skirts (albeit complemented by sweatpants underneath, tennis shoes, and T-shirts with English-language writing) and keep their hair in braids, whereas younger generations of girls often choose modern fashions (designated as *de vestido*).

Despite these realities, rural villages of the Azuayo-Cañari region continue to hold a cherished place in Ecuador's national imagination as an

---

indigenous peoples who attempt to pass themselves off as mestizos. (A similar term, *chazo*, is also used in Cañar and Azuay.) A tremendous literature in the Andes addresses the multivocal meanings of *cholo/a*. For Bolivia, consult Buechler and Buechler 1996. Examinations of the term in Peru include Bourricaud 1975; de la Cadena 2000; and Seligmann 1989. Weismantel (2001) provides a stimulating synthesis of this literature while addressing underlying constructions of race and sexuality in the Andes.

6. I documented a wide range of ethnic self-identifications and ethnic markings of others in Jatundeleg and its neighboring villages, many of which contradicted each other. For instance, some families who were identified to me as *Indian* identified themselves as *campesinos* (simply "peasants," though with the connotation that they were mestizos). These same families reserved the label *Indian* to identify others in the region only in disparaging ways, often choosing the most derogatory terms, such as *mitayo* and *longo*. Others, however, who chose to identify as indigenous did so almost as a badge of honor. Moreover, a significant number of people identified themselves as having a "*cholo* culture" but did not identify themselves as *cholos/as*.

embodiment of the fictionalized harmony of *mestizaje,* or race mixing. In Cuenca in particular, idealized images of the countryside have found their way into literature, art, and music, as well as into artistic photographs that grace the pages of coffee-table books and postcards produced for the tourist industry. *Pollera* skirts, humble adobe homes tucked away in the foliage of *maíz* fields, elderly campesinos gracefully maneuvering backstrap looms in the production of *ikat* shawls, and fields being plowed with draft animals form part of the imagery of local residents that have led to the characterization of them as *nuestro folklórico* (our folklore) by middle- and upper-class urban Ecuadorians. For Cuencanos, especially members of the city's upper class, a group self-described as *nobles,*[7] the evocation of *nuestro folklórico* calls forth an imagined bygone era when, above all, rural peoples knew their place in the social order: as industrious workers on the land, producers of artisanry, and humble servants of *hacendados* (hacienda owners) (cf. Miles 1990). More sophisticated and refined than Indians but not quite as modern as urban mestizos, Azuayo-Cañari peasants are persistently taken to be the living embodiments of a fictionalized colonial past.

In Jatundeleg, despite multiple networks that linked villagers to family, employment, and education in Cuenca, there existed clear antagonisms between rural peoples and urbanites. Hidden under a veneer of reverence and respect, residents of Jatundeleg I knew confronted *nuestro folklórico* as racial and economic marginalization by means of the seemingly benign "country folk" characterization—a marker that ultimately worked to discount their contributions historically to the country's economic development. In the discourse of "modernizing" Ecuador, gentile country folk are meant to serve as representations of a mythic past, of where Ecuador had once been, not where it is going (see Radcliffe and Westwood 1996).

---

7. Cuenca, Miles notes, is a city "deeply committed to a rigid class system, one that harkens back to its colonial past" (1997, 59; see also Miles 1991). *Nobles* occupy the top of this class system, holding many university, ecclesiastical, and civic appointments. Their wealth is concentrated in land, but much of their power lies in social capital and prestige, concentrated in kinship relations and endogamous marriage practices (Brownrigg 1972; Hirschkind 1980; León 1997). By the 1970s, a "nouveaux riche" class emerged from fortunes made in oil, agribusiness, and other commercial activities, further threatening *noble* hegemony.

It is therefore not surprising that both regional and national elites have come to resent the alternative course of modernity that Azuayo-Cañari peoples have been paving through international migration since the late 1960s. As urban elites have watched throngs of largely young, uneducated, dark-skinned men from the countryside leave for the United States and send back what the elites perceived to be hundreds of dollars a month to build ostentatious houses in the countryside, they have reacted against migration with a range of actions—from derisive racial comments and jokes to organized legal processes. In the late 1970s and early 1980s, return migrants donning new fashions and *iony* pretensions were derided in Cuencan newspapers as "*cholo* boys" and "*cholos lisos*" ("slick" *cholos*), a reminder that the symbolic capital of Western attire and the addition of a few English words into their vocabulary could not erase their indigenous and rural roots in Ecuador's racial hierarchy. Seemingly little had changed by the mid-1990s, when I taught English at an upper-class English-language school in Cuenca. My students would frequently regale me with incredible stories of life turned upside down in rural villages as a result of migration. Many stories mined the themes of urban legend. One described the plight of a "poor aunt" living in the *campo* left in charge of twenty-five children when all her brothers and sisters migrated to the United States. Others perpetuated exaggerations regarding the existence of *pueblos de mujeres solas* (communities of only women), created by the absence of husbands and fathers. However, by far the most pervasive characterizations in the national and local media depicted the woeful ignorance of migrant families and their pathetic inability to manage their modern fortunes. A 1989 issue of *Vistazo,* a national news magazine, featured an "exposé" of the changes in Corpanche, a migrant-sending community fifteen kilometers from Cuenca. The hybridity of rural lifestyles where adobe homes with dirt floors nonetheless housed new refrigerators and stereo systems drew the *Vistazo* reporter to the conclusion that the countryside of Azuay and Cañar had become "una mezcla de costumbres casi grotesca" (a mix of almost grotesque customs). He excoriated:

> When immigrants return to visit relatives, they arrive weighted down
> with gifts for family. They bring sound systems that they don't know how

to use, electric typewriters that are destroyed in the excrement of rab-
bits, *cuy* [guinea pig], and other domestic animals that just walk through
the recently finished houses. They buy cars and leave them in the garage
"until they return," and they are damaged by lack of use. It is so pathetic
it's almost comical to see frightened hens springing out of the windows of
houses built in the purest "Californian style." (Artieda 1989, 39)[8]

I witnessed a similar critique being made when I attended a conference devoted to the implementation of a law "in defense of the migrants"
against the exploitation of human smugglers and unscrupulous employers in the United States. The meeting, held in Azogues, the provincial
capital of Cañar, brought together notable regional figures, including a
prominent Azuay *diputado* (senator) and the rector of the Universidad de
Cuenca, along with local clergy, social workers, and lawyers. Dressed in
business attire, they stood in awkward contrast to the handful of Cañari
Indians and *pollera*-clad *cholas* who occupied the auditorium's back row.
The speakers scarcely addressed the proposed themes of the conference,
and little consideration was paid to the root causes of migration or the
risks involved. Rather, the forum dwelled on migration as a "problem of
reclaiming national identity"—an affront to *nuestro folklórico*. One panel-
ist, for example, the author of a book on Ecuadorians in New York City,
lamented that rural communities now resembled nothing of "the culture
that made Inga Pirca and the great Tawantinsuyu [the Inca Empire]."
"They have lost their culture," he pronounced.[9] Months later I came across
a similar sentiment expressed by a noted scholar of migration in the pages
of *Cántaro,* a usually left-leaning Cuenca-based journal of development.

8. The rhetorical strategies that Ecuadorian journalists have employed to portray the
effects of international migration on Ecuador's countryside are surprisingly similar to the
visual and textual techniques of juxtaposing modern and "primitive" elements found in
the periodical *National Geographic* (Lutz and Collins 1993, 110–15, 247–53). Rather than
showing active participation in modernity, these journalists have depicted "natives" as passive and bewildered receptors of Western culture. By juxtaposing the modern and the traditional (e.g., the adobe home with its new stereo system), the images form a visual narrative
of the pollution of the pristine Andean countryside.

9. Inga Pirca is considered Ecuador's most important archaeological ruins.

In the writer's estimation, not only identity but also local economy were threatened by the massive U.S.–bound exodus:

> The importation of architectural styles from the big city, the excess and abuse of cement and concrete block have made the areas with the highest levels of migration lose their identity and heritage and harmonious architectural styles to the truly hideous monsters of cement [*monstruos de cemento*]. This also signals a loss in the potential of these places as rural tourist attractions for both national and international use. (Borrero 2001, 40)

The varied meanings of *nuestro folklórico* and their ideological implications for Azuayo-Cañari households reflect a long history of rural-urban relations that the remainder of this chapter explores. The chapter tacks between a history of the economic and political development of the Azuayo-Cañari region and of the Ecuadorian Andes more generally, on the one hand, and a microhistory of the village of Jatundeleg from the pre-Columbian period through the late twentieth century, on the other. Although readers may initially find descriptions of the forced relocation policies of the Inca who settled Jatundeleg as a community or of the economic policies of the Spanish colonizers that shaped rural livelihoods tangential to an understanding of the migration of modern Ecuadorians to New York City, this chapter is built on the premise that current migration patterns cannot be grasped without first examining the historical development of the region within the world economy. An in-depth historical examination is essential to explaining the high rates of international and transnational migration from Jatundeleg and the region (to the exclusion of other areas) as well as the meanings given to it by both those who leave and those who stay behind.

From Empire to Empire: The Inca and Spanish Invasions of the Azuayo-Cañari Region

The many villages that freckle the modern provinces of Azuay and Cañar are the vestiges of what once were loosely confederated kin-based indigenous communities. Details about the sociopolitical organization of pre-Incaic groups in the region are spotty at best and the source of some debate. Prior to the Inca and Spanish conquests, the inhabitants of the region, referred to as the Cañari, lived in small village units of extended families and cultivated subsistence crops such as potatoes, maize, beans, squash, and quinoa (Caillavet 1996; Hirschkind 1995; Idrovo 1986, 49–56; Murra 1946, 799–801). These family units, or *ayllus,* shared responsibility for and access to community lands, herds, and other material resources needed for survival, organized geographically along a pattern of vertical exploitation (Murra 1972).[10]

Inca expansion into the region was initiated sometime in the 1480s under the empire's ninth ruler, Inka Tupac Yupanki, but it was his son and heir, Huayna Capac, who would solidify a strong imperial presence. Huayna Capac was born in Tumipampa (modern-day Cuenca) and during his short reign transformed the city into a mirror image of Cuzco, the Inca capital. Inca hegemony in the region would be short-lived, however. The Inca most successfully ruled areas with dense populations, so the dispersed communities of the rugged south-central highlands proved

10. Ecuadorian historian Juan Chacón Zhapan speculates on the presence of "count- less" *ayllus* throughout the region (1990, 37–38), many of which correspond to village names in the modern provinces. He further points out that *ayllus* fell under larger units linking two or more extended families into small chiefdoms *(cacicazgos).* Archaeological evidence confirms the presence of two principal administrative sites predating the expan- sion of the Inca into the region. One site lay in Hatun Cañar, at the pre-Inca and Inca ruins of Inga Pirca, where the most powerful chief of the local "confederation" reportedly ruled (Jamieson 2000, 21). The other was Guapdondeleg at the present location of Cuenca. To what degree these centers reflect the establishment of a larger, unified "Cañari confedera- tion" linked through such basic indices as language, trade, and cultural tradition is an open question. Proponents of a common ethnicity theory include contemporary Cañari Indi- ans, who presently occupy upper Cañar province and claim to be direct descendants of the original builders of Inga Pirca (see Burgos Guevara 2003; Confederación de Nacionalidades Indígenas 1989, 193). A different line of reasoning supports the idea that Cañari identity and unity represent an instance of "ethnogenesis" of group identity formed in its opposition to Inca domination and later to Spanish encroachment (Engwall 1995; Fock and Krener 1978; Hirschkind 1995; Salomon 1987).

difficult to control, playing host to near constant warfare (D'Altroy 2002, 78–80; Idrovo 1986, 55). The abrupt death of Huayna Capac to smallpox put further in doubt the future of the Inca Empire in a region where it had only a tenuous hold. The ruler had died without choosing an heir from among his sons, touching off a dispute between two of his male offspring, Atahualpa and Huáscar, as to the legitimacy of the kingship. The brothers' inability to resolve their differences resulted in a destructive dynastic war (1525–32), pitting Atahualpa's stronghold in Quito against Huáscar and his Cuzco-based forces. The peoples of the Azuayo-Cañari region had sworn allegiance to the doomed Cuzco-based Huáscar, considering his faction a liberating force to lift the yoke of local Inca rule. Atahualpa, however, eventually triumphed over his half-brother and in retribution ordered the complete destruction of Tumipampa and a massacre of the local population, a retaliation recorded as particularly gruesome, including the intentional murder of pregnant women and the extermination of whole villages (Cieza de León 1965, 142–47). According to chronicler Miguel Cabello de Balboa, writing in 1586, Atahualpa proclaimed the region to be filled with "such bad people, they deserved to die twice" (1951, 435).

When the Spanish chronicler Pedro Cieza de León passed through the Azuayo-Cañari region in 1547, the consequences of war were close at hand and palpable in the area's skewed demography. He observed that women greatly outnumbered men and that many women had taken over male roles, serving as porters and guides for the conquistadors. As he described the situation,

> Some Indians are accustomed to saying they do this because there are so few men and an abundance of women, due to Atahualpa's cruel punishment of the natives of this province[...].They say that, in spite of the adults and children having gone out with green branches and palm fronds to beg for mercy, with a severe and angry expression he ordered his troops to kill them all; and thus a great many men and children were murdered. . . . Because of this, those who are alive now say that there are fifteen times more women than men; and because there are so many women, they work in this manner and do everything else husbands and fathers tell them to do. (compiled in L. León 1983, 58)

Cieza de León's comments are noteworthy because they suggest an interesting irony connected to the modern description of *pueblos de mujeres solas*. More important, however, they reveal some of the first insights into the demographic upheavals that have shaped the region up through today. The decimation of whole communities opened the area for future migrations to the region after the Spanish invasion.

After the execution of Atahualpa in 1532 by Francisco Pizarro in Cajamarca (modern northern Peru), the Spanish set about the daunting transition from military invasion to social control. As historian Susan Ramírez notes, the post-Inca Andean highlands—still a mix of different cultures, languages, and livelihoods—encompassed a "social geography whose scope, dimensions, and profile had not yet been totally explored, or perhaps even grasped" (1995, 145). Creation of a new city was one of the first steps toward control. In 1557, Huayna Capac's Tumipampa was renamed Santa Ana de los Rios de Cuenca (or simply, Cuenca). As payment for their efforts in subduing the local native populations, individual conquistadors were given authority over native groups through the gift of *encomiendas,* grants of Indian workers. Spanish lords *(encomenderos)* forced Indians to build houses and churches, plant fields of imported crops, spin and weave cotton, and tend to herd animals imported from Europe. In return, indigenous peoples were instructed in Spanish customs and religion. As a solution to the region's labor shortage, however, the *encomienda* system ultimately proved inadequate. During the 1550s and 1560s, the Azuayo-Cañari region, like much of the Andes, experienced a drastic reduction in its Indian population, attributable to epidemic disease and harsh working conditions. A 1567 census enumerated a tribute-paying population of only 5,470, suggesting an Indian population of no more than 24,615 (Hirschkind 1995, 329–30). At the same time, the European immigrant population began to increase along with European demand for local goods (especially fruit and sugar), outpacing what *encomienda* labor could produce.

The Azuayo-Cañari region, because of its shortage of labor and the seemingly haphazard dispersal of Indian groups, was one of the most heavily targeted areas for the Spanish Crown's ambitious program of *reducciones* starting in the 1570s. Initiated under the ambitious Viceroy Francisco de Toledo, the reforms called for Indians to be "reduced" into discrete and manageable Spanish-style towns, organized around a central plaza and chapel. Distinct from the *encomiendas,* the new reforms coupled economic measures with a far-reaching social-policy of bringing Indians into the emerging folds of Spanish society—what Toledo termed a policy of "gobierno y pulicía" (governance and refinement). Among other goals, the reforms specified that "local councils should be charged with the control of good hygiene [*limpieza*], vigilant that the streets as well as the houses are clean and that in each house there are wooden beds where they sleep" (Toledan Reform XXXIII, quoted in Chacón Zhapan 1990, 63).

Jatundeleg first appears in colonial administrative records under these circumstances as a satellite community of the established *cacicazgo* (chiefdom) of Déleg (Chacón Zhapan 1990, 53; *Libros Parroquiales* 1615 [civil registry in Déleg maintained by a local priest]). As inhabitants of the region claim today, Déleg and its surrounding communities were most likely populated in the fifteenth century by a loyal Inca *mitamae* (Inca state colonist) community transferred from the Cuzco region.[11] Lending evidence to this claim, many contemporary surnames in the area are similar to Quechua names found in southern Peru (Hirschkind, 1999).

The Spanish Crown had hoped that *reducciones* would streamline the management of Indian labor and the collection of tribute, a goal unrealized in the south-central highlands owing to the lack of a comprehensive regional industry and the erosion of local native economies. In contrast to the northern reaches of the Real Audiencia of Quito where large weaving workshops on rural estates *(obrajes)* forced Indians to produce fine woolens for export (Andrien 1995; Phelan 1967), in the Azuayo-Cañari region the Spanish continued to siphon what tribute they could from Indian agriculturists. Although inefficient from the perspective of Spanish landholders, tribute collection under the *encomienda* partly mimicked the tribute practices of the Inca. By contrast, the Toledan reforms ushered in a "depersonalization of tribute" (Ramírez 1996, 117) in that what was collected

11. Inca presence in the region is less clear. Archaeologist John Hyslop notes that a branch of the royal Inca highway (Capacñan) ran through Déleg (1984, 22), and it is possible that a small imperial settlement was located there.

became akin to a tax, increasingly paid in cash (silver) rather than assessed in labor or local goods. Déleg's *libros parroquiales* demonstrates how this transformation of tribute often undermined the urban elite's ability to tap Indian labor in the countryside. Although no tribute lists *(cartas cuentas)* have survived for the area, references to tribute payers as *mitayos de yerba y leña* (Indian laborers who served as pasture keepers and collectors of firewood) suggest that *encomenderos* were paid either in service or in fuels needed for cooking, a resource Jatundeleg villagers would likewise collect for themselves. Under the *reducciones,* tribute demands in silver found many Indian households unable to pay. In 1651, Jatundeleg's *cacique* (indigenous authority) was jailed for failure to collect tribute from local Indians in the form of silver. Along with others incarcerated in Cuenca, villagers drafted a petition stating that unless the *caciques* were released to find their missing community members, no tribute would be paid.

The Colonial Era: Consolidation and the Rise of the Noble Class

Although Cuenca was established as a *corregimento* (administrative and commercial center) of the Real Audiencia of Quito because of its close proximity to the important port city of Túmbez (modern northern Peru) and its strategic midpoint location between Quito and Lima, the city passed much of the colonial period in isolation. Geography was largely to blame, with its rough terrain, formidable rivers, extreme weather, and poor-quality roads. In addition, in an economy based on mercantilism and heavily driven by the extraction of metals, the Azuayo-Cañari region lacked the dazzling mineral wealth the Spanish desired and had found in great abundance farther south in Huancavalica and Potosí (Chacón Zhapan 1990, 131–90). Agriculture, which continued to be the backbone of the regional economy, carried on sluggishly, hampered by an overabundance of poor-quality soils. In this context, two distinctive features of the region developed: (1) a self-ascribed nobility, which "abstained from intensive participation in commerce, trade, and manufacturing" (Hirschkind 1980, 40); and (2) a *minifundio* land-tenure system, whereby each individual household held an extremely small plot of land and practiced subsistence farming. Both of these developments fueled antagonisms between the urban elite who sought, often unsuccessfully, to harness rural labor and resources and the rural producers who tried to maintain autonomy and self-sufficiency.

Although urban elites maintained only a loose grip on rural producers, the relationship was anything but smooth. Protest over the autonomy of Indian landholdings frequently prompted critics to question whether it was labor shortage that created the *minifundio* or the other way around. As small *minifundio* landowners held tenaciously to their land, would-be and small-scale *hacendados* expressed their dismay at being unable to harness Indian labor. In 1764, Romualdo Navarro, a judge in the *audiencia,* wrote of the Azuayo-Cañari region:

> It is true that there are many who do nothing whatsoever, just as there are almost anywhere; the only thing special about here being that one cannot find people to cultivate the land or who want to serve on estates, which is due to the fact that everyone has his plot of land, though it be small, and since, as I have already said, this region is very fertile; with almost no work the land provides for all needs. (quoted in Hirschkind 1980, 52)

Despite Navarro's claim that the region was "very fertile," Indians' lands often lacked this quality because they were located on high slopes in arid rain shadows and cursed with rocky terrain *(canguaga)*. The few haciendas often inhabited the best-quality lands, a complaint frequently mentioned by liberal "reporters" in the *Relaciones de Cuenca*. By way of justification, hacienda supporters pointed to areas in the region where the Indians had "all of the land [in some areas] . . . without any *hacendado* and they have a lot of cattle" (Merisalde y Santistéban 1994, 411, written in 1765). Another visitor noted, "Thanks to the abundance of produce, the Indians here manage to find greater comfort and rest in their lives, as compared to the bare subsistence of those miserable Indians in other parts of the province" (quoted in Albornoz 1960, 39).

Over time, the freedom that Azuayo-Cañari campesinos enjoyed would not go unnoticed by Indian laborers in Ecuador's central and northern highlands. Consequently, thousands of Indians fled their native villages to exempt themselves from the *mita* (required labor service) and, whenever possible, to find land of their own to settle. Owing to the complacency of the Spanish elite, *forasteros* (Indians not living on their own comunal lands) gravitated to the Azuayo-Cañari region in hopes of obtaining their own *minifundios*. By the late eighteenth century, more than 75 percent of the Azuayo-Cañari region consisted of emigrant *forasteros* (Andrien 1995, 41), making it the most populous and crowded area of the Real Audiencia. Already small parcels of individual *minifundios* were made even smaller.[12] In fact, by the beginning of the nineteenth century, the modern provinces of Azuay and C nar had the smallest individual landholdings, averaging between 0.5 to 0.7 hectares.[13]

The Long Nineteenth Century: Poverty, Protest, and the Consolidation of Agri-artisan households

By the close of the eighteenth century, a modest *minifundio* landholding less than a hectare in size served poorly as a unit of agricultural production to meet a single household's needs in the expanding cash economy (Rodas 1985, 158). Families frequently had to seek supplementary income working on haciendas or collecting cinchona bark, an easily harvested plant used for the manufacture of quinine. Rural households additionally relied on the help of extended kin. Reciprocal labor agreements, known locally as *cambiamanos* (literally "changing hands") and *prestamanos* ("borrowed hands") allowed families to acquire resources and labor without needing access to cash.

Likewise, the entrenched *minifundio* system left Cuenca's entrepreneurial elite with few viable options to tap the rural population for economic gain. A partial solution to this problem came in the form of artisan

12. To the best of my knowledge, scholars and agronomists do not identify a specific size of landholding to define *minifundio*. The *Diccionario económico juridico y político* defines *minifundio* as simply "any tract of land where the means of production to obtain results are too scarce and insufficient to assure the normal life of its proprietors" (n.d., 122). A sense of what an "extreme *minifundio*" would be is indicated by what the average landholding in Ecuador is: approximately five hectares (Espinoza and Achig 1981, 151; see also Chiriboga 1988).

13. One hectare is equal to 2.47 acres.

production and the development of a regional textile industry. In the final decade of the 1700s, colonial merchants had learned hard lessons about the mass production of textiles as the once vibrant *obraje* sector of the northern highlands collapsed. Struggling with issues of liquidity and the lack of credit, merchants looked to a smaller cottage industry model to lower costs (Andrien 1995, 44–48; Phelan 1967). Numerous households in the Azuayo-Cañari region, themselves plagued with crowded and underproductive farmlands, began to spin and weave low-quality cotton cloth *(tocuyos)* and wool textiles *(bayetas)* for both local and distant Andean economies. The cottage production complemented the farming schedules of planting and harvesting and allowed households time for each activity (Palomeque 1990). Primarily women and children spun and wove cotton, leaving men free to tend to the needs of farming. The economic potential of this new cottage industry gradually attracted the attention of Cuencan merchants, and over time a system of middlemen developed to facilitate the process further. Merchants purchased raw cotton from Peru, which they sold to weaving households in the Azuayo-Cañari region. In turn, they purchased finished *tocuyos* and *bayetas* to sell in markets from Peru to Panama.

Textile production had a profound effect on shaping agri-artisan households in villages such as Jatundeleg. The principle behind the household was simple: what basic needs families could not acquire through agriculture they made up in textile production. This shift reflected the increased involvement of the Azuayo-Cañari region in distant markets at the same time that it further entrenched rural-urban relationships and the influence of urban control. Although the combination of *minifundio* agriculture and weaving afforded households a degree of autonomy, it simultaneously cut off direct relations from a variety of labor options in the city (such as mule driving and liquor production) and discouraged group mobilization (Espinoza and Achig 1981). Households came to rely on middlemen to purchase their goods and to supply them with raw materials at a reasonable price. In this process, peasants often complained about unscrupulous intermediaries because they were commonly paid only a fraction above the cost of raw materials for their labor. A common refrain, as recalled by some of Jatundeleg's most senior residents old enough to remember their grandparents' reminiscing, went that "for every ten yards of textile produced, they gave the middlemen two 'dead yards' [*varas muertas*]."

In addition to the reorganization of production, households experienced greater efforts on the part of urban elites to control and manage their livelihoods by turning peasants into consumers. Indeed, more than ever, relationships were mediated through an influx of consumer goods entering all classes of Azuayo-Cañari society. Along with raw cotton from Peru, merchants brought to Cuenca *efectos de castilla*, high-priced imported goods from Spain. Urbanites became discriminating consumers of fine threads, velvet, silk, books, and paper, as well as cheaper household goods imported from Great Britain (cf. Krüggeler 1997). The thriving economy also brought new consumer goods from the north—*efectos de Quito*—such as hats, rosaries, spices, and shawls.

The textile market that shaped the agri-artisan structure of Azuayo-Cañari households and brought a degree of economic diversity would ultimately be short-lived, cut off prematurely by the rebel shouts for independence from Spain. Prior to the founding of the Republic of Ecuador in 1830, the region was a department capital under Simón Bolívar's confederation of Gran Columbia.[14] Fearing that links to Peru would lead to the annexation of a new nation and the breakup of Gran Columbia, Bolívar cut off trade ties. Peru's demand for Azuayo-Cañari textiles fell sharply as cheaper textiles flowed in from Europe (Palomeque 1990, 19). Simultaneously, the regional market for cinchona bark—the southern highlands inauguration into the world market—declined as world consumption waned. The combination of isolation and a lack of elite initiative translated into a stagnant economy that would persist for much of the period between 1830 and 1860.

In communities such as Jatundeleg, where household incomes depended heavily on the production of what came to be called *tejidos de la tierra* (weavings of the land or countryside), living conditions deteriorated significantly. Annual production of *tocuyos* that had once reached an astonishing volume of 698,480 yards per year in 1787, for example, plummeted to 261,961 yards by 1828 (Palomeque 1982, 122).

---

14. The modern province of Azuay was formed in 1830. Cañar followed in 1884.

The most immediate effect of the economic crisis was widespread food shortage. In the words of Azuay's governor, unthinkable "horrores de la escasez y del hambre" (horrors of scarcity and hunger) plagued rural villages across the region (quoted in Palomeque 1990, 101). During the stable years of the weaving economy, many households that also worked on nearby haciendas had let their lands lie fallow. As the haciendas equally felt the effects of independence, regular harvests also diminished, causing widespread shortages of basic staples. Families responded most readily by sending fathers and able-bodied sons to work on the coastal cacao plantations, leaving wives and daughters to maintain agriculture.

From the vantage point of Cuenca, however, antagonisms between rural producers and urban elites hampered a unified response to the economic crisis. When hunger-stricken rural *"vagos"* (vagrants), as the newspapers called them, began to flood Cuenca's streets to beg for food, responsibility for the situation shifted from structural factors of isolation and poor economic development to criticism of male out-migration to the coast. The absence of men generated reports that migration was starving native communities. One journalist reported that "the continuing migration of men to the coast causes the calamity of hunger that afflicts this entire province" (quoted in Palomeque 1990, 108). More sophisticated in their analyses, though no less accusatory, were explanations for the food shortage claiming that migration robbed communities of adult men who were "more qualified [*más calificados*]" for agricultural work than were their female counterparts. Women left behind, the author argued, would be inclined toward the monocultivation of *maíz*, considered the easiest crop to grow, thus raising the potential for crop failure and food insecurity (Palomeque 1990, 109). The historical data do not reveal the answer regarding whether men's out-migration and the loss of agricultural labor (not technical expertise) contributed to the hunger in the highland villages. Instead, revealed in the reporters' claims are the ways in which urban concerns over the faltering regional economy began consistently to find rural households, the most vulnerable sector of the local society, at fault for the crisis. As time went by, blame would give way to the fear of rural populations.

Urban fears of rural unrest in the highlands fomented throughout the late nineteenth century. Subsequent to the collapse of the weaving economy, native communities attempted to consolidate their resources, including their obligations to the state (*servicio al estado*) (Larson 2004, 117–18). In particular, peasants tried to skirt church and state taxation, forced participation in public-works projects, and obligatory military service. They also struggled to protect their dwindling communal lands from the expansion of would-be *hacendados*.

Jatundeleg and Déleg, like many surrounding communities, were the sites of numerous peasant uprisings and protests throughout the 1800s (González Aguirre and Vásquez 1982; Vintimilla 1982), although they had passed much of the colonial period in relative calm, a situation owed in large part to fact that the parish experienced few land invasions and encroachment by Spanish and mestizos. The first registered protest appears in 1784, when it is noted that the "Mestizo M. Rubio" moved to usurp community lands. By 1786, however, two haciendas had taken shape in the area. In Déleg's *libros parroquiales,* a reference to the climate of unrest mentions that protest gripped "*all* of the population, save some of the most prosperous families." In August 1824, an internal report issued by the governor of Azuay warned of Déleg's "insolent and uproarious mobs"[15] that, in their organization in the town's plaza, were "rebellious to the point of arming themselves with shovels, rocks, and some even with firearms" (all quoted in Vintimilla 1982, 172–73). Villagers mounted their largest protest against the building of the Naranjal road, an ambitious construction project that would connect Cuenca to the coastal port of Guayaquil via the town of Naranjal in the Jubones Valley to the south. Peasants understood the road-building project as favoring hacienda owners, providing a convenient and quick route to transport their commercial items to the coast, but offering few direct benefits for rural producers. Moreover, the building of the road placed workers in particularly unfavorable labor conditions, ranging from the frigidly cold *páramo* to the malarial-ridden coastal lowlands (Larson 2004, 118; Vintimilla 1982). On July 27, 1869, the *teniente político* (police lieutenant) of Déleg issued a report to the governor concerning local protests against the project:

15. "Turbas insolentes y bochincheras."

I should inform you that the riot instigated by a group of *indígenas* was commanded by José Manuel Llayta, decisively refusing to obey the high command orders to lend [*prestar*] their services for the public works. [The rioters] stated that to participate they would have to abandon their planting and their families would die of hunger. (quoted in González Aguirre and Vásquez 1982, 212)

By the middle of the century, an unwavering urban criticism of male out-migration to the coast mixed with a growing fear of rural protest to form a unified critique of Indian communities as slowing the region's progress and development. Urban anxieties over the region's isolation found a comforting scapegoat in the construction of an unproductive and morally bereft rural Indian population (Espinoza and Achig 1981; Palomeque 1990; Prieto 2004). A member of Cuenca's town council detailed the problem: "Robbery and assault are the most common crimes. . . . The main cause is poverty and the lack of moral and religious education for the Indian classes, and second because of the public drunkenness, prostitution, and vagrancy that have spread through the region" (quoted in Palomeque 1990, 100). Another council member called for direct action, placing his faith in a renewed economic progress to sweep away the ills of the countryside: "A law of measure against vagrants and beggars [*mendigos*]—plain and simple—would be the most honorable act for the nation and of profound utility for society. It is imperative that local authorities see to it that [these people] dedicate themselves to *some kind of industry* lest they all end up in a house of refuge" (quoted in Palomeque 1990, 100, original emphasis).

The author's plea for social reform was to be delivered through the regional dedication to a new cottage industry: the production of *sombreros de paja toquilla,* or "Panama hats," fine-quality straw fedoras that had been produced on the coast since the early 1800s. More comprehensive in scope than earlier weaving ventures and more readily adopted by rural households, this industry would transform the local economy for nearly a century and would further integrate peasant households into distant markets. In the process, however, the unequal rural-urban relations that had structured previous elite ventures in the Azuayo-Cañari would persist and strengthen.

Panama Hats, Consumo, and Advancement, 1850–1960

By the mid-1850s, the towns of Biblían, Cañar, Gualaceo, and Déleg, among others, had become noted hat-making centers. Demand for the hats quickly stretched from internal markets in Ecuador to distant buyers abroad, including gold miners passing through Panama on their way north during the gold rush (hence the name "Panama hats").In the early years of production between 1856 and 1873, exports totaled more than one million pesos (Domínguez 1991). By the late 1850s, Azuay's governor spoke proudly of the new industry "so generally found throughout this region that there is almost no individual who is incapable of making these kinds of hats" (quoted in Palomeque 1990, 49).

In Jatundeleg, hat making likely occupied at least some of each household's time and contributed a significant portion to its overall earnings. In 1852, a church scribe visiting the village commented on the "industriousness of all peasant families . . . who, it seems, constantly

2.3. Finishing Panama hats for sale around the world, ca. 1930.

have their heads down and their hands quickly moving in the production of *sombreros de paja toquilla.*" No living persons remember the advent of the hat industry, but many village elders born in the early decades of the twentieth century still vividly recall the way hat making captured the hands, if not the hearts, of the local residents. Alfredo Uruchima, born sometime around 1910, was one of those who grew up learning to make hats. His recollection captures a number of common themes of the hat-making livelihood:

> Every family in Jatundeleg wove hats back then. We were poor, and there was no way to get money. You could go to the coast, but it was far! It could be months before you would return. No, working at home was better. When the husband would leave, the wife would have to do all the agriculture. Weaving kept everyone at home. . . .
>
> We all had a job, my brothers and sisters and me. When my father would bring the bundles of raw *paja* home, it was my job to sort the straw. My father told me to pick out the best strands, lest we make a hat the *comisionistas* would not want. . . . Before, my family never worked in artisanry, no *bayetas* or other weavings. We were poor farmers only. . . . We worked with other families to share harvests, and we traded labor [*cambiamanos*][. . .].I can remember times when we could make some real money [*hacía agosto*][16] from the hats. My parents would try and work extra hard to make more hats. While you could make between six and eight per week, if we were diligent, if you really worked all the time, you could maybe make twelve or more. My parents bought new pots and pans, dishes . . . sugar, and my dad bought and sold liquor [*trago*]. When you work that fast, though, some of the hats were *ushuros* [hats of poor quality] that wouldn't fetch much of a price. Some people who didn't want to farm anymore tried to make it as hat makers. It was very difficult.

As Alfredo Uruchima's reflections hint, hat weaving, in contrast to the production of crude *tocuyos* and *bayetas,* ushered in a new kind of livelihood. The hat economy became a force to organize schedules and so

---

16. The phrase *hacer agosto* literally means "to make August." It refers to the harvest month when rural highland households sit on the most wealth.

competed with agricultural and religious cycles in rural communities. Depending on the day of the week, individual households prepared hats to sell at different markets, and weavers frequently worked themselves into exhaustion to finish hats for market deadlines. As quickly as the hats were made, they were rushed to the middlemen purchasers before they became water stained, gnawed by animals, or soiled by the dirty conditions of rural homes.

The boom years of the hat-making industry dovetailed with Ecuador's liberal revolution powered by the dynamic general-turned-president Eloy Alfaro. In the final decade of the nineteenth century, Ecuador found itself following the zeitgeist of modernization that was sweeping Latin America, buttressed by strong convictions of nationalism and a unified and progressive nation-state (Clark 1998; Love and Jacobson 1988). In this context, many of the local initiatives aimed at bringing "progress" and "advancement" to rural Azuayo-Cañari households reflected the deliberate social engineering of the new liberal state. Distinct from raw materials, such as cinchona bark, and crude textiles, *sombreros de paja toquilla* stood as icons of modernity and a clear sign that the long-endured isolation of the region had ended. As ethnohistorian Kim Clark describes in her history of railroad building in liberal Ecuador, concepts of "movement" and "connection" enjoyed a wide circulation in the liberal state's justifications of itself (1998, 45). Hat exporters, for their part, frequently touted the far-reaching demand for their products in markets, expos, and fairs across the world (Domínguez 1991).

The global demand for hats also required a new organization of labor. A cornerstone of the emerging liberal state discourse was the creation of a new society of moral citizens who, above all else, found their sense of purpose as Ecuadorian citizens within the space of work. Liberal reformers championed work as a "moralizing force" in the face of vagrancy and idleness (Clark 1998, 46–48; Prieto 2004). Amidst the excitement generated around hat making, the local government granted town leaders sweeping powers to remove vagrants from the streets and to turn local jails into de facto weaving training centers and sweatshops (Domínguez 1991). In a report to Ecuador's president, a member of the Cuencan elite lauded the industrious nature of hat-weaving households:

We are not exaggerating when we assume that at least two-thirds of our population, rural and urban, lives in dedication to this profitable occupation. It is a curious observation how in peasant households are grouped 3 to 4 persons of a modest and hardworking family on the patio and under the eaves of the poor homes passing their days content in the profitable duty of whose product assures comfortably sustenance all week long. (quoted in Domínguez 1991, 78)

The transformation of new forms of productive work, however, represented only one-half of the project of making full citizens in the Azuayo-Cañari hinterland. In reformers' eyes, producers also had to become consumers who, through the acts of purchasing, could realize the fruits of their labor and appreciate hard work. Since the first impulses of Ecuadorian nationalism, reformers had long complained that despite economic incentives, rural *indígenas* seemed to lack proper *necesidades* (needs) for consumer goods, a response they translated as a sure sign of laziness and an absence of ambition (cf. Krüggeler 1997, 49). Hat weaving arguably represented the first integration into the Ecuadorian national economy, complete with its own currency and a host of inexpensive consumer goods to purchase. As the *jefe político* (political chief) of Azogues declared in 1855, "The advancement of hat weaving in the region promises to be the only branch of industry to bring the hope of riches to the countryside" (quoted in Palomeque 1990, 49).

Hat production in no way offered a sure-fire route to enrichment, yet it did afford some poor households the chance to engage in new forms of consumption. Like Alfredo Uruchima's family, it allowed for the purchase of practical items such as sewing needles, shovels, and iron hoes, which lessened the travails of rural life. It also permitted rural families to extend reciprocity pacts further and to amplify the fiesta cycle in both size and the lavishness of food and drinks. Recollections of these changes, which I gathered from village elders, were generally positive and looked upon as signs of progress and advancement. Some elders, though, held the augmentation of the fiesta cycle in contempt. Increased spending on alcohol and dancing was a tool used by affluent families to solidify and extend their reciprocity networks, while ultimately stratifying the community and destroying the sanctity of the patron saints and religious histories they were designed to honor.

Policies directed at "civilizing" indigenous peoples through the creation of a consumer culture ultimately did not prove to be the panacea reformers had hoped they would be. Rather, they ran up against contradiction and paradox: the urban elite encouraged Indian participation in markets as a way to bring progress to the hinterland, but at the same time fretted about the effects of unrestricted consumption.[17] It was agreed that if campesinos were to become part of the "nation of consumers," they would have to do so along with an *espíritu de ahorros* (spirit of saving). For households in Jatundeleg, such policy issues mattered little. More important than what they consumed and how much they consumed, *consumo* proved to draw peasants further into a web of market relations, including the fluctuations of the prices felt by all and new desires for goods previously unknown.

Hat making also subtly changed the notion of work in agri-artisan households. Although the new industry ostensibly represented a cottage enterprise, with each household enjoying an enormous amount of freedom, it subtly served to keep wages low for weavers, to increase competition between households, and ultimately to discourage resistance and labor organizing. Luís Monsalve Pozo, a Marxist sociologist with a sharp pen, provided in 1944 one of the most trenchant attacks against the hat-weaving industry: "Thousands of hands, white and smooth, fine hands of women, girls' hands weaving *toquilla* fiber, weave the illusion of obtaining their bread and water, when in reality the illusion is converted into mere *centavos* [pennies] for them, but for others the conversion is to palaces, Cadillacs, villas, tourism, and other things" (1953, 6).

The plight of woefully exploited agri-artisan households equally captured the minds of the literary world.[18] A poem from the era entitled "Juan

17. Stephenson (1999) draws out a similar set of contradictions in her analysis of Bolivian pedagogical manuals from the early 1920s.

18. See also Alfonso Cuesta y Cuesta's 1963 novel *Los hijos* (The Children), which tells the bittersweet tale of a little girl (nicknamed "La Tejedorita," the Little Weaver) who devotes all her energies to weaving the best Panama hat for a citywide contest in Cuenca only

Cuenca—Biography of the Hat-Making People" draws out the gendered facets of the trade, the male hat finisher and the female weaver, who each in his or her own way pays for the work done:

> Many times the straw, strong and slippery,
> Cut his fingers like a twisting knife.
> Always at the meat of his tired finger,
> Leaving the imprint of fiery, yellow canals . . .
> Fiber which the *chola* weaves, weaving tuberculosis[19] and hunger,
> Mixing anemia with the ruin of her body, shrinking Her body, shrinking
>   her thorax . . .
> Twisting her spine, always leaning toward her work
> *Carloduvica Palma*
> Executioner disguised in white clothing . . .
> Exalted assassin of the Brown Virgin of the Rosary
> Wearing a lovely sombrero woven by the hands of a *chola*
> Who dies as she lives . . . (G. H. Mata, quoted in T. Miller 1986, 161)

Criticism of the hat economy was quickly muted when hat production took an irreversible nose dive in the late 1940s as international demand for the *sombreros* decreased. Unable to compete with cheaper "straw" hats mechanically produced in various parts of Asia, the production of *sombreros de paja toquilla,* as a percentage of total regional production, fell from 22.8 percent in 1945 to 1.6 percent in 1954 (Domínguez 1991, 214). Despite efforts by rural elites to streamline production and eliminate usurious

---

to find that the church has collected all the hat contest entries for itself to export to and profit from in New York City.

19. The boom years of Panama hat production coincided with a regional tuberculosis epidemic that claimed the lives of a number of hat makers. Social critics such as Monsalve Pozo were quick to link the disease to the hat industry, citing the cramped living quarters where most weavers worked as a prime risk factor for the disease's spread. To the contrary, epidemiological studies conducted in the 1960s found that seasonal migration to the coast from highland communities (and the drastic climate changes that accompanied it) was a stronger correlation than hat making for tuberculosis in Azuayo-Cañari villages (personal communication, Department of Public Health, Azuay Province, Feb. 1999).

middlemen in the export process, the production of Panama hats would never regain its once-celebrated vitality.

Rural households had few safety nets in which to catch themselves when the hat economy collapsed. Total rural income derived from weaving in the Azuayo-Cañari region plummeted from 15,599 sucres in 1950 to 6,955 sucres in just four years (Espinoza and Achig 1981, 159). The number of full-time weavers registered in the region dropped from 47,280 in 1950 to 12,000 by 1959 (Sempértegui 1991, 57). Elite efforts to stem the economic crisis were limited in scope, again leaving rural villages to cope with food shortages and the absence of alternative income-earning opportunities. And, as previously, the central image of the misery was that of the rural beggar on the streets of Cuenca. Monsalve Pozo, taking up his pen after the industry's fall, lamented how "the streets . . . have become filled with the manifestation of hunger—weaver women dressed in tatters and rags carrying children on their backs" (1957, 109). Such visual reminders aside, the disarticulated nature of the hat economy and the lack of a collective consciousness among hat-weaving households commingled to make the social and economic dislocations that rural peoples experienced a quieted series of tumultuous events, what Cuencan sociologists Leonardo Espinoza and Luis Achig (1981) term a "silent struggle" for peasants to regain their livelihoods.

Migration and Rural Development, 1960–1980

During the 1950s and 1960s, the country's coastal provinces experienced an intense agrodevelopment, including a "banana boom" in the 1950s and a significant increase in the country's cultivation of sugar and rice (Lentz 1991; Striffler 2002). These developments brought with them considerable labor needs, drawing workers from throughout the highland region. Jatundeleg was among a number of Azuayo-Cañari villages that had become regular seasonal stops on plantation *enganchadores'* (recruiters) worker-seeking tours. On busy market days in Déleg, older men from Jatundeleg recalled crowding around the recruiters to hear promises of daily plantation wages five and sometimes ten times higher than wages in the sierra. Before a road connecting Cuenca and Guayaquil was built in 1953, recruiters went to great lengths to transport workers to the coast. Some of Jatundeleg's elderly recommended traveling by airplane from Cuenca to Quito and then by train to their work destinations. Other workers would walk to the coast, a week's journey along the muleteer trails and railroad tracks. Between 1950 and 1974, more than ninety thousand men and able-bodied boys (called *gente de palas, lampas y picos* [men of shovels, spades, and picks]) migrated from the Azuyo-Cañari region to work plantations in the coastal provinces of Guayas and El Oro (Borrero 1991).

Few households involved in labor migration sought to settle permanently on the coast, a decision that altered Azuayo-Cañari domestic organization immeasurably.[20] Although some women and children did accompany men, largely in search of jobs selling goods in the markets, most migration activity remained male oriented and seasonal. Migrants earned the label *golondrinas* (swallows) for their seasonal patterns of mobility—working from June until December on the coast and then returning to their highland villages for the first part of the year. Plantation work ultimately made possible the formation of households and minor investment. Although some families continued to make handicrafts, the majority of households directed their wages to the purchase of land. Years of partible inheritance, whereby parents bequeath a small parcel of land to each child (see chapter 4), had left many new couples with extremely small plots of land, a problem greatly relieved by weaving incomes. Seasonal migration to the coast again allowed peasants to purchase land and, in some cases, even to build houses (Hirschkind 1980). In fact, almost one-third of the households that participated in my census had constructed their homes between 1970 and 1980. Other households put their remittances toward specific business ventures: three established *tiendas* (small stores) in the village; one household purchased a commercial oven to start a small bakery *(panadería);* three other families forged links with farmers on the coast and began importing vegetables and fruit to sell during market days.

Although seasonal out-migration did little to alter the core structure of rural life, it did contribute to a new gendered division of labor, one that

---

20. See Lentz 1991 and 1997 for an elaboration of the effects of internal migration on rural communities.

would later define the structural qualities of international migration. Although the hat-weaving economy had spelled greater dependency on cash through the need for imported food stuffs and other consumer goods, social relations in Azuayo-Cañari households, especially gender relations, remained relatively stable in that economy. Both men and women contributed to agriculture duties, and both dedicated themselves equally, as time permitted, to the production of *sombreros de paja toquilla*. Under seasonal migration, women were forced to assume greater roles as household managers, taking on many of the tasks of planting, weeding, and maintenance of animals before their husbands' return for the harvest. At the same time, those aspects of the household economy reserved for hat-weaving and other artisan production became almost exclusively female centered. This "feminization" of the handicraft industry led to its devaluation in village life, therefore cutting off a potentially valuable economic strategy for young men (Balerzo 1984; Kyle 2000, 60). Indeed, when I queried young men about why they did not learn hat-weaving, the response was often the same: "!Es un trabajo de las mujeres!" (That's women's work!) For some households, too, women's subordination to men's wages was exacerbated by the influx of children into the school system and the demands of a school schedule on a parent's time (see Weismantel 1997b).

Although altering gender roles and responsibilities, seasonal migration made possible the "repeasantization" of some Jatundeleg households through the purchase of land, the construction of new homes, and, to a lesser extent, the purchase of cattle. At the same time, significant national initiatives to modernize the country in the 1970s and early 1980s brought other transformations to village life (Martínez 1984). Buttressed by high state revenues from the discovery of petroleum in the Amazonian lowlands, the military-led government of General Guillermo Rodríguez Lara (1972–76) implemented a series of social and economic reforms aimed at eliminating poverty, improving national infrastructure, and spurring economic development (see Schodt 1987, 115–34). High on the agenda and aggressively supported by the United States and the Alliance for Progress was the enactment of agrarian reform legislation calling for the redistribution of land and an agribusiness revolution. The 1973 legislation, which included provisions to break up large hacienda landholdings, enjoyed widespread support, yet ultimately benefited only a fraction of peasant households.[21]

By contrast, what villagers in Jatundeleg recount as the most important development of the era was the construction of a road connecting the village to Déleg and to the Pan-American Highway. Both practical and symbolic, the road demonstrated to villagers that their future would come through the connections they could forge beyond its limits rather than from within. Ironically, though, even while the population began looking elsewhere for its future, other state-led projects further established Jatundeleg's community status. In 1972, a primary school with three classrooms was erected. Health services and the construction of latrines followed. Electricity would reach the village in 1984.

National modernization reforms did little to curb the tide of labor migrants to the coast. Moreover, locally directed initiatives aimed at modernizing Cuenca—billed as the *tercer polo* (third pole) of development (after Quito and Guayaquil)—also went unfulfilled (Espinoza and Achig 1981). Unable to attract investment on par with that made in Ecuador's largest cities, Cuencan elites instead drew in smaller industries, a tire-making plant and a cement factory, that did little more than temporarily shore up urban unemployment (Hirschkind 1980, 171). Consequently, chronic rural development problems continued to persist without a remedy in sight. Rural producers with few economic opportunities looked again to migration, although this time beyond Ecuador's borders.

International Migration

Jatundeleg's history demonstrates a logical and patterned past of migration— from the forced movements of Inca *mitamaes* to different cycles of coastal migration, first to harvest cacao and later to work the banana and sugar plantations. Uncovering the exact context of the initiation of international migration within this history, however, is anything but straightforward. In many

---

21. By 1978, only 7 percent of farmland in both the sierra and the coast had been redistributed under agrarian reform. By the early 1980s, the severity of the *minifundio* system continued, with 67 percent of farms less than five hectares in size (Schodt 1987, 122).

villagers' memories, the specter of the hat-market collapse loomed large. Echoing the words of many elderly residents in the village, my seventy-year-old neighbor don Miguel Cusco told me, "People migrated to escape the *llachapa vida* [literally, the 'ragged life'] when we couldn't sell our hats." However, if the decline and collapse of the hat-weaving economy defined many of the structural features of international migration, missing from the accounts I heard were clues to the decision-making processes that influenced where people migrated to and the actual networks that linked highland Ecuador with the United States.

How did peasants who were practicing circular seasonal rural-rural migration begin to initiate a new international migration stream? Sociologist David Kyle (2000) notes that although highland peasants began migrating to the lowland coastal plantations, an equally important migration network linking Azuay and Cañar provinces with New York City began taking shape through the efforts of thousands of Panama hat *comisiónistas* who still had well-oiled business connections in the United States. As Kyle posits, this incipient stream of well-to-do white and mestizo immigrants settled in New York in the late 1950s and used their influence to facilitate the migration of rural weavers north (2000, 65).

Jatundeleg and the other villages that dot the countryside of the *cantón* Déleg are considered the original migrant-sending communities of the Azuayo-Cañari region (Carpio Benalcázar 1992; Cueva Malo 1991; Preston 1974; Sempértegui 1991). They also composed the seat of the Panama hat-weaving industry. Jatundeleg residents, like their neighbors, boasted about their *pionero* (pioneer) migrant, Hugo Callaguaso, who journeyed to the United States in 1976, before it was uncommon to do so. In his migration account to me (which opens chapter 4), Hugo could not confirm or deny Kyle's thesis that campesinos of the Azuayo-Cañari region piggybacked on the migration of Panama hat exporters. Instead, what is most striking in his migration story and in others like it is the importance of social and kin networks. Contrary to the theory that migrants make economic calculations and seek out "immigrant markets," Hugo went first to New York merely because he had a cousin there who offered him a temporary place to stay. In Ayaloma, the first villager migrated directly to Chicago, where an uncle had established himself. Over time, and especially after 1986, when

the IRCA ushered in the possibility of citizenship for thousands of Ecuadorians living illegally in the United States, as well as for their immediate
relatives still living in Ecuador, family and social networks solidified.

Throughout the economic crisis of the 1980s, as villagers weathered
falling wages and rising prices on basic necessities, migration from the
region intensified, and the networks that facilitated it grew. A 1990 survey conducted by the Universidad de Cuenca's Insituto de Investigaciones
Sociales (IDIS, Institute for Social Research) found that 33.8 percent of
households in Azuay province alone had at least one family member in the
United States (Borrero and Vega Ugalde 1995, 72). While other parts of
Ecuador suffered under the economic crisis, households fortunate enough
to have a relative abroad were cushioned by the influx of remittances.

Because of Jatundeleg's early entry into U.S.–bound migration, a number of returned migrants resided in the village at the time of my research.
Their histories provided a useful contrast to the stories of migration I was
collecting from younger migrants. More important, though, their influence
in village politics and economic life meant that by the late 1990s nearly an
entire generation had come of age in a local economy dominated by international migration. In the way their parents had valued work on the coastal
plantations, young people growing up in Jatundeleg understood migration
as more than simply another outlet to earn money. Rather, migration had
profoundly affected both their expectations and their obligations. For village
youth starting their own households as married couples, the *ñaupa tiempos*
of subsistence agriculture punctuated by occasional wage labor had become
an inappropriate model for trying to make a living in a village increasingly
defined by the priorities of migration and the influx of dollar remittances.

In the next chapter, I explore the rural context of migration as I experienced it during a year's residence in Jatundeleg in 1999 and during
return visits in 2001 and 2002. Although migration has delivered on some
of its promises—bringing individual prosperity to some and leveling a
challenge against the marginal status assigned to villagers in the *nuestro
folklórico* ideology—it has equally exacerbated and more clearly exposed
underlying tensions between rich and poor households. These tensions
are no better revealed than in the desires and motivations of migrants
themselves and of those who hope to follow in their footsteps.

3

Jatundeleg

The Rising Cost of Everyday Life

An Embarrassment of Riches?

A few days before the meeting was announced, word had already spread through Jatundeleg that representatives from the Ministerio de Agricultura y Ganadería (MAG, Ministry of Agriculture and Livestock) wanted to hold a *charla* to discuss "new farming opportunities." Villagers appeared suspicious. Carmela Quispe told me, when I stopped to buy dry goods at her *tienda* a day before the meeting, that she was unaware of the representatives' plans, yet she was convinced they were a veiled attempt to inhibit villagers from going to the United States by keeping them tied to the land. Seventy-year-old don Andrés Saldañes, Jatundeleg's bus driver, qualified his comments by praising MAG regional officials for their *buenas costumbres* (good practices) and fair dealings with Jatundeleg farmers in the past. Yet this time he was convinced MAG did not have the campesinos' best interests in mind. "This isn't about farming," he presaged. "This is about taking what they can." He joined his neighbors in the belief—fueled by months of rumor—that MAG would force villagers to acquire official title to their land, a proposition many assumed to be just one step away from taxation.[1] The weather also threatened to dampen spirits. When an official

---

1. Villagers throughout the region had been mounting a steady resistance to titling since the mid-1990s. They opposed titling because, in addition to threatening taxation, it would require landowners to demarcate lands officially and to show proof of ownership, sometimes over multiple generations. Many families with little or no land feared that they

announcement of the meeting came crackling over the village public-address system (a loudspeaker positioned in the church belfry), I was sitting on my neighbor María Dolores Uruchima's patio, watching as she adeptly maneuvered her fingers over the unwieldy palm strands of an unfinished *sombrero de paja*.

"Are you going?" I asked.

"No," she snapped back. "¡Achachay! [It's too cold!]" Indeed, the weather had been unusually chilly for late July, with what seemed like weeks of endless rain and strong winds. By many residents' estimation, the success of the meeting hung in the balance.

Despite the night's chill and the land-titling rumors, the meeting fetched a large crowd. As soon as the *convento* lights had been illuminated, villagers quickly filled the room. Elderly campesinas in wool hats and thick wool shawls bundled up over their mouths to combat the cold huddled together against one wall. Their husbands accompanied them—many thin, wiry older men in frayed polyester sweaters, ripped trousers, tattered ponchos, and rubber boots. The meeting was also attended by a number of younger men, many of them returned migrants, distinguishable by their pressed shirts and slacks and, in some cases, fine leather coats and cowboy boots. By 8:00 P.M., the room was bursting at the seams; kneeling benches were brought over from the chapel to meet the demand for seats. The village council, comprising Jatundeleg's president, the community's liaison to residents in New York, and a secretary, sat at a table off to one side. In the middle, two MAG representatives, light-skinned mestizos in dress pants and sweaters, addressed the crowd.

As it turned out, the topic for discussion was not land titling, but indeed a proposition for a new farming opportunity—the use of large greenhouses *(invernaderos)* to grow vegetables for market. The representatives described a community-led program with MAG technical assistance in the building process, crop yield monitoring, and the location of produce markets. The cost of the project—including materials, seeds, and fertilizers—was nominal (under $500) and would be covered by a pooling of

---

would be exposed as "squatters" on land they thought abandoned or that mere "handshake agreements" would not be recognized under official titling.

community funds and donations of labor. For farmers who were experiencing one of the worst growing seasons in recent memory, the prospect of stable and productive yields prompted a visible excitement in the room. The representatives recounted the successes of an *invernadero* project in a nearby village, boasting of tomatoes weighing "más que una libra" (more than a pound). Villagers asked about vegetable varieties and potential profits. A couple of women held imaginary one-pound tomatoes, trying to comprehend the size.

With the excitement at its apex, one of the representatives silently addressed the eager crowd with an outstretched hand as if to say, "So, what do you think? Can a program of *invernaderos* be successful in Jatundeleg?" The room abruptly fell silent. After a few moments, an elderly man stood up, adjusted his wool poncho, and addressed the two men: "In those communities that are purely *indígena*-campesino, they are a community [*comuna*] because they have to be. They have to work together because they are poor. We are not—we are rich people [*ricos*]. We have our own property. Everyone has their own land. We have to be really organized to do something here." The president of the community, Juan Mishquire, framed the problem in the context of migration: "[H]ere people are going to leave if they have the money—or even if they don't, and maybe even more so if they don't have it. If they have enough money to put into this project and they are interested, they are going to pay for it themselves. Why wouldn't they? If something goes wrong, they can take care of it themselves. We are a community, but a community of families that can look out for themselves. . . . The problem is unity." Although the speaker's words were a harbinger of the project's doomed future, the evening ended with an agreement that villagers would confer among themselves and contact the MAG representatives at a later date. The later date never transpired, and few people talked of the project again.

The meeting that promised to be a show of stereotypical "peasant suspicion" at best,[2] village apathy at worst, had turned into a revelatory anthropological snapshot to be questioned and analyzed. What had happened?

2. For an informative discussion of the depictions and stereotypes of peasants in anthropological writing, see Kearney 1996.

What did the statements put forth by the elderly campesino and the village president about being "rich people" and "a community, but a community of families that can look out for themselves" represent? Did these words capture the community's general sentiment? Many of Jatundeleg's households who did not enjoy the benefits of migrant remittances could certainly have profited from the greenhouse project. Why had *they* not spoken up?

This chapter places the greenhouse meeting within the context of village poverty and wealth and the politics of everyday life through an exploration of important changes taking place in Jatundeleg and other villages of the Azuayo-Cañari region. Far from a seamless ethnography of contemporary village life, the chapter looks at specific ways in which the influx of remittances and the dominance of activities surrounding transnational migration in the local economy have led to a reordering of social and economic commitments, new meanings of rural life, and new assumptions about wealth. I address two broad processes. First, I examine the material consequences of migration in the community and analyze how, as remittances make their way into the local economy, the need for cash (particularly U.S. dollars) both to maintain households rooted in agriculture and to ensure the agriculture future of the next generation has increased for nearly all village households, in some instances escalating the tensions and making larger the divisions between village rich and poor. Second, I look at the role of social capital and new claims to status and prestige afforded by expanding forms of commodity consumption and the outlay of remittances. As I explore more intensively in later chapters on the form and definition of transnational families, commodity consumption provides a key arena in which migrant families can maintain status and mediate tensions by redefining commitments to community life. Building new homes in the community, sponsoring fiestas, spending lavishly on children, and contributing generously to public works projects are just some of the ways migrant households contribute to the "production of locality" (Appadurai 1996). Although, at one level, people recognize that these actions challenge the racist and patronizing position of *nuestro folklórico,* new consumption practices have simultaneously introduced powerful new standards of material success by which people judge their own and others' status, ultimately raising the cost of everyday life.

Village Wealth and Poverty

When I started my research in Jatundeleg, previous waves of international migration beginning in the early 1970s had left a heavy stamp on almost every aspect of village life. A number of the richest households were headed by returned migrants whose successes abroad were evidenced, most clearly, in their ownership of new homes, cars, land, and livestock. More recent migrant households were just beginning to make their presence known through the skillful allocations of remittances. Although the community's history through different economic booms—the Panama hat industry and coastal migration in particular—attests to the fact that Jatundeleg has always maintained "rich households" and "poor households," migration to the United States had widened this gap significantly by the time of my research. Households that had no migrant kin remitting from the United States could hope to bring in an average monthly income of between $90 and $170 by cobbling together agriculture with local wage labor, mostly by farming other people's land in sharecropping agreements *(medias)*, construction, and, in some cases, seasonal migration to the coast (see figure 3.1). In contrast,

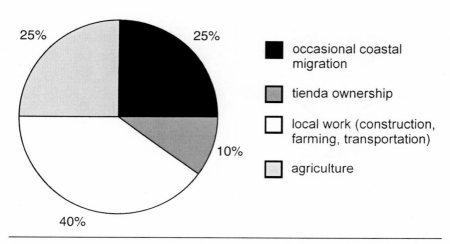

Figure 3.1. Sources and percentages of household income of non–international migrant households. *Source:* Study data, author's household census, 1999. Percentages are based on survey of forty-five domestic units.

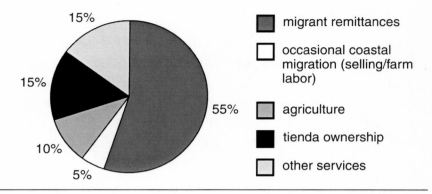

Figure 3.2. Sources and percentages of household income of international migrant households. *Source:* Study data, author's household census, 1999. Percentages are based on survey of forty-five domestic units.

households with a migrant relative abroad (most often a husband) could see an average *monthly* remittance of between $200 and $250 (see figures 3.2 and 3.3). As I elaborate in the coming chapters, although migrant families spent much of their money servicing debt, a considerable amount eventually went to schooling children and to purchase a wide array of consumer goods including televisions, stereo systems, furniture, and *electro-domésticos* (household appliances). Over time, their monies would be put toward building new homes and purchasing more land.

Despite the fact that remittances were responsible for a new level of inequality in local social relations, villagers of all social classes consistently described this transformation in positive terms, as a sure sign of the poor region's "development" *(desarrollo)* and "progress" *(progreso).* Some of the poorest families I knew who benefited the least from migration nevertheless could point to a number of advantages resulting from the elevated wealth in the community. The most important improvements they cited were the yearly repairs made to the two rutty dirt roads that connected Jatundeleg to Déleg, roadways that would periodically wash out, leaving the town isolated for weeks at a time. In addition to opening up the village to a

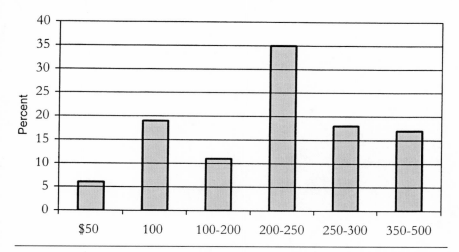

Figure 3.3. Average amount of monthly remittances sent to international migrant households. *Source:* Study data, author's household census. Percentages are based on survey of forty-five domestic units.

far greater number of services (from the delivery of cooking gas to an expanded number of foodstuffs sold in the village *tiendas*), the increased access had also convinced local officials to construct the Seguro Campesino health clinic and to get a doctor in the village two days a week. The increase of cash in the village had other positive effects as well. Through communitywide efforts to pool cash resources and with money collected from migrants in the United States, Jatundeleg's church was completely renovated with new cement walls, fresh paint, and a new roof. When I returned to the village in July 2001, concrete had just been poured for a new combined soccer and volleyball court.

Such new, lauded conveniences, however, could not drown out subtle, yet persistent criticisms from members of households whose own access to money was frequently unstable. My discussions with villagers about the increasing demands for cash in the community often took a decidedly historical tone, with villagers comparing the need for cash in the past with current demands. Alejandro Sinchi, a village elder who supplemented his

3.1. Jatundeleg's church under reconstruction with remittances from the United States. Photograph by the author.

subsistence farming with what he complained of as "too little"[3] cash sent from his son working in New York, explained:

> It used to be that only the *ricos* had cash, the ones who made hats or had jobs [outside the village]. They could buy new land, livestock, and build houses. My family was poor, but my father had lots of land where we grew tremendous crops. You can't believe it! Tremendous fields of nothing but corn [*puro maíz*]! We grew just corn because everyone wanted corn. And that was our money at times. We could trade the corn for whatever we needed—sugar, kerosene, tools; whatever we needed. . . . Today everyone needs cash every day. I tell my son I better join him in Yoni [New York City, also adapted from "I ♥ NY"] since I am always chasing the *dolarcito* [little dollar].

Although increased affluence worked to differentiate families "with cash" from those who were more intensely tied to a subsistence livelihood, it was the influx of U.S. dollars, as opposed to the national currency, the sucre, that

---

3. The "too little" he complained about was approximately $100 every three months.

posed the greatest challenge for poor families. U.S. dollars—mailed, carried by returned migrants, and sent directly through banks and money-wiring agencies—entered the local economy in remarkable ways. For migrant households, incomes in dollars provided a level of wealth well above that of households involved in domestic wage labor. Moreover, the high exchange rates between the dollar and the sucre allowed dollar-rich households to speculate with their money and increase their overall wealth. Well-off migrant families I knew, although often tight-lipped about money matters, periodically admitted to keeping large dollar reserves—safeguarded jokingly in "el banco de abajo del colchón" (the under-the-mattress bank)— for purchases of land and livestock. Having dollar reserves was helpful for outbidding nonmigrant neighbors who managed only with sucres.

My neighbor María Dolores, a woman in her early sixties whose family name villagers commonly associated with migration to the United States (although nobody in her immediate household had migrated), shared with me the following experience:

> Everyone talks about them, and everyone wants those *dolarcitos*—no sucres anymore. Their value is nothing. . . . For example, there was a family in Shullín that my sister said was selling pigs. The prices were good, and we had been looking to buy a pig to roast for [my son's] confirmation. When she said the price, I was confused until I realized she meant dollars. She looked at me and said, "You are from the *familia* Uruchima, yes or no? You have relatives over there [in the United States]. You must have dollars." This is the way life is in the village here, too.

María Dolores's access to dollars was in actuality very limited. After the incident, she began probing her sister-in-law for information on exchange rates, and for months she would make a weekly trek down to Déleg to check the exchange rates at the town's two money-wiring agencies. On days when the sucre had advanced closer to the dollar, she would convert her sucres to the more stable and powerful currency. Almost a dozen families I knew in Jatundeleg engaged in this practice.

The upper hand that migrant households had over their nonmigrant, dollar-poor neighbors reached a feverish intensity during the period of my fieldwork, as Ecuador's economy slipped deeper into crisis. In early 1999, the rate of exchange hovered between 6,000 and 7,000 sucres to the dollar; by early 2000 the sucre had fallen to 24,000 to the dollar, with the plummet showing no signs of abating. Soon after, Ecuador's Central Bank stabilized the currency at 25,000 sucres per dollar, foreshadowing plans to fully "dollarize" the economy by September 2000. Many residents complained.

Historically, wealth in the Azuayo-Cañari region had been tied up in having land, in the ability to harness labor (through *prestamanos* and *cambiomanos* agreements), and, to a lesser extent, in the ownership of livestock. However, as remittances were transformed from a source of income that families used to manage households to a currency of exchange *between* households, the costs of subsistence living increased for everyone. Not only did cash become an essential part of everyday life, it also became an increasingly important component for the maintenance of status in the village. Before I address some of these different arenas of change, an exploration of a cross-section of Jatundeleg households is useful to demonstrate the different experiences of village families vis-à-vis their varying needs for cash. Many of these needs played directly into villagers' decision-making processes with respect to migration.

For as long as villagers could remember, *la familia* Cajamarca-Quispe had been the wealthiest in Jatundeleg. The patriarch of the family, sixty-three-year-old don Andrés Cajamarca, a tall man with short graying hair and a leathery face, enjoyed a wide reputation throughout the *cantón* for his business acumen and his abilities as a public speaker. In 1999, he owned well more than ten hectares of farmland (an usually high concentration; see figure 3.4) and a large home built in the early 1980s. When don Andrés had married Alejandrina Quispe, he had moved to Jatundeleg from an adjacent village. Alejandrina's family were large landowners in the community, and she, as the eldest daughter, inherited a generous five hectares of land upon her marriage to Andrés. In contrast, Andrés's inheritance *(herencia)* of land was considerably smaller, prompting him to sell it and put the earnings toward improving his wife's fields. In a three-room house built on Alejandrina's property, the couple raised five children (two others died in infancy): Miguel, age fifty-five; Miltón, fifty-two (?); Andrés, forty-eight; Clemencia, thirty-three; and Carmela, thirty. When Miguel and Miltón were in their

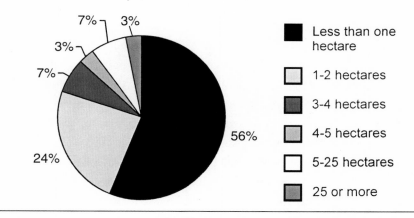

7% ⌐ 3%

3% ⌐

7% ⌐

24%

56%

- ■ Less than one hectare
- □ 1-2 hectares
- ▨ 3-4 hectares
- ▨ 4-5 hectares
- □ 5-25 hectares
- ▨ 25 or more

Figure 3.4. Distribution of land holdings in Jatundeleg. *Source:* Study data, author's household census. Percentages are based on survey of forty-five domestic units.

teens, they accompanied their father to work on the coast. For four months out of the year, they plowed, planted, and harvested rice on a plot of land they rented from a local hacienda. They would ultimately sell their yield to a rice farmers' cooperative. The profits were used to maintain farming, to purchase more land, and to fulfill don Andrés's dream of having his own *tienda* and animal feed store. As Miltón remembered,[4] "Almost all of our money went to buy more land. [My father] said we could keep what we earned, give some to my mother if we wanted, or we could buy land. Either way it would be our *herencia*."

By the early 1990s, don Andrés's family was clearly one of the village's wealthiest. Their feed store, selling cracked corn and green bananas (for feeding pigs), held a monopoly on their services; at the time of my research, don Andrés was in the process of building a set of greenhouses. Although their business successes were self-evident to many in the community, don Andrés and doña Alejandrina's pride rested with their children. Neither of them had any formal education, but both of their daughters had completed high school and married men outside the community. The sons had had less schooling, but had done well for themselves nonetheless. The eldest

4. I interviewed Miltón during a return visit he made to Jatundeleg in June 1999.

sons migrated to the United States in the late 1970s and had received citizenship under the IRCA in the late 1980s. The youngest, Andrés, worked closely with his father at the *tienda* and on the greenhouse project and would be first in line to inherit a large portion of his parents' assets.

By many people's estimation in Jatundeleg, don Andrés and doña Alejandrina lived comfortable lives. Despite don Andrés's repeated comments to me about "having more money in the past" and the rising costs of daily life, he nevertheless maintained a steady access to cash. As Miltón told me, his parents had been adamant that their children hold on to their own money, stressing that they were "humble people" *(gente humilde)* whose overall needs were few. Indeed, their spacious Spanish-style house made of wood and concrete and the adjoining *tienda* showed signs of age and a lack of upkeep. Still, when they needed cash, they were not at a loss for it. For example, when don Andrés suffered a severe heart attack in the early 1990s that required surgery in Cuenca, Miguel and Miltón quickly wired money to Ecuador so that the operation costing more than $4,000 could be performed. Miltón expressed to me, "Without our help, my father and mother would be in debt for the rest of their lives, or he just wouldn't have had the surgery in the first place."

The household of Luís Callaguaso and María Carmen Cusco represented an only slightly less prosperous example of village wealth. The couple, both in their early forties, had five children (ranging in age from thirteen to twenty-two), all of whom had received primary school educations in Déleg, and two of whom were attending high school in 1999. Luís, the cousin of one of Déleg's original migrants, overstayed a tourist visa and spent five years in the United States. Tragically, he returned to Ecuador just one year before the IRCA was announced in 1986. Although he missed his chance to obtain residency, his time abroad was anything but fruitless. Together with a small inheritance of land that he later sold, he was able to purchase a truck and build a house in Déleg with his savings. When I met him, he was shuttling people and goods throughout the *cantón* six days a week as one of seven four-wheel-drive pickup drivers in the local transportation cooperative. The job earned him approximately $70 per month. He earned an additional $35 monthly by renting out the house in Déleg. For her part, María Carmen supplemented the family's income by making dresses for fiestas, baptisms, and other events. Instead of living on the Déleg property (which María Carmen complained was "demasiada ciudad" [too city]), the couple and their children occupied a modest home owned by María Carmen's parents in the center of Jatundeleg and farmed two hectares of land. The couple's two oldest children (Mario, twenty-two, and Lucho, eighteen) worked in construction outside the village. The next three children, also boys, divided their time between school and helping with agricultural chores.

The Calluguaso-Cuzco household managed a higher-than-average income for a family not directly involved in migration and were considered "well off" by village standards, but they joined their neighbors in a constant need for cash. Gasoline prices, critical to the amount of income Luís could make with the transportation cooperative, fluctuated tremendously. (In 1999, for instance, the price of gasoline doubled under the economic crisis and restructuring.) The rental property also proved unstable as a source of income as tenants frequently skipped paying rent and utilities, and the family had no legal recourse to hold them accountable. Although Luís and María Carmen enjoyed a certain level of prosperity, they, like others in their position, fretted over their children's future. "Without land, they can't have a simple farming life." Indeed, as I rejoin their story in the next chapter, both boys were aware of the possibility that they would not inherit land, a realization that pushed them to consider migrating to the United States.

The lifestyles that Mario and the younger Lucho desired were not necessarily embodied in the fruit of their parents' hard work and in the way they cobbled together diverse means of earning cash. Rather, like many youths their age in Jatundeleg, they looked for models in the newly forming households headed by young couples whom villagers collectively glossed as the *nueva generación,* whose wealth was nearly or completely derived from remittances. At the time of my fieldwork, most of these households were in the formative phase of constituting their household: paying off debt, buying land, building houses, and, for some, starting businesses. As such, their cash reserves were often limited. By comparison, the household of Miguel Solano and Sandra Pañora, both in their early thirties, and their three children (two boys, ages sixteen and thirteen, and a girl age nine) represented one of the wealthiest migrant families at the time of my research. Their successful allocation of money was setting new standards for economic livelihoods in the village as well as for status and prestige.

Between 1992 and 1998, Miguel worked in an Italian restaurant in New York City. In 1994, Sandra joined him and found work in a garment factory; detesting life in the United States, she returned to Jatundeleg two years later. Miguel described himself as a "good saver" and was quick to point out the rewards of his time abroad. In 1996, the couple hired an architect to build a three-bedroom home with a large courtyard situated on a small parcel of land in the *centro*. On the front of the house, they apportioned a space for a *tienda*, which quickly became one of the most frequented shops in the village. A carport housed the family's early 1980s four-wheel-drive pickup truck and a small Skoda-brand compact (which Miguel owned jointly with one of his brothers). In addition to the *tienda*, the couple held eight hectares of land, where they pastured twenty head of cattle. (They farmed another five hectares on land owned by another of Miguel's brothers, who lived in New York.)

In 1999, Miguel was considered one of the richest residents in the community and had recently held the village presidency. Still, the effects of the economic crisis had delivered his family considerable financial hardship. Falling prices for their cows' milk and the high cost of stocking the *tienda* gouged into their once healthy profits. Their problems were compounded when Miguel and Sandra were among the thousands of bank account holders whose dollar assets were "frozen" by the Ecuadorian government in February 1999 in an effort to maintain its cash reserves.[5] The measure left the family with little cash to cover their expenses, ultimately forcing them to sell a few head of cattle at below-market price. As I prepared to leave Jatundeleg, Miguel was seriously planning another trip to the United States and hoped to leave within the year. His oldest son, he claimed, was chomping at the bit to join him. As Miguel told me, "Puede ir si Dios quiere" (God willing, he can go).

---

5. Bank accounts in dollars were frozen for the second half of 1999 and into 2000. Bank customers were allowed to withdraw only a small percentage of their money and were required to exchange their dollars for sucres at a fixed rate below the actual rate of exchange.

The examples of well-off households represented by the families Cajamarca-Quispe, Callaguaso-Cusco, and Solano-Pañora stood in stark contrast to the livelihoods of Jatundeleg's poorest residential units, most of which were situated on the periphery of the *centro*, scattered along the pathway up to Loma Lanzacay. With the exception of a few homes partially made of cement block, most houses in this area consisted of one- and two-room wattle-and-daub structures (some with dirt floors, but most outfitted with crude wooden planks) topped with rusty corrugated zinc roofs. All had limited electricity, yet no residents in the sector enjoyed the benefit of piped water, and most families cooked over open-fire hearths. Accounting for approximately 30 percent of village households, these residents also had the least access to cash, both sucres and dollars, and depended greatly on subsistence farming. Land holdings for the poorest families amounted to less than one hectare, with the average equaling 0.8 hectares.

Alberto Sinchi, his wife, María Dolores Pullo (both in their late thirties), and their four children (ranging in age from nine to nineteen) composed one of these poorer households. I met the couple on a house call with my physician colleague from the Seguro Campesino. María Dolores had been bedridden for nearly two weeks, weakened by a persistent cough that appeared to be tuberculosis. Their house was a two-building structure with a badly warped and rusting roof that extended between the two structures to form a covered porch. A television, a blender, and a small refrigerator adorned the otherwise spartan surroundings.

Despite his small and bony physique, Alberto–a man of thirty-seven who looked older than fifty—had massive hands, muscled and rough from being curled around the fat wooden handles of hoes and pickaxes in a life devoted to farming. As one of eight siblings vying for his parents' land, Alberto received a small inheritance of less than a hectare. When he and María Dolores married, she contributed an equally meager parcel. Together, they grew *maíz* and beans, in addition to raising pigs, chickens, and *cuyes* (guinea pigs) that they occasionally would sell or barter. Farming posed frequent financial risks for them as it did for other poor families in the village. In 1999, heavy rains and unusually cold temperatures left Alberto and María Dolores with an unsellable corn harvest. After a good season, the family typically used its corn profits to purchase dry goods and supplies. Without other cash sources, Alberto and his eldest sons sought jobs as *jornaleros* (day laborers) who worked their wealthier neighbors' fields. Considered by villagers to be the least desirable (and poorest paid) form of wage labor, *jornalero* work earned between $2.00 and $3.00 a day plus lunch and alcohol. For her part, María Dolores would occasionally weave straw hats, although she claimed that the labor-intensive activity did not justify the small return.

Near the end of my research, things had begun to improve for Alfredo and María Dolores. The couple's oldest son married a neighbor girl and soon thereafter migrated to the United States. Although they had lost their son's labor, they gained a daughter-in-law who could help around the household and care for the still sick María Dolores.[6] The extra help also freed Alfredo to work away from home with greater frequency. When I revisited Jatundeleg in 2001, Alfredo had found work tending roses and carnations at a flower plantation near Azogues, which assured him a more regular flow of cash.

Patched together, these households present a complicated picture of rural life and livelihoods in the Azuayo-Cañari countryside. They point to the increasing importance of cash, especially dollars, for all village families and the variety of ways that households satisfied this need, including labor migration to the United States. In each case, a family's level of wealth was strongly determined by its members' success in finding and sustaining wage labor and, in some cases, in operating their own cash-generating businesses. Although wage labor and its ability to increase the divisions between rich and poor were nothing new in Jatundeleg, the effects of international migration in village life dug these divisions deeper. In particular, as new transnational households fashioned lives that combined subsistence farming with remittances, their actions raised the costs of everyday subsistence for all villagers. Inflated land prices, the decrease in reciprocal labor, and elevated costs of agricultural inputs created tensions between

6. As much as poor crop yields, sickness was a constant worry for Jatundeleg's poorest families. See Carey 1987 for an analysis of the relationship between sickness, labor loss, and poverty in the Peruvian Andes.

those who had access to cash and those for whom access was more difficult. These tensions took various forms, ranging from idle gossip and under-the-breath comments to the dissolution of reciprocal ties and open hostilities between families. Many people, however, like those whose livelihood required seeking out wealthy villagers for loans or in some cases for their *compradrazgo* ties (god-parent relations), could not afford to pursue their grievances and potentially risk jeopardizing alliances with wealthy patrons. Many eventually accepted, if only tacitly, changes afoot in the village as the inevitable costs of progress and more comfortable lives.

The Rising Costs of a Comfortable Life

Residents of Jatundeleg whom I knew often drew on the concepts of the *ñaupa tiempos* and of *iony* modernity as bookends to capture the great intensity of change they had experienced in their lives. Especially among residents older than forty years of age, there was a profound feeling that although they ultimately remained *pobres* (poor people), there was greater convenience in rural life than there had been decades earlier. A man in his late fifties told me: "¡Por fin! Finally! We have a community where there is development [*desarollo*]. Back then, in the *ñaupa tiempos,* we were just a hamlet of families working our fields, not even a recognized village. There were no roads; you had to walk to get water. Food was something you grew, not purchased. . . . Life is more comfortable [*más cómodo*] now, but it comes with a price." In one sense, discussions of *desarollo* and of being *progresivo* referenced forms of state-sponsored development that invaded the community in a smattering of campaign stickers pasted on bus windows and imposing roadside billboards trumpeting public-works projects, as well as the familiar television spots of a perpetual presidential candidate charging "¡Adelante Ecuador, Adelante!" (Forward Ecuador, Forward!). In another sense, villagers located the source of these changes in the mental outlook of residents themselves and of returned migrants in particular. Returned migrants were often described to me as "más despiertos y avivados" (more awake and ready) than villagers who had not gone to the United States. This expression described the excitement and leadership that many returned migrants brought to initiatives of community development. Although nearly everyone shared the desire for a more comfortable life—in initiatives to bring potable water, better roads, and improved telephone and electricity service to the community—not everyone shared access to these conveniences.

As many residents would concur, development in the village began in the early 1970s with the construction of the dirt road connecting Jatundeleg to Déleg and later with the extension of electricity into households in 1984. Both developments worked toward the same goal: to open the community to regional, national, and international influence. The new packed dirt roads, funded in part by the boom in national oil revenues, facilitated the entry of a host of products into the village by truck and allowed villagers easier access to goods, services, and jobs outside the community. The advent of electricity brought the possibility of, among other things, television and, only later in 1997, telephone service.

One of the key effects of the opening of the roads was a proliferation of village *tiendas*. In 1999, Jatundeleg boasted an unusually large number of small stores for a community of its size, with seven strategically located at the busiest points of village life. Aside from two *tiendas* that were built from the capital of households who had sent migrants to work on the coastal plantations, all shops were recent additions built by families with migrants in the United States. In the 1950s, anthropologist Orlando Fals-Borda referred to the *tiendas* in highland Columbia as the "country clubs" of rural Andean life (1962, 166); the same could be said for the *tiendas* in Jatundeleg in the late 1990s. In the absence of restaurants, bars, or other meeting establishments, people went to the *tiendas* to socialize, to talk politics, or simply just to be seen. At night, even though the *tiendas* were rarely open past ten o'clock, men crowded around the few tables and benches in front of them, sharing drinks, cigarettes, and jokes.

Tiendas were also, of course, places where people could buy goods that they would otherwise have to produce for themselves or, more likely, simply live without. In addition to tobacco, alcohol, soda, matches, and medicines, each *tienda* sold a variety of prepared foodstuffs, including packaged white bread, "Maggi" brand soup mixes, cooking oil, coffee, dry noodles, and candy *(caramelos)*. Women occasionally cursed the *tiendas* for helping their husbands *ponerse borracho* (become drunk), but they frequently acknowledged the conveniences the shops brought to their lives. One woman expressed the convenience in the following way as I sat down in her kitchen to enjoy a spread of white bread, cookies, and sweet coffee (all purchased at a *tienda*):

> In my mother's generation, a homemaker [*ama de la casa*] always would have some *tamales* or *quimbolitos* [sweetened cornbread snacks] that she had made from scratch on hand. But it was hard; they take a long time to make, and they must be fresh. My husband would always have friends coming by, local officials, relatives, and would have something for them to eat. Now, you just give a child a little money and send them running to the *tienda* to buy a little something.

The same was true for everyday cooking. Packaged soups, canned beans, and instant coffee, for example, could cut preparation times considerably, lessening the burden of kitchen work and allowing women more time to attend to other tasks.

It was clear, however, that villagers welcomed the variety of goods available at the *tiendas* for more than just their convenience. Different foods also allowed individuals to demonstrate refined tastes and status (see Weismantel 1988). For example, a returned migrant whom I interviewed about his plans to spend his remittance nest egg described wanting to open a *tienda* that would sell "special beers like Budweiser and Corona" because current *tiendas* offered only Ecuadorian brands. In a similar vein, on more than one occasion of visiting a village household, I could hear family members discussing in hushed tones what to serve me before an interview. During one particular visit, the wife of a returned migrant I had come to interview put a plate of the regional mainstay *mote,* a kind of large kernel boiled hominy, and hard-boiled eggs in front of me as I waited for her husband to arrive home. Once he laid his eyes on the spread, though, he quickly excused himself from the room to speak with his wife. A few minutes later the wife reappeared, made a brief apology, and replaced the original plate with another featuring packaged cookies and a yet-to-be-opened jar of instant coffee. In the poorest of households, where families could offer little more than *mote,* the desire to present something else to me was also clear. Members of these households repeatedly apologized for what they saw as a meager offering. Some would proceed to ask me about what I received to eat when visiting other households.[7]

The introduction of electricity to Jatundeleg in 1984 also brought welcomed conveniences to the community. In 1999, all households included in my village census had electricity, although some of the poorest families claimed that they had lost their connections when they could no longer pay the bill. The level of conveniences afforded by electricity was largely contingent upon a household's access to cash to purchase electronic goods, but there was a collective acknowledgment that electric service extended daily possibilities, allowing people, as they would say, "to let the day march on" *(continuar la marcha)* and to mix work with relaxation. Indeed, television viewing provided a welcomed distraction to accompany tedious tasks such as weaving hats, sorting seeds for planting, or cleaning and sharpening tool blades (cf. Colloredo-Mansfeld 1999, xi). Don Miguel Cusco, my elderly neighbor, admitted to me that having a television helped seal the decision to keep his *tienda* open late because he "now had a way to pass away the hours." Televisions outnumbered telephones in the community almost three to one. In living rooms and bedrooms, they joined "boom box" stereos, floor lamps, clocks, and, occasionally, video game players. Some owners of these devices fashioned their living rooms and bodegas into video parlors where they charged villagers a small fee to watch poor-quality bootlegged copies of dubbed North American films.

Electricity also had a tremendous impact on defining the modern kitchen. No couple, for instance, would think about beginning their household without a blender, an essential convenience for quickly making fresh juices and soups, as well as *ají,* the indispensable chili pepper condiment found in all Ecuadorian kitchens. For many new households, a refrigerator was quickly becoming de rigueur.

Beyond augmenting status and fulfilling the desire to live a more convenient life, the choice to buy goods in the local *tiendas* or to purchase a television was a personal act that villagers could take or leave, depending

7. This treatment was reserved not only for me, an outsider from the United States. Schoolteachers, regional authorities, and the local priest also received coffee and snacks purchased at a *tienda.*

on their access to cash resources. A wife, for example, could respectfully avoid purchasing processed food at a *tienda* by invoking the culinary superiority of cooking in the tradition of the *ñaupa tiempos*. By the same token, the cost of a television could be justified by the fact that, like other *electrodomésticos,* it was viewed as a safe investment, an item that could be easily sold for cash at difficult times. Adjusting to other newly emerging standards of village life, however, proved more difficult. Specifically, greater levels of wealth prompted many households to seek out modern conveniences they associated with being *más urbano* (more urban), including potable water, better roadways, and increased security. Both migrant and nonmigrant households roundly welcomed these conveniences, but the increase in the number of community development projects represented one of the central arenas where many residents acutely felt the rising costs of subsistence life. As opposed to making personal consumption choices, not coming fully on board with development projects had ramifications beyond failing to appear "modern." A family's nonparticipation could raise accusations that they were *cerrada* (closed or reserved) and antisocial in relation to community activities.

Development projects in Ecuador and in the Andes more generally—ranging from the construction of latrines and potable water systems to agricultural improvement—are often funded and implemented by a combination of governmental and nongovernmental actors (Bebbington and Theile 1993; North and Cameron 2003). NGOs specifically, representing such diverse interests as faith-based organizations, environmental groups, and outside governments (including organizations such as the U.S. Peace Corps), have come to assume a critical role in development projects as the Ecuadorian government has steadily retreated from this function under neoliberal restructuring (North and Cameron 2003; Sawyer 2004). In the transition to nonstate actors and market incentives in the development arena, top-down models have been replaced by community partnerships whereby sponsoring organizations look to local residents to aid in the planning process, to donate labor, and to assume a portion of the financial costs necessary to see a project to completion. In Jatundeleg, the influx of migrant remittances greatly complicated this process. Simply stated, many of the development projects that wealthy villagers fought hard to bring to Jatundeleg often required extensive labor and financial contributions. For wealthier households, "sign-up" fees or a monthly bill for utility services amounted to little in their overall budget. Moreover, wealthier families were often in better positions to provide their own labor for development projects or, in some cases, to pay others to fulfill their labor contribution. By contrast, poor households, like that headed up by Alberto Sinchi and his wife, who were dependent upon *jornalero* work to earn a living, struggled to meet the labor requirements and to take advantage of the new conveniences. As Alberto complained, "For village work parties [*mingas*], people work one or two days a month. However, to have these new things, we have to work four or five days at a time. . . . Sometimes we forget who we are working for. Is it the *comuna* or *los ricos* [the rich]?" Although the goals of these projects received overwhelming support, Alberto's question regarding for whom he was working signaled the difficulty such ventures posed for some village residents. The brief examples provided here explore this situation further.

The 1999 rainy season, registered as one of the heaviest on record, had badly washed out a number of roadways, leaving deep ruts and cavernous potholes to navigate. Entryways to some of the nicest homes in the *centro* had become formidable fields of mud. In response, the community president and others with ties to the municipal government contracted with a private road-building company to bulldoze and repair some of the damaged community roads. Additional funds were secured from the Japanese government, which had sponsored other road-building and repair projects in Azuay and Cañar provinces since the devastation of the 1997 El Niño. For their part, community members were expected to contribute several days of free labor. In just three days of work, an overwhelming show of support from villagers from all parts of the community restored all the main *centro* roads. The work had been arduous, requiring the removal of a number of large boulders that had blocked roadways. At a village meeting the next day, the president announced that the project was complete and that no more roads would be bulldozed. Villagers who lived along the roadways leading away from the *centro* (roads that had not been repaired) questioned the announcement, asking why their roads would not be included. The president snapped back that the contract covered only the *centro*, where the majority of villagers lived and where "the majority of village activity takes place." The angry villagers fired off a petition that claimed they had provided free labor to those living in the *centro* and had received nothing in return. If their roads were not included in the project, the petition explained, residents from this sector would never again participate in a village work project. In its strongest language, their letter mentioned a number of families by name whose houses were in the *centro* but relied on the secondary roads to access their farm and pasture lands. After a week of bitter argument, the president and other villagers acquiesced to the angry dissenters and extended the project.

Some projects ultimately did not include all community members. One such example entailed the replacement of a pumped-water system that delivered water to households via a series of above-ground pipes *(agua entubada)* with a new well *(pozo)*. Residents often complained that the current system consisting of above-ground pipes was prone to breakages and clogs, and often debilitated by heavy rains, so that it became unusable to produce water for drinking, washing clothes, or bathing for weeks at a time. A group of households headed by returned migrants spearheaded the project by bringing together engineers from the Ministerio de Obras Publicas (MOP, Ministry of Public Works) and additional funding from an Ecuadorian NGO. Participating households were required to pay for a portion of the supplies and to contribute many days of community labor—digging ditches, laying pipes, and construct- ing the actual well. The water project received wide support from many families who either had a home in the *centro* or were in the process of building one. Many of the newest domiciles included new rural luxu- ries such as multiple bathrooms, kitchen sinks, and elaborate cement clothes-washing boards—new conveniences that required large amounts of clean water. Two months after the project was proposed, almost two dozen households had jumped on board, each agreeing to pay nearly $180 in material fees and to donate labor during the *mingas*. In total, the project required all participating families to send one person from their household to work a minimum of two days a week for a month. (At times, however, the labor requirement could be as much as three or four days a week.)

3.2. *Minga* (work party) in Jatundeleg to build new water system. Photograph by the author.

The fact that some village women no longer had to trudge to the river with their dirty laundry or that households experienced fewer water shortages were marked improvements that residents thoroughly embraced. However, as the divide between those connected to the well and those not connected grew more obvious, some residents in Jatundeleg's poorer households began to feel left behind. For example, during dry spells, poorer households connected to the *agua entubada* found themselves borrowing water from neighbors connected to the new system.[8] Alejandro Cuzco, a thirty-seven-year-old Loma Lanzacay resident who headed up one of those poorer families, expressed his desire to replace his aging *agua entubada* system with the more reliable connection. Although the price tag ($90)

8. Some residents claimed that a couple of households connected to the well had even begun to charge their neighbors for water during periods of excessive rain and drought.

was high, he was confident he could save the money or, if need be, borrow it from extended family members. The obstacle that stood in his way, however, was the labor requirement. Most migrant households could afford to donate their own labor or buy their way out of the labor requirement, but unremunerated labor was not an option for many poor families. When Alejandro realized that connection to the new system was, at least for the time being, unattainable for his household, he vented:

> The village is changing tremendously, this is true, and it is a positive thing. Thanks to God for the United States [Gracias a Diós por los Estados Unidos] that people here can have better lives for themselves. But these *proyectos* [projects] are no longer projects of the *comuna*. They are not for the whole of the community. . . . Soon there will be two *mingas*— those for the rich and those for the poor. In all, the village is moving forward, but some people are going to be left behind.

Another young man and his wife struggling to build their household remarked, "[The well-off families in the *centro*] set the agenda in this community. They decide how much we can pay for things." Their resentment was fueled by a rumor that the true costs of the project were actually much lower and that the "excessive needs" of new houses in the *centro* were elevating the costs of development.[9] Again, rarely did these hostilities move far beyond the level of gossip and the occasional disparaging remark against "*los ricos*." To be sure, many poor households simply could not afford to dissolve their ties to more affluent households, on whom they counted for support, including the patronage of *compadrazgo* ties. Indeed, by the close of my research, these ties, in the form of short-term loans and the security of steady *jornalero* work, were becoming important ways for some villagers to realize their goal of being connected to the well.

Migrant affluence, although lessening the burdens of rural life, also came with its own set of problems that in turn created new village needs. One such need was that of increased safety and security. Migration clearly

9. I was frequently told that some households needed the well in order to operate "high-powered" washing machines, but I was never able to confirm this claim.

meant that some households sat on more wealth than others did, much of it stored away in people's homes. Migrant households also commonly converted their earnings into electronic goods and jewelry, items that held their value better than sucres and could be easily sold for cash in city shops. During my fieldwork, news of at least a half-dozen burgled homes worked its way through the pipelines of village gossip. However, after the houses of three prominent families were burgled in the same night while their owners attended a wedding in Déleg, discussions of village security shifted from trite gossip to a plan of action. Villagers could recall very few acts of theft and burglary in the past, aside from occasional incidences of cattle rustling. When such crimes did occur, villagers were apt to blame "outsiders," *gente sin razón* (uncivilized people). Fueled by sierra-wide suspicions of coastal peoples, villagers readily accused itinerant merchants from the coast who periodically peddled plastic buckets, blender parts, and other household items in the region. Some residents also blamed the escalation of crime on *pandillas,* gangs of "roving boys" who many feared had access to guns.

Throughout many parts of rural Latin America, where state law enforcement is lacking or altogether absent, strong traditions of popular justice have taken hold to quell a host of social problems, ranging from cattle rustling to domestic violence and adultery (Colloredo-Mansfeld 2002; Starn 1999; Stavenhagen and Iturralde 1993; Wray 1993). In spring 1999, a group of Jatundeleg families, including several victims of the recent burglaries, tapped into this rich tradition and explored the possibility of forming their own justice system. For the next three weeks, villagers devoted a portion of the Sunday meeting to discuss the issue. Advocates proposed a system of nightly "rounds" *(rondas),* whereby members of each household would take turns walking the village and monitoring its security. The idea quickly divided the community. For some families who were already feeling the squeeze on their labor from other proposed projects, commitment to a *ronda* presented itself as a burden on top of burdens. One resident who had yet to benefit from the well project complained, "I can't keep giving more days to the *comuna.* Sure, I want to see the village be safe and calm, but I am a farmer, and I must work." Poorer households grew to believe that the recent crime wave did not affect all residents equally, but instead was largely driven by the increases of cash and consumer goods acquired by migrant households. At one village meeting, Alberto Sinchi blasted the proposal by saying, "I will join the day someone wants to steal my pigs, *cuyes,* or chickens. The problem is not everyone's yet." Others took direct aim at migrant families, blaming the escalation of gangs on "irresponsible households" where the parents had gone to the United States, leaving their children behind to find their way into trouble. By the close of my research in the village, nobody had yet to make the "rounds."

When I visited Jatundeleg in 2001, one of the first things I noticed was the addition of a large red-and-white sign posted at one of the community's most important crossroads. Littered with misspellings and grammatical errors in its original Spanish, the sign read:

> Jatundeleg and its neighboring communities united in the same idea of progress welcome tourists, sellers of goods, and foreign visitors. For our security and yours, we ask for your cooperation in supporting our laws. If you are a native or a foreigner, please respect both public and private property. We will bring suspicious people to the attention of the community secretary.

The sign went into the ground shortly after the final discussions about organizing the *rondas* ended without support for the initiative. As don Andrés Saldañes reported, the sign was a gesture of "saving face" on the part of those whose proposal failed. The sign's warning—"to bring suspicious persons to the attention of the community secretary"—was also nothing but symbolic. Without a *ronda,* the secretary could act in ways no different than ordinary villagers could, which was to report incidents to the ineffectual *cantón* police. Unable to achieve consensus on the proposal, those whose wealth made them targets for robbery proceeded to minimize the threat in the ways they had been doing for some time: by fortifying their homes with high iron fences and steel window barricades.

Don Andrés was not alone in his criticism of the sign. He and others forcefully questioned the proclamation that the village was "united in the same idea of progress." For him, the idea of unification in progress was ironic given the vastly different perspectives that villagers maintained with respect to local development. Don Andrés especially liked to point out the differences between the *invernadero* project and the *ronda* proposal. In the first case, households linked into the remittance economy had essentially squelched the greenhouse discussion by arguing that few households would need the extra assistance and that, if they so chose, they could pursue it on their own. In the second case, it was nonmigrant households, who generally had fewer valuables, that stood firm against contributing to the *rondas*. This splintering of village priorities was obvious to others in the community, though at times it seemed of little serious concern. Most agreed that such disparities were the inevitable growing pains that Jatundeleg had to endure if it was to experience the *progreso* and *desarrollo* villagers perceived other parts of the country to be enjoying. Nevertheless, many wondered to what extent migration would erode commonalities between households. Don Andrés again was particularly pessimistic on the issue. "Pretty soon," he said, "there will be a total *dolarización de los maizales* [dollarization of the cornfields]. Then what will we do?"

Don Andrés's mention of cornfields was not an isolated utterance. In fact, frequent references to corn and cornfields in discussions of village politics pointed to one of the most fundamental aspects of changing rural life. Signaling more than just another commodified component of their agricultural existence, mention of corn in conversations of migration, village wealth, and change simultaneously played into a richly symbolic local arena of meaning. The "dollarization of cornfields" suggested that not only economic livelihoods were in flux, but also people's sense of a specific Azuayo-Cañari identity. In the next section, I explore how key transformations in the production, consumption, and meaning of *maíz* reveal fundamental redefinitions of village life.

Agricultural Lives, Identity, and the Dolarización del Maizal

Although households in Jatundeleg cobbled together income from a diverse number of sources, including remittances, all of the participants in my household census counted subsistence farming as their primary occupation. By their own self-identification as campesinos, rural peoples of the Azuayo-Cañari region continued to identify their history and livelihood with working the land. In the absence of other discernible and distinct ethnic identifiers, the crops that villagers grew, the foods they ate, and the pace and rhythm of an agricultural calendar made claims on and formed the basis of local identity. Moreover, on top of the images that villagers had of themselves as campesinos and *gente de la tierra* (people of the land), these same images were enforced, exploited, and often ridiculed in urban conceptions of *nuestro folklórico*.

The agricultural history of the Azuayo-Cañari region is one of villagers coping with a legacy of poor-quality soils and uneven terrain, the lack of formalized irrigation, and sluggish markets in which to sell crops (Brownrigg 1972; González 1988; Hirschkind 1980; Jokisch 1998, 2002). Villagers regularly complained "que la tierra no produzca más" (that the land doesn't produce anymore). One resident explained, "You have to keep putting more and more damn fertilizer on your crops, and they just don't produce. Pretty soon you might as well just grow fertilizer." Although the majority of crops were grown for subsistence, the yields accounted for far less than half of the foodstuffs Jatundeleg households consumed.

The exception to this pattern was *maíz*, in particular the soft corn variety *(choclo)*, identifiable by its plump, teethlike kernels. Although villagers commonly grew only a couple of principal crops or limited their crops in the *chacras* in order to concentrate on fruits and vegetables in small garden plots *(huertas)*, almost no family ever went a season without planting *maíz*.

3.3. Jatundeleg cornfield. Photograph by the author.

In fact, for young people, the host of crops raised in their parents' and grandparents' generations—barley, quinoa, wheat, potatoes—meant little because they had grown up with fields of *puro maíz* (nothing but corn). In the *cantón* Déleg, well more than 50 percent of total agricultural production was dedicated to corn (Sempértegui 1991, 36).

Corn, though, did not always figure so prominently in the Azuayo-Cañari market basket. Before Inca expansion into the region, potatoes (of numerous varieties) played a much greater role in the local diet. According to Murra (1973), the introduction of corn, an imperial prestige crop requiring irrigation, transformed potatoes into a humble food associated with commoners. In the daily exigencies of the Inca Empire, corn was both a basic food crop and a critical medium of exchange and tribute (e.g., see also Bauer 1996; Silverblatt 1987). Specially designated cornfields were cultivated for the veneration of major Inca deities and as the source ingredient of *chicha,* a fermented corn alcohol at the center of state ritual and ceremonial life (Sánchez-Parga 1997; Weismantel 1991). Corn harvests were times of great celebration honoring the Mama Zara (Mother Corn), whereby village households kept vigil over a shrine dedicated to her by wrapping the harvest's choicest ears in fine textiles (Murra 1973, 398).

In contemporary times, corn continues to symbolize aspects of life-giving fertility and fecundity (Isbell 1978; Millones and Pratt 1990; Vega Delgado 1998). In Jatundeleg, the fact that the development of *maíz* closely mimics the nine months of human gestation, from the time seeds are placed in the ground to the point when the plump ears of *choclo* can be harvested, is not lost on campesino minds. Children born according to harvest cycles are said to be strong and so will have long lives. Resonant with this belief, Jatundeleg midwives *(parteras)* exploit the roots and husks of corn plants for their life-sustaining and fortifying qualities. In general, the consumption of *maíz* embodies ideas of personal strength and longevity. In his seventeenth-century treatise to the king of Spain, the half-indigenous chronicler Guamán Poma trumpeted the virtues of corn as a source of vitality and brawn. In a comparison of different Andean groups, Poma noted, "The Colla are Indians of little strength and courage, with large bodies fat and tallowy because they eat only *chuño* [freeze-dried potatoes]." The Chinchaysuyus of the northern Peruvian highlands, in contrast, "although small in stature, are brave, are fed on maize and drink corn *chicha,* which gives them strength" (1936, 336).[10] In the Azuayo-Cañari region, consuming corn, more precisely the large-kernel hominy-like variety known as *mote,* also indexes ideas of strength and vitality. In the colloquial speech of the region, a person who is tired from sickness or appears sluggish in their work can expect to be chided by the accusation that "le falte mote" (he or she lacks *mote*).[11]

The *maizal* is also symbolically constructed as a place of sexual exploration and adolescent innocence (Millones and Pratt 1990; F. Vega 1996). "In the *maizal,*" as an elderly woman from Shullín remarked, "more than just the corn grows." Villagers often describe fields as "safety zones" where young people can engage in premarital hetero- and homosexual experimentation. Although perhaps not officially sanctioned, their actions are conveniently overlooked by elders, hidden by the tall stalks and thick leaves. "El amor en el maíz" (love in the corn) is a common theme of Azuayo-Cañari folktales, ballads, and jokes (see, e.g., Einzmann and Almeida 1991; Martínez and Einzmann 1993). Similarly, as many of Jatundeleg's elderly residents contended, the positioning of cornfields around village houses formed part of a loose ideology of village unity and strength, as a "buffer" between the values of *ñaupa tiempos* and the changes of modern times.

In addition to *maíz*'s symbolic properties, practices related to its production significantly shape the rhythms of rural life. In Jatundeleg, planting takes place in August and culminates with the harvest in April or May. In June and July, as the plants start to dry and wither, and it seems there is nothing left to salvage, peasants sweep through the fields again to collect up the dry ears *(los secos),* which are destined to become cornmeal. Harvest also entails piling all the corn stalks and husk stubble *(calcha)* into a perfectly rounded and delicately formed *parva,* or haystack. For the coming months, the empty field will be used for pasture, and the *parva* will be feed for cattle. When the nutrient-rich stalks and leaves of the

10. The translation comes from Murra 1973.

11. *Mote,* at different stages of the cooking process, also indexes human characteristics. McKee notes that *cauca* (half-cooked *mote*) is used as a metaphor to describe a person considered "half socialized" (1980, 113).

parva decay, the whole thing is plowed back into the earth for the process to begin again.

Villagers grow corn for nourishment. However, *maíz* also serves as an important exchange commodity, in both economic and symbolic senses. At the symbolic level, the exchange of food in the Andes enacts social relations based on reciprocity and trust between and within households (Allen 2002; Corr 2002; Weismantel 1988). Any time I helped a family in their fields or gave them a copy of a photograph I had taken, I would invariably receive an open invitation that I come "compartir motecito" (to share a little plate of *mote*). Similarly, no *almuerzo* (lunch) in an Azuayo-Cañari household is ever complete, especially when guests are present, without a steaming bowl of boiled *mote* placed in the center of the table. Hungry hands grab for it to fortify otherwise thin soups and to satisfy hunger before a main course is served. In some cases, everyone is given a spoon to scoop up the *mote,* each spoon placed systematically around the lip of the bowl like spokes of a bicycle wheel fanning out from the axle.

In decades past, *maiz* also played an equally important role in ritual life as the base ingredient of *chicha*. Elders recalled how in the *ñaupa tiempos minga* hosts would offer endless cupfuls of *chicha*[12] as workers broke land for planting, erected houses, or repaired washed-out roads. As villagers told me many times, only those households with ample stores of corn could harness enough labor. Although in recent times, *canelazo* (a hot spiced drink made from sugarcane alcohol) had replaced *chicha* at *mingas* (because it requires no fermentation process), corn beer continued to be an important component of village fiestas. Fiesta sponsors had to make sure they had enough corn in their stores to produce the beverage, or they would have to purchase it from other villagers. Maintaining a steady supply of corn in various forms—cornmeal, *mote,* or the main ingredient of *chicha*—served the important function of meeting the obligations of village social life even as other forms of status and cultural capital were emerging.

12. Corn-based *chicha* has an alcohol content of between 3 and 4 percent. Its brewing predates Inca occupation in the region by many centuries. Cuencan anthropologist Gustavo Vega Delgado speculates that the province name *Azuay* likely came from the traditional importance of corn *chicha* in the region, known locally by the name *Azhua* (1998, 24).

The symbolic importance of *maíz* was evident to me from my first days in Jatundeleg as I took in the cuisine and hospitality of my hosts. Less evident and more complex to tease out, however, were the economic relationships fashioned around the production and consumption of corn. Early in my fieldwork, I had accepted the working hypothesis that the remittance economy was, albeit slowly, ultimately undermining local agricultural practices. During conversations with campesinos and Ecuadorian migration scholars, I had grown accustomed to a common refrain (and lament) that rural lands were increasingly becoming *tierras botadas*, lands "thrown out" of production as a result of out-migration (see Jokisch 1998). Echoing the findings of a number of well-known studies on the impact of migrant remittances on agriculture in Mexico (e.g., see Durand and Massey 1992; Reichart 1981), as well as studies addressing internal migration in the Andes (e.g., Collins 1988), the combination of labor scarcity, environmental degradation, and remittance economies suggested the fate of local farming. In some instances, this change surely was the case. Among the wealthiest migrant households (whose migration histories stretched back to the 1970s), farming had been steadily displaced by more profitable ventures, such as raising dairy cattle and opening small businesses. For these households, all their *maíz* needs could be met by purchasing it from neighboring families. In other cases, some migrant households simply ceased to farm altogether, instead allowing poor villagers to sharecrop their land. The tactic assured a constant access to corn but the freedom to pursue other economic activities.

Geographer Brad Jokisch (1998, 2002) has systematically explored the relationship between land-use patterns and migration in the Azuayo-Cañari region. Assessing competing theses that propose that migration has the potential either to improve agriculture (by channeling remittances into production) or to diminish its importance, Jokisch (2002) describes Azuayo-Cañari campesinos as pursuing a "middle-path." Migrant households have not given up agriculture, but they have tended not to improve it either. Jokisch argues that among return migrants and transnational households, for instance, participation in the remittance economy has not prompted families to channel their new wealth into agricultural inputs (i.e., fertilizers, new crops, enhanced seeds, irrigation,

etc.). In a comparison of two migrant-sending communities with significantly different migration histories, Jokisch (2002) found few substantive
differences between nonmigrant and migrant households with respect to
agriculture. On average, both communities recorded near equivalent per
capita *maíz* yields.

Why then do households enmeshed in the remittance economy continue to devote time, energy, and capital to the production of unproductive
maíz? I frequently posed this question in different guises to the farm families I knew in Jatundeleg, and I frequently received the same pat response:
"Así somos" (That is who we are). Jokisch explains this phenomenon as a
kind of security against fluctuations in the local economy and especially
against inflation (cf. Colloredo-Mansfeld 1999). In Jatundeleg's migrant
households, maintaining crops is especially crucial during the first years
after a migrant's absence, when household costs are greatest and the regularity of remittances not yet guaranteed. As I detail in chapter 7, agriculture
plays a particularly important role for women by giving them a security
cushion if husbands should fail to remit or should not remit enough to
meet household needs. "[Women] continue to cultivate their land because
it allows them the security of procuring much of the household's food, re-
duces overall food costs, and provides them with a modicum of economic
independence" (Jokisch 2002, 541).

Because of the many ways in which *maíz* approximates in Azuayo-
Cañari society what Mauss (1967) called a "total social fact"—anchoring
villagers' social, cultural, and material lives—the communitywide commitment to its production provided, at the time I was living in Jatundeleg, a
certain level of comfort for those who saw migration as disruption from
the *ñaupa tiempos.* At the same time, however, some village households
who depended on *maíz* for a significant portion of their subsistence worried about the ways an incipient *dolarización del maizal* was threatening
their farming livelihood. In particular, the infusion of cash into the production of corn was reorienting the basic principles of reciprocal exchange
that had long governed village relations. In the past, corn could be bar-
tered for tools, other foodstuffs, and labor. A common refrain I heard on
the topic was that "before there was money, the poor had *maíz.*" These
kinds of agreements were still present in Jatundeleg in the late 1990s, yet

were quickly becoming marginalized in the dollarized economy. Many of Jatundeleg's poorest families still relied on their corn surpluses to stand in for cash in local transactions. For example, one returned migrant told me that in years when he did not want to cultivate all his fields, he would occasionally purchase corn from one of Jatundeleg's poorest households, even though he could get a better price elsewhere. "They [the poor households] don't have cash, and besides I think there are family, too—distant relatives. We help each other with corn." Similarly, Carmela, the *tienda* owner, maintained an almost ten-year relationship with a family in Shullín with whom she traded goods from her store for the family's *calcha,* which she used as animal feed.

Although everyone had noticed the decline of *maíz* as a medium of exchange, the rising costs of *maíz* production presented itself as a more constant worry for households with the least access to cash. Under favorable circumstances, most households managed to meet their farm labor needs by recruiting extended family members. However, at certain critical times of the year, during the labor-intensive stages of weeding and planting, for instance, extra help could become indispensable. This was especially true for households with more than five hectares of land. Many elderly villagers spoke fondly of the ways in which households met their labor needs in the past through reciprocal work exchanges *(cambiomanos* and *prestamanos).* By the early 1980s, these exchanges were in marked decline as migration took able-bodied men from the community and the cost of sponsoring work parties greatly increased.

I recorded only one *prestamanos* party during my year of fieldwork in the village. The sponsor was a returned migrant who had marshaled together approximately thirty residents to break ground on a new field; workers also helped construct a barbed-wire fence around the perimeter of the property. The event was awash in alcohol, cigarettes, and even music in the form of a hired disc jockey spinning highland *sanjuanitos* and *cumbia* favorites, as men and women slung pickaxes and uncoiled spools of fencing wire. The workday concluded with more alcohol and a roasted pig served in a traditional style *(pampamesa)* on a large piece of cloth laid upon the ground. The expense was clearly far greater than most households could ever hope to spend in a communal work party. Afterwards, many joked, probably correctly, that it would have cost less to hire a group of *jornaleros* to do the work.

In fact, *jornalero* work had come to replace many of the farming needs previously met through exchanging labor. Within migrant households, where labor shortages could occasionally be acute because of the absence of husbands, sons, and even daughters, it was customary for families to hire *jornaleros*. In 2000, the rate for agricultural work ranged between $2.30 and $3.00 per day, including an *almuerzo* and sugarcane alcohol, given seasonal demand. At times, these labor costs could rise with the scarcity of available workers in the *cantón*. Similarly, with the decline in reciprocal labor, cash had become critically important in the preparation of fields for planting. Plowing season requires a pair of oxen, together referred to as a *yunta,* to break ground. Owing to the considerable land required to pasture bulls, few families in Jatundeleg owned their own *yuntas* and in most cases rented them. In 1999, rental costs for a *yunta* hovered between $9.00 and $10.00 per hectare plus labor costs. Within migrant households, the expense represented a small amount of the domestic budget. For nonmigrant families, however, saving enough money to rent a *yunta* proved difficult without the possibility of trading labor and bartering *maíz.*

In actuality, few households, even among the poorest in Jatundeleg, ever completely lacked the ability to maintain their farming practices. Although poor families spent each year worrying about the next, wondering if they would get their crops in the ground, they fretted most about the next generation's ability to own land. As I develop more fully in the next chapter with respect to youth, land scarcity has a long and problematic history in Jatundeleg in that generations of partible inheritance have contributed to the decreasing size of property holdings. This phenomenon was only exacerbated with the expansion of the remittance economy.

Ironically, as the flow of remittances into Azuayo-Cañari villages has done little to provide incentives to improve and develop agriculture, land itself has become a highly valued commodity. As Jokisch describes, the sale of land has led to a burgeoning "peri-urban landscape of cultivated real estate" wherein the value of land unhinged from its actual monetary value for crop production has steadily increased (2002, 547). In the mid-1990s, a hectare of cultivatable land in Jatundeleg fetched $3,000 or higher (a price tag already higher than the national average). By the time of my research, the same parcel of land sold for between $7,000 and $10,000, with prices set in U.S. dollars. Migrants owned on average twice as much land as nonmigrant households. In the highly charged rhetoric that surrounded the high prices, villagers whose access to cash was minimal accused their migrant neighbors of "parcelando los cerros" (parceling up the hills). Mention of *los cerros*—land held in common—was significant, for it linked together the purchase of individual land with a metaphor of community history. Land-grabbing households would commodify not only available farmlands, but community relations as well. In reality, the *cerros* had been spared the intense real-estate boom. Instead, the most significant parceling of land was under way in the expanding and urbanizing *centro*, where the goal of land ownership was not so much the cultivation of crops, but rather the cultivation of new forms of status.

The Commodification of Status in Jatundeleg

In the face of the emerging gulf between rich and poor households in Jatundeleg, I was often surprised at the uniform ways residents adamantly clung to a portrait of their community as anchored in the idiom of the *comuna*. Villagers referred to the *comuna* to speak simultaneously about the actual group of community members and the property that the community held in common. Members of the *comuna,* or *comuneros,* described their community as sharing a common livelihood and mutual obligation to one another. As already mentioned, the glue traditionally holding *la comuna* together was different forms of reciprocal labor—villagewide *mingas, prestamanos,* and *cambiamanos,* at times backed by the formalization of *compadrazgo* ties. Thus, a household's status could be defined by its ability at any moment in time to secure mutual aid in the form of labor, the borrowing of goods (such as *yuntas* and other farm implements), and access to credit.

Although the necessity of cooperation had begun to wane for many households, the social forms buttressing it had not. Because such acts had long organized forms of cooperation, often in ritualized ways, they were quintessential to the formation of group identity and community membership. In short, *comuna* rites were socialized and subject to rules, sanctions, and social pressures even after their economic necessity had slackened. Thus, as much as households desired more comfortable lives based on new definitions of *progreso* and *desarrollo,* they felt compelled to pursue their new goals within the traditional avenues of participation. For many migrant households, what counted most was not so much the accumulation of status as the activity of status management.

Nowhere was the management of status more prominently displayed than in the villagers' religious lives. Contributing to the well-being of community religious life promised the positive judgment not just of other villagers, but also of God. By happenstance, my fieldwork dovetailed with an important metamorphosis of the village church. In my first days in Jatundeleg, I saw the church's skeleton without its plaster skin—a matchstick arrangement of eucalyptus poles and concrete reinforcements—as workers tore down crumbling facades and cracked inner walls. Over the coming months, the church would be transformed into a towering edifice with a shiny tile roof, a belfry taller than it was previously, and colorful stained-glass windows. Hired construction workers tended to the physical reconstruction of the church, but the persuasive oratory of and persistent rallying by the community's president and the self-appointed leader of a *directiva* (directive or campaign), Segundo Pañora, had made the project fiscally possible. With little support from regional church authorities, the community took it upon itself to raise the estimated $8,000 needed to complete the reconstruction. From the beginning of the capital campaign, efforts to raise funds were steadfastly transnational. Segundo Pañora spearheaded a campaign in Queens and Brooklyn and would periodically call out at Sunday meetings the names of migrants and the amounts they had contributed. Donations by migrant households outstripped local contributions in both size and quantity. By purchasing stained-glass windows, wealthy households could also choose a more permanent way to contribute and display their status.

To my surprise, evidence for what migration researcher Patricio Carpio Benalcázar condemns as a "dollarization of the faith" (1992, 171) spreading throughout the Azuayo-Cañari highlands did not carry over to religious fiesta life in the ways one might think. Quite simply, in contrast to the church directive, the patronal fiestas remained patently local affairs that corresponded more closely to influential farm families than to migrants seeking opportunities to reestablish their identity and status in the community. The lack of migrant sponsors, or priostes, however, spoke less about a desire to participate and more about the limits of participation. In particular, many migrants' undocumented status limited the feasibility of their returning from the United States. It also made fiesta sponsorship an unwise goal in the cultural economy of transnational status. As a migrant in New York told me, "Being a prioste 'without papers' is like paying for your own birthday party and not attending." Rather, because of the ways the structural barriers of illegality impeded migrants' mobility, managing status in Jatundeleg often took more permanent forms localized around the priority of family life.

For many households, the connection between family life and village status was established in the building of new homes. In 1999, migrant-sending villages throughout the Azuayo-Cañari region were riding a wave of new home construction unprecedented in previous eras. Even as the economic crisis began to envelop Ecuador in early 1999, the Cámara de Construción de Cuenca (Cuenca Chamber of Construction) reported almost double-digit increases in new construction projects and an increased demand for building materials.[13] In Jatundeleg, the blossoming of new homes added to an already diverse built environment comprising three general architectural styles and types. The oldest housing type in the community, as noted earlier, generally occupied by the village's poorest residents, consisted of one- and two-room wattle-and-daub structures with red clay–tiled roofs. One of the rooms served dual purposes, as sala (living room) and sleeping room; family members typically slept together. The second structure was reserved as a kitchen and storage room. Just as important, and perhaps more important than the interiors, was the outside patio space, where much of a family's activities would center. Beginning around the late 1970s, a second class of housing emerged, driven by the earnings of seasonal migrants to Ecuador's coast.

---

13. See news reports in El Mercurio ("Construcción en la desocupación" 1999; "Construcción incrementó" 1999).

3.4. A new house on the Andean landscape. In contrast to more traditional housing, such homes are sometimes referred to as *chiri wasis* (cold houses).

Houses built in this era were generally larger and made of cement and concrete block. Although the materials differed, the style of new homes preserved the central features of older housing, including the autonomy of the kitchen from the rest of the house and the centrality of the open patio space.

By contrast, a new generation of housing in the 1990s took its cues not from Spanish or local Andean designs, but rather from North American designs. Most homes were multistoried edifices based on suburban tract-style plans. Gone were the open courtyards and patios, replaced by indoor washrooms and enclosed work areas. Newer houses also included multiple windows, skylights, high ceilings, garages, and fenced-in yards. Migrants not infrequently took their ideas for their new homes from what they saw overseas. They sent snapshots of homes they admired in the United States for local architects to replicate in the rural Andes. A three-bedroom North American–style home built largely of inexpensive cement and rebar could be had for between $6,000 and $9,000.

3.5. Houses built with remittances at various stages of construction. Photograph by the author.

I began my fieldwork in Jatundeleg by plotting the approximate ages of new developments in the community and the different housing styles. During my observations, I could scarcely stop and photograph a home without someone passing by and commenting, "¿Casitas lindas, no?" (Aren't they beautiful little houses?) Despite the praise, however, villagers often questioned the "place" of these new homes in community life, sometimes inciting comparison with houses of the *ñaupa tiempos*. Older-style homes, including those built in the 1970s, were invariably constructed by means of a *wasi pichana,* or communal house raising that utilized the donated labor of kin and neighbors. By contrast, the complicated designs and specialized electrical and plumbing requests for new domiciles often precluded the use of community labor. Similarly, new domestic construction also operated on a different time line of completion than previous projects. During a *wasi pichana,* in most cases, a home could be built to a livable standard in a matter of days. Conversely, new homes could take many years to complete, and many never made it to completion and were left like empty shells on the landscape. Complaints about stacks of unused concrete block, rusting rebar, and piles of loose gravel were common.

Again, although it was widely agreed that these measures reflected the growing pains of a community poised for development, such additions could not help but leave some people confused. For many residents, such as Luís Callaguaso, who owned a home built in the early 1970s, it was difficult to articulate exactly what they disliked about the new construction. Luís admired the aesthetics of new homes, but felt that something was experientially lost. With respect to older homes, he told me vaguely, "Todo era mas real antes" (Everything was just more real before). When I pushed him to explain, he just repeated the phrase. Catherine Allen, in her vivid descriptions of changing housing styles in the Peruvian Andes, captures some of what perhaps made older homes "more real" for some villagers like Luís:

> The low doors in the old-style houses force you to bend over as you cross the threshold, whereas you enter the new ones standing upright. Entering the old house implied a qualitative change in consciousness, an experience confirmed every time one crossed the threshold, straightened up, and readjusted the senses to different light, temperature, smells, and spatial dimensions. The perceptual contrast was strong and definite, confirming the cultural salience of the opposition between inside and outside. (2002, 236)

To describe the "unreal" qualities of new housing styles, villagers often called forth the idea of the *chiri wasi* (cold house). Rendering the phrase in Quichua (as opposed to *casa fría* in Spanish) no doubt lent their critique an air of tradition. A cold house was not simply one where propane gas stoves had completely replaced radiant open-fire hearths, but more substantially where the signs of symbolic warmth emanating from the visible activities of family life were difficult to detect. To be sure, newer homes tended to shift people's domestic activities out of sight from the casual passerby. Once-mundane chores such as shucking beans, peeling potatoes, and doing laundry were now hidden behind high fences and replaced by empty yard spaces. Accordingly, new housing styles were not conducive to the types of casual socializing to which families were accustomed. For instance, in the newer styles, one was less likely to happen upon neighbors working out of doors. The entertainment of guests at new homes, instead, often took place in *salas*, which added a degree of formality to social encounters (see Fletcher 1999, 78).[14]

No family I knew who occupied a modern house wanted the reputation of living in a *chiri wasi*. Nor did they necessarily always use their domestic spaces in the ways the architecture might suggest. For instance, wives who lived in new homes would at times continue to do their laundry in the open yard; some families allowed animals to wander and nest in the new homes, as would be standard in older homes, much to the consternation of urban cultural critics.[15] In addition to these small attempts to "relocalize" their decidedly nonlocal domiciles, migrant households also used their homes to make more public claims to status and to communicate a sense of modernity that their family was moving ahead *(adelantando)*. Eschewing fiesta sponsorship as a means to garner status and respect, migrant households instead often chose less public rituals to convey and maintain their status.

Parties for baptisms, first communions, confirmations, and birthdays occupied the place that fiesta sponsorship might have in other contexts—a claim to community participation. The price tag for such events, as for fiestas, also could be quite large. Most events were announced in hand-delivered invitations, including specially made cards and envelopes with the child's name printed on them that hinted at the lavishness of the celebration to come. Houses would be liberally decorated with crepe streamers and festooned with custom-made glittery Styrofoam cutouts appropriate to the event (crosses, for example) that villagers purchased in Azogues or Cuenca. Whenever possible, the cutouts also included personal touches

---

14. The custom of entertaining guests in the formal living room is as much a middle- and upper-class Ecuadorian convention as it is a North American one. Lynn Hirschkind writes, "One of the more notable of Cuenca's domestic institutions is that of the *sala*, or living room. *Salas* are meant to impress more [than] to provide a comfortable setting for gatherings. . . . [They] are formal statements to all of the status, wealth, and tastes of the owner" (1980, 297).

15. Recall the *Vistazo* reporter's comments quoted in chapter 2.

3.6. Jatundeleg children at a confirmation ceremony. Photograph by the author.

specific to each child, including his or her name and a photograph. Most events took place in the large *salas* of the new homes, where families were most likely to have displayed the fruits of migrant labor, such as televisions, stereo systems, clock radios, and new furniture. The Styrofoam cutouts were occasionally built around and accentuated a family's fortune and would be left in place months or years after a celebration had passed.

The all-day and sometimes all-night events centered on eating and dancing. Alcohol consumption often played only a minor role in these celebrations, in contrast to its prominence at fiestas. As one mother sponsoring an event informed me, "These celebrations are for the kids. They see enough [drinking] already." The foods served typically followed holiday convention, though in greater quantities and more elaborate in presentation. Helpings of traditional roasted *cuy,* potatoes, and soups often came in specially purchased paper dishware with plastic utensils as opposed to in everyday chipped enamelware. Specialty cakes topped off an afternoon of feasting, again with special writing identifying the child and his or her celebration. Finally, critical to sustaining a celebration's energy required hiring a disc jockey and sound system *(disco movil)* to play throughout the night. Even though sixty or more people usually attended a household celebration, that was not everybody, and the sound system could make an event strangely public as music echoed throughout the village.

In a testament to the importance of food in these celebrations, a village wife who together with her migrant husband orchestrated a large confirmation party for her twin sons castigated my wife and me when we failed to attend the event despite receiving an invitation. To right things, she demanded we stop over for a "piece of cake." Far from just offering leftovers, María Vivian went about meticulously re-creating the event for our benefit. As we sat alone at a specially arranged table in her living room (the decorations still up and music still playing), we were treated to a four-course meal consisting of soup, guinea pig, potatoes, salad, and colored champagne served in plastic flutes. Few details of the actual celebration were spared for our visit.

In many cases, a well-orchestrated children's celebration spoke as much about the parent's achievements as it did about the children's. As a night of festivities passed into the early hours of the morning, parents would often ask the disc jockey to make a public announcement thanking those who made the event possible. Invariably, the generosity of a father in the United States was roundly praised, and, at times, a prayer followed asking God to safeguard the migrant relative abroad. Well-prepared families would also read emotional statements from migrant fathers so they could express their love and appreciation for their children. Additional attempts were made to link children with their absent parents. On some occasions, families used bulletin boards to assemble photographs of migrant parents alongside current photographs of them with their children. Viewed in their entirety, children's celebrations held in the houses built through migrant remittances assumed the function of what Douglas and Isherwood describe as "rituals of consumption," special events in which "[t]he patterned flow of consumption goods . . . show a map of social integration" (1978, xxii).

Household celebrations that simultaneously featured the claims of *iony* modernity with a celebration of family life also worked to combat criticism and to sway opinion about the negative effects of migration on children. Families in Jatundeleg, Ayaloma, and Shullín were well informed of the critical opinions held by journalists and an array of experts (including lawyers, psychiatrists, physicians, social workers, and teachers) who persistently linked migration with the rise of rural so-termed *"hogares desorganizados"* (disrupted households). These critics closely connected the migration of one parent (and in some cases both parents) to a litany of conditions and problems in children and adolescents, including, though not limited to, depression, explosive anger, violent behavior, animal abuse, poor school performance, "gender identity confusion," homosexuality, stuttering, timidity, and bed-wetting (see Ochoa Ordóñez 1998; Pinos and Ochoa 1999). Villagers peppered their conversations on the subject with a host of technical terms taken from developmental psychology, such as *abandono* (abandonment) and *negligencia familiar* (parental neglect), borrowed from newspaper and television coverage. Some among the migrant households, of course, knew the children's afflictions firsthand, which they typically glossed as *nervios,* a standard idiom of distress (Pribilsky 2001b).

Although not every child of migrants experienced problems, nearly all migrant parents went to some effort to distance themselves from negative associations of migration. In particular, families countered such images by emphasizing their commitment to providing a "modern" childhood for their children. In the same ways that critics of migration drew legitimacy from popular psychology, migrant families linked their modern aspirations for *iony* modernity with modern child-rearing techniques (cf. Kanaaneh 2002). During a visit I made to the home of Miguel Solano and Sandra Pañora, Sandra showed me how she had taken to buying a couple of copies of Ecuador's newly inaugurated parenting magazine *Crecer Feliz* (Growing Up Happy) while shopping in the Azogues market. The glossy magazine pages were filled with tips on how to improve parent-child relations and to boost school performance, in addition to advertisements for the requisite items of a modern childhood. The magazine's intended audience was likely *blancos*-mestizos and urban professionals (as evidenced by its high price tag at the newsstand), but Sandra found it a useful model to convey the kind of life she and her husband desired in their newly built Jatundeleg home. When she obliged my request for a tour of her home for my research, she spoke to me about how the priorities of family life had changed since when she was a child. "Before," she said "children worked all the time. Now they go to school and play, and parents play with them." As we passed through the hall and peeked into the children's separate rooms, she noted authoritatively, "Children should have their own rooms," as if quoting from the pages of *Crecer Feliz*. She then paused for a moment and looked at me. "Right?"

Although poor households in Jatundeleg could occasionally pool together their resources with other households to host fiestas or make community donations, individual family endeavors such as large baptismal or confirmation parties were often far out of their reach. In this regard, the kinds of status claims migrant households made through children's parties represented an especially insidious affront to poorer people's ability to maintain status in village affairs. Placing the needs of children before those of parents linked moral responsibility with modernity. If parents could not provide for their children, what did this say about the parents' commitment to their children? Perhaps most distressing for parents of poor households were their children's acknowledgments of these subtle messages. One non-migrant villager shared with me his feeling of horror when after a weekend of festivities following a confirmation, his son asked if he would go to the United States for him so that they too could have a celebration.

The Pain of Dollars

The experiences of Jatundeleg villagers as they grapple to realign their identities with the rising costs of subsistence livelihood reflect challenges nearly all rural Andean communities face as part of an increasingly globalized economy. Families I knew approached these challenges not as hapless victims, but rather as agents with their own aspirations for "progress" and "development." By doing so, they articulated a new standard of living for themselves, one heavily influenced by a desire to challenge the disparaging images of *nuestro folklórico* and to adopt those of *iony* modernity. As this chapter underscores, however, the means to achieve these communitywide goals were not uniformly available to all villagers. Decades of remittances served to create an ever-expanding chasm between rich and poor. Nevertheless, villagers experienced these changes not in open hostility, but rather through reconciliation and a recognition of the growing pains of becoming *progresivo*. Along the way, they experienced what I often heard cleverly labeled as "el dolor de dólares" (the pain of dollars). Progress in the form of better water systems, improved roadways, more efficient agriculture (e.g., greenhouses), and better security required increasing amounts of cash to acquire. At the same time, some families found their ability to garner and maintain status in the community slipping as costs elevated. These factors, in part, intersected with particular household dynamics to shape young people's decisions about migration. However, as we shall see in the following chapter, the decision to migrate is in general shaped by more than economic need. Migration is as much about chasing *dolarcitos* as it is about gaining some of the emblems of *iony* modernity and new markers of village status.

4

Rural Youth, Migration Decisions, and the Constitution of Transnational Households

Jatundeleg's Hometown Hero

I was fortunate to meet Hugo Callaguaso, Jatundeleg's *pionero* migrant, during a return visit he made to the village to join in the annual fiesta for its patron saint San José. Well on his way to intoxication, he singled me out as the only foreigner in a crowd of ponchos and *polleras*. Flicking off clumps of mud from his otherwise brilliantly shined cowboy boots and new blue jeans, he engaged me in near perfect English: "Can you believe this? I never get as dirty as I do when I am here, and there ain't no hot shower and half the time no electricity." I understood Hugo's desire to fraternize with me about how "dirty" and inconvenient life in the *campo* could be as an indication that he saw himself as more American than Ecuadorian. Having left for the United States in 1976, he certainly had spent most of his life away from his natal home in the rural Andes. When, at the age of seventeen, Hugo joined two other men from Ayaloma on the sojourn north, villagers knew little about the United States, aside from its association as a major importer of the Panama hats. Some village elders could remember ogling merchants' photos of their *sombreros de paja toquilla* on display in the glass cases of fashionable New York hotels and convention centers. One villager recalled, "With skyscrapers [*rascacielos*] and wide avenues, you thought you were peering into El Dorado."

For Hugo Callaguaso, the son of subsistence farmers with less than two hectares to divide between three sons, the United States indeed felt like El Dorado. When his tourist visa expired six months after his arrival, he began a ten-year undocumented adventure, cycling through dozens of restaurant and janitorial jobs in New York City, Miami, and Chicago. With passage of the IRCA in 1986, however, all that changed. Hugo applied for amnesty, and by 1990 he received U.S. citizenship. Two years later, while he was bartending at Chicago's O'Hare International Airport, a television commercial advertising the life of long-haul trucking caught his attention, prompting him to pursue a commercial driver's license and begin driving a semi. Divorced and with two children born in the United States, Hugo settled down comfortably in rural Virginia, where he purchased a home and new car. In Jatundeleg, it was no exaggeration to equate Hugo's stature with the cultural icon of the "hometown hero" because it seemed virtually everyone admired—and many envied—his life, including the woman from Shullín he recently married and planned to take back with him to Virginia.

Hugo wasted no time, though, in pointing out that his story was not the norm—and probably never was. He quickly sobered up to share the contrasts he saw: "I left when nobody was going, and it was easy. *Pooh!* I flew right into the Miami airport with a visa. I feel for these guys because it is so much harder. I could have stayed here and probably would have made it OK. My father didn't have lots of land, but I would have gotten by. By now, well maybe, I could have had a dairy farm or a small store where I could sell feed grain or something. But that would have taken years! But for these guys, there ain't nothing. They don't have land. I tell you they have it hard. En este país no les ofrece buenas oportunidades por eso se van [This country doesn't offer them any good opportunities, so they leave]."

I asked him, "What is so different about today?"

"To be a man and to have a family you have to migrate. Girls here they only want a migrating man. To say, 'No, I am gonna stay here and work,' that will get you nowhere. You can work and work and work. You'll be in your grave. Now, in this region, to go the United States is a feverish epidemic [*como una fiebre epidemia*]. If you're a young man, you better catch it and go. It takes a lot to go. It is hard for me to even imagine now how expensive it is. But not to go can cost more."

Hugo Callaguaso was not alone in his description of U.S.–bound migration as a feverish epidemic. In the early 1980s, men left only *poco a poco* (little by little), yet by the start of the 1990s, as personal networks began to solidify and many villagers were able to take advantage of their relatives' newly awarded U.S. citizenship through IRCA, the numbers of those seeking to leave greatly increased. Aiding this rural exodus was the proliferation of a long-standing regional tradition of informal moneylenders *(chulqueros),* who brought a "democratization of credit" to the Azuayo-Cañari countryside (Carpio Benalcázar 1992, 103). For the first time, families with few resources or connections abroad could realistically send a loved one north by contracting a migrant smuggler. During my fieldwork, the momentum to migrate was palpably high, and the metaphor of an unchecked feverish epidemic was more apt than ever. As my community census revealed, more than three-quarters of village households had at least one family member in the United States.

In the previous two chapters, I discussed how particular economic and social conditions within Ecuador have shaped transnational migration strategies in the Azuayo-Cañari region. However, consideration merely of those factors that "push" migrants out of unproductive areas and "pull" them toward new economic and social opportunities provides just a partial analysis. For instance, we cannot yet answer the following question: Why in communities with long traditions of multiple economic strategies for the reproduction of society has migration to the United States become the singular goal of rural youth? Nor can this analysis explain the gendered demographics of migration or the multiple meanings that migrants and their communities attach to their mobility. Instead, steps toward accounting for these aspects require first taking a closer look at the ways specific migrant decisions reflect the increasing complexities of rural life in southern Ecuador.

This chapter focuses on the lives of rural youth and discusses the social and cultural factors that propel migrants to the United States. Because migration continues to draw young *men* from rural villages, I focus specifically on the lifeworlds of male youth and the paradoxes of manhood they confronted growing up in Jatundeleg in the late 1990s. Although previous migration strategies served to ensure the social reproduction of households in Azuayo-Cañari villages, modern youth found, in the reverberations of transnational migration at this time, that the basic costs of reaching adulthood had risen sharply. Irrespective of their decision to migrate to the United States or not, many young men discovered that the time-tested steps to manhood—land ownership, marriage, and the initiation of one's own household—had become nearly unattainable without the kinds of economic and cultural capital that migration afforded.

Over the past two decades, migration researchers have consistently stressed the need to embed the ethnography of migration within analyses of the life course (e.g., see Boisvert 1987; Buechler 1987; Gardner 2002; Heyman 1990; Mills 1999; Osella and Osella 2000; Setel 1999). As articulated by Hans Buechler, this approach "plots individual life histories, stages in an individual's life cycle, and the crucial events or periods in an individual's life (such as migratory experience) against those of other members of a family, the development and composition of the family as a whole, and specific historical events or conditions" (1987, 222). To be sure, situating the migration decisions of Azuayo-Cañari youth within a life-course perspective reveals both gendered and generational tensions regarding a rapidly changing rural livelihood. Because life cycles in the Andes bind individuals with families and households (see, e.g., Bourque 1995), the decision to migrate marks a three-way intersection whereby young men's obligations to their parents to begin new households and their dreams of *iony* modernity merge and clash with newly raised conceptions of what it means to be a man *(ser hombre)* in the Ecuadorian Andes. In a comparable context, writing about the relationship between men's life cycles and migration in Kerala, South India, Osella and Osella note that "[m]igration may accelerate an individual's progress along a culturally idealized trajectory towards mature manhood . . . [and] may accentuate characteristics already locally associated with essentialized categories of masculinity" (2000, 118).

First, I place rural youth in the context of village life and discuss longstanding societal expectations in Azuayo-Cañari villages, including gender roles, marriage choices, and the initiation of new autonomous households. Then I analyze the ways the shifting economy and new possibilities for migration have reoriented these expectations and the implications for young adults. The chapter ends with an examination of the different means by which the constitution of new households has become the constitution of "transnational households" through the imperatives of migration to the United States.

Rural Youth and Everyday Life in Jatundeleg

Ecuador, like much of Latin America, is bottom heavy with young people. In 2001, more than 20 percent of the population was between the ages of fifteen and twenty-four; 33 percent was fifteen or younger (Instituto Nacional de Estadística y Censos 2001). The local situation was not much different: 32 percent of Jatundeleg's population fell below the age of twenty-four. Contrary to what seemed like constant reminders by villagers that nearly all *(casi todo)* of the village's young people had left for the United States, a critical mass of youth could always be found—at *tiendas* consuming sodas and cigarettes, whispering among themselves during evening church services, or participating in weekend pickup volleyball and soccer games. On Friday nights, I made sure not to miss hanging out on the benches in front of the church, where casual conversation and playful antics made for pages of fruitful field notes later. It was not uncommon for boys as young as sixteen to migrate to the United States, so my pool of informants stretched across age groups. Ecuadorians typically make a rough distinction between adolescents *(adoloscentes)* (roughly ten to seventeen years of age) and youths *(jóvenes)* (seventeen to twenty-four). It was this latter group of young people quickly, if fitfully, becoming Jatundeleg's next adult generation who were my closest confidants.

Young people in Jatundeleg had grown up in the shadows of Latin America's "lost decade" of the 1980s. Because the core economic problems of debt crisis, high inflation, and unemployment afflicted all parts of the nation, Azuayo-Cañari households were unable to escape their regional problems by migrating to the coast as they once had. Stable work on the banana and sugar plantations disappeared as exports dropped in the latter half of the century (Striffler 2002). Exacerbating local hardships, reformist government policies for import-substitution industrialization resulted in higher prices on basic commodities and foodstuffs, increasing rural households' need for cash (Larrea 1998; Weiss 1997). Jatundeleg families weathered the crisis in much the same way as they had in the past: by cobbling together what piecemeal wage labor they could find with subsistence agriculture. Households that had invested in land and cattle as well as in *tiendas* and other small businesses did their best to retain their investments and profit from them.

Many elderly residents in Jatundeleg clung adamantly to a belief that the economic crises of the 1980s and 1990s paled in comparison to the poverty and misery of the *llachapa vida* that accompanied the collapse of the Panama hat economy, but many young people remembered distinctly how the later economic crisis affected them. By far the most salient memories were those of interrupted and abandoned educations. Although public education is ostensibly free in Ecuador, matriculation fees, supplies, and mandatory uniforms can make schooling children prohibitive. In Jatundeleg, education costs could easily gobble up a month's worth of a family's earnings and were often the first "unnecessary" expenses to be forfeited to make ends meet.[1] As a consequence, the education histories of many rural youths were spotty, with missing years and delayed completions. Compounding matters, the national school teachers' union, Unión Nacional de Educadores (UNE), in its efforts to gain better pay and benefits, staged frequent strikes *(paros)* that halted classes for up to a month or more at a time. By the end of my fieldwork in Jatundeleg, Ecuador's education system was again facing serious economic and political challenges, plagued by budget shortfalls and more UNE strikes. The disillusionment catalyzed by missed classes and unmotivated instructors, coupled with students' own frequent evaluation of their high school educations and with the promises of *iony* modernity, worked to transform the completion of one's education into a low priority among Jatundeleg youth and increasingly among their parents, too (cf. Levinson 2001, 314–19).

Although migration consumed many of their thoughts and desires, it by no means represented the only route Jatundeleg youth pursued to economic independence. To be sure, among the high school students (as well

---

1. In 1999, matriculation fees and other costs amounted to approximately $60, accounting for approximately one-third of an average household monthly income for a family not receiving remittances.

as among youths not attending school) whom I interviewed, some clearly had no interest in going to the United States. By way of demonstrating this lack of interest, many young men tried persistently to find work locally that would allow them to gain independence and eventually start their own families and autonomous households. When young people reached the age of seventeen or eighteen, it could be expected that they would produce their own income, some of which they contributed directly to their parents' household and the remainder they set aside for seeking out a marriage partner. In many parts of the Ecuadorian Andes, where there are no steadfast rules about income pooling or explicit obligations of maturing children to contribute to household economies, most youth in Jatundeleg saw it as a duty of good will *(buena voluntad)* to give a portion of their earnings to their parents. Again, this subtle expectation affected boys more than it did girls, whose assistance in childcare, cooking, and other domestic chores was essential to smooth household operations. Birth order also played a role. Among male youth in their late teens, the oldest would be expected to seek employment first, and the next male child in age might never feel the same pressure.

Most youths followed in their parent's footsteps as farmers, working the older generation's land, which they hoped to inherit someday. In some cases, young people assumed full responsibility for their families' *chacras,* from preparing the fields to orchestrating the harvest, to allow their parents to seek more lucrative employment elsewhere. In addition to farming family land, young men also worked other people's fields as *jornaleros.* Few opportunities for work existed outside the village. In a few cases, young women were able to find jobs in urban areas as seamstresses. Opportunities for *jornalero* work frequently took young men no farther than the fields that surrounded the village. In rare instances, young men found highly coveted construction jobs in Azogues.

Only in a few cases did young men find work opportunities in Guayaquil, Quito, or even Cuenca, despite its close proximity. In Jatundeleg, many cash-strapped villagers considered prohibitive the idea of venturing into the city for work. If a migrant lacked family ties in the city, a good portion of his wages would end up going to cover food and lodging costs. In some instances, particularly daring young men I knew found construction jobs where they were able to sleep on site, though not without the fear of being robbed. The risks of urban employment were heightened for those who tried their luck as street vendors *(ambulantes)* who peddled everything from kitchen gadgets to lottery tickets. A young man from Jatundeleg who eventually migrated to the United States told me how he had borrowed a large sum of money from his uncle to buy an inventory of soaps and tooth-brushes only to find a glutted and competitive street market. Well-estab-lished family networks controlled the market, structuring who could sell goods where in the main commercial areas of the city. When he could not liquidate his inventory, the young man tried unsuccessfully to locate the wholesaler he had purchased the goods from as the man had prom-ised to buy back any unsold items. With no other options, he eventually unloaded his toothbrushes and soap on another vendor at below-market value and returned to Jatundeleg broke and humiliated. Other young men and women from the village shared similar stories, although not always as extreme, of being burned in the *ambulante* market.

Young people also shunned urban employment out of fear of the racist reception they would get in the city. "In Cuenca," Marco Cajarmarca re-marked to me, "I have been called *longo, mitayo, indio sucio* [dirty Indian] when I tried to find a job."[2] Another young man told me how he spent the better part of two days waiting in the Plaza San Francisco in Cuenca (a well-known location for employers to find day laborers) only to be told by one potential employer that he didn't "hire *longos*." Complicating matters of urban racism regarding Azuayo-Cañari youths' indigenous-sounding surnames, dark skin, and rural backgrounds were the association many in Cuenca drew between rural villages of the Déleg region and migra-tion. Many people described to me incidents where disclosure of their hometown prompted people to view them as "rich Indians," making them especially vulnerable to corruption and bribery. Applications for visas, military conscription, or auto registration were prime opportunities for

---

2. *Longo, mitayo,* and *indio* are common derogatory labels for indigenous peoples in Ecuador and in the Andes more generally. For a closer look at their etymology and usage in the Andes, see Weismantel 2001, xxviii–xli.

officials to overcharge clients from migrant communities. For instance, a twenty-year-old man from Ayaloma told me how when he was stopped for a traffic violation in his uncle's truck in Cuenca, the officer imposed an unusually high fine *(multa)*. When the young man contested the exorbitant charge, the officer called him a *"mitayo* with dollars" who could surely afford to pay any fine amount.

Whether young people found work in the fields around Jatundeleg or in the streets and small workshops of Cuenca, overwhelmingly their earnings could do little to alter their situation. Making the predicament of poverty particularly vexing, however, was the realization of their marginal status within Ecuadorian society and the world beyond them—a world transmitted daily into their rural households through televisions and radios. When electricity reached the majority of Jatundeleg households in the mid-1980s, televisions quickly followed. More than 90 percent of families in the village owned televisions at the time of my research (many since the 1980s). On the four channels available to them, villagers particularly enjoyed watching evening *telenovelas* (soap operas) and comedy shows. The *telenovelas,* almost all from Colombia and Mexico, portrayed stereotypical images of white Latin American urban sophistication packaged in highly formulaic story lines peppered with issues of wealth, love, jealousy, and corrupted power. By contrast, popular Ecuadorian-produced comedy programs presented skits and routines that poked fun at Ecuador's campesinos and *indígenas.* In particular, these programs brought campesinos face to face with the disparaging images of *nuestro folklórico* that painted indigenous peasants simultaneously as quaint relics of the past and as an ignorant inferior race. One evening at a *tienda* I watched a program that I later recorded in my field notes:

> The episode featured what was presumably a mestizo pharmacy owner who had grown bored selling over-the-counter medications. Seeing an opportunity to seduce his female clientele, the owner clad himself in a poncho and hat typical of highland indigenous groups along with exotic accouterments supposedly belonging to a shaman, or traditional healer. As scantily clad female clients came to him with different ailments, the shop owner would convince them that what they needed was a *"limpieza,"*

or spiritual cleaning to cure them of their sickness. In his back room, atop a long table, the shop owner rubbed a cleansing egg over the women's bodies, ostensibly healing while all the time seducing them. Finally, after performing this sham on a number of women, the pharmacy owner gets a taste of his own medicine, when his former "patients" return, tie him up, and torture him with the ritual cleaning.

Although the skit initially prompted everyone to laugh, a sense of unease eventually was cast over the viewing. One male viewer asked, "Is this what people in the United States think of *indígenas?*" When I said I did not think so and suggested that it reflected prejudice and racism in Ecuador, the viewers agreed. Another added: "We would be treated better in the United States than we are here! Here, they just don't tell the truth. They think we are living in the old-fashioned times [*ñaupa tiempos*] and we don't know any better." Many of the men who appeared in agreement with this statement began laughing when I followed by asking if maybe what was needed was a show about real life in Jatundeleg. "Maybe a *telenovela?*" I suggested.

"Who would watch it?" a campesino in tattered slacks, polyester pants, and wool poncho queried. "Who wants to watch something about our tough life?"

"Maybe [they would watch] if it was about those who return from the United States and live in those big luxurious houses," qualified a similarly looking man.

"But we'd still be campesinos *humilde* [country folk]," a man in his early twenties retorted.

Young people confronted these disparaging images of themselves the best way they could: by channeling their meager earnings into conspicuous consumption that they hoped would approximate the urban sophistication they had come to know on television. For unmarried men in Jatundeleg, money went foremost to the purchase of alcohol and cigarettes, and occasionally to fashionable clothing, digital watches, and faux gold jewelry. Equally important were outings to Cuenca that briefly allowed young people to escape their rural surroundings. Indeed, few Sundays passed without a group of young people organizing a day trip into the city to see a movie, eat in a restaurant, or otherwise pass their time in the city's main plaza. Youth anxiously awaited these events and took great care in their planning and preparations. Unmarried young women exchanged their soiled campesina clothing for fashionable jeans and blouses and spent hours fixing their hair and applying makeup. Similarly, men's knee-high rubber work boots and wool hats gave way to brand-name tennis shoes, denim jeans, and Nike and Adidas nylon sweat suits.

As many young people in Jatundeleg were learning, though, they need not turn on their televisions or make a special trip into the city to experience the modernity that simultaneously intimidated and attracted them. Increasingly, the desires of what it meant to be *iony* were not just in the fictional lives of characters on television, but close at hand and palpable in the speech, clothing, spending patterns, and attitudes of return migrants and their families. Young people in the village watched as their peers left to the United States and then sent back money to their families to be spent on consumer purchases. When migrants themselves returned, they often did so with a small nest egg of savings that they quickly exhausted in their efforts to pad their return with a certain degree of comfort. Although not all migrants met with success abroad and were able to send back large remittances or return with sizeable savings, those who did presented young villagers with powerful images of possible success and markers of status that were hard to ignore.

However, for many youth I knew, mere status and identity markers alone did not fuel an irreconcilable animosity between villagers. Rather, many accepted the pressures to keep up with peers and neighbors as an inevitable part of the changing economy. Instead, the more far-reaching effects of the new remittance economy worried many youth. Specifically, the new levels of wealth that expanded competition from one merely for the emblems of *iony* modernity to one that took place in the playing field of courtship and the eventual selection of marriage partners made youth resentful of their peers and fearful for their futures. The exclamation of one youth—and echoed by others—that migrants were taking "all the women" reflected the subtle ways young men viewed migration as beginning to alter men's trajectories along the life cycle by intensifying the competition for available marriage partners. Increasingly, young men I knew found a trip to the United States to be a certain inevitability, rather than merely a possible alternative path, in order to move from being a youth to being a socially recognized adult as defined by marriage, fatherhood, and autonomy from parents.

"Considering One's Parents": Youth, Obligation, and the Life Course

As a number of ethnographers have noted, children in many parts of the Andes are taught from an early age to assume a great deal of responsibility by assisting their parents with household chores. Such acts form an integral part of the socialization process and a formalization of parent-child relations. Anthropologist Ann Miles aptly captures the situation: "Children's contributions to household labor not only serve [an] instrumental purpose . . . but also helping out at home is considered an intrinsic moral good" (1994, 142). By age six or seven, children in Jatundeleg are expected to help their parents by fetching water and firewood, taking care of guinea pigs *(cuyes)*, shucking corn and beans, and serving as village messengers and couriers. In some households, children as young as seven learn the intricacies of *paja* weaving. By age nine or so, children begin looking after younger siblings, hike to the *cerro* to feed pastured animals, and help with cooking responsibilities. Most of these tasks, aside from cooking, are not gender specific.

Many parents of migrant-age youth I knew in Jatundeleg halfheartedly bemoaned the "lack of respect" that they now received from children in comparison to how it was in the often romanticized *ñaupa tiempos*. Older residents, for instance, noted how it was once common that each time a child entered the home after leaving for more than an hour or so, he or she would seek his or her parents' blessing *(bendición)* by kneeling before them. Twenty years ago parents also expected children to address them using the formal *vos* rather than the informal *tu* (you) in spoken Spanish. In the absence of such acts of deference, one general facet of respect that had not gone away was the expectation that children should "consider their parents" (have *considerándoles*). To "consider" his or her parents in Azuayo-Cañari villages, a child must anticipate and feel his or her parents' needs, understand their point of view, and, above all, treat them with unwavering respect *(respeto)* (see McKee 1980, 61). By aiding their parents, children enmesh themselves in webs of reciprocity and mutual obligation. In return, respectful children receive their parents' love and affection *(cariño)*. Casual observers of highland households often note that children do not receive direct praise for the tasks they perform. Children, parents frequently explained to me, should perform their chores without having to be asked and without requiring constant acknowledgment when tasks are completed. Instead, a well-behaved and respectful child is said to be filled with *buena voluntad* when he or she does not need to be reminded of a task. By contrast, parents label children who fail to carry out the tasks expected of them as misbehaving ("está malcriado") and not fully considering their parents. To forget to complete a chore may be grounds for punishment.

Considerándoles does not end with childhood, and ideally the reciprocal bonds should continue and strengthen over time. Elderly parents, for instance, rely on their adult children to help them in their fields, to escort them into the city for appointments, and, although less explicitly defined, to help them out financially when necessary. At the time of a parent's death, it is the children's responsibility to arrange and pay for a funeral at the church. On All Souls' Day, adult children continue to consider their parents by cleaning their gravestones and adorning them with freshly cut flowers and decorated *guaguas de pan* (bread babies). As an informant in the highland village of Los Flores told anthropologist Lauris McKee regarding the perpetuity of *considerándoles:* "The [bonds] never wind themselves up ['No se liquidan']" (1980, 61).

As children mature, the most endearing and respectful way they can demonstrate consideration for their parents is to make an initiative to marry and start a new household. At around the age of nineteen or twenty, and even earlier in some cases, young people begin to feel their parents' good will and generosity running thin and begin receiving subtle cues that it is time to think about marriage. Adult unmarried children, unless they are contributing significant amounts of their income to the family, can be a drain on the household economy.

In the past, children needed little prompting in the ways of marriage because parents strictly arranged most unions, often pairing together already

4.1. *Guaguas de pan* (bread babies) to honor deceased parents on All Souls' Day. Photograph by the author.

closely related families in a strategic merging of resources. More recently, I was told, parents had taken to "letting open their children's hearts" and to allowing the power of romantic love some leeway. In practice, however, few parents proceeded in such a carefree manner with respect to their children's choices of partners. More than a union of two individuals, marriage brings together families in social and economic relationships, where each party can call on the other for exchanges of labor *(prestamanos)* and resources. Even in the late 1990s, who was deemed a suitable partner differed considerably between concerned parents and reflected the varied resource bases and specific kinship positions of diversified households. For instance, one partner was desirable because his or her family had ample land to share; a different partner had a *yunta* that could be used at no charge during the planting season; yet another could bring numerous heads of cattle or sheep into the relationship. Surely, though, the most desirable partners were those who in some ways had links to U.S.–bound migration, either directly through migrant relatives, through having migrated themselves, or through participation in the business of money lending.

Male youth in Jatundeleg felt acute pressures to marry and form new affinal links with outside families. A playful regional tradition of jokes and rhymes chides young men and warns them of remaining single *(ser soltero)* forever—of having to cook for themselves while peers look on in ridicule. However, the most immediate pressure to marry came from parents who consider a son's marriage one of the only sure-fire ways to increase household wealth. Because the rewards of conjoining households varied greatly among the families I knew, young men repeatedly told me of their parents' desires for them to marry and fulfill *considerándoles.* Girls, by contrast, faced less pressure to marry. Parents valued daughters for the indispensable contributions they make in the household even as they reached a marriageable age. Marriage, many agreed, often stole daughters from their natal families.

Although no steadfast rule of patrilocality exists in the Ecuadorian Andes, newly married women in Jatundeleg often saw it as their duty to attend first to their mother-in-law's household. Conversely, boys became less useful in the domestic arena long before marriage, with opportunities in wage labor frequently pulling them away from the household. As one elderly woman with four sons and no daughters confided in me, "A daughter can cook and clean, but a son after a while can only drain your resources." Parents thus readily guarded unmarried young women and were more apt to seek control over their choice of spouse. Parents especially grimaced at the possibility of a widowed daughter or a single mother *(madre soltera)* whose husband had died or left her. Such women were generally considered ineligible for remarriage and customarily wound up living with her parents again. Mindful of these potential consequences, parents of marriage-eligible daughters found themselves in a tight spot with respect to suitors who planned to migrate. Although the possibility of enrichment through a son-in-law's dollar remittances enticed poor households, the fear of abandonment could quickly temper such desires, inhibiting parents from rushing too quickly to bless a new union.

For their part, young people also saw great advantage in getting married. Throughout the highlands, as McKee notes, "marriage and the advent of children offer the most commonly available, surest route to adulthood, to recognized social maturity, and to the kind of autonomy valued in culture" (1980, 103). Unmarried youth in their late teens, especially males, stand in an awkward and ambiguous social position vis-à-vis marriage. Unmarried men I knew could easily earn the same income as their fathers performing largely the same work, but they were ineligible to participate in most social exchanges that defined relationships between adults.[3] What these young men lacked, however, was not simply a wife, but also a separate household, or at least the assurance of a future new household based on the ownership of land. As one young man hopeful of getting married told me, "You can be the richest person in the village, but if you are not married, no one will listen to you."

Although multiple factors informed the initiation of new unions, in many cases it was a youth's alcohol consumption that tipped the scales and brought a parent's guarded wishes for a son's marriage to the surface of discussion. One village mother shared with me a common sentiment among village women: "[The problem] is young men who have just enough [money] to 'wet their throats' [*mojarse el garganta*] but not enough to become the heads of their own households." During my research, I closely monitored such tensions in one household headed up by my neighbors Luís Antonio Cuzco and Ximena Aucaquispe, with whom I shared a special relationship as a godparent *(padrino)* to their second-to-youngest son. My closeness to the family permitted me to watch, in particular, as Ximena's patience evaporated with her twenty-two-year-old son Juan Carlos, who lived at home and showed no signs of moving toward marriage. Although I was most familiar with this family's case, the same tensions I witnessed in this household burdened other village families I knew as well.

Juan Carlos was the eldest of seven children in one of Jatundeleg's poorest households. Because of his family's persistent money troubles, Juan Carlos dropped out of school at age twelve to work alongside his father in construction. The partnership was short-lived. Both father and son were heavy drinkers, and they had come to blows many times in drunken

3. Throughout the Andes, unmarried men occupy a stigmatized status (see, e.g., Carter 1977; Isbell 1978). Among the Aymara, for example, unmarried men maintain the status of *yokalla*, or adolescent, for their entire lives and are generally shut out of opportunities for fiesta sponsorship and community leadership (Buechler and Buechler 1971, 36).

Table 4.1

Comparison of Average Age at Marriage in Two Decades by Sex

	Male	Female	Age Range (male and female)
1970–1979	21	19	15–52
1990–1999	24	21	17–49

Source: *Libros parroquiales y civiles*, Déleg, 1999.

bouts. When I met Juan Carlos, he was working as a carpenter on the reno-vation of Jatundeleg's church. The job provided a certain level of security, giving him money to spend while he continued to live in the comfort of his parents' home.

As indicated in the civil registry of the *cantón* Déleg, average ages for marriage in Jatundeleg, Ayaloma, and Shullín had risen slightly since the decade of the 1970s (see table 4.1). The reason for the increase could be convincingly attributed to the difficulty young people faced with respect to starting their own households in the unstable economy of the 1980s, coupled with the shortage of land in highland communities. Thus, given the fact that men married in Jatundeleg at an average age of twenty-four, there was little cause for alarm over Juan Carlos's seemingly disinterested stance toward marriage. Instead of remarking on age, villagers were more likely to gauge the likelihood of a youth's advancement toward marriage based on the length and seriousness of particular courtships *(noviazgos)*, of which Juan Carlos had none serious enough to mention.[4] Rather, like many young men his age, he appeared enamored only with the emblems of *iony* modernity.

What money Juan Carlos did not spend on alcohol often went to fashion. He almost always wore trendy baggy cargo pocket jeans, hooded

4. Formal courtship *(noviazgo)* was not a socially recognized practice to which most village households adhered. Although some couples did go through traditional courtships, they did so usually at their parents' request and not out of a sense of societal obligation. In the central Ecuadorian Andes, Stølen (1987) found that a typical courtship before marriage lasted five months.

sweatshirts, and name-brand Nike and Adidas nylon athletic jackets; an American flag bandanna perpetually covered his head and neatly held back his shoulder-length jet black hair. His interest in North American fashions and popular culture was paralleled only by his interest in migrating to the United States, the prospect of which he discussed with me incessantly. However, as the eldest son in a large family, Juan Carlos also carried a special obligation to "consider" his parents and to look after them in old age. His father, Luís, had two brothers legally residing in the United States, and the family held out constant hope that their connections could someday help get Juan Carlos or one of his brothers into the country without having to resort to illegal means. Luís himself had illegally migrated to the United States in the 1970s, though he had returned empty-handed after just two years. His sour experience abroad greatly affected his hopes (and fears) for his sons.

Juan Carlos, feeling that he was "buying time," frequently occupied his idle hours drinking with friends. Many nights Luís Antonio and Ximena waited in worried anticipation of their son's arrival home from a night of drinking after work on the church ended for the day. On a number of evenings that I spent visiting with Luís Antonio and Ximena, Juan Carlos would barrel through the door, intoxicated and yelling at the top of his lungs. In these moments, Ximena often came to her son's aid, both in an attempt to calm him down and to avert the curious eyes of siblings, the youngest of whom was only five. Ximena usually could successfully pacify Juan by luring him into the kitchen for a late-night *merienda* (light supper) before he retired to bed.

Luís Antonio and Ximena would not admit to having arranged their son's marriage to Sonia, a neighbor woman three years younger than Juan Carlos, but all evidence pointed to their heavy hand in their son's affairs. As Luís Antonio confessed, "A time comes when a son must marry. Sometimes parents declare this time, sometimes it is children." However, for Juan Carlos, there appeared to be few options for marriage. His villagewide reputation as a *chumado* (drunk), despite his handsome looks and his family's good reputation, made him an undesirable potential partner. Sonia, however, was a logical choice for both families. Both households were already linked through marriage, and they had for many years shared pastures and fields. As such, there was little gained in the union; it was but "half a mar-riage," Ximena lamented. For her part, Sonia complained to her parents that it felt like an arranged union. Her dream, like many girls her age, was to marry a migrant and eventually to live in Cuenca. Although her parents approved of the wedding and strongly exercised their opinion with their daughter, they continued to have reservations about Juan Carlos's heavy drinking. Their decision ultimately rested on the fact that Sonia was their only daughter. In this context, Juan Carlos was considered a safe pick. Few felt that he possessed the dedication to migrate and therefore would not abandon their daughter or, worse yet, try and convince her to go the United States with him.

After an inexpensive civil service, the couple moved into a small apart-ment space (one room and a bathroom) above a sewing shop owned by Sonia's aunt. During my last visit to Luís Antonio and Ximena, it seemed that their efforts to marry off their son had proven successful. Juan Carlos and Sonia had begun the process of forming a new household that would eventually result in a new home with their own kitchen. For the time being, they shared the hearths of both of their parents, where they took their meals and contributed to providing food. In the prescribed duties of a daughter-in-law, Sonia divided her time between the tasks she had always carried out for her parents and the new ones set forth by Ximena. Although the couple received only a small portion of land *(una media cuadra)* from both parents at the time of their wedding, they had taken to working it, planting corn and potatoes. Much of the burden of the planting and harvesting fell upon Sonia as Juan Carlos continued to work in construction. For Ximena and Luís Antonio, the situation was as close to perfect as they could hope given their limited resources. Luís Antonio told me during our last visit that Juan Carlos was again "considering" his parents.

Land Scarcity, Migration, and Generational Conflict

Tensions between unmarried sons and parents in Jatundeleg families al-most certainly lessen when young people marry and begin the process of forming their own autonomous households. Although relationships based on *considerándoles* continue, marriage provides some autonomy for young couples. To be sure, parental demands on married children become largely confined to asking them to provide occasional labor at stressful times of the agricultural cycle and occasionally to help with household expenses. In general, marriage was often described to me as the way couples *asentar cabeza,* a phrase translated literally as "to establish a head" but carrying the more encompassing meaning of "to take responsibility." As dependent children become socially recognized adults with their own households, they can properly stake a claim in the community and are able to call upon other village households for labor exchanges. In turn, they assume obligations to help others.

Although highly desired by both children and parents, the prospects of marriage in Jatundeleg at the time of my research were far from straight-forward because land—the prerequisite for a new union—was in scare supply. Specifically, the majority of village youth at this time composed the first generation, as far as most residents could remember, that did not stand to inherit land from their parents, or at least not in the crucial first years after marriage. Indeed, most unmarried couples *(novios)* were not as lucky as Juan Carlos and Sonia to begin their unions with the merging of family land and the possibilities for an agricultural future. In response to the land crisis, villagers frequently reminded me of the supreme importance of land as *lo basico* (the bedrock) of a new marriage and eventually a new, autonomous household. Without land, as one man in his fifties who worried for his own unmarried sons confided in me, one is "con la chulla" (fighting with one hand) to make it in the community. He continued: "No one should marry without land because it is very hard to live. Who will trade with you? What can they offer their neighbors? What will you give your children?"

A number of factors accounted for the scarcity of land. Since the shortcomings of Ecuador's agrarian reform (initiated in 1964) were first identified, several researchers have written about the dwindling size of individual landholdings, a transformation often described as a shift from the *minifundio* to the *microfundio* (Carpio Benalcázar 1992; Jokisch 1998; Kyle 1996, 2000). In addition to unproductive farmland in the region, perhaps the greatest factor contributing to land scarcity was the result of generations of divisions and subdivisions of land between family members in inheritance to a point where parcels could no longer be meaningfully (or economically) divided. Similar to other regions of the Andes, Azuayo-Cañari communities practice parallel partible inheritance whereby both male and female children inherit from each parent. Inheritance *(herencia)* refers foremost to land, although it can also include houses and livestock. Older Jatundeleg residents, although they had long merged their lands with their spouses, could still clearly identify their own personal *herencia*. An orderly system of dividing and passing down land had sustained itself for many generations, but the triumph of lower mortality and higher fertility rates beginning in the early part of the twentieth century brought new pressures and land scarcity (see Clark 2001).

The problem of inadequate land size was additionally compounded by an incongruity in generational life courses. Simply put, at the time of my research the problem was not just that parents did not have enough land to give away. Parents were also living longer and could not readily bequeath lands they continued to use for their own subsistence needs. How this situation played out in Jatundeleg differed little from what Weiss hypothesized for the central Ecuadorian Andes two decades ago:

> If we set up a hypothetical couple who marry at age 20, have children soon after, and then die at about age 45, we can say that the eldest son would inherit property (in a bilateral kin system) when they are about 25 years old, at about marriageable age. They could then set up their own household on their own parcel of land and establish labor exchanges, and so on. . . . A structural problem would arise if the senior generation started to live longer, for their children would remain in a structurally dependent position for a longer period of time. (1985, 477)

Although data capturing the severity of land scarcity over time do not exist for Jatundeleg, oral testimonies regarding inheritances and land division confirm that a problem of land scarcity was identifiable by as early as the late 1950s. However, as many elderly residents informed me, the conditions of being placed in what Weiss identifies as a "structurally dependent position" vis-à-vis parents could be and often was averted by the purchase of additional parcels of land. Wages earned on coastal plantations allowed villagers, in part, to "catch up" and supplement their meager *herencias* with newly purchased plots. For Jatundeleg youth in the late 1990s, however, this option had all but dried up as a result of the inflationary effects of dollars on the local economy. Wealthy migrant households had initiated what amounted to a "land grab," buying up scarce premium land at inflated prices. (Many parcels of land were subsequently transformed into pastures for dairy cattle.) When I returned in 2001, I learned of one case where a wealthy returnee had purchased a large swath of land in Loma Lanzacay where he intended to grow pine trees for Japanese lumber companies. In this climate, with high sticker prices often set in dollars, young people who wished to purchase land outright realized they could do so only with the kind of wealth afforded by migration.

Beyond the clear association of land with marriage, many young people had difficulty imagining a future without land and especially without growing their own *maíz*. Because parents could not promise an inheritance, they could no longer exercise the same degree of control over their children in the areas of marriage and work as they had in the past. In a profound way, the absence of inheritance unraveled adult children's bonds of *considerándoles* as they faced a future based less on inherited property and more on their own initiative. The possibility of migration as a means for children to assert themselves in village life played a paramount role in these changes and, as such, facilitated the introduction of alternative sources of authority into parent-child relations.

During a focus group discussion among five village men and myself, all with adult children, the topic of dwindling inheritances loomed large.

PARTICIPANT 1: Many of the young people leave on account of there not being enough land. A *media cuadra* doesn't produce enough to live on.

JCP: Why is there not enough land?

PARTICIPANT 1: They [the soils] are bad and don't produce. But there is also not enough land to give away. Parents need that land just as much as children.

PARTICIPANT 2: I have three sons and two daughters. My oldest son works with [my wife and me], and he will get the land when we die. The others? I don't know. They will have to find a different future.

JCP: . . . So, the lack of land has affected what children will do?

PARTICIPANT 3: If we have nothing to leave them, how can we expect them to stay? How can we expect them to respect the family?

Young people I interviewed on the same subject rarely blamed their parents for their inability to bequeath them land. Instead, they generally understood the situation as an inevitable part of seemingly irreversible economic conditions in the village. One man who talked at length about these issues with me was twenty-two-year-old Mario Callaguaso (whose family story is detailed in chapter 3):

> It is *la chulla vida,* no? Life is just changing in the village. Everyone in my family for generations had been a farmer. I would be a farmer too, but I can't wait. . . . Here is an example: my cousin, he is older than me [the cousin was twenty-six] has been working his parents' land ever since he left school. And what does he have to show for it? He and his wife live with her parents. He makes nothing . . . fifty or sixty dollars [monthly]. He cannot afford to send his children to school, to buy new things. How will he ever buy land? No, young people now want something else.

Mario's reference to his age set as "wanting something more" was readily understood by many in his parents' generation and even more so by many in his grandparents' generation, who viewed village youth as unwilling to make the sacrifices they themselves had made in order to get land. Don Lucho Misquire, age sixty-three, had one son who migrated permanently to the United States in the early 1970s and who regularly sent back money. Don Lucho chided the "new generation," in contrast to his own children, who presumably had only money—not their parents—on their minds: "Most [young people] think they can go to Yoni and pick the money off the trees and buy land back in the village. And because they have this belief, they sit around and wait in the village, waiting to go the United States, all the time treating their parents horribly. Parents will share their land with children because they love them. But children won't wait anymore." Another father in his fifties who had no children in the United States expressed a similar sentiment:

Puhh! [Adult] children have no patience! When I was young, you "considered" your parents because they would take care of you. And you knew someday you would take care of them. It is not like that now. Children do not want to farm with their parents. They want their own land, or they don't want land at all. They don't want to work with their parents. The problem, I think, is what they see all around them—the big houses, cars, pastures full of fat cattle. They tell themselves this is all I want: "Es que esa es mi única esperanza, traer un poquito de plata a mi vida" [This is my only hope—to bring a bit of money to my life]. It is a new mentality here.

What adult children supposedly no longer desired, and what parents claimed the children had no patience for, was the slow, laggard process by which new households typically form in Andean communities. The advent of new households entails more than the physical construction of domestic structures. Rather, it is, as Mary Weismantel has articulated, a "constituted process . . . [focused on] the steady accretion of minute alterations in everyday domestic habits, out of which come the major transitions of an individual lifetime, as well as the evolution of new households and families" (1989, 69). In the Andes of Peru and Bolivia, though increasingly less common today, the process of new unions often begins in a "trial marriage" *(sirvanakuy)*, whereby newly formed couples start their lives together in their parents' home for approximately a year (Bourque and Warren 1981, 99; Carter 1977; Price 1965). If during the trial period things have gone smoothly, an official wedding will be arranged, and the couple will slowly receive the resources needed to build their own home. In the Ecuadorian Andes, further variations define this process. In the highland province of Chimborazo, Carola Lentz reported a six- to ten-year lapse between a couple's wedding and the construction of their own home. Remarkably, she notes that this time frame is "early" and that during the hacienda period young couples typically had to wait until their own children were old enough to begin contributing labor in the fields before a new household would be considered economically viable. Similarly, Weismantel (1989) describes how marriage in Zumbagua merely starts a process that may culminate many years later, even after children are born to a married couple. In contrast, the development of new households in the Azuayo-Cañari region during my fieldwork was slightly faster, with an average of two years after marriage. During this period of time, it was often expected that adult children would initiate the process of starting a new household by entering into a sharecropping relationship with their parents, helping with all stages of farming. In exchange for their labor, married children claimed a portion *(una chala)* of the harvest that they could trade, sell, or consume.[5] Over time, the accumulation of resources went toward building a new home for the young couple.

The idea of working for *chalas* struck many youth in Jatundeleg as highly undesirable in the late 1990s, if for no other reason than that the process of patiently waiting for land would have few discernable payoffs. In the past, married children could expect to receive not only land from parents, but also a home when parents deemed them worthy. At the turn of the last century, with parents living longer and clinging more desperately to their land, children began estimating these rewards to be far out of reach. Moreover, new couples equally looked with envy upon the handful of highly successful migrant households in the village's *nueva generación* for whom the process of marriage and starting a new household happened nearly simultaneously.

The village youths' impatience also reflected different gendered positions. Although young women shared with their male counterparts a reluctance toward "working for *chalas,*" their desire to start their own households—by means of migration—in a much quicker fashion than accomplished by their parent's generation spoke to different imperatives. Soon after marriage, young women typically found themselves under the thumbs of their mothers-in-law in the "standard" practice of patrilocality.[6] Many young women such as twenty-five-year-old Catalina Pomaguiza argued that deference paid to mothers-in-law did not come with the same rewards today as it had in the past: "When my mother married, she went and

5. In Spanish, *chala* literally means "cornhusk," although in the context here it refers to an actual portion of the harvest. Although cornhusks hold value as animal feed, the phrase "working for *chalas*" can carry a connotation akin to "working for peanuts."

6. As other anthropologists have pointed out (see, e.g., Belote and Belote 1977; Weismantel 1988), patrilocality in the Ecuadorian Andes is a standard practice, not a practice prescribed by kinship rules.

lived with my father's family there [pointing to a two-room adobe home]. Can you believe it? They all lived there. And she had to prove herself worthy to my grandmother. She did all the work—planting, weeding, feeding the animals. And she still had to cook, too. But over time, she inherited a lot of land, and things were good. She did not have to worry. Girls today wouldn't get that much."

For their part, older women acknowledged the predicament of female youth. When I shared Catalina's statement with my close neighbor María Dolores Uruchima to get her reaction, her mouth fell open as she considered what I was telling her. "I lived with my *suegra* [mother-in-law] when my husband went to the coast. All day I felt like I stirred a large pot [olla] of *mote* for her. I always cried, and I did not like her. So I understand these young girls. . . . But ultimately they have no respect for their *suegras*. They don't believe the *suegras* can give them anything, which is true with their husband's money raining from the north. But they can learn something, but they don't care to."

Other older women were less forgiving of the changes María Dolores expressed to me. It was not simply young women's reluctance that led to the inversion of authority. As remittances flowed back to wives, daughters-in-law gained new powers and autonomy through wealth, a situation that placed in-laws in compromising positions.

Cumplir Su Destino: *Changing Expectations of Men, Marriage, and Migration*

If dwindling inheritances and expanding possibilities for migration brought new tensions to the traditional authority of parent-child relationships, the same set of factors also affected the gendered expectations of village youths as they went about their activities of courtship and marriage. In the Andean region, gender roles and ideologies reflect the historical stamp of cultural clash—of five hundred years of accommodation, residence, and hybridization of Spanish traditions (circum-Mediterranean cultural traits more generally) with pre-Columbian indigenous traditions (Bourque and Warren 1981; Silverblatt 1987). Gender roles in the Azuayo-Cañari region blend ideologies and practices of the pre-Hispanic

Andean model of "complementarity" and the more patriarchal model of Hispanic and circum-Mediterranean cultures.[7] Although I am careful not to reify these two traditions, their prominence and, at times, distinctiveness were evident in Jatundeleg courtship practices during my time there. Mestizo values, for instance, influenced men's aggressiveness in courtship. Jatundeleg parents delightfully told stories about the persistent antics of young men courting their *novias* in the middle of the night, waking entire families as they pledged their love in a drunken serenade. Similarly, young men pursued their *novias* by writing them endless letters and insisting they borrow personal items such as clothing and compact discs. Many courtships were solidified and simultaneously made public when girls acquiesced to sporting their boyfriends' baseball caps, which girls preferred over the white flat-topped hats worn by their mothers. Courtships also included older mestizo traditions. In at least two households, I observed in practice the symbolic vestiges of a dowry system *(dote)* as the parents of girls came to a marriage proposal brandishing kitchen supplies for the new couple.[8] However, accompanying what appeared to be young women's passivity in courtship was their strength as equal contributors of land and resources at the time of marriage. Many older residents thus

7. Andean complementarity composes part of a larger set of nested beliefs and ideologies surrounding cosmology, economics, and kinship, based on dualisms, parallel descent, and generalized reciprocity (see Silverblatt 1987; Zuidema 1977). Men and women's relationships are reflected in these beliefs through patterns of inheritance and an expressed equality in work (Allen 2002; Harris 1978; Isbell 1981). A woman and man, as heads of households, make decisions together, but each may also follow her or his own decisions (Hamilton 1998). The Hispanic model is predicated on a firm distinction drawn between *la calle* (the street) and *la casa* (the home). At the representational level, the former is associated with men and their activities, the latter with women. As is true of most Hispanic, circum-Mediterranean societies, the *casa* is valued less than the *calle,* women's work less than men's. In the Ecuadorian Andes, especially in contexts where mestizo and indigenous practices overlap, most scholars note a dynamic interplay between the two gender systems. As detailed ethnographic cases illuminate, such factors as age, status, wealth, development, urban versus rural, education, and occupation create unique scenarios that no appeal to static models can fully explain (see, e.g., Belote and Belote 1988; Herrera 2001; McKee 1980, 1997; Miles 1991, 1992, 1994; Miles and Buechler 1997; Stølen 1987, 1991; Weismantel 1988).

8. McKee writes about the *dote* in highland traditions (1980, 107).

described marriage to me as ultimately a "partnership" where the responsibilities of starting a marriage and a new household rested equally with
husband and wife.

With the decline of inheritance, how was this situation changing? How
did migration play into young people's conceptions of these roles in the
formation of new households? Addressing a similar set of issues in rural
Andalusia, Jane Collier notes that as the importance of inheritance lessened for Spanish youth in the 1980s, men's and women's roles vis-à-vis
property changed, raising the stakes of success for both genders, though
significantly higher for men. Collier describes a situation in which men are
the primary managers of property, but her comments are no less applicable
to Jatundeleg in the late 1990s:

> In contrast to a manager of a family household, who was not held respon-
> sible for his family's poverty unless he wasted his and his wife's inherited
> resources, a breadwinner was held responsible for his family's income. . . .
> Moreover a breadwinner had far more chances to fail than did the ad-
> ministrator of a family household. Whereas most men could manage to
> avoid losing status in a social system where men strived to preserve the
> family properties and reputations they and their wives had inherited,
> only some men could succeed in a social system where men competed
> for apparently unlimited wages and profits. (1997, 128)

Indeed, as men's out-migration became the principal means by which new
households formed, young people in Jatundeleg began to see men less as
"co-managers" and more as "breadwinners."

The significance of this transformation was made explicit to me one
evening after I had attended the nineteenth birthday party of Juan Moya,
the son of a couple whom I had interviewed in Ayaloma many times. After the party, I walked home accompanied by Sonia and Rosa, the teenage
daughters of one of my neighbors, and we talked about the birthday party.
"Now that Juan is nineteen," I started to ask, "He'll probably be looking to
get married soon?"

"Yes," they replied in unison.

Rosa followed up: "It is time for him to fulfill his destiny [*cumplir su
destino*]."

Assuming the clichéd phrase must hold a rich euphemism, I continued probing. "Fulfill what destiny?"

"Oh, he'll probably be starting to look for a wife and leave to the United States soon," Rosa answered.

Sonia confirmed her sister's statement. "Yeah, that is what the men do." The conversation ended as the three of us joked about who would be Juan's lucky girl. Over time, I grew accustomed to hearing this phrase and began to question its significance. In Andean cultures, I wondered, where mobility and migration are distinguishing features of society and people's arrivals and departures are often marked by ritual activities (see, e.g., Lund Skar 1994), had teenage birthdays become de facto send-off parties for male youth? How did the emphasis placed on men's roles in setting up households change both the expectations and negotiations surrounding marriage? A handful of Jatundeleg youth I knew well acknowledged my comparison. As one male youth in his early twenties told me, "Young girls want to marry *only* migrants." In my high school survey, 74 percent of the female respondents answered affirmatively that they would want to marry a migrant or a man who had the potential to migrate.

An example attesting to the kinds of pressures young men felt as they entered the arena of courtship and marriage is found in the story of Roberto Sinchi, a twenty-year-old from Ayaloma. Since Roberto's early teen years, family and friends had joked that he would marry María Eugenia Aucaquispe, the daughter of a Shullín couple with a considerable amount of land and cattle. Although both sets of parents strongly approved of the union, María Eugenia expressed discontent. In the months leading up to their marriage, Roberto spent numerous weeks away from the village working in construction, trying to earn money for the wedding. In the couple's separation, María Eugenia began spending more time with a neighbor, a returned migrant named Carlos. María Eugenia and Carlos had been childhood playmates, but during his adolescence Carlos had lived in New York City with his father, a legal resident. As a U.S. passport holder, Carlos returned to Shullín yearly for a month or so at a time to visit his mother and married sisters. During his last visit, he told people that when he returned to New York, he was going to school at York College in Jamaica, Queens. Near the end of his stay, Carlos asked María Eugenia to marry him and move to the United States. It would take months to secure a visa for María Eugenia to travel abroad legally, but Carlos urgently wanted to elope to Cuenca or Guayaquil. Once married, María Eugenia could tell her parents and wait for a visa.

Although ecstatic, María Eugenia disapproved of the elopement plan and informed her parents of the idea. Although marriage to Carlos would bring substantial benefits to the family, María Eugenia's parents feared losing their daughter to the United States. Moreover, they feared what would happen to their long-standing ties with Roberto's parents if they broke their obligation to them. After considerable deliberation, they announced that the wedding would go as planned. Roberto and his parents moved forward with a formal marriage proposal, a *palabriar* (from *palabra*, meaning "word" in Spanish). They arrived at María Eugenia's parents' home weighted down by traditional marriage offerings: *trago* (liquor), cigarettes, packaged bread, *humitas* (steamed corn cakes), and bananas. Roberto wore a suit; his father wore his poncho, which he almost never did, and his mother donned elegant jewelry and a clean felt hat. As Roberto recalled, the event went poorly because María Eugenia refused to show her face. A week later, when it came time for María Eugenia's family to reciprocate with a similar celebration and outlay of gifts, the daughter protested and refused to attend, again announcing her love for Carlos and her desire to marry him. Realizing they had no room to move, María Eugenia's parents agreed to the marriage with Carlos, and the courtship with Roberto ended. Over time, Roberto grew increasingly preoccupied with going to the United States. After unsuccessfully trying to secure a loan to go, he moved to Guayaquil to look for work.

Although most marriage negotiations that had migration in the mix did not take on such dramatic proportions as the case described here, for young women the goal of "entregarse de un hombre bien" (catching one's self a good husband) was increasingly bound up with finding men who had the potential and capital to migrate. By the same token, young men meant to fulfill their destiny abroad sought potential wives who possessed a high degree of trust *(confianza)*. Indeed, for many couples, the issue was not if a new husband would migrate, but *when* and *how*. Such was the emerging trend in Jatundeleg as couples sought to marry while preparing men to migrate north. However, as the examples I turn to in the next section demonstrate, no one single pattern of household formation dominated.

Constituting the Transnational Household: Three Examples

How was the transnational household constituted in Jatundeleg at the time of my research? What was the process? Although indeed some migrants left as single men and others did so after many years of marriage and autonomy from parents, the majority of youth who migrated from the Azuayo-Cañari countryside in the late 1990s did so in the process of constituting their own independent households. To be sure, for many couples whose stories I collected, the decision to marry was rarely made irrespective of the decision to migrate. Thus, paradoxically, many men understood that leaving Jatundeleg was a critical first step to stake a claim in their community years later. The reasons for getting married before migration varied considerably, however. Some adult children married out of respect for parents who realized that, without the promise of *herencia,* marriage to villagers served as one of the only anchors keeping their children tied to the community. Indeed, as Case A demonstrates, marriage sometimes served as the only guarantee that a migrant would return and fulfill economic and familial obligations. In other cases, marriage played an opposite role by helping young people distance themselves and their remittances from the interests of extended family.

Regardless of the pattern new households took, one decision loomed above all others: how to finance a trip north. As I discuss in considerable detail in chapter 5, the costs of smuggling rose substantially in the late 1990s as the pathway north became littered with more and more obstacles. In the early 1990s, migrants paid between $2,000 and $4,000 to be smuggled to the United States.[9] By 1999, this price had quadrupled. In

9. In the early 1990s, Carpio Benalcázar (1992) and his colleagues (Cajamarca 1991; Cueva Malo 1991; Sempértegui 1991) documented the cost of illegal travel to be seven million sucres, approximately $3,000. Similarly in 1989–90, Sarah Mahler's Ecuadorian informants in the United States reported the average cost of passage from Ecuador to be $2,880 (1995, 60). Grünenfelder-Elliker points out that in 1993–94 smuggling costs at her research

Table 4.2
Sources Ecuadorians Have Used to Finance Undocumented Migration

Source	No. of migrant respondents	Percentage
Own capital	189	14.3
Family	282	21.3
Bank loan	78	5.9
Friends	82	6.2
Chulqueros/as (chulco)	626	47.4
Other	51	3.9
No response	13	1.0
Total	1321	100.0

Source: Catholic Diocese of Azogues 1997.

response, migrants pursued every option possible to fund their trip, including seeking loans from extended family, selling personal possessions and land, and asking for help from migrants already abroad (see table 4.2). Some migrants received financial help from family and friends already in the United States.

However, by far the most common source of funding was a long-standing tradition of quasi-legal moneylenders (Carpio Benalcázar 1992, 103; Kyle 2000, 66–67). For decades, villagers had turned to *chulqueros* or *prestamistas* (loan makers), for credit to purchase land and livestock, to build houses, and, in some cases, to start businesses. These loans *(chulcos)* were crucial elements in an economic climate where standard banking services proved altogether prohibitive because of astronomical interest rates, impractical payment schedules, and racial prejudice. In Déleg, as was true in other communities, the most prominent *chulqueros* were members of powerful families that had amassed capital in lucrative

---

site of Gualaceo, Azuay, varied depending on who was being smuggled. She reports that men cost an average of $5,000 and women $7,000. The rare practice of smuggling children fetched a price of $10,000 or more (personal communication, Sept. 7, 2001).

construction and cattle businesses, in addition to years of usury. Interest rates in 1999–2000 were between 8 and 12 percent, compounded monthly. In addition, *chulqueros* often demanded significant forms of collateral to safeguard the extension of credit. Providers of collateral might receive in exchange a portion of the migrant's remittances, the use of a migrant's land in his absence, or labor help from the migrant's family.

The following three cases also demonstrate the interplay between generational and gendered tensions that emerge in migration decisions. Each highlights a different aspect of the constitution of transnational households, including the role of extended families, women's relationships with in-laws, and the importance of children to justify a new couple's desire for autonomy. Although some events are more dramatic than a random sampling of cases may provide, many of the issues discussed here played out in similar ways in the lives of other couples as they went about forming their own households.

Case A. Twenty-seven-year-old Luís Sinchi returned to Jatundeleg from Queens in 1996 after a five-year absence. A year later he moved with his wife and one-year-old child into a four-bedroom concrete block house built from his remittances. Seven years earlier, Luís had been residing in the village with his widowed mother, who owned a little more than two hectares of land. The family eked out a modest living selling fruits and vegetables in the local market. When I met Luís in 1999, he was adamant that the market business was just his way of killing time, just long enough until he could find a way to migrate. Indeed, as the second-to-youngest child in a family of four children, he was unlikely to inherit land and would instead have to find an alternative future for himself.

Very little kept Luís anchored to Jatundeleg aside from his *novia,* María Rosa Quispe, whom he had been courting for more than a year. Although the couple was "deep in love," as Luís described in his limited English, they did not want to marry. Indeed, María Rosa's feelings mirrored those of many village girls for whom the prospect of marriage constituted an internal battle between wanting to marry a migrant who could provide both support and avenues to modernity and not wanting to be left alone without a husband. As Luís recalled, María Rosa declared, "If you love me, you will return and marry me then." For Luís, postponing marriage represented part of the symbolic importance he placed on his "journey" *(la ida)*. Not only did he set high goals for himself, including getting residency in the United States, but he also hoped he would one day be able to take María Rosa there.

As I elaborate in chapter 5, planning an illegal trip to the United States requires patience and tenacity. Its success depends on the cooperation and organization of a number of people, beginning with family members, who often provide funding, and ending with the smugglers, who demand it. Luís's smuggling costs were largely assumed by his maternal uncle, who had been like a father after Luís's biological father passed away prematurely. In particular, the uncle agreed to provide the collateral needed to secure a *chulco*. In exchange, his uncle hoped that Luís would be able to send some extra money to expand his dairy cattle business. Plans for their mutual enrichment, however, came to a halt when the uncle learned of Luís's plan not to marry before he left. Having been privy to Luís's many diatribes about the "boredom in Jatundeleg" and the adventures he would have in the United States, the uncle grew leery of the plans. He questioned his nephew's bonds to the community: What would ensure that he return to get married? Who would manage his money? The uncle ultimately demanded that before he would help him, Luís would have to marry.

When Luís told María Rosa of his uncle's demands, she refused to give in and not "simply marry for money." She insisted that Luís stay in the village and with her settle an independent household first. Luís felt anxious over the decision and became resentful of María Rosa. Why, he asked, would she not get married and let him go? As María Rosa told me, it was fear that motivated her decision—fear that they would marry and that Luís would never return, making her unfit for marriage. Over time, it was María Rosa's two sisters (both of whom were married to migrants in the United States) who helped to persuade her. In my notes, I paraphrased María Rosa's discussion with her sisters:

> If you marry him now, they said, he will leave and be faithful and send you money for the things you want. He will miss you so much and be overcome with *pena* [sadness and heartache] that he will treat you right.

But if you wait, and you marry him and years go by, then forget it! If then he goes to the United States, he will do so thinking you are comfortable left behind. . . . If you cook with *leña* [firewood] and your husbands grows accustomed to that, then when you ask him [from the United States] to send money to buy a gas stove, he won't.

The sisters' advice and stories from their own transnational relationships eventually convinced María Rosa to rethink her position on marriage. Luís was elated. The couple married a few months later, and Luís's uncle followed through with his promise to provide the collateral for the *chulco*. In the end, nearly two years elapsed before all the necessary arrangements could be made for Luís to migrate. In that time, the couple began the process of building the house that Luís's remittances would finish years later.

This episode captures some of the ways in which obligations to family forced marriage on young couples in situations where men sought to migrate. In many respects, marriage represented the only sure-fire way villagers believed youth would stay active in their families and home communities. However, in other cases, marriage and the departure of a migrant husband caused tensions in, rather than facilitating the creation of, transnational households. This situation is revealed in Case B.

Case B. In almost half of the cases of couples I profiled in Jatundeleg, Ayaloma, and Shullín, new wives moved in with their in-laws after their husbands migrated. One such arrangement affected twenty-four-year-old Carmela Ayaguaso who went to live with her in-laws soon after her husband, Alfonso Correa, migrated north. As I have previously mentioned, some wives dread living with their in-laws and especially fear potentially contentious relations with their *suegras*. In contrast, Carmela seemed genuinely open to the idea. Her situation, however, was somewhat unusual in that both her parents had died of tuberculosis only a few years before she married Alfonso. Beyond the security provided by familial relationships, Carmela valued the arrangement as a money-saving maneuver for a young couple with aspirations to build a modern house and buy pasture land. "We can save more money and build our house faster," she expressed to me. In the first six months after Alfonso's departure, the situation went swimmingly; Carmela delighted in helping her mother-in-law and enjoyed preparing the family's fields.

The situation began to change, though, after Alfonso started sending regular remittances. Although the money was wired directly to Carmela, Alfonso's mother was well aware of the nearly $300 coming into the household each month. Alfonso's father felt uncomfortable taking his son's money, but his mother viewed the situation differently. For years, she had suffered from debilitating back problems that required repeated costly visits to a doctor in Cuenca. When her expenses grew especially high, Alfonso's mother approached him for help, and Alfonso generously responded. Over time, his mother resorted to calling Alfonso in the United States instead of going through Carmela. Even after she stopped seeing the doctor, her requests for monetary assistance continued. Carmela grew increasingly restless with the situation and pleaded with her husband. Over the telephone and in letters, she complained to Alfonso that living with his mother stymied her ability to save for their future, and she feared it would be years before they could initiate construction on their own home. Alfonso was torn between his wife and his mother and pleaded to his father for help, although there was little his father could do. When Alfonso finally confronted his mother, she grew angry and resentful that her daughter-in-law had suspected she was using the money for something other than doctor's appointments. She lashed out angrily, claiming that the reason she needed the money was to compensate for the expense of having Carmela live with them.

After that point, relations soured between Carmela and her in-laws. In response, she placed pressure on Alfonso to send more money so they could start their own home sooner. Without a household to move into, she felt stuck in an obligation to her mother-in-law and to her mother-in-law's demands on the young couple's money. Carmela told me that Alfonso had even threatened to return to the village just to arrange a new household and lessen the tensions. However, because of his success in the United States, a return home only to have to pay smuggling costs again would have been a serious setback. A year before Alfonso's return, the couple partially solved their problem. Carmela continued to live with her in-laws, but the couple found a way to guard their remittances. Alfonso's monthly remittance did not amount to enough to buy land outright or build a house, but the couple was able to take out a second *chulco* that allowed them to purchase a plot of land and begin building a new cement house. The demands of the loan proved significant enough to justify keeping the remittance within the nuclear family.

Case C. A final case highlights another prominent pattern of how young couples went about constituting their transnational households, that of married couples with children. In Case B, what kept Carmela from moving out of her in-law's house when relations broke down was more than simply money; it was the stigma of doing so as a woman in a *matrimonio* (simply, a "marriage"), as opposed to in a *familia* (a married couple with children). In Jatundeleg, as is the case throughout highland villages, it was unheard of for a married woman without children to live alone, and only women with children could safely begin their new households in the absence of husbands. Although some new wives such as María Rosa's sisters in Case A believed that the optimal situation for transnational households was the one wherein the husband left soon after marriage, others disagreed. To protect themselves and keep their husbands faithful, some women demanded that men postpone migrating until after a union could be solidified by having children or, in some cases, by first conceiving children. As a woman in her forties whose husband left in the early 1980s explained,

> When my husband and I began to "go with each other" ["to walk with one another," in the local parlance], he was como un diablo en una botella [like a devil in a bottle]. He acted so anxious to go the United States. But he was filled with tenderness, too. He used to tell me how beautiful I was and that I deserved more than just being poor. That's why he wanted to go the United States, he said. I told him no, that if he left, he would lose me. I told him, "I didn't get married so I could be alone. We have to be a family first." So he waited. He didn't leave until after our first child was born. . . . Sure, it was harder, but we were a family, and families have tenacity.

For some younger couples, the reasons for forming a *familia* before migration extended beyond concerns over stability. In the case of Carolina Pomaguiza and Julio Pañora, the choice to have children before Julio migrated was in part a conscious decision to consolidate the demands that would potentially be placed on Julio's remittances by outside family members. As Julio told me frankly, "If you are just a *matrimonio,* everyone will ask you for help, for money and such. A family, though, is protected." Although few Jatundeleg couples spoke of having children in such functional terms, it was obvious to many that a married woman with a child or children could more ably exert her independence and dominion over her husband's remittances than if she were simply married.

Being married with children also gave women license to live independently with their families if they so chose when their husbands migrated. A number of women saw no benefit to living alone, but for others such as Carolina Pomaguiza the option allowed them to avoid what could potentially become a difficult relationship with their *suegra.* Many wives found themselves in situations like that of Carmela Ayaguaso—struggling to keep a hold on their husband's remittances while at the same time pushing their husbands to send more. For many couples, however, autonomy was a long process in the making as they waited for the accumulation of remittances to allow them to build a house of their own.

Carolina and Julio took advantage of another option that worked to speed up the development of their independent household. As I mention in chapter 3, newlyweds could also take advantage of various rental options in the village, serving as the caretakers of homes owned by absent migrants. When Julio left for the United States, Carolina took charge of a vacant three-bedroom home in Jatundeleg's center, where she and her two small children lived. Just a little way down one of the dirt arterials of the village was the plot the couple had purchased inexpensively from one of Julio's uncles. On it was a cement skeleton of a house they were building, complete with the spiny poles of steel rebar that sprouted from unfinished homes, signaling hope for the future.

Single Female Migrants: "We Won't Be Able
to Keep Them Here for Long"

As my fieldwork in Jatundeleg came to a close, I went about the village tying up loose ends: collecting last-minute interviews, clarifying field notes, and saying my good-byes and thank yous. In this context, my stop at a Loma Lanzacay household headed up by sixty-three-year-old Alfredo Mishquiri was routine. Two of his sons, Rómulo and Alejandro, were living in Hackensack, New Jersey, and don Alfredo had many times expressed to me his wish that I visit his sons and take them a package of *recuerdos* (mementos). Like most village fathers, he worried about his sons' safety and often looked to me, the *gringo*, to assuage his fears. During this particular visit, however, Alfredo expressed a different fear to me: "She is going—mi guagua—and we can't stop her," he exclaimed. "She has her brothers helping her!" The *guagua*, or baby, he spoke of was Lethia, his youngest daughter, twenty-two years old. For some time, Lethia's brothers had been encouraging her to come north, a prospect that excited her very much. She tried to talk to her parents about the possibility, but each time she did, her parents kept pushing marriage on her. When marriage proposals were not forthcoming, her desires to leave only multiplied.

Just weeks before my last visit to don Alfredo, Lethia's on-going conversation with her parents about migration had erupted into fights, prompting her to take refuge with an aunt in Ayaloma. Although don Alfredo understood his daughter's frustration ("What is there for her here in the village?"), he hoped she would wait patiently for a marriage proposal, and then, if her husband desired, she could migrate with him. For her part, Lethia's mother, Rosa, viewed herself the better judge of her daughter's character and tried to convince Alfredo otherwise. Rosa considered Lethia "too independent" to get married and doubted she could ever conform to the discipline of being a wife. After considerable debate and assurance from his sons that they would take care of Lethia once she reached the United States, don Alfredo acquiesced, and Lethia returned to her parents' household. A compromise was reached that she would leave just as soon as Rómulo and Alejandro could wire enough money to hire a *pasador* (migrant smuggler), but not before the next harvest.

Men had for decades clearly monopolized flows of out-migration from the Azuayo-Cañari region, but it was impossible during my fieldwork to ignore an incipient stream of young women leaving the village. As don Alfredo claimed, "In most cases, it is the fathers. But, little by little, go the brothers, the husbands, the sons, and now, yes, the daughters." Other migration researchers in the region have observed that to some degree women have always participated in undocumented migration (Borrero and Vega Ugalde 1995; Cajamarca 1991; Camacho 2004; Kyle 2000; Miles 1997). However, the actions of women such as Lethia represented a clear departure from earlier patterns whereby women who traveled north did so almost exclusively as the wards of husbands, fathers, or brothers. In contrast, Lethia was part of a new generation of women leaving on their own volition, often securing their own sources of funding, and working through their own networks to find work abroad.

The extent of this new female exodus, like all undocumented migration from the region, is nearly impossible to quantify. Guayasamín Cruz and Moya Herrera provide one of the first preliminary studies to focus specifically on women migrants. They point to the many publicized cases of Ecuadorians being apprehended as they attempt to travel north clandestinely and note the increasing numbers of women among the male cohorts in smuggling rings (2002, 97). Although women's migration is clearly shaped in part by the same forces that impact male migration, a great deal more of a "pull" accompanies their decisions. In particular, women experience a much greater demand for their skills as sewers and seamstresses (Grünenfeld-Elliker 2001; see also M. Chin 2001). In fact, several young women who left for the United States did so at the behest of friends and family abroad who knew of lucrative jobs in garment factories. Near the end of my research, women were also being pulled in another direction, to Spain, and by another attraction, the promise of domestic servant jobs. For a hefty price tag (approximately $2,000), though considerably less than the cost of illegal passage to the United States, women from across Ecuador's different ethnic and class lines began migrating to Spain (Jokisch and Pribilsky 2002). During a short visit to Jatundeleg in 2001, I learned of three single women who had left or were in the process of leaving to prearranged jobs in Barcelona and Madrid.[10]

10. These job prospects were sometimes too good to be true. Stories of women who migrated to Spain under the false pretense of work as domestics only later to be forced into prostitution were common during my fieldwork. Nervous parents would frequently use these horror stories to dissuade daughters from going abroad.

Because of the new female exodus, it behooved villagers from Jatun-deleg, Ayaloma, and Shullín to evaluate the changing status of women in village life. A general sentiment prevailed that women's lives had become much freer and that they had begun to enjoy many of the rights and privileges of men. Although, as I discuss in greater length in chapter 7, many of these changes were related to the absence of migrant husbands and the pragmatic response women were forced to have, more long-term and fundamental changes were also at work. For example, I was frequently told that women were "abriendo un apetito" (developing an appetite) for new things in village life. Villagers pointed to developments as varied as women's greater say in marriage and a recently inaugurated girls' soccer club, complete with glitzy uniforms and high-profile matches played at fiestas alongside the celebrated men's team.

In contrast, discussions of restrictions on women's mobility in the past often conjured up Andean folklore. By far the most popular story was the one about the *chuzalongo*. This figure, who has a child's body but an accentuated penis, preys on girls and young women innocently playing in the hills and high *cerros*. He typically finishes off his victims by raping and then strangulating them with his long penis. The metaphors of guarding women's sexuality that appear in the *chuzalongo* story were not absent in areas of village life I observed. Women, for instance, rarely walked about the village alone at night; being alone in high hills and *cerros,* sometimes a necessity for feeding animals, was widely seen as dangerous. Similarly, a woman inviting a man into her home when she was alone could become the victim of witchcraft. As young women transgressed these implicit cultural boundaries through migration, their actions provoked startling new reformulations of feminine identity for all women in the village.

Nevertheless, certain factors worked to maintain the gendered divisions of migration. In July 2001, when the popularity of migration to Spain was rising fast (see Jokisch and Pribilsky 2002), most women I spoke with did not express the same exuberance about migration that I often noted in men. Some expressed a belief that women who migrated did so at the risk of disgrace *(desgracia)* and community disdain because their movements conjured up long-held beliefs linking women's mobility with unbridled sexuality. One woman told me bluntly, "Women who leave [alone] are seen to be like whores [*putas*]." Considered most disgraceful, however, were married women with children who migrated alone, leaving their kids behind to live with relatives, usually grandparents or aunts and uncles. Their actions called into question not only their sexuality, but their obligation to family as well. For others who wished to migrate, either as single women or as wives desiring to be reunited with husbands abroad, migration posed other risks. As Guayasamín Cruz and Moya Herrera (2002) report, women who migrate are frequently put in compromising positions by smugglers who demand sexual favors in addition to standard monetary compensation. Moreover, a general fear of rape preoccupies women who must travel through the underworld of shady towns and ports along the migrant trail north. Sociologist David Kyle reports that in early 1990s female migrants in the community of Checa near Cuenca were asking doctors to prescribe them birth control pills before traveling north, so serious was their fear (1996, 109). Although many young women possessed the desire, the means (through access to *chulcos*), and their parent's begrudging approval to migrate, factors such as gendered violence and social stigma worked to keep migration primarily a male vocation.

Jatundeleg youth found their decisions regarding migration impacted by two sets of contrasting processes active in village life. On the one hand, land scarcity and parents' inability to ensure sons and daughters a solid future in agriculture motivated children to seek alternative paths. On the other hand, the same economic conditions of migration responsible for driving up land prices were simultaneously also responsible for rising expectations and the introduction of alternatives models of what constituted a "comfortable life" in the rural Andes. Not only did the lessening of intergenerational obligation and the growing desires for *iony* modernity reorganize new relationships between parents and children; they equally ushered in new responsibilities and roles between the genders. Given this ethnographic context, migration decisions cannot be profitably examined by addressing only the economic and developmental factors that reduce labor migration to "push" and "pull" factors. Greater attention must be paid to the ways in which both the demands and desires of labor migration intersect with youths' life-course priorities and expectations. Piecing together how young male migrants often merged their desire to migrate with the societal pressures to marry and initiate autonomous households, I came to view their journeys as personal transformations and struggles experienced in triplicate—becoming socially defined men, negotiating roles as husbands and fathers, and adjusting to life as undocumented laborers. The next two chapters examine these transformations and struggles more closely by exploring men's lives as migrants in New York City.

5
Undocumented Migrants in Yoni

New York is the most perfect city. It never sleeps. It dazzles all its visitors. In this city, the richest man of our poor country would feel like a beggar, the most corrupted person like a saint, the most ignorant like a wise person, the wisest like an ignoramus. Here, anything can happen.

New York is like a sponge. It absorbs you, empties you, and then throws you out to dry.

—Excerpts from letters sent by migrant men to wives in Ecuador, in Galo Galarza, "Viaje por el filo del mido" (1987)

A combination of social, cultural, and economic forces propel young men from rural Azuayo-Cañari villages into low-wage jobs in New York City. With hopes of claiming a stake in their rural livelihood through marriage and the initiation of their own autonomous households, young men see a trip to the United States as indispensable to earn money and, as is often the case, to purchase land. In fact, as discussed in the previous chapter, a large number of migrants arrive in the United States already in the process of "constituting" their transnational families from abroad, with wives and small children left behind in Ecuador. In addition to economic goals, young migrants arrive in search of new opportunities and experiences, as Luís Sinchi explained it to me, "to be a part of something big, something larger than here," and to adopt some of trappings of *iony* modernity. In New York City, young men from Jatundeleg have joined thousands of other Ecuadorians, the majority from the Azuayo-Cañari highlands. Life in New York, though, often proves to be less than they hoped, and they quickly learn that their goal of earning money for families back home and their goal of finding a modern urban adventure contradict one another. For many, the *chulla vida* becomes the *vida dura* (hard life), as they realize their access to an *iony* lifestyle is highly attenuated by the necessities of saving money, working long hours, and adhering to a strictly disciplined life.

This chapter closely examines the lives of young Ecuadorian men as they negotiate their way through New York City as undocumented migrants. Built around fieldwork with migrants in Queens and interviews conducted with returned migrants in Ecuador, it considers how young men organize and interpret their experiences abroad. In the changes that accompany new living conditions, employment options, and social activities, migrants undergo a number of transformations and dislocations from their premigration lives. Perhaps the most sobering aspects of a migrant's life in New York are the dislocations caused by the necessities of work and earning money—dislocations from the value of work, from fellow migrants, and from access to the emblems of *iony* modernity they hoped to acquire. Ultimately, men's responses to these changes reveal the gendered experience of migration, a topic developed in detail in the remaining chapters of this book. Here I focus specifically on the constraints of living and working on the margins of U.S. society as undocumented migrants. However, because the profound transformations that accompany migration begin long before men set foot in New York, I begin with an exploration of the dangerous journeys taken by Ecuadorians to get to the United States.

Coming North *por la Pampa*

Before young men could *cumplir sus destinos* in New York City, they had to get there first. Although I never accompanied migrants I knew on their surreptitious travels north,[1] I frequently saw the expectations of their journeys written on their faces when I had a chance to interview them before their departure, expressions that ranged from uncontainable excitement to

1. In summer 1999, however, I did travel from Ecuador to New York City's John F. Kennedy International Airport with a twenty-two-year-old from Shullín who had residency in the United States. I relay his story and our encounters in Jatundeleg and New York in Pribilsky 2002.

intense fear. In part, both expressions reflected the fact that they knew not exactly what to expect. Human smuggling, precisely because it is illegal and unregulated, is an enterprise full of clandestine practices and unscrupulous characters and con artists.[2] Ecuadorian newspapers run stories almost daily exposing the cons and scams *(estafas)* of people who pass themselves off as smugglers in order to bilk the unsuspecting and vulnerable. Like Wild West towns, storefront windows in Cuenca and Azogues frequently display wanted posters with the pictures of fugitive *pasadores* and announcements reading, "Se Busca Coyote. ¡Recompensa!" (Looking for Coyote. Compensation!) Given the climate, villagers approached smugglers with suspicion and trepidation. With few laws to protect would-be migrants and their families from *pasadores'* botched efforts, simply beginning the negotiations of a passage north could incur incredible costs and risks.

Caesar Pañora's predicament is exemplary of the many problems migrants I knew faced with respect to securing passage north. Twenty-four years old and single, Caesar lived with his parents, whom he helped cultivate less than two hectares of land, in addition to working construction in Azogues. As a man in his early twenties, Caesar felt pressure to marry his girlfriend from Shullín. Migration north played into his plans to begin his new household. As the oldest child and only son (among five children), Caesar was able to convince his parents to mortgage both house and truck to pay for his trip. Soon after, Caesar successfully located a *pasador* who went by the name "El Conejo" (the Rabbit). The Rabbit promised a "smooth route" to the U.S.–Mexican border, flying Caesar on a forged visa to Guatemala City. The entire journey would take less than fifteen days, a promise Caesar remembered as too good to be true, but not worth questioning: "No pensaba en nada solo en llegar a los Estados Unidos" (I wasn't thinking about anything besides getting to the United States).

To Caesar's surprise, the Rabbit followed through on his promise, passing him before both Ecuadorian and Guatemalan border agents on a falsified visa. The next day, though, Caesar's luck ran out when the cramped "safe house" where he was staying before traveling farther north

2. See Kyle and Dale 2001 for a useful history and introduction to human smuggling issues.

was raided. For the next two months, Caesar lingered in a Guatemalan detention center *(corralon)* with other migrants, including what he remembered as "hundreds" of Chinese whose boat had sunk in the Atlantic Ocean. Dipping into the savings he had brought with him, Caesar bribed his way out of the detention center and slipped into Guatemalan society. He quickly looked for work because he would need between $2,000 and $3,000 to finish the last leg of his trip, up through Mexico and across the Mexican border. He tried earning money on a farm in Guatemala, yet payment in Guatemalan quetzals amounted to little. Frustrated, Caesar returned to Jatundeleg just six months after he had first left, humiliated and deeply in debt. Two months later, when his lenders realized that his plans had been foiled, thugs who worked for the *chulqueros* seized Caesar's father's truck and threatened to take their home unless at least some of the $8,500 Caesar had borrowed was repaid. The family also started receiving disturbing phone calls threatening to kidnap and kill Caesar's sister if the money was not delivered. Near the end of my fieldwork in Jatundeleg, Caesar started planning another trip to the United States. He had cobbled together $3,000 from various sources, including his in-laws and an uncle who had residency in the United States. Again, he was forced to borrow the remainder from a *chulquero.* If and when he made it to the United States, he would be $15,000 in debt before he could begin sending money home to his family. Although Caesar's situation presents an extreme example, it is by no means an isolated case. About one-third of the migrants I interviewed had experienced a major setback in their attempts to get to the United States. Still, for every failed attempt, many others met with success.

To travel undocumented is to go *por la pampa* (by land), *por el camino* (by road), or *caminando* (walking), in the colloquial speech of migrants I met. In reality, *pasadores* smuggled migrants using a variety of different routes to enter surreptitiously into the United States, often following an itinerary that included a combination of land, water, and, in exceptional instances, air travel. Throughout the 1980s, illegal passage was partially eased by the option of flying directly to Mexico or Guatemala on either a legitimate or professionally forged or falsified visa. From there, a *pasador* would secretly ferry migrants across the border.

By the early 1990s, the implementation of U.S.–backed antismuggling efforts in Mexico and numerous Central American countries forced *pasadores* to utilize new strategies to circumvent authorities. By the time of my research, local *pasadores* had reacted to their new challenges by raising prices, parceling out their services into per leg costs, and diversifying their modes of travel.[3] Most important, though, was the formation of a maritime smuggling route whereby migrants were channeled via the Pacific Ocean, from Ecuador's coast to the Central American isthmus and secretive points of entry in Costa Rica, Nicaragua, El Salvador, and Guatemala. Ecuador's El Cuerpo de Guardacostas de La Armada (Coast Guard) would frequently intercept smuggling vessels that left daily from the country's port towns and cities Jaramijó, Machalilla, Puerto Cayo, Salango, and Puerto López.[4]

Coast Guard reports of intercepting smuggling vessels detailed situations of hardship, danger, and sometimes death. To save money, *pasadores* would cram anywhere from 150 to 200 persons into boats designed for fishing crews of between 12 and 20 people. In Jatundeleg, villagers also told stories about stowaways freezing to death in the refrigerated holds of boats and drowning when vessels capsized. Compounding would-be migrants' fears was the fact that many of them, as rural children growing up in a

3. During follow-up interviews conducted in Ecuador in July 2001, I found that prices for *pasador* services had increased substantially, and more *pasadores* were quoting prices in per leg units. Thus, for example, an itinerary may include one price to go from Ecuador to Guatemala, another for Guatemala to the U.S.–Mexico border, and yet another for passage into the United States and arrival in a migrant's final destination. The highest overall price I recorded in 2001 for travel from Ecuador to the United States was $13,500.

4. In fiscal year 2000 (October–September), U.S. Coast Guard cutters intercepted 1,244 Ecuadorians, more than any other nationality attempting to journey north illegally. In the following year, an additional 1,020 Ecuadorians were detained by U.S. officials in conjunction with Ecuador's Cuerpo de Guardacostas (Jokisch and Pribilsky 2002, 82). The demographic profile of apprehended passengers was nearly identical to the profile of Ecuadorians leaving Jatundeleg: 70 percent male, most between the ages of eighteen and twenty-five, and overwhelmingly from the provinces of Azuay, Cañar, and Chimborazo. For a discussion of maritime smuggling operations, see Jokisch and Pribilsky 2002.

region without a significant body of water nearby, had never learned how to swim. One man whom I interviewed soon after he arrived in Queens described the conditions as "the worst experience of his life":

If you go by sea, you can come up in either a *pesquera* [fishing trawler] or a *bananera* [banana cargo ship]. Thankfully, I came in a *bananera*. I had heard they were cleaner, and you don't freeze to death. But the storage holds are small, and we had, maybe, one hundred guys in there. I was crammed next to my brother, which made it a little nicer. The smell was horrible by the third or fourth day. . . . The smell of vomit pervaded the cabin as people who had seasickness couldn't make it outside. . . . And those guys [the *pasador*'s operatives] lied! They said they would let us out every day, but they didn't. It was always something, usually an excuse about getting caught. They would say, "There are too many boats, and we don't know which of them are agents."[. . .]My brother thought he was going to die. He couldn't stop coughing in the hold, and we were given

5.1. Migrants smuggled on the open seas in the late 1990s. Photograph given to the author by a migrant informant from Jatundeleg.

very little water. Each day we had only a banana and a hard-boiled egg to eat. The nights they were cold, and we weren't given a blanket or anything. We thought we would never make it out alive.

Migrants I knew often arrived in their Central American destinations disillusioned with the risks they had taken. "I paid thousands of dollars to be starved nearly to death," exclaimed one man after an anticipated two-week boat trip turned into nineteen trying days at sea with little food and no fresh air. What lay ahead, though, rarely afforded a respite. The journey north tested migrants' physical endurance and stamina, as well as their abilities to withstand hunger and to maintain an almost constant vigilance against con artists and thieves. In this context, the last major hurdle of crossing the border *(la frontera)* into the United States often seemed ironically anticlimactic to many men. "La frontera, la frontera, la frontera," repeated a twenty-six year-old returnee in Jatundeleg. "I kept saying the word the whole way up from Ecuador. I had so much fear about crossing. But it was easy going over." His friend, who crossed the border a year later, took what appeared to be the absence of a strong border patrol as a sign of U.S. tacit acceptance of undocumented workers: "Man! You couldn't imagine the scene. It was like the door was left wide open, and anyone was welcome. . . . The United States needs us to work for less; that's why you can get through. The United States has incredible amounts of money. If they wanted to, they could build a one hundred foot wall and stop everyone from coming in. They don't want to. They need us."

Despite some migrants' perception of a "wide open door," U.S. Border Patrol agents did successfully apprehend large numbers of Ecuadorians. Approximately two-thirds of the returned migrants I surveyed in Jatundeleg had been detained at least once during a border-crossing attempt. However, because it is a common practice for Border Patrol agents to "throw back" alien Mexicans caught crossing illegally, if Ecuadorians can convince authorities they are Mexican nationals—requiring little more than the recitation of the name of the country's president or a basic knowledge of Mexican geography—they, too, are simply sent back over the border. Almost all those who failed the first time crossed successfully in their subsequent attempts. A major factor contributing to their eventual success was the "cat-and-mouse game" that transpires between smugglers and U.S. INS officials (Andreas 2000; see also Conover 1987). Migrant smugglers skillfully exploit authorities' vulnerabilities, knowing exactly when and where to sneak migrants across the border. They also frequently employ a strategy that involves "sacrificing" one group of migrants as a diversion so another group can pass through.

The act of smuggling physically moves people from one place to another; it also, however, transforms people's identities. As Sarah Mahler describes the situation, "The individual who emerges from a tunnel or trailer or trunk of a car and steps onto U.S. soil is not the same person who left Peru, El Salvador or Columbia. Her identity has become the near antithesis of the woman left behind. She has gone from citizen to foreigner, law abider to law-breaker, legal to illegal, independent to dependent, social member to social outcast; and her personhood is degraded" (1995, 75). Every migrant I met who had attempted to cross into the United States carried with him a story about how his trip north had affected him. Each story reflected a different combination of individual agency and overarching structural factors. To be sure, although a strong psychological disposition and personal resources (e.g., extra money and family networks) could lessen the discomfort and hardship of illegal travel, structural factors largely out of migrants' control—including the quality and honesty of their *pasador,* the dangers encountered en route, and encounters with local authorities—could play a major role in shaping each migrant's own personal experience. Anthropologists studying migration have described these movements of people across borders as rites of passage writ large (Alvarez 1987; Chavez 1992; Mahler 1995). As individuals leave one place for another, exchanging stability for liminality, they enter a time of being "betwixt and between" and find themselves straddling states, in psychological as well as political terms (Turner 1967; van Gennep 1960). Writing about undocumented Mexican migrants in California, Leo Chavez points out that although border crossings are monumental personal transformations that separate sojourners from their previous statuses, initiates rarely move into new and comfortable positions. Rather, they remain "liminals" who quickly "find full incorporation into the new society blocked because of their undocumented status" (1992, 62; see also Coutin 2005). Mahler adds that undocumented migration inverts the typical stages associated with rites of passage: "[R]ather than emerge through this process into full-fledged men and women like cultural heroes, they emerge from the border wilderness as children again" (1995, 58).

The experiences of Ecuadorian migrants crossing *por la pampa* were repeatedly shaped by feelings of being separated from their sense of being Ecuadorians, then estranged from the community of their illegal peers. Many men described undergoing a process of loss and of discarding bits and pieces of their old lives on the journey north. In a way that almost constituted a narrative convention, migrants often began their stories by noting how they had "left so much behind." This story-telling pattern usually opened with a recounting of trip preparations wherein migrants packed too much stuff and then were abruptly instructed by their *pasadores* to discard many of those belongings. Crossing stories were routinely peppered with emotional recollections of having to leave behind small photo albums, mementos, religious icons, and other items that connected migrants to their home villages and families. One man told me how he had bundled together cobs of freshly harvested *choclo*, a small bottle of *trago*, and pictures of his family that he would occasionally open up and look at during difficult points in his journey. For poor rural people who have few possessions to begin with, the prospect of doing away with a cherished item could be unbearably painful. Some well-prepared migrants sewed pockets into coat and shirt linings and pant legs, places where they could secretly stow family photos, small keepsakes, and money.

The loss of personal effects speaks symbolically to a greater sense of loss—of identity and belonging. Migrants-in-waiting begin their smuggling journeys with coaching from *pasadores* and learn that shedding their identities will improve their chances of making it across the border. As one youth from Shullín preparing to leave explained to me, "In the United States, we are Latinos, or so you think. But coming up from Ecuador, going through the different countries, people know. A Guatemalan knows a Mexican from someone from Honduras. I know, too. We talk differently, and we have different words for things. But as we get close to the border, we won't be Ecuadorian anymore. Maybe I will be Honduran. Maybe a guy from Peru. Whatever it takes."

Many migrants, though, are not naïve to the potential hardships they will encounter traveling north or to the kinds of chameleon tactics they must employ in order to be successful. In Jatundeleg, the anticipation of migration, the desire for *iony* styles, and the push of village poverty mix to form a vibrant oppositional popular culture. Among both youth who are waiting to leave and returnees—groups who celebrate the quest of migra-tion—resistance against *la migra* (INS) and the camaraderie of sharing a similar experience as *indocumentados* (undocumented migrants) flourish. Toward the end of my fieldwork, T-shirts glorifying a fictitious "Ilegales Club" (Illegal [Migrants] Club) were becoming standard issue for return migrants, as well as for those who dreamed of leaving for the first time. Saturated with American icons of rebellion, the T-shirt brought together a Harley-Davidson motorcycle insignia with images of waving American flags against a jet black background.

Similarly, a giant mural in a community a few miles from Jatundeleg glorified the solidarity between *paisanos* (countrymen) that migration supposedly creates. Occupying an outside wall of the village's community center, the mural depicted an indigenous campesino clasping hands with an Ecuadorian migrant in New York City. The campesino is short and thin and wears clothing typical of highland *indígena:* a red poncho, short white pants, and a felt hat. In the foreground stand the Cañari and Inca ruins of Inga Pirca; an Andean condor flies overhead. By contrast, the migrant shares an undeniable likeness with Sylvester Stallone's cinema character Rambo, outfitted in denim jeans, an American flag bandanna, and a skintight tank top that barely contains his bulging muscles. The Manhattan skyline and another American flag flank his impressive frame. Together, the contrasting images of the mural suggest the transformation migrants undergo in their journeys north. Although the migrant himself is surely Ecuadorian, evidenced by his black hair and dark skin, he has undergone profound changes. As the mural suggests, he has overcome the odds of his perilous journey north and is stronger because of it. His resistance, presumably to corrupt *pasadores,* Border Patrol agents, and

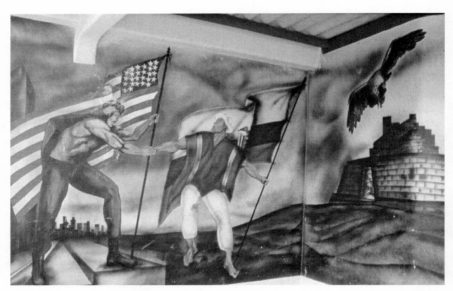

5.2. Mural glorification of migration to the United States. Photograph by the author.

a generally unwelcoming U.S. society, comes alive triumphantly in his imposing physique and resemblance to the rebellious Rambo character.[5] All along, he maintains his grip on his compatriot, yet it is unclear if he is merely holding onto to his campesino counterpart—celebrating their transnational union—or pulling him to the United States.

Like much of Latin American mural art, however, the painting suggests a transformation that often does not match reality. Although migrants

5. Rambo is a well-known cultural icon in Ecuador. Poor-quality bootlegged copies of the movies he appears in are a mainstay of long bus trips through the country. The fact that Rambo is chosen as a symbol of migrant resistance is more intriguing in light of alternative receptions that Rambo films have received in other parts of the world. Michaels, for instance, points out that Rambo's popularity among Australian aborigines is owing in part to the ways the character is fashioned as a symbol of Third World resistance to white colonizers (cited in Kottak 2003, 243). Native Australians imagine tribal ties between themselves and Rambo and the unjustly incarcerated prisoners he frees. Similarly, Roger Lancaster has described how Nicaraguans saw an anti-American freedom fighter in Rambo during the U.S.–backed war against the Sandinistas (1992, 191–92).

believe their journeys will create camaraderie among similars—the Ile-gales Club—they invariably find that their border-crossing experiences are marked by the need to keep a distance from one another as a measure to make it into the United States. As Jesús, a young man from Jatundeleg who despite being only twenty-four had already made two border cross-ings, put it, "You really learn to trust no one. You have your money, and it is your journey. Someone else in the group is for sure to be robbed, maybe killed. If you depend on others, you may not make it. I crossed with my brother. Good thing—I didn't trust any of those other *cabro-nes* [fuckers]." They are stripped of their identities as husbands, brothers, sons, and *comuneros,* and the first months in the United States represent, in part, a building up of their new identities. As soon as they reach the city, the necessities of getting on their feet—finding a job and a place to live, making money and sending some back home, and just learning their way around—require a period of "orientation" *(orientación).* But, as one Jatundeleg migrant youth boasted, "¡Somos grosereos! [We're tough guys!] I don't care what we face. My great-great-great-grandfathers were *mitamaes,* dropped here by the Inca. They didn't even know where they were going! I will! My father worked in Guayaquil; I worked in Guayaquil. That is a tough city. I can handle New York."

Héctor's *Orientación*

In an ironic way, the New York borough of Queens as it would have ap-peared in the eighteenth century, with its farmsteads of sprawling corn-fields, would have been more comforting to Héctor Ayaguasa than the concrete jungle he entered on a cold February evening.[6] Like many of his contemporaries growing up in Jatundeleg, Héctor had never visited Quito, the capital city of Ecuador, and could barely recollect a short trip to Guayaquil he took as a child with his father. Also, like his peers, Héc-tor's knowledge of and preparedness for life in New York was colored by the stories returned migrants told about "la Gran Manzana" (the Big

---

6. Sanjek presents an illustrative picture of Queens in colonial North America as a bu-colic farming community (1998, 19–23).

Apple). During one of our conversations, Héctor spoke of his first days
in New York:

> I arrived in February when it was freezing. I didn't have a coat, and my
> clothes were full of holes and threadbare. I was afraid to look at myself
> in a mirror and see what I looked like since my legs and back were badly
> covered with thorns from our desert crossing. Almost all of my money
> was gone. The smuggler instructed me to buy a plane ticket in Texas, and
> I flew right into the airport. He also gave me a phone number that I was
> supposed to call when I got there. [Then], somebody would pick me up
> and take me to Miguel's [Héctor's brother-in-law] apartment. A guy who
> spoke Spanish, though not like in Ecuador, picked me up. He told me
> the ride would cost fifty dollars to get to my brother-in-law's apartment.
> He said because I didn't have papers he would be forced to take a longer
> route to Miguel's apartment to avoid the police. . . . I later learned the
> airport was only eight blocks away, and I could have just walked! There
> weren't any police to avoid!
>
>   . . . Miguel wasn't there when I arrived at his apartment. [Héctor
> later learned that Miguel had taken a temporary construction job in up-
> state New York]. The guys in the apartment—all from Cañar—invited
> to me stay, but I would have to pay rent. When I told them I didn't have
> money, they told me I could pay them later, but I had better quickly look
> for work. I was lucky to find work right away using the tips Miguel's
> roommates gave me, on the street [as a day laborer]. I probably worked
> every day for three weeks. No days off. No rest. And almost all the money
> I made seemed to go to paying to stay at Miguel's. His roommates de-
> manded a little bit of money each day. I didn't know any better. . . . That
> kind of stuff happened all the time! People ripping me off.
>
>   When I finally really went out—I couldn't believe it. I thought it
> would be nicer, cleaner. What surprised me most [*me sobrecogio*] was the
> stress all the people have, the traffic, and the constant noise [*la bulla*]. It is
> true, I was scared. But I learned. I found a place to live and places to shop,
> and I didn't have to pay people for things anymore.
>
>   It is these little things like that you need some *orientación* about. No
> one is going to help you. Everyone makes it; just some make it quicker
> than others. They have to. And some have money left over when they
> figure it all out. . . .

Like Héctor, most migrants I knew arrived in New York City with the assistance of friends or kin. Ties in Jatundeleg helped not only secure *pasador* services and *chulcos,* but also places to stay and occasional job contacts. Nevertheless, as Héctor's particular situation demonstrates, familial and friend contacts alone could not shield migrants from the hardships of starting out their new lives with an undocumented status. Many new migrants discovered that their family contacts provided little more than an assurance that they would have a place to sleep, a foot in the door to apply for a job, and directions for how to get around. Already established migrants, as discussed in the work section of this chapter, were often taxed by their own search for employment, demanding job schedules, and tight budgets, making the extra task of providing an initial welcome to a familiar face a burden (cf. Mahler 1995, 94–102).

"Somos Indocumentados": The Ecuadorian Community in Queens

New York City is the epicenter of Ecuadorian immigrant life in the United States. As Ecuadorians both at home and abroad commonly joke, Manhattan and the surrounding metropolitan region is their third largest city, edging out the ever-growing city of Cuenca in the country's southern highlands. Return migrants talk passionately about New York as Yoni or, with a hint of transnational patriotism, of "nuestra chica patria" (our little homeland). Although significant numbers of Ecuadorians populate other American cities, including Miami, Los Angeles, and Chicago, their primary destination continues to be New York. The 2000 U.S. census enumerated 122,472 Ecuadorians in New York State, the majority (nearly 60 percent) concentrated in the New York City metropolitan area (U.S. Bureau of the Census 2000). However, precisely because 70 percent of the Ecuadorian population in the New York City metropolitan area is considered to be undocumented, this figure surely underestimates their actual numbers. Corrected estimates push them considerably higher, suggesting that as many as 250,000 Ecuadorians reside in the region (Logan 2001).

The majority of migrants from Jatundeleg, Ayaloma, and Shullín settled in the north-central region of Queens, in the community district of Elmhurst-Corona and the adjoining neighborhoods of Jackson Heights

Map 5.1. The Elmhurst-Corona neighborhood in Queens, N.Y. Source: Sanjek 1998. Used by permission of Cornell Univ. Press.

and Woodside (map 5.1).[7] More than 80,000 Ecuadorians are estimated to be clustered in this area (Logan 2001). Here they have joined one of the most ethnically diverse populations in the world, what sociologist Louis Winnik has described as "an ethnic cross section of the planet" (1990, 69)—an eclectic mix of different languages, nationalities, and ethnic backgrounds. The area crossed the "majority-minority" threshold early in the

7. A sizeable Ecuadorian population also resides in the borough of Brooklyn. In the past two years, there has also been an incipient movement of Ecuadorians into the traditionally white suburbs of Westchester and Rockland counties. Many of these newcomers are indigenous Cañari from small villages in northern Cañar province (Pribilsky 2001a).

1970s, such that by 1980 only 34 percent of the population was considered white, and by the year 2000 less than 18 percent was (U.S. Bureau of the Census 2000). In these figures, anthropologist Roger Sanjek (1998) sees Elmhurst-Corona as revealing the "future of us all." Moreover, this future, as political scientist Michael Jones-Correa describes, is one of "communities overlapping but not touching" and the persistence of the ethnic and national pride of a dizzying number of immigrant groups (1998, 32).

One of the initial tasks of my research in New York was to outline the contours, boundaries, and institutional structures that defined this community. Stated somewhat differently, my goal was to map the areas where the Ecuadorian community "overlapped," as Jones-Correa puts it, with other Queens communities, while simultaneously to identify the mechanisms by which it kept from "touching" and becoming indistinguishable from its ethnic neighbors. I took as an obvious starting point a standard research agenda built into many immigration studies: to look at the ways the immigrant community would be constituted in ethnic businesses, village associations, political parties, and specific labor niches. Indeed, I proceeded to plumb the importance for newly arrived migrants of what had been presented in the Ecuadorian media as "over 125 Ecuadorian social and cultural clubs distributed throughout the neighborhoods of Queens, Brooklyn, Manhattan, and in neighboring Newark" (Statman 1989, 10A).

This straightforward research task was quickly derailed, however, during an interview with Ruben Cajamarca, a migrant from Jatundeleg. I obtained Ruben's address from his wife in Ecuador, who asked that I "check up on him" because she was not sure if he was still employed; she had not received a telephone call for months and could not verify his current address. In five years' time, Ruben had cycled through five different living situations (most of them shared one-bedroom apartments) and countless restaurant and cleaning jobs. When I met him, he had been working in an Elmhurst pizza restaurant for six months, the longest stint he had spent in any one position. Anxious to learn more about the importance of Queens-based organizations and clubs whose names I had collected in my preliminary research, I spewed out my list to the veteran Ruben. He reacted with an initial silence. Among the ten or so organizations I shared with him, the only one he recognized was the Comité Cívico Ecuatoriano

(CCE, Ecuadorian Civic Committee). When I pushed Ruben to elaborate, he stopped me and made a curious statement. "Somos indocumentados" (We're undocumented). "We're not Ecuadorians here." After I asked him to elaborate, he said, "We come here to Yoni and think we will all be together. Quickly you start working, all day, and then you have to sleep. And maybe you see people, and maybe you don't. Some guys I have lived with I didn't even know. They were gone when I came home from work and at home when I was gone. Some were not from there [Ecuador]. No, they were from many different places. . . . Sometimes I didn't understand their accents. But really I wanted to know other people—Americans—and I wanted to learn English. But that is hard, too. You can watch the TV, but that is not the same."

"But there are *a lot* of Ecuadorians here," I said. "What groups are there? Soccer groups? Civic groups? Are there places where other Ecuadorians meet?"

"Oh, of course there are groups. But it's like Ecuador—you have *ricos* [the rich] and *pobres* [the poor], and they live in different worlds. It is true, in Flushing, there is a tremendous number of soccer clubs. Yeah, I have friends, but they are player-friends, not family. You see them once a week, maybe have a little drink or something, but you don't see them again . . . maybe for weeks."

"You have been in New York for five years now, no? Do you feel like this is 'home'?"

"New York is exciting, and it is easy to do things here. But, ultimately, we are the undocumented ones [*los indocumentados*]. We are not part of life here. We float above it. We are here, but we are not. We want to belong [*pertenecer*], but it is hard . . . even frustrating."

Ruben's statements convinced me that the idea of a homogenous "Ecuadorian community" would not hold up against the ethnographic realities of my informants' lives. Indeed, looking for such a community ultimately belied the internal differences among Ecuadorian immigrants, differences formed along axes of class, ethnicity, and race (indigenous as opposed to mestizo); regional background (highland versus lowland, urban versus rural); and legal status (documented versus undocumented). More important, it masked ways that newly arrived immigrants from countries and cultures as disparate as Ecuador, Pakistan, and Senegal share a common culture as undocumented migrants, one that is arguably closer in experience than a hermetically sealed Ecuadorian community "overlapping but not touching." When I made this discovery, my inquiry quickly changed from a search for a homogenous Ecuadorian community to questions about how a community constitutes itself when 70 percent of its membership is undocumented.

In the initial stage of my New York research, I hypothesized that undocumented migrants weathered their *orientación* and settled into their transplanted lives through involvement in an invented immigrant community based foremost in Queens. Simply put, I believed I would find a community where many of the class, ethnic, and regional differences that divide Ecuadorians would partially dissolve in the creation of an "Ecuadorian American" identity and solidarity. It quickly became obvious, though, that much of what is officially represented as the "Ecuadorian community" *(comunidad Ecuatoriana)* in New York differed sharply from the actual lives of the newly arriving undocumented migrants from Azuay and Cañar provinces.

The most visible signs of the immigrant community reflected the particular backgrounds of the first wave of Ecuadorian immigrants, a group significantly different from the highland campesino migrants who began flocking to the city in the early 1990s. The first immigrants who ventured to the United States in the late 1950s and early 1960s were white and upper-class mestizos, drawn largely from the professional classes of Guayaquil, Ecuador's banking and finance center. According to Zambrano Castillo, many of these early immigrants relied on contacts within Standard Fruit and other influential banana exporters to secure tourist visas, which were later converted to work visas and permanent residency (1998, 52). With enclaves of Ecuadorians not yet established, resourceful immigrants streamed into the cities, including New York, where they already had established business contacts.

Since the first wave of immigration, this elite corps of Ecuadorians has continued to maintain a strong presence in Queens and Brooklyn. For instance, the CCE and Profesionales Ecuatorianos en el Exterior (PRO-ECUA), the business organization that lobbies on trade issues, are staffed

largely by second-generation elites who have strong family ties in Guayaquil and Quito. These organizations frequently coordinate fund-raising
efforts for projects back in Ecuador. In 1999–2000, for example, the CCE
raised relief funds to help families affected by the eruptions of the Tun-
gurahua volcano.[8] By contrast, when I inquired about specific services for
immigrants, representatives from both CCE and PROECUA looked puzzled. They instead directed me to services such as the Catholic Diocese,
food pantries, and even a homeless shelter. One CCE representative told
me that the lack of services for undocumented migrants was the result of
the migrants' own outlook and ways of living in New York: "Most of the
migrants don't care about settling. They think they will just make lots of
money and leave when they do. They don't even put their bags down! They
don't have roots. . . . So you see it is hard for [established] people to offer
services to them."

Signs of the significant gulf between Ecuador's undocumented migrants and the established immigrants who came decades earlier were
evident elsewhere. The pages of *Ecuador News,* the "official" monthly
newspaper of the Ecuadorian community in the United States, include
almost no articles that deal specifically with undocumented migrant issues. Amidst its vast advertising for Ecuadorian restaurants and dance
clubs, the paper presents little in the way of useful information to undocumented migrants in need of health, employment, and legal services.
Public-health officials in Corona were dumbfounded when an alarming
outbreak of twelve cases of tuberculosis were discovered among a household of undocumented Ecuadorians, and they could not locate a single
community liaison or activist among the Ecuadorian community to assist
them in their contact investigation (New York City Department of Health,
Corona, personal communication, September 2001).

By late July 2001, I had completed the bulk of my research in New
York, but as August approached I still had one event to see and analyze:
the Tenth of August Parade commemorating Ecuadorian independence
from Spain. Migrants I knew commonly agreed that if an expression of

8. In 1983 and 1987, the group also successfully raised more than $450,000 to aid flood
victims in Ecuador (Jones-Correa 1998, 103).

the Ecuadorian community existed anywhere in New York, it was the parade. Similarly, a CCE executive assured me that the parade represented the most important cultural demonstration of the immigrant community, showcasing the rich culture of Ecuador. On the day of the parade, hoards of Ecuadorians lined the blockaded sidewalks of Roosevelt Avenue, from Thirty-Seventh to Seventieth (the area with the greatest concentration of Ecuadorian businesses), waving tiny flags from all of Ecuador's provinces. Immigrant parades have been analyzed as important sources for immigrant groups to solidify a sense of tradition while simultaneously forging new identities in their host communities (see Kasanitz and Freidenberg-Herbstein 1987; Paerregaard 2001), but the vast majority of symbols employed in the Tenth of August Parade suggested a celebration of the two Ecuadors I had come to know in Queens: the established legal community with roots in upper-class Guayaquil, on the one hand, and the much larger undocumented and lower-class population, on the other. Floats and elaborately decorated cars ushered in a gallery of special guests (including the former president of the Ecuadorian Congress and the mayor of New York), beauty queens straight from Ecuador, as well as displays of important religious symbols, including the highly venerated Virgen de la Nube from Azogues[9] and the Virgen del Cisne. Almost no floats, for instance, aside from the PROECUA and CCE floats and two representing local soccer clubs, were of local groups to which migrants may have belonged. Instead, the New York presence focused more on the promotion of those businesses and service agencies catering to the transnational community: Saeta Airlines (advertising daily flights from JKF to Quito and Guayaquil), Delgado Travel (the largest remittance-sending business), along with various other money- and package-sending agencies.

9. Our Lady of the Clouds is a representation of a Marian apparition in the south-central Andes before World War II. Peasants reportedly sighted the Virgin Mary in the clouds above them. Over the years, her apparition has been indigenized: she often appears with a *sombrero de paja toquilla* and long dark braids, common to the *cholas* of the Azogues region. Special celebrations of the patron saint have become popular among the newly arrived migrants in Westchester County ("Patron Saint Festival" 1999).

5.3. The Tenth of August Parade in Queens. Photograph by the author.

For migrants I spent time with in New York City, the Tenth of August Parade offered little more than a gateway into a day of drinking or an organized soccer match. It did not provide them with a long and lasting connection with their homeland or provide them with a sense of community borne out of being *paisanos*. For instance, the political candidates and officials who appeared in the parades meant little to men who had no involvement in electoral politics back in Ecuador.[10] In contrast to these public displays of Ecuadorian unity, more private affirmations of faith filled a vacuum and provided an alternative kind of community, linking migrants with their homeland. In New York, many migrants, if and when they were not working, would attend one of the Spanish-language Catholic masses held in various Queens and Brooklyn

10. For legal immigrants, the parade of political leaders and candidates was immensely important. In 1995, dual citizenship was constitutionally guaranteed to Ecuadorians living permanently outside of Ecuador (Jones-Correa 1998, 163), allowing immigrants to participate in elections in both places. Immigrants were able to cast votes from abroad for Ecuador's president in 2006.

locations. At special times, some churches invited Ecuadorian priests from rural parishes to spend a month or more serving their expatriate parishioners and performing masses.

Not surprisingly, much of religious life and Catholic worship by undocumented Ecuadorians speaks directly to the experience of migration. As sociologist Peggy Levitt has pointed out, transnational migrants often seize upon religious symbols and practice as means to "imagine and locate themselves within a religious landscape that may be superimposed on to, run parallel to, or obviate the need for one defined by national boundaries" (2001, 19). For instance, it was rare for me to meet young Ecuadorians in New York who before their journeys north had not made a visit to the sanctuary of the Milagrosa Imagen del Señor de Andacocha, a pilgrimage site in the Azuayo-Cañari countryside. After trudging up a steep path, often with family and picnic baskets in tow, migrants-in-waiting enter the sanctuary to seek protection from the Señor de Andacocha. Etched in the stained glass above the sanctuary's altar is the hopeful claim "From Pilgrim to Migrant." Before leaving, migrants write their prayers and wishes on the sanctuary walls. Successful return migrants will often go back to Andacocha to pay their respects by placing shiny marble plaques on the walls attesting to the Señor's powers.

Similarly, a visit to the Santisima Virgen de la Cisne (Virgin Mary of the Swan) has also been transformed into a specific migrant devotion. The Virgen de la Cisne is one of the oldest popular Catholic devotions in Ecuador, with reports of her apparition dating back to the 1550s. In a highland lagoon near the city of Loja (in southern Ecuador), the Virgin Mary reportedly appeared to an indigenous peasant in the form of a swan. When the peasant tried to capture the swan, the bird ascended into the sky and was transformed into the Virgen. Since the colonial era, pilgrimages to the Virgen have been a central part of popular faith in Ecuador and are now nationwide events that draw almost two million people annually to the site of the apparition. It was not until 1995 that statues of the Virgen were first brought to the United States to be venerated at masses, fiestas, and parades. Soon after, the bishop of Ecuador, presiding over a mass in Saint Patrick's Cathedral in Manhattan, ordained the Virgen as the protector of the "ausentes Ecuatorianos" (absent Ecuadorians).

5.4. Prayers for migrant relatives written on the walls of the Sanctuary of the Señor de Andacocha. Photograph by the author.

Although, no doubt, masses that infuse Catholicism with civic pride are important markers of community, it would be naïve to assume that such events supply migrants with long-lasting support. To be sure, for many migrants, busy work schedules leave little time to attend masses or otherwise become active members of a church congregation. Rather, more often migrants confine their worship to their own daily prayers and devotion. During my conversations with migrants, the subject of their belief in Catholicism would invariably arise, most often in the context of discussing the difficulties of their illegal travel north and the hardships they had faced in the United States. One young man told me, "There are a lot things that change when you come, some things good, some things bad—a new mentality. But I still believe [in my Catholicism] with everyone back in my village." Another shared how his beliefs connected him directly with his parents back in Ecuador: "My parents are very religious, and they pray all the time. When I pray, I feel like I am closer with them." In their living spaces, many migrants had assembled small shrines to the

Señor de Andacocha and the Virgin de la Cisne. Often accented with plastic flowers and miniature Ecuadorian flags, devotions captured in postcardlike pictures or in glass icons with glittery tin foil and lace worked "to delineate an alternative cartography of belonging," as Levitt puts it, reminding migrants of their pasts in Ecuador while at the same time creating new spaces in their transnational lives (2001, 20). Ruben's Señor de Andacocha icon, which he had kept hidden among the few possessions he brought across the border, was particularly special to him. On the back of a rectangular piece of colored glass decorated with foil stars and the image of the Señor was a prayer that Ruben had scrawled on the walls of Andacocha: "Help me to my destiny that I hope to reach, Señor. I ask this of you with my whole heart." Pointing to the icon positioned next to his bed, he spoke of the role of religion in his life: "When I pray, I know that I am being watched. Back in that little church [Andacocha] and in my home village. [The lord] knows I am here, but that my heart is there. . . . [Life] can be hard here, and the Señor watches over us. He will help me when I return. The Señor protects us all."

Undocumented Work in New York

Although faith can help ground transnational lives by linking home and host communities, migrants' experiences of living in New York are arguably most heavily mediated by the kinds of jobs they find. Migrants I met worked a variety of jobs in restaurants and construction, and as parking attendants, night shift office janitors, cabinet makers, pizza deliverymen, mechanics, laboratory aids, coffee bar attendants, landscapers, and illegal taxi drivers (see table 5.1). A large number of men also found work in both legal and illegal factories, manufacturing everything from designer clothing to bullet-proof vests and packaged cookies.

As table 5.1 demonstrates, despite the large numbers of Ecuadorian migrants and their relatively long history in the United States, their labor has not been concentrated in one area of specialization. Labor patterns nevertheless do exist, both in the types of jobs migrants can find and in the types of jobs they consider desirable. Indeed, just as important as the wages earned were jobs that resembled migrants' work lives back in

Table 5.1

Most Frequently Reported Employment for Undocumented Ecuadorians in the New York City Metropolitan Area, 1999–2000

Employment Type	Number of people
Restaurant worker	36
Supermarket/market	22
Day laborer *(esquinero)*	19
Factory/sweatshop	10
Commercial cleaning	8
Construction	18
Laboratory aid	3
Commercial driving *(taxiando)*	3
Cabinetmaker *(ebanista)*	3
Total	122

Source: Interviews and spot conversations compiled by author, from January 2000 to January 2002.

Ecuador, that offered different levels of autonomy and respect from employers, and, when possible, that expressed their sense of and desire for *iony* modernity. The following cases illustrate the range of work options that young Ecuadorians I knew found in New York and the different ways they sought to gain some control over their labor conditions.

Esquineros

"At one time or another you find yourself on the corner," Victor Saldañes told me, reflecting back on his first work experiences when he came to Queens at age nineteen. "But usually it's just your first job." Having worked as an *albañil* (brick mason) in Déleg, building the dream houses of return migrants, Victor predicted he would have little trouble finding a job in New York. However, he had the unfortunate luck of arriving in Queens in late autumn, the worst season, along with winter, to find

5.5. Day laborers *(esquineros)* wait for work in the early morning. Photograph by the author.

construction employment. Without work, Victor immediately joined the ranks of the day laborers, or *esquineros* ("street corner men"). The types of jobs he found varied tremendously, including doing masonry, cleaning swimming pools, moving furniture, washing commercial trucks, stuffing envelopes, demolishing buildings, canvassing parking lots with restaurant menus, doing landscaping, and hauling debris.

In an ironic way, *esquinero* work thrust migrants I knew into the public eye at exactly the time when they felt the most vulnerable. Carlos Quispe, who migrated at age seventeen, remembered having mixed feelings of fear and amazement when he started doing day labor: "I thought the *migra* would sweep down and take me the minute I hit the street. But they didn't. There we were—Mexicanos, Cubanos, Salvadoreños—all standing around with the cars passing, and I bet the bunch of us were all *sin papeles* [without papers, undocumented]." In Queens, migrants frequented a parking lot of a McDonald's restaurant where the management left the *esquineros* alone despite their long hours of loitering. "As long as at least one or two guys buys a cup of coffee or something, we are left alone," an *esquinero* from

Mexico explained. By 6:00 A.M., both sides of the roadway (and not necessarily the corners) would be dotted with small groups of between four and five men; at peak time, more than one hundred men would converge on the area in search of work. Time spent waiting for work was by no means passive, and migrants watch the street intently like hawks, watching for the slightest signal from potential employees driving by. On days when there were few or no employers, *esquineros* worked hard to fight off boredom. Pulling up discarded milk crates to serve as make-shift seats, men would share cigarettes, huddle around someone with a Spanish-speaking newspaper, or strain to listen over the rush of traffic to a lucky recipient reading from a letter sent from a loved one back home.

Most migrants put *esquinero* work at the bottom of a list of favorable jobs. Nearly all complained about the unpredictability of the work in terms of its availability and the wages it paid. Victor elaborated for me the difference between a "good" and "bad" day on the street:

> There are bad days when there is no work at all. When I was first here, I didn't know how to get them [how to be chosen for a job]. I was shy and scared, and sometimes nobody would come to hire us. I would stay around until the afternoon and then leave, go home. . . . I would be so sad [*con pena*] those months, hiding under the bed covers wondering why I came. . . .
>
> A good day is when you get to the street early. If it is winter, when you are cold and maybe it is dark, it is so hard to make it there early, but if you do, it is better. There are some corners that are better than others, and you don't want to be on a corner where there are too many people. That [too many people on one corner] intimidates those who are looking for workers. They [employers] like to talk with fewer guys to set the price and day's plan. . . . A good day is also making a good wage and getting all your pay at the end of the day. . . . Sometimes you have to wait a number of days to get paid. . . . That scares you.

Migrants complained most bitterly about the instability of *esquinero* wages and how they could vary greatly from week to week and job to job (cf. Valenzuela and Meléndez 2003). Much depended on the negotiations between employers and day laborers regarding pay. The most important factors in deciding a fair day's wage included the type and difficulty of the job, hours to be worked, how far away the job was from the *esquina* (street corner), and whether the employer would provide food. According to most migrants, a fair day's wage ranged anywhere from $50 to $100, depending on the individual constellation of factors just mentioned. Construction work paid upwards of $70 a day, but other types of "odd jobs," such as hauling debris or cleaning swimming pools, generally paid less. Most men I knew averaged *esquinero* wages of between $60 and $70 daily.

Over time, as new migrants learned that waiting for work would not draw them into the hands of INS authorities, they discovered that the greatest hazards of day-labor work were those surrounding employer deceptions. It was not uncommon for employers to offer one wage for a job and then pay much less when the work was finished. To mask their deception, employers would claim that a job was not satisfactorily completed or that the *esquinero* had misunderstood the terms of the work agreement. When, after a long and arduous day of hauling debris from a construction site, for example, men would be paid $65 instead of $85 as promised, they had little to no recourse to recoup the difference. Even migrants' attempts to alleviate such situations by sending their best English-speaking worker into negotiations were no guarantee against employer deceptions. As one young man lamented, "We want honest work, and we will work hard. But they know we can't go to the police and can't speak English well, so we are trapped."

Some of the jobs *esquineros* accepted also posed significant health and safety risks. Because pickup work is routinely off the books, constituting part of the borough of Queen's massive informal economy (Sanjek 1998, 119–40), laws and regulations that protect workers from harm are infrequently applied. For employers, the high costs associated with projects such as asbestos removal and building demolition, as well as those that require working amidst noxious chemicals and fumes, can be lessened by using inexpensive immigrant labor. However, because these projects often constituted the best-paying day-labor work, migrants were likely to take them without assessing health risks. When accidents did occur, though, the costs were often high. A week without work might mean a family back home would have to reevaluate their month's expenses. In extreme instances, accidents forced migrants to return to Ecuador when they could no longer work or, in some cases, were fearful of seeking out medical care. Migrants also reported chronic health problems associated with long-term *esquinero* work. Those who spent multiple years as *esquineros* earned reputations as being *agotados* (literally, "exhausted ones") who were, as I heard many times, "slowly killing themselves." Particularly strenuous work tended to aggravate already existing health problems, particularly latent infections of tuberculosis that migrants brought with them to the United States or acquired on their journeys north. Without insurance and easy access to medical attention, many let health problems become aggravated before they sought care.

Laboring as an *esquinero* meant a life of unpredictable schedules, inconsistent wages, and the constant potential for physical harm, but at the same time it also provided familiarity and occasionally a degree of autonomy to men's working lives. In their early youth, almost all migrants from rural Azuay and Cañar had spent at least some of their working lives earning money as *jornaleros*. Like pickup work, *jornalero* jobs were contracted daily at fixed meeting places. Away from their rural homes and distanced by time, some men were apt to romanticize the life of the *jornalero,* stressing the work's flexibility and the cordial relations between employers and employees. As one twenty-seven-year-old migrant in Queens tried to convince me,

> [i]f you have trouble making money, if your own fields don't grow or your milk cows don't produce milk, you can usually find work as a *jornalero.* In Azogues, we would go in the mornings and wait for work. It didn't matter who you worked for, they were usually fair, and they always fed you. . . . You always knew what the price would be. During the *almuerzo,* the boss [*patrón*] would sit down with us and share some *motecito* [a bit of hominy corn]. You could talk, laugh, and have fun. But then, you would get up and finish the job.

Migrant men were also attracted to day labor because of its close identification with masculine qualities of work and the way it afforded opportunities for men to socialize that could be limited in other work situations. Particularly because pickup jobs often included physical labor that was performed out of doors, it matched a criteria that placed it squarely in the cultural category of "men's work," as opposed to patently gendered women's work conducted indoors, such as jobs found in the garment industry discussed later. "Both men and women do hard work, but only men are *jornaleros*. Here [in the United States] it is the same. Women wouldn't be able to do the work we do here. It is harder than work back there [in Ecuador]," opined one Ecuadorian *esquinero*. His friend on the corner agreed, though he lamented how the all-male work pool limited his abilities to meet and socialize with women: "Yes, only the men do [pickup] jobs. It is better that way. . . . I can't imagine women here with us on the streets. There are a lot of machos on the streets, and they talk badly and tell nasty jokes. . . . The work, too, is very hard [*muy duro*]. No, the women, they all have indoor jobs, and we don't see them. I wish we did." Still, for many, waiting on the *esquinas* provided camaraderie between men that they often could not find elsewhere.

Despite the romantic comparisons some men drew between *esquinero* and *jornalero* work, others were quicker to dwell on the rigidity and discipline of working the corner. With little doubt, what Roger Rouse has described of Mexican migrants in California holds true for Ecuadorians in Queens: "[They are] not immigrants undergoing an inexorable shift into wage-labor but migrants turning from localized petty producers into members of a transnational semi-proletariat" (1990, 8). In particular, *esquineros* lacked the safety net of land and family that by contrast made *jornalero* work an *option* and not necessarily a daily necessity.

Day-labor wages can also be extremely erratic. Some men reported to me how they would have to work seven days a week in order to make enough money to cover their expenses and be able to remit something to their families. The results could be devastating and ultimately self-defeating. "After a few weeks, you're *agotado,* and you just have to take a break for a few days," explained a twenty-four-year-old migrant who returned to Jatundeleg after doing pickup work for three years. "Your body just won't do it anymore." But, as he explained to me, taking time off, even only a few days, can launch a migrant back into a situation where he can no longer send money, again necessitating a search for more work.

Migrants also expressed frustration over the lack of meaning in their work. This problem manifested itself in two fundamental areas of their work experience: relationships with employers and the imposition of hourly time and clock schedules. In the first instance, perhaps owing to the amicable relations migrants had experienced as *jornaleros,* they frequently lamented the limited contact that they had with employers when they did *esquinero* work. Distinct from the brief recollection of *jornalero* work presented earlier, interactions between employers and *esquineros* were usually short and formulaic, centering on the transaction of payments and the explanation of jobs. Some migrants explained away the sour relations with employers as the result of not sharing the same language; others expressed it as a "fear of people who speak Spanish." Whatever the reason, in their explanations of the mistreatment they frequently faced at the hands of employers, they implicated a lack of rapport. Although they placed the lion's share of the blame on their employers, they also blamed themselves and at times what they understood as their failure to adapt and "to belong" *(pertenecer)* in a foreign culture.

The imposition of times and schedules in day-laborer work further distanced employers from employees and workers from ownership over their own work, a consequence that plagued men even as they moved into more rigidly defined jobs. Men in rural Ecuador had come to know *jornalero* work as almost always calculated by the task at hand rather than by hourly wage. Wage labor was commonplace for migrants, but the extreme emphasis placed on time in their day-laborer jobs was not. *Jornalero* work schedules were punctuated by the necessity of eating, breaks for ritualized drinking, and the coming of nightfall. If a job was not completed by the time of one of these natural breaks, it could be resumed later or the next day with little thought about it. Digging a row of ditches and plowing a field with a *yunta,* for example, were tasks in which they could "dedicarse a su trabajo" (dedicate themselves to their work). Although they labored on someone else's land, they still perceived themselves as having some personal control over the activity of work. Men were often initially surprised that they did not find the same kind of satisfaction in their *esquinero* jobs. Although they would be hired for a specific job, bosses often demanded that they complete it by a certain time. Not infrequently, employees threatened to withhold portions of a day's wage if a job were not completed on schedule. As Carlos Quispe complained about a particular day of work, "I will do a job and get it done. But the boss was always yelling, 'I want this done in two hours! I want this done in three hours!' Allá [back in Ecuador], when the job is done, the job is done."[11]

Compounding feelings that *esquinero* work was not work men could easily "dedicate themselves to," employers also would frequently incite competition between workers to increase productivity. Not uncommonly, workers in the middle of a day's work would hear comments such as, "Whoever can haul more bricks will earn an extra twenty dollars." Although *esquineros* readily welcomed the chance to make more money, they equally expressed their dismay, noting how the practice created divisions between laborers. Again, migrants often evoked the idyllic image of the *jornalero* as a contrast: "As a *jornalero*," Luís Sinchi described, "you are a little group. Everyone gets the same amount of money, and you all work the same. The work can be *duro* [hard] or *pesada* [tedious], but at least you have each other."

I met few Ecuadorian men who did not seek to get off the *esquina* and find more stable employment, even if that meant settling for lower wages. In addition to seasonal fluctuations, the availability of *esquinero* work could change dramatically from one day to the next. If not enough jobs were available on a given day, if a migrant did not exercise enough aggressiveness in order to be picked up for a job, or if rumors about INS sweeps were circulating about, long stretches could go by without income. In most cases, men willingly forfeited the positive qualities of *esquinero* work—including its flexibility and immediate associations with masculine work—for more

---

11. The distinction Carlos made between time and work echoes the concerns of British historian E. P. Thompson, who in the contrast between "task-oriented" time and "clock-oriented" time located the roots of industrial capitalism's hold on workers alienated from their labor: "[T]here is a sense in which it [task-oriented time] is more humanly comprehensible than timed labour. The peasant or the labourer appears to attend upon what is an observed necessity. Second, a community in which task-orientation is common appears to show the least demarcation between 'work' and 'life.' Social intercourse and labour are intermingled—the working day lengthens or contracts according to the task—and there is no great sense of conflict between labour and 'passing the time of day'" (1967, 60).

regimented and steady jobs. Such jobs included opportunities in highly sought-after restaurant jobs and with Korean employers in grocery stores and light manufacturing.

"Trabajando por los Chinos"

Miguel Quispe from Cochahuayco, a town twenty miles north of Jatunde-leg, arrived in Queens in the winter of 1998 with few marketable skills and a $4,000 debt to pay. After spending two months as a day laborer, he found a job in Elmhurst in a Korean-owned grocery store only a few blocks from his apartment off Roosevelt Avenue. At first, he and his Korean boss could communicate only by using the limited English they had between them and a few mutually understood hand gestures. Over time, Miguel became one of his boss's most trusted employees. He worked as a jack of all trades, cleaning floors, stocking the shelves, and making deliveries. He was eventually promoted to running the register, one of the most coveted of jobs. He still held the job when I met him in 2000 and boasted about his $7.00-an-hour wage, more than any of his compatriots earned. He described his job as "buen trabajo" (good work) and remarked that "los Chinos are good to us."

In 1999, Luís Uruchima injured himself while working on a construction site on Long Island. The accident robbed him of his ability to capitalize on his construction skills because long hours spent on his feet left him in excruciating pain. After almost two months of trying to continue working in construction, Luís began looking for another job, in particular one that would allow him to sit for part of the time. For almost two weeks, he aggressively canvassed a number of clothing and textile factories in lower Manhattan and Queens. The factories he visited were divided up ethnically. As he recalled, all the Jewish-owned factories required that he have documentation, but the Koreans never did. He took a job in one of the Korean-owned shops and began sewing garments for $5.25 an hour. According to Luís, work in a factory was not particularly difficult, but very *pesada* (boring and tedious). The pay, however, was consistent, and his bosses told him if he worked hard, he could expect a raise.

The fact that Miguel and Luís found work with Korean employers, people they called "los Chinos,"[12] was no coincidence. Although the past two decades of migration to New York may not have been accompanied by the development of a distinctly Ecuadorian labor niche, specific ethnic hiring practices have provided one of the most convenient means for newly arrived migrants to find work in a tightening immigrant labor market. In Queens, I grew accustomed to the barrage of leafleters on Roosevelt Avenue passing out fliers from Korean temp agencies. The fliers, printed in Spanish on one side and Korean on the other, targeted newly arrived Latin Americans with little or no skills, willing to work for low wages. In the 1990s, Korean business owners began turning to Latino immigrants (specifically Ecuadorians and Mexicans) to fill entry-level positions that newly arrived Koreans were unwilling to accept. In these freshly arrived Latino immigrants, Koreans found an appealing labor force desperate for work and with few resources to bargain for better wages (Kim 1999, 583).

Many of my Jatundeleg informants in Queens confirmed the importance of the Ecuadorian-Korean connection. Manuel Pomaguiza, who worked in the same garment factory as Luís Uruchima, remarked, "Yeah, when you get here, everyone will tell you, try the Chinos. They will hire without papers." Another migrant told me, "They [Koreans] were offering jobs all over the place. I didn't have to look very hard for a job."

Within Korean grocery stores and fish markets in Queens, Latino employees maintain a high profile, running about mopping floors and stocking shelves. Yet the bulk of Ecuadorians I knew who worked for Koreans did so less noticeably in numerous garment factories scattered throughout the city. Different from work in grocery stores and restaurants, work in the garment industry landed migrants in some of the most inhospitable environments they had ever experienced. Garment businesses, in particular, run the gamut in terms of legality, safety, and suitable work

12. In the Andes, the term *Chino* (which literally means "Chinese") is used to refer to anyone of Asian background. In Peru, former president Alberto Fujimori, although widely known to be of Japanese descent, was nevertheless nicknamed "El Chino."

conditions;[13] even many legal garment shops operate under sweatshoplike conditions. Sealed up tightly, factory interiors can become sweltering hot and humid with constant streams of steam saturated with dust and other particles coming off machines. Most of the shops are nestled in ware-houses with covered windows and unmarked doorways in out-of-the-way industrial sections of Queens and Brooklyn.

The bulk of migrant workers from Azuay and Cañar found jobs in shops that specialized in making designer clothing. Migrants could best recall the brand names they produced because they were accustomed to the counterfeit knock-offs of the same name sold in the Déleg market: Ralph Lauren, Calvin Klein, and Tommy Hilfiger. However, there was no mistaking the difference in price between the costly garments they produced and the fake ones they wore. Before sharing with me his ex-periences working in a garment factory, Luís Uruchima told me a story about shopping: "I was away on my free time, on Sunday, and I went to Manhattan. We know someone who lives in Harlem from Ayaloma, and he invited us to come to the city. We were walking around the downtown and looking into all the shops, and I saw a piece of clothing that I made . . . a woman's jacket. The price was visible, and I looked . . . I couldn't believe it. That one piece cost more than two weeks of my earnings." Although experiences like the one Luís had could cause a migrant to question the inequalities of his work conditions, the men for the most part seemed sat-isfied with the wages they made in the garment shops, ranging from $5.15 to more than $7.00 an hour for an employee with years of experience. On average, men reported having to work between forty-five and fifty hours a week in order to cover their expenses and be able to send money home to their families.

As opposed to *esquinero* work, the garment industry employs large num-bers of both men and women (M. Chin 2001). Factory shop floors where Ecuadorian men work have long been heavily populated by Mexican, Salva-doran, and other Latinas from Central and South America. Many of these women have backgrounds in weaving and handicraft production and easily

---

13. My descriptions of factories and sweatshops are drawn from interviews with mi-grant workers and therefore are highly subjective. I was not allowed to enter these facilities.

find specialized sewing positions. Given the gendered nature of this work, some male migrants I knew often fretted over making sure I understood that their work was not the "fine" *(fino)* sewing work performed by women. Instead, they stressed that their work was the most physically demanding, often requiring the operation of heavy machinery. Men cut the thick rolls of fabric, flattened the fabric in large steam presses, and bagged up the finished clothing items to be shipped out. Therefore, any gendered stigma that may have come from working in sewing shops (strictly the occupation of women in Ecuador) was reconfigured in men's formulation from that of garment sewing to "factory" work *(trabajo de fabrica)*.

Although migrants appreciated the formality and predictability of the garment industry, they identified drawbacks as well. In particular, Korean hiring practices inevitably serve to create a climate whereby migrants are discouraged from helping friends obtain jobs in their place of work. As Chin points out, Korean garment factory owners often perceive migrants with connections to other migrants as being "too connected" and established. Instead, owners prefer to hire new arrivals based on an assumption that the immigrants will work for less because they have yet to learn about competitive wages (2001, 298). As I discovered, not only did this practice diminish men's abilities to tap their personal networks, it also limited the development of interpersonal relationships between employers and employees. For instance, employees could not easily curry an employer's praise by bringing a new loyal worker to the shop floor. As a migrant from Ayaloma explained to me,

> I was already working in the factory in Chinatown for about three months. It was the best job I have had so far. I am a cutter, meaning I cut the fabric and stretch it out into the [cutout] forms in the suits for the sewers. It is a better job than many, not so *pesada,* and it pays pretty well. A cousin of mine back there [in Ayaloma] wanted a job, and I told him he should come to my factory. He did, but he wasn't given a job. I thought maybe there were no jobs at the time, so a couple of weeks later I brought him back in. Again, no job. A Mexican guy told me, "Hey don't bring him in here again." I didn't, but later I learned that they wouldn't hire him anyway. The Mexican, though, feared they would take away his job and give it to my friend, who would work for less.

Workers also complained of a lack of loyalty among employers. A twenty-two-year-old garment worker from Cuenca told me, "Our bosses here are very competitive. They only want to make money. If they don't make money, they start getting rid of people. The ones that are paid the most are usually let go first." The practice of letting go of experienced workers when business was slow affected men in the factory more than it did women. Because women possessed more skills than men, employers were less likely to get rid of them and face the cost of training new employees. With regularity, migrants lost their jobs when employers could no longer afford to pay their relatively high wages. This reality was never far from the minds of the young migrants I knew in Queens, prompting them to be on a constant lookout for other jobs.

Most men I knew hoped their work would give them a way to be "part of" *(parte de)* as well as to "belong" *(pertenecer)* to American society. Working for Korean businesses, however, often constrained this desire as migrants found themselves in an insular world dominated by Koreans and Korean culture. One young man who stocked shelves and cleaned the back room of a grocery claimed that work time was constantly filled with "Korean music, Korean videos, Korean newspapers." The topic of isolation was sparked in another migrant I interviewed when I asked him how his attempts to learn English were going: "*Poooch!* I haven't learned any English here. Maybe Korean. . . . Yeah, maybe I have learned some Korean. But seriously, it isn't Yoni. . . . It's a different United States." Restaurant jobs, although harder to come by than the well-oiled networks linking Koreans and Ecuadorians, often filled this void.

Restaurant Work

As a significant component of the "new international division of labor" (cf. Sassen 1984, 1991), restaurant jobs represent some of the most consistently available work for newly arrived and poorly skilled immigrants in New York City (Bailey 1985; Talwar 2002). Even when undocumented migrant workers are not counted, well more than one-third of the city's restaurant workforce is foreign born (Winnik 1990; Zukin 1995). More stable than doing day labor, though less isolating than working for Korean-owned businesses, restaurant jobs offered migrants the best possible opportunities to balance the necessities of remitting money with the desire to engage in an *iony* lifestyle. Yet not all restaurant work was valued equally, and some jobs were clearly more aggressively sought than others. Almost all restaurant jobs nevertheless offered opportunities for promotion in ways that factory work and grocery jobs typically did not.

Migrants found work in three sectors of the restaurant industry: dishwashing and prep cooking, waiting tables in upscale restaurants in Manhattan, and working the counter (in delis, donut shops, and fast food). A number of factors guided men's search for restaurant work. At one level, migrants I knew felt that restaurants were safer for undocumented workers than other labor niches. Because most restaurant shifts for migrants were in the evening or overnight, many felt less threatened by a possible confrontation with *la migra*. (Factories, by contrast, were notorious for high-profile raids by INS and U.S. Department of Labor agents.) Restaurant work also offered migrants a cost-effective way to feed themselves as employers often provided free meals before shifts or would allow employees to take home food that was about to spoil.

Restaurant work also provided one of the most consistent forms of community for migrants, both among other migrants and between themselves and employers. As opposed to the hiring practices of Korean business owners, New York City restaurateurs actively solicited referrals from their migrant staffs for new hires. Migrants I knew constantly tapped their kin and friend networks to bring those they knew into their place of work. By implication, the trust employers would place in their workers to bring in new employers would extend to those implicated in the networks. In other words, a newly arrived migrant would be implicitly required not to make the one who provided the recommendation look bad. A twenty-five-year-old Ecuadorian male migrant told me, "My boss has trust in us [*con confianza*]. When he needs a new person to wash the dishes, he asks me. He knows we are without papers, but he doesn't ask. He just asks if I know someone who is responsible. . . . When one friend was hired here [at the restaurant], I was embarrassed on account that he only worked one day and then left. Other [referrals], though, have been good, and my boss was pleased."

Equally important in the development of enduring ties between kin and other *paisanos* and of new *confianza* ties cemented between employer and employee was the actual space of restaurant work and the physical closeness between workers. Sociologist Gary Fine argues that restaurant settings almost necessitate the forming of communities: "Whether or not [restaurant] workers choose, they belong to a community. In sharing a place, they are forced to accept the presence of others. . . . This reality leads us to understand how the communal life of a work organization contributes to the occupational identity of the worker. . . . These interactions provide the worker with a sense of personal possibilities that defines his or her identity" (1996, 226–27). Sharing the cramped spaces of a restaurant brings workers closer together. Where everyone knows the components of everyone else's job, migrants can, as Fine describes, "develop a sense of identity from their own occupational socialization" (1996, 227). Migrants told me many times that because they could see their role in the entire production of the restaurant, such work constituted a job they felt they could truly dedicate themselves to *(dedicarse)*.

Not only did the small spaces of the restaurant bring workers together, they equally and arguably in a more remarkable way brought employers into contact with their undocumented staffs. Many who described having good relations with their bosses credited their experiences to a shared reciprocity. If migrants worked hard, remained loyal, and perhaps on occasion helped to bring in a new employee, they could hope to be taken care of by their employer. For example, some migrants told of how restaurant employers would offer them free food, occasional transportation, and, in rarer instances, short-term loans. Alfredo Uruchima, who had worked at the same Italian restaurant for twelve years in Brooklyn, described that in his first year of work his boss paid for him to study English. Héctor Ayaguasa shared a story of how in the bakery where his cousin worked, the boss allowed his employees to use one of the large baking ovens to roast an entire pig overnight for a fiesta. Although a cynical interpretation of such examples might suggest such acts are but a small price for an employer to pay to ensure hegemony over his or her workers, in many cases the rapport and trust seemed to be more genuine.

An extraordinary example of work relationships that could form between migrant employees and employers is the story of Manuel Cusco and his employer at an Italian restaurant in Manhattan's Little Italy. In 1998, after Manuel had returned to Ecuador, his boss visited Jatundeleg during a vacation to the Galapagos Islands, Ecuador's most important tourist destination. The employer spent days walking the hills around the village and practicing Spanish with Manuel's family. As it happened, he never made it to the Galapagos, opting instead to spend the duration of his vacation in the Andes. It was also not uncommon for villagers in Jatundeleg to display pictures of the bosses who employed their migrant relatives in New York.

Among researchers who study restaurants, a distinction is made between low-paying "back work" and the relatively well-paid "front work" performed by wait staff and hosts (Fine 1996; Zukin 1995). Migrants I knew, because of their undocumented status and lack of English-language skills, typically performed "back work" jobs—washing dishes, stocking inventories, chopping vegetables (a slightly better job described to me as being the "salad man"), restocking kitchen ingredients, and cleaning. Not surprisingly, the least desirable restaurant job was also the most plentiful and easiest to come by for migrants—dishwashing. Dishwashers put in the longest shifts, usually from 11:00 A.M. or 12:00 P.M. until 2:00 or 3:00 A.M. the following day or, alternatively, from 4:00 or 5:00 in the morning until 6:00 or 7:00 in the evening, and they performed the lion's share of kitchen cleaning, including scrubbing down the stoves and rubber mats that cover the floors, along with changing the oil on deep-fat fryers.

Few migrants I knew worked for long periods as dishwashers. Either they moved up the ladder of jobs, or they changed positions altogether. Unlike the competitive garment industry, the high turnover rate for dishwashers created a culture of referrals. Indeed, more than any other employment sector, restaurant jobs came word of mouth and through *paisanos'* recommendations. Migrants also found unskilled restaurant jobs through "migrant friendly" employment agencies that targeted the most desperate and vulnerable of the undocumented migrant population. In a fictionalized work about the lives of Ecuadorian migrants in New York City, Jorge

Cevallos constructs a conversation between Miss Betty of the "Iris May I Help You Employment Agency" and a newly arrived migrant:

> MISS BETTY: Do you Speak English?
>
> EMILIANO: Is it necessary for washing dishes?
>
> MISS BETTY: No, not so much. However, I do recommend that before you go to your interview you learn words like soap, sponge, lids, dishes, plates cups, glasses, frying pans, buckets, and all those different saucepans that you have to identify in a restaurant. . . . Now get rid of that face from a child's funeral! The bosses are good people!
>
> EMILIANO: And they will give me a job?
>
> MISS BETTY: Oh yes. I am completely sure, since I have provided them with so many workers. They have always been pleased with the employees we send them: young, agile, thin [*flaco*], undocumented, and all of them Latinos. (1997, 24)

Paying one's dues as a dishwasher, though, often had its returns, and good workers found themselves promoted up the ladder. With wait-staff positions almost impossible to obtain, migrants I knew aspired "to work with the knife," as they described in their limited English. This included work as prep cooks and, with years of experience, as full cooks.

In most cases, migrants worked close to where they lived, securing jobs in ethnic restaurants (Italian, Korean, Chinese, and Latin American) or, in some cases, as counter support staff positions at nearby fast food restaurants and bakeries in Queens and Brooklyn (Talwar 2002). A subset of migrants, however, found work in Manhattan in upscale restaurants. Although no doubt migrants could find dishwashing and even prep cook jobs on the island, the appeal of jobs in Manhattan was the hope of finding "front work" rather than "back work." Both Jhonny Callaguaso (eighteen years old when I first met him in Jatundeleg) and Victor Sinchi from Azogues worked as waiters at a high-priced fashionable restaurant in midtown Manhattan that I will call "Celebrity." Celebrity's interior mixed elements of postmodern architecture with Latin American folk art. Similarly, its menu offered a number of dishes best described as pan-Latino, with an emphasis on health-conscious offerings and an eye to aesthetic presentation. In this ambiance of traditional and modern—a restaurant, in Sharon

Zukin's words, that delivered "a global product tailored to local tastes" (1995, 182)—Jhonny and Victor complemented the establishment's culti- vated sophistication. They stood out among their Azuayo-Cañari mates of the same age. In their home communities, they would most likely be de- scribed as *"medio indio"* (somewhat Indian) because of their high cheek- bones and darker-than-most complexions. Adding to his "exotic" look, Jhonny wore his jet black hair long and neatly pulled back in a ponytail. These features would be discriminated against in the wider Ecuadorian society in which they lived, but at Celebrity they served as the basis of a marketable cultural capital. As Zukin notes, "A restaurant's style is both implicitly and explicitly negotiated by waiters and management. The ac- cents and appearance of waiters affirms distinctions between restaurants as surely as menu, price, and location" (1995, 155). Rushing among the tables at Celebrity in their stylish black shirts and slacks, the men embod- ied the restaurant's spirit. Although fluent in English, their accents, indig- enous features, and mannerisms helped them get their foot in the door of one of the most desirous of immigrant jobs.

Young men like Jhonny and Victor, who were hired as much or more for the cultural capital they brought to a restaurant's unique style as for their particular skills, remained keenly aware of their market value. As Jhonny bragged to me, "Everybody in Yoni is into Indians. They all think we have some kind of powers, that we live in the Amazon, that we can turn into jaguars. We are something they want." Victor elaborated, noting that in Cuenca "to be an *indio* is to be bad, but here it is something cool. Here [in New York], people don't like blacks. But *indios* are alright." Similarly, another migrant told me how his boss at an Italian restaurant in Little Italy came right out and told him that he was hired because he looked "Italian enough" to pass for an "authentic Italian waiter." The boss added that he had trouble finding "real" Italians to do the work.

"Front work" at upscale Manhattan restaurants had a number of other recognizable benefits. Because the sophistication of such establishments came at a high price, migrants usually received large tips and were gener- ally better paid than their counterparts working in less fancy restaurant settings. Celebrity's wealthy clientele, for instance, often left Jhonny and Victor with nightly tips of between $100 and $120. But, as many who were lucky to find front work in Manhattan restaurants explained, the jobs also afforded an opportunity for migrants to be part of a larger American society that most of them only dreamed about. *Esquinero* work confined men to marginal and sporadic groupings of other undocumented laborers, and jobs taken with Korean employers could, at times, make migrants feel as though they were sealed off into a separate ethnic world, but work as waiters brought them squarely into a world of *iony* modernity. Migrants welcomed the modern interiors and slick clientele, in contrast to the harsh conditions of these other types of jobs. Jhonny was particularly cosmopolitan in his outlook; as he told me, "I have friends from everywhere. My girlfriend is a *gringa* from Holland."

"From Home to Work and From Work to Home"

Whether migrants found day-labor jobs, swept floors and cut fish in a Korean grocery store, washed dishes, or waited on customers in a chic Manhattan restaurant, all worked remarkably long hours. Indeed, as I explore in the next chapter, to be able to balance living expenses in New York with the necessity of sending remittances, the overwhelming majority of a migrant's time had to be spent working. On average, migrants I met worked twelve hours a day, six days a week, without the luxury of paid sick time or vacation days. Some migrants worked even longer hours, with a fifteen-hour shift being not unusual. Such demands shaped one of the most sobering aspects of migrants' lives abroad: the way work bisected their time between their place or places (in the case of *esquinero* work) of employment and their place of residence. When I asked men about their work schedules and free time, they frequently described their situation as nothing but "de la casa al trabajo y del trabajo a la casa" (from home to work and from work to home).

Although demanding work schedules structured an inordinate amount of a migrant's time, nonworking hours could be equally constricted by domestic tasks and the need for rest. With typically only one day free from work per week, migrants I knew often found their free time gobbled up by chores and errands *(quehaceres)* such as washing clothes, shopping for groceries, and attending to transnational issues (calling and writing to families, wiring remittances, and shipping packages). Likewise, limited discretionary income curtailed the kinds of experiences men could have on their free days. To the extent that time and finances allowed, many migrants looked to participation in sports and informal gatherings centered on drinking as ways to build their networks of friends and feel camaraderie. Such outings, however, represented the exception, not the norm, for men I knew, who felt their lives overwhelmingly hemmed in by the demands of work and the need to send money home. In Ruben Cajamarca's words, "I am only working and in my home am locked up [Estoy solo trabajando y en la casa encerrado]. But I like my job, and it makes me happy. . . . Still, I have to work almost all the time to be able to make even a little something, to be able to send something home. You work and work and work . . . and for what? So little! Everything costs dollars. . . . It's so frustrating [*tan frigado*].

As Ruben's comments suggest, it was not work per se that made a migrant's life difficult in New York. In fact, work proved to be one of few rewarding parts of a life otherwise characterized by regimented schedules and undesirable living conditions. Although no doubt migrants who occupy what is arguably one of the most vulnerable sectors of the U.S. economy face exploitation by their employers, the Ecuadorian migrants I knew perceived such aspects of their lives to be largely out of their control. Instead, as I explore in the following chapters, many of their struggles revolved not around making money at the jobs they found, but rather how their money should best be handled, including practices of saving and spending. Men found themselves in a constant struggle between their desires for and inability to obtain what they considered to be *iony* style, on the one hand, and the demands of meeting obligations to families back in Ecuador, on the other. As we shall see, these central tensions over managing money reveal not only the political economic textures of undocumented immigrants' lives, but also the shaping power of gendered constructions of reality, the necessities of transnational ties, and the enduring importance of family and rural life.

6

Adapting to Consumption

Spending, Saving, and Transnational Ties

[In Jatundeleg] life is more *tranquila* [laid back and calm]. Here it is
much harder. For us, the life is often *triste* [sad], and you can miss your
family terribly. . . . When you just work and come home, it is as if you are
in a locked tomb.[. . .]We don't always feel like we belong. But, sometimes, you have a little money left over, and you can buy some things.
[Back home] I could never do that. There was nothing. Here, I can aspire
to have things [Yo puedo aspirar a tener cosas] for myself and my family.
                                    —Luís Uruchima

The multiple entertainment, clothing, speaking, and cultural styles of
Spanish-, English-, and French-speaking immigrants are constantly
recast with a New York flavor, woven into the fabric of everyday life and
consumed as elements of authentic New York experience by natives and
visitors alike. The fact that their contributions are not well recognized
can partially be attributed to longtime colonial status within the U.S.
economy, but the complexity of their experience remains to be written.
                       —John Calagione, "Working in Time: Music and Power
                           on the Job in New York"

For the young Ecuadorian migrants I knew in New York City, the *iony* life
they dreamed of before leaving their rural Andean villages invariably paled
in comparison to the realities of their "shadowed lives" (Chavez 1992) on
the margins of U.S. society. Although few migrants arrive in New York
without a sense of the hardships they will endure, many remain steadfast
in a belief that with hard work and determination they can beat the odds.
By premigration standards, dollars earned in low-wage jobs often appear
high, but migrants quickly learn that daily life—in the form of rent, food,

and transportation—exacts a hefty price, diminishing what can be converted into remittances and purchases and sent home. For many migrants, disentangling the dreams of quick enrichment from the realities and necessities of strict money management proves to be one of the most fretted over aspects of their lives abroad.

However, alongside low wages, unsavory work conditions, cramped and dilapidated housing, and feelings of isolation, migrants I encountered often partook in a vibrant, though little analyzed, world of consumption. Watching American television. Window shopping. Grocery shopping. Bargain hunting for long-distance telephone cards. Going to the movies. Sorting through used clothing at a thrift store. Buying liquor. Sharing cigarettes with friends and coworkers. Picking out a necklace for a daughter's birthday back in Ecuador. Budgeting money to purchase an appliance for a wife. Seemingly mundane and quotidian, these and other consumption practices constituted for migrants I knew some of the most meaningful aspects of their lives abroad. To be sure, as Luís's comments that open this chapter suggest, up against the isolation of his "locked tomb" and the loneliness that came from being separated from family, it was his ability "to aspire to have things" that made an otherwise difficult life not only tolerable, but full of options. Still, the possibility of consumption constitutes more than just options. Consumption also lies at the heart of the tensions that transnational migrants face with respect to the seemingly incompatible goals of maintaining obligations to provide for families back in Ecuador, on the one hand, and experiencing *iony* adventure, on the other.

This chapter examines the consumption practices of Ecuadorian migrants living in New York City. Agreeing with Douglas and Isherwood that analyzing consumption reveals ways that "culture is fought over and licked into shape" (1978, 57), I isolate specific spending, saving, and budgeting practices, as well as activities related to the consumption of images and media (such as television viewing and window shopping), as key arenas for understanding how Ecuadorian men construct and give meaning to their lives abroad. In the past decade, a number of anthropologists and historians have turned their attention to the meanings behind commodity consumption. In a variety of contexts, such studies have addressed, for example, the ways African American girls in the urban United States perceive notions of inequality and racism through their purchases of dolls and other toys (E. Chin 2001), how everyday shopping practices in the north of London reveal meanings of love and the commitment to family (D. Miller 1998), and the means by which native Zimbabweans developed a desire for soaps, lotions, and other hygiene products in the process of becoming colonial subjects (Burke 1996). In examining these topics, they have challenged social scientists to consider Daniel Miller's assertion that consumption represents "the main arena in which and through which people have to struggle towards control over the definition of themselves and their values" (1995, 277). Struggles of self-definition play out in the Ecuadorian context also, as migrants negotiate between obligations to wives and family back home, on the one hand, and their quest for adventure and modern *iony* identities abroad, on the other. Indeed, although never before experienced consumption possibilities help migrants shape a sense of self in the face of their positions as invisible workers at the bottom rung of U.S. society, they equally serve to define their roles as husbands and fathers in the lives of families thousands of miles away.

Toward an Ethnography of Migrant Consumers

Within studies of migration, the theme of consumption has long commanded considerable attention, beginning perhaps with anthropologist Manuel Gamio's (1930) cataloging of the goods that Mexican migrants brought back with them across the U.S.–Mexican border in the 1920s. For much of the past century, research addressing consumption practices in migration contexts has reflected Gamio's original concerns, focused largely around questions of economic development (Brettel 2000; Kearney 1995). In particular, scholars have spent much of their time analyzing the potential of remittances (and of their related consumption practices) to foster local development and to lessen the necessity for future migration.[1] By contrast, a generation of anthropologists inspired by the symbolic

1. Researchers have overwhelming recorded cases confirming the latter, arguing that not only are remittances used unproductively, but the forms of consumption that ensue from these expenditures frequently lead to cycles of dependency that discourage

and practice approaches taken by Mary Douglas (Douglas and Isherwood 1978), Pierre Bourdieu (1984), and more recently Daniel Miller (1995), among others, has pursued a line of investigation that unhinges the analysis of consumption from questions of development and redirects it toward issues of identity, status, and the refashioning of livelihoods (see, e.g., Colloredo-Mansfeld 1999; D'Alisera 2001; Fletcher 1999; Gamburd 2000; Salih 2002). By way of example, Peri Fletcher's (1999) ethnography about the *casas de sueños,* or "dream homes," that Mexican migrants build in their natal communities puts aside questions of development in order to focus on the cultural meanings that accompany new construction. As remittances transform houses from sites of production to ones of consumption, Fletcher ably considers the different ways migrants use home construction to convey messages about their continued commitment to and claims to status in communities in which they no longer reside permanently.

Although Fletcher's study and others like it present vivid portraits of the ways consumption choices shape and articulate changing modes of livelihood, they tell only one side of the story. In most cases, readers are invited into local worlds of commodity consumption only after budgets have been hammered out, money has been allocated, and particular consumer choices have been made. Indeed, the autonomy and agency afforded in the practices of consumption have captured scholars' attention, but the obvious constraints that shape consumer behavior have not been mined for what they can tell us about the construction of social identities. For example, returning to the case of Fletcher's *casas de sueños,* we learn much about the messages that migrants choose to send when building their

---

autonomous development. For example, in a review of thirty-seven migrant community studies from Mexico, Durand and Massey conclude that researchers were "remarkably unanimous in condemning international migration as a palliative that improves the material well-being of particular families but does not lead to sustained economic growth within sending communities" (1992, 25). Up against these findings, a recent line of research has paid greater attention to the actual circumstances that lead migrant households to invest or not invest in development ventures back home (Conway and Cohen 1998), as well as the degree to which remittance flows help already existing local economies (Durand, Parrado, and Massey 1996).

dream homes, but almost nothing about the other practices rightfully falling under the aegis of consumption, such as the money-making, saving,
and budgeting strategies that also inform particular consumer choices. We
fail to see, as Elizabeth Chin warns, that "[c]onsumption does not take
place in a vacuum-sealed world of signs and symbols, but rather in a messy
material world where other processes are also at work" (2001, 12). These
other processes prompt the asking of new questions: What is the relationship of new forms of consumption to long-standing traditions of spending
and saving? What kinds of new cultural practices emerge from savings for
homes? How do migrants balance the desire to save for dream homes with
the immediacy of other types of instantly satisfying consumption? What
can an examination of the practices of saving reveal about the ways migrants adapt to their host communities?

If these questions are put aside for the moment, an equally important
concern emerges in a critique of this selective ethnographic framing: the
implicit division of labor it assigns to migrants and their communities. Simply put, migrants themselves are defined almost exclusively by their actions
as workers and producers, whereas those left behind in sending communities are typically cast in the role of consumers. As historian Andrew Heinze
notes in his study of mass consumption among Jewish immigrants in nine-
teenth-century New York, scholars have consistently privileged production
as the basis of social relationships: "Not what a person buys and uses, but
what a person does for a living, has been perceived as the key to his or
her social identity" (1990, 8). By equating migration with labor, researchers often unwittingly cast migrant consumption practices as unproductive
and, in the context of migrants' ability to adapt and prepare for the future, even as potentially counterproductive. A refreshing exception to this
tendency is Mary Beth Mills's (1999) well-crafted analysis of the spending
practices of young female Thai migrants in Bangkok. Mills demonstrates
how rural women, as low-wage factory workers, struggle to balance their
desires to become *thansamay* (up-to-date), which first drew them to the
city, with their obligation to be "good daughters" by remitting a portion
of their income to parents still living in their natal villages. The attention
Mills pays to the actions that *inform* consumption, rather than simply to
the symbolic role of consumer goods, productively indexes the numerous

contradictions poor women face as rural-to-urban migrants and the hard choices they must make. In Bangkok, women refashion their decidedly unglamorous lives as factory workers into brief moments of urban sophistication through inexpensive and well-budgeted urban leisure activities. They also find ways to conjoin their "up-to-date" identities with their daughterly obligations by recasting trips home as "vacations" and skillfully displaying their urban consumer goods to their rural counterparts. The Thai case closely mirrors the experience of Ecuadorian migrants who confront similar dilemmas as they weigh their desire for *iony* adventure up against the need to maintain status and produce their locality through the sending of gifts and remittances to home communities.

Finally, closer attention paid to migrants as consumers in their host communities also allows for a greater understanding of the role consumption practices play in processes of immigrant adaptation. In the United States, where historians have repeatedly linked a particular brand of "Americanization" with consumer activities (Heinze 1990; McCracken 1988; Peiss 1986; Potter 1966), this understanding may be especially true. Again, as the Jewish experience described by Heinze suggests, consumer activities have long been at the heart of processes of "becoming American": "[Although] acquiring American speech, participation in American institutions, and making economic advantages were important to the search of cultural identity . . . vast numbers of people with little sense of language and limited exposure to institutions were engaging, virtually from the moment they entered the streets of the city, in a new cycle of consumption that defined a uniquely American approach to life" (1990, 10). For undocumented Ecuadorians, as well as for other groups like them blocked from legal routes to citizenship and participation in civic institutions, involvement in the all-inclusive and unabashedly democratic world of American consumerism clearly serves as one of the surest routes to a sense of acceptance and cultural citizenship.

Money Matters

After Héctor, Miguel, Luís, Victor, Jhonny, and the other young migrants introduced in the previous chapter slipped clandestinely into the United

States—having evaded border agents, con artists, and corrupt local officials—they were able to breathe a sigh of relief. But only for a moment. Saddled by debt and in need of money to start their new lives, they found their first days in New York marked by an overwhelming urgency to find work. Certainly, just as soon as many newly arrived migrants could scrape enough money together in their first employment, they rushed "to send a sign" *(enviar una seña)* to a *chulquero,* demonstrating their intention to pay back what they have borrowed. However, for migrants with large debts loads of more than $10,000, sending a "sign" added up to little more than servicing the compounding monthly interest on a crippling *chulco.* Nonetheless, all migrants are keenly aware that if a sign is not sent in a timely fashion, *chulqueros* may threaten family members back in Ecuador and in some cases begin the repossession of the loan's collateral. Almost as important as the mad scramble to remit to a *chulquero* was the sending of a sign to anxious family members in Ecuador fretfully waiting to learn that the migrant is alright. Along with token amounts of money, migrants hurriedly packaged up modest gifts, such as a piece of clothing or jewelry, to give the appearance of instant success. Photos—of a migrant's apartment, a workplace, or even recent purchases—round out the well-scripted story of initial good luck in Yoni that many migrants wish to tell (cf. Mahler 1995, 88; Miles 2004).

As most migrants I knew soon realized, however, initial impression management is much easier than money management. Manuel Pomaguiza arrived in the United States with a plastic baggie containing $300 sewn into a pant leg. Together with an offer from a friend from Ayaloma to let him sleep on his apartment floor for a month or so, Manuel anticipated having little trouble landing himself on his feet. Unfortunately, the money went much faster than he imagined. "The three hundred dollars didn't last two weeks. Everything costs money . . . a little here and a little there . . . and then it was all gone. I couldn't believe it." For Victor Sinchi, all the little costs associated with living in the New York did not occur to him:

> When I got my first job in a restaurant and my boss told me the wage, it seemed like so much. I was sleeping on a friend's couch and giving him just a little something [money] for food and the lights. I wrote

it all down—how much I made, how much I could save, how much I needed to buy this and that. . . . Having my own place cost a lot, and in winter the heat took much of my money. I had to pay rent for my place, for food, for clothes, the lights, the water. . . . I wasn't really making that much.

Similarly, Luís Uruchima felt as though the harder he worked, the less money he earned. "When I first I arrived, I told myself I would work all the time if I had to since I was young. With more work, I guess I was spending too much or something because I could never seem to have enough money." Like Victor, Luís resorted to drawing up a budget of his expenses, which he shared with me over the course of interviews (table 6.1). The budget reflected average monthly earnings of $1,050. With slight variations, the budget permitted Luís to send between $250 and $300 to his wife and family each month, barring unforeseen expenses.

The frustration that migrants I knew in New York City experienced with respect to saving money reflects the difficult transition that many

Table 6.1
Luís Uruchima's Monthly Budget

Expense	Amount (in dollars)
Housing (rent)	400.00
Food	150.00
Utilities*	75.00
Household furnishings/appliances	20.00
Transportation	30.00
Communication (telephone/postage)	60.00
Clothing/toiletries	15.00
Liquor	20.00
Other	20.00
Total Monthly Expenses	790.00

* Monthly average of natural gas and electricity consumption.

rural migrants from Latin America face as they shift from an economic mindset of maintaining subsistence to one oriented toward generating surplus. As Sarah Mahler notes, migrants "face the task of stretching their meager salaries past self-sustenance . . . [and] achieving a surplus to cover debts and family obligations," which is different from the goals governing economic livelihoods in their home countries (1995, 2). Of course, most rural migrants, including those from the Azuayo-Cañari region, did not come from strict subsistence economies, but instead had extensive experience of working in wage labor and a cash economy. Nevertheless, the kinds of money-management skills necessary to generate income far and above that needed to live in the United States were qualitatively different from the tasks to which most migrants were accustomed.

Frustration over how to increase and stretch earnings ran high among migrants I knew. However, my desire to understand these difficulties was initially hampered by my inability to comprehend the terms men used for personal budgeting. "It is so frustrating [*tan fregado*]," Miguel exclaimed to me one afternoon in Queens as I showed him photos I had taken of new home construction in Jatundeleg, Ayaloma, and Shullín. "How do they do it? How do they have the money to buy those big houses?" He continued: "I can make a living [*ganarse la vida*] just fine here. But that is not good enough. It is working for money [*para plata*] that frustrates me so! How am I to save money?"

Other migrants also used the distinction Miguel had made between "making a living" and "working for money." Although at first the two terms appeared the same to me, both products of wage labor, each constituted a different approach to the management of cash. *Ganarse la vida* includes not only the act of making money in order to meet one's needs, but also the other constituent parts of the peasant economy, including reciprocal labor pacts and barter.[2] Since childhood, most migrants had

2. The meanings of the phrases *ganarse la vida* and *trabajando para plata* as described here correspond roughly to their similar use in the Andes as described by others (see Gudeman and Rivera 1990; Mayer 2002). Because of the established use of these terms, I present them here as glosses and, for the sake of consistency, as stand-ins for a host of related terms men employed to describe their money-saving practices.

lived in an affective world of reciprocities—from *mingas* to *prestamanos*—whereby not all economic relations were grounded in cash exchanges (see chapter 3). Although monetization was not new, the degree to which it shaped migrants' lives abroad was significant. In New York, migrants were able to tap into kin and *paisano* networks to meet some needs, such as help in obtaining initial household furnishings (mattresses and bedding, for instance) and useful information about where to find thrift stores and community centers offering free services. By contrast, the notion of working *para plata,* which most male migrants associated with women's control of money, delineates a wholly different approach and goal with respect to making a living. Over time, urbanized migrants I spoke with employed various strategies to minimize their expenses and save money. Formal saving measures, such as bank accounts, were impossible to obtain without a social security number, so migrants exchanged a host of information regarding informal cost-saving measures and budgeting techniques.[3] In fact, the list of tips and tricks that men shared with me and that filled my field notes is not easily summarized, and many strategies go unrecognized here.

By far the most critical cost-saving measure begins with housing. Catering to its swelling immigrant population, Queens is home to some of New York City's most notorious examples of illegal housing, typified by the popular "slapdash" conversions of single-family homes undertaken by unscrupulous landlords: "Plywood room partitions, basement and garage units, and self-installed water, sewage, and electrical connections creat[ing] dangerous, overcrowded conditions" (Sanjek 1998, 189). As U.S. census takers can attest, it is this form of "complex housing" that often belies the true numbers of the country's new immigrants. For instance, many Ecuadorian men shared studio and one-bedroom conversions with five or more roommates to minimize expenses. Others lived as *bordantes* (lodgers) in small, single-occupancy rental spaces (garages, attics, and large closets), usually in private houses and without their own bathrooms or kitchen facilities.

3. In only a few cases did migrants I knew utilize informal credit systems (known as *sanes* or *sociedades*). A number of men were suspicious of *sanes* because they were operated by non-Ecuadorians.

Migrants also strategized to lower their food costs. While I was working in Cuenca in the early 1990s, my English-as-a-second-language students passed along numerous urban legends about migrants in the United
States, including one that described their subsisting off "SuperCan" dog
food, which migrants apparently found "inexpensive, yet nutritious." In
addition to generating a few laughs, these stories tended to propagate a
misconception that migrants scrape by while abroad. To the contrary, most
migrants claimed to eat better in the United States than they had back in
their home villages. Although food prices were generally higher than in
Ecuador, migrants found prices on desired foods such as meat to be considerably lower, making it a luxury they could afford. As one young man
told me, "[Back there] I was lucky to eat meat once a week. Now I eat it all
the time." Apartment freezers attested to this fact in that they were often
full of the packages of meat that thrifty migrants purchased on sale. Still,
most migrants I knew went to great lengths to spend the bare minimum
on food. Migrants working in restaurants took meals at work when they
could. They also had their pick of expired food and often took to pilfering
inventories. Beyond exercising thrift in procuring food, migrants also had
to combat the tendency to give in to the convenience of buying prepared
foods. In the living arrangement Jhonny Callaguaso had with two other
migrants, each man took turns cooking meals on his day off. The men
would mostly prepare large batches of inexpensive and easy-to-prepare
rice dishes *(arroces)* that would keep for days and were easily transport-
able. In other households, men pooled their money to hire a cook, usually
a woman living in a nearby apartment. In one household I knew well, the
men had struck a deal with a Haitian woman in their building. She willingly cooked for free as long as the men provided her with ingredients that
they stole from their restaurant jobs.

In Luís's monthly budget, approximately $60 went to communication
costs, mainly telephone calls and occasional shipments to his family in Jatundeleg; other migrants reported higher communication expenses. As I
detail in the next chapter, frequent communication with family and friends
back in Ecuador fulfilled more than simply an emotional need. It was also a
logistical necessity for the smooth functioning of transnational households
and, as such, was not an expense that migrants I knew could jettison easily,

even during hard financial times. As many migration scholars have noted, both a drastic reduction in the cost of long-distance telephone charges and improved technology have greatly facilitated transnational communication (see, e.g., Basch, Glick Schiller, and Szanton Blanc 1994; Foner 1997b). Aiding in this revolution has been the rise of discount phone cards with advertised "cheap talk-time minutes" that allow undocumented migrants without credit histories easy access to long-distance services (see Sachs 2002). In 2001, prices for Ecuador-specific prepaid phone cards ranged widely, with a low cost of $5.00 for ninety long-distance minutes. Men would often travel throughout the city in pursuit of the cheapest available cards. Jhonny Callaguaso's roommates ribbed him for (though ultimately admired) his relentless search for low-cost long-distance phone cards. His long subway rides up to the Bronx to purchase phone cards from a discount vendor earned him the nickname "Haciendo Agosto" (Making a Killing) from his roommates and friends.[4]

In addition to remittances, migrants also sent packages back home to their families, typically coinciding with holidays as varied as Christmas, Carnaval, and Mother's Day.[5] Most of the items I documented could be properly considered gifts—household items, tools, toys for children, clothing, and shoes. Migrants would also occasionally send medicines that were too difficult to find or too expensive to buy in Ecuador or that held symbolic value as "local products." Homemade videos *(videos caseros)* and cassette tapes also showed up in the mix. In the six- or seven-block stretch of Roosevelt Avenue with the heaviest concentration of Ecuadorian businesses, literally dozens of shipping companies compete for migrants' business. Over time, skillful migrants learn which of these businesses reward repeat customers and which have seasonal discounts. In 2000, prices for shipping goods to Ecuador varied considerably, reflecting intense competition. To ship a

4. See note 16, chap. 2, for a definition of the phrase *hacer agosto*.

5. In 2001, Ecuadorians abroad shipped home a weekly average of 272 kilograms (598 pounds) worth of gifts and other merchandise. At holiday times, this number can increase significantly. In the month of December 2000 alone, Ecuador's Office of Customs registered 816 kilograms (1,800 pounds) entering the country weekly from the United States ("Los réditos escondidos" 2001, 8).

package from New York to Ecuador within eight days (an industry standard) ranged between $2.50 and $3.50 per pound; at Christmas time, prices could drop as low as four pounds for less than $10.00.

Although not all migrants paid serious attention to long-distance phone cards or shipping costs, almost everyone I knew in Queens closely monitored the crippling surcharges attached to sending remittances. Distinct from other transnational migration contexts where sending and receiving communities are in relatively close proximity to one another (e.g., El Salvador, Guatemala, and Mexico), Ecuadorian migration does not play host to a system of affordable couriers who shuttle back and forth delivering remittances.[6] Rather, nearly all migrants who remit money to Ecuador must do so at the mercy of money-wiring services; few will take their chances and send cash through the mail. In 2000, handling charges for sending remittances averaged $22 per $200 remitted (a standard remittance), or just higher than 11 percent.[7] Because such a hefty surcharge could gouge into remittances, migrants tried hard to locate services with the lowest charge.

To North American readers routinely familiar with comparison shopping and bargain hunting, the transparent acts of migrants combing the streets of Queens for discount phone cards or low money-wiring fees can appear mundane and of little consequence. To be sure, in many ways these acts *are* of little consequence in that their cumulative effect is usually not enough to boost migrants' earnings or, more important, the amount of their remittances qualitatively. In fact, migrants I knew grew frustrated in their pursuits as they found that almost no amount of strict fiscal discipline ever substantially raised their earnings. Rather, their financial successes invariably came only with fitting extra work into their already overtaxed schedules and, in some cases, profiting off the needs of other migrants. For instance, soon after I met Jhonny Callaguaso, he began selling to his friends and acquaintances the $10.00 phone cards that he purchased from

6. See Mahler 1999 for a description of formal and informal courier services operating in Salvadoran transnational migration.

7. See Orozco 2001 for a comparative analysis of money-wiring charges for various Latin American countries.

a wholesaler for only $7.00 each. Nevertheless, small acts of budgeting were important as migrants put faith in them to bring a semblance of control to their precarious experiences as undocumented laborers. In the context of high debts and obligations to their families, fears of missing work and failing to generate remittances were threaded through my interviews with migrants. These men had little control over an employer's whims, debilitating sickness, and the potential for work-related accidents, any of which could cause them to miss work and lose earnings, so mastery over budgets provided a psychological buffer against uncertainty. As Victor Saldañes confided in me, "I go to sleep with those numbers in my head, and I can't sleep. But I have to know."

In Search of *Iony* Identity: Overcoming Marginality

Migrant workers in New York, including the young men I knew from Jatundeleg, Shullín, and Ayaloma, often told me that the attraction of the United States lay not just in an economic impetus shaped by land scarcity and a lack of jobs in Ecuador. The other side of the *chulla vida*—one life to live—was the world of adventure. On the walls of smoky kitchens and dusty living rooms inside many Jatundeleg homes was a large, framed color photograph of the Manhattan skyline at night. The scene resembles nothing in the Andean countryside; Quito and Guayaquil, with their fair share of modern edifices, pale in comparison. However, for many villagers, the image was a compelling one and often served as a springboard to get them to talk about their perceptions of urban life in America. They imagined New York to be "clean," "exciting" and full of adventure. By contrast, they described rural life as lonely, isolating, and "too quiet." Especially during the long rainy season, when torrential downpours and bone-chilling winds kept people indoors for weeks at a time, the community could easily resemble a ghost town. The city, as one returned migrant summed up, "is alive and vibrant, while my village is sad." However, new migrants never really saw this New York because demanding work schedules invariably overshadowed and curtailed their urban experiences. One migrant explained to me that because he began work at 4:00 in the morning and did not stop working until the early evening, he rarely saw the city in daylight for months on end. Unless men possessed the extraordinary luck and significant cultural capital to find work in a sophisticated restaurant setting or similar venue, as Jhonny Callaguaso and Victor Sinchi did, they often had to find their *iony* modernity in more trivial, though no less important, social experiences. Coming to terms with the ways work overshadowed their lives required migrants I knew to carve out what free time they could in which to explore *iony* life. Across the East River and buried deep in the seemingly endless neighborhoods of Queens, migrants found themselves far from the glimmering skyline they had come to know in the popular photograph that adorned Jatundeleg living rooms.

I was often reminded of just how insulated and marginalized migrants' private lives could be during my many attempts to locate my informants' homes. Deceptively straightforward street addresses, apartment building names, and unit numbers often represented just the general landmarks for what ultimately proved to be secret dwellings located behind labyrinths of alleys and hallways. Finding apartments meant locating doors behind doors, back staircases, cellar entrances, open windows to yell up to, the right unlabeled buzzer. The apartment occupied by Luís Uruchima reflected many migrant domiciles I visited during my research. With three other men, Luís shared the back portion of a dilapidated house that had been illegally converted into four spacious studio apartments. The apartment consisted of one large room with two windows overlooking a back alley, a tiny bathroom, and a nooklike kitchen not big enough for two persons to occupy simultaneously. The cramped kitchen housed a two-burner electric stove, an extra hot plate, and an aging refrigerator with a rusty door. The countertops were cluttered with covered pots and pans filled with leftover food.

Four inhabitants with four different work schedules (two of Luís's roommates worked night shifts for a Korean cleaning service) necessitated the division of the main portion of the studio into separate living spaces. Bed sheets nailed to the ceiling acted as partitions, giving each man a small portion of the studio to call his own. Each personal space had a mattress and a makeshift bed stand fashioned from either a milk crate or a cardboard box. Because of the limited space, one of the roommates' mattresses had to be pushed against the wall when he was not there to clear a path to a rundown and foul-smelling bathroom. Although small and in poor condition, the apartment had a comfortable and orderly feel to it. In a mutual space beyond the kitchen and bathroom, a television, VCR, and CD player sat atop a large table strewn with VHS cassettes and CDs.

Each man's personal space also revealed the ways the apartment served as more than a mere crash pad. When I made a connection with one of Luís's roommates, Romero, by informing him that I had visited his home village, he eagerly directed me over to his corner of the apartment to show me a display of framed pictures. Pointing to a photograph of his parents' house, he told me that he and his wife owned a piece of land nearby where they hoped to build their own home. Romero had propped up the photo against a plaster Ekeko figurine, a traditional Andean symbol of abundance and good fortune, rendered as a plump, cigar-smoking merchant weighted down by a valuable load of merchandise. As a devotional, Romero had placed a matchbox-size car and a magazine photograph of a home with a swimming pool next to the figurine. In the meantime, as he waited for his luck to improve, he had been remarkably successful in acquiring the emblems of an *iony* lifestyle. In addition to a CD player and a modest collection of discs, a makeshift clothesline suspended above his mattress held a cherished set of stylish shirts, pants, and jeans. In fact, when I first met him at his apartment, Romero had just returned from his shift at a nearby restaurant. He immediately apologized for his appearance and ran to his section of the room to change quickly into a pair of jeans, an athletic sweatshirt, and a UCLA baseball cap. When I asked why he had so many clothes and why it seemed he was so taken by appearance, he looked at me blankly. Only when I qualified my statement, suggesting that such expenditures must cut into the money he would save for remittances and building a home, did Romero take interest enough in my line of inquiry to respond: "Everyone has their own look. You have to be that way. What am I going to do? Be like they are [back in Ecuador]? Where, when work ends and your clothes are dirty, you just go to the next thing? No, not here. Here, you come home and wash up. It is cleaner and nice, but it is also kind of a necessity. . . . I don't want to be a campesino here, not if I want to get ahead."

I probed further. "But since you have a uniform for work, when do you ever get to wear your clothes?"

Luís interjected into the conversation, "He doesn't have anywhere to go! He is a dog . . . that works all the time! There isn't anywhere he can go to be able to wear those clothes. He better not gain any weight so he can at least take them home with him!"

Romero ultimately had to agree that in fact he had little free time. This, however, did not stop him from dressing up whenever he could, if for no other reason than to walk the busy streets in Queens and to socialize with friends. As Luís told me later after my conversation with Romero, "There are a lot of guys trying to fit in like that. It's just something you do."

Luís's point that Romero had little time to wear his fashionable clothing was no doubt overstated. Demanding work schedules and a lack of discretionary income certainly often colluded to make migrants feel their lives were nothing more than "from home to work and from work to home." Many migrants I knew found their dreams of *iony* adventure greatly reduced to the consumption of "cheap amusements": renting (or in some cases borrowing) movie videos and watching television (Peiss 1986). Although migrants fortunate enough to own televisions sometimes eschewed Spanish-language networks in order to watch English-speaking channels (a choice many told me was to help them with their English), such adventures in escape were only partial at best.[8] Nevertheless, opportunities for excursions out were not only welcomed distractions, but in some cases hard to ignore. Outings that allowed migrants to forget, if only briefly, their lives as undocumented labor migrants, could be as minor as going window shopping in Manhattan and hanging out with friends at malls or could be more elaborate excursions to entertainment events.

Contributing to the Ecuadorian transnational imagination of a seamless community extending from South America to the United States is the flood of national entertainers who travel to New York to perform for ex-

8. Television also provided a common experience that migrants could share with family members back home. Because of the global reach of large Spanish-speaking networks such as Univisión and Telemundo, men could watch programs that their families were viewing simultaneously. Some migrants told me this activity provided them with a sense of togetherness because they could share their reactions to the program during phone conversations.

patriate audiences. In Queens, announcements for *merengue* and *cumbia* bands, comedy acts, and Ecuadorian dance shows fill the pages of *Ecuador News* and the airwaves of local Latino radio stations. When a particular event caught their eyes or ears, migrants I knew were anxious about the possibilities. However, such events often required a sizeable outlay of cash for the right attire and entrance fees. Although many found these kinds of events out of their budget, subtle pressures from peers to take part often worked to convince them to go. Some, such as Miguel Quispe, dismissed the events as "not for *indocumentados*," however. He spoke from his own experience: "Yeah, I went to one of those shows—a *merengue* group from Guayaquil. Some *monos*[9] worked at the same restaurant I did, and they told me to go. 'It's an all-night party there with the best-looking girls you have ever seen,' [they said]. So I went. What a humiliation! I didn't have the right clothes, and I couldn't afford to drink. After a while they threw me out since I couldn't buy drinks."

Whereas clubs and other venues tended to represent the "other Ecuador" described in the previous chapter—legal, professional, and predominantly coastal in orientation—highland migrants could find alternative social activities that placed them among their peers and equals. In months of good weather, much of immigrant life in Queens revolved around Flushing-Corona Park, located a few train stops from where many Ecuadorians I knew lived. For migrants who worked five and often six days a week, a Saturday or Sunday spent in the park usually constituted their only weekly social engagement. A visit to the park represented a stark departure from the drudgery of work, requiring that they trade their soiled work clothes for more fashionable apparel.

Most would agree that on weekends Flushing was for playing soccer (*fútbol*) (see Sanjek 1998, 225–26). Virtually all migrants grew up playing and attending village soccer matches and spontaneous games of what Ecuadorians call "*indor*."[10] Soccer in Flushing, though, represented a different sport altogether, with a level of sophistication closely tied to commodity consumption and markers of *iony* style. Some prominent

9. Highland Ecuadorians often refer to coastal people as *monos,* or monkeys.

10. Despite the sound of its name, *indor* is soccer played outside, usually on quiet streets and plazas.

Ecuadorian towns and villages, for example, have their own organized migrant soccer teams in the United States, with jerseys and complex game schedules. Although a handful of men I knew played on organized teams, most attested that this level of participation was largely reserved for Ecuadorians *con papeles* (with papers) who had more lenient job schedules and discretionary income to pay club fees, purchase jerseys, and attend all the matches. Even among informal soccer groups, a tacit dress code was enforced for hopeful players. To play often required special shorts, socks, cleats, and jerseys—all apparel and equipment needed as much for play on the field as for socializing afterward.

During a visit to the park I made with Jhonny to see his cousin play soccer, I was warned not to expect much of the game. It was, after all, as he put it, "not a league [*liga*] game." When the game became slow and uninspiring, Jhonny followed with more apologies. Rather than comment on the team's evident lack of athletic prowess, he grew fixated on the team's lack of style. He was embarrassed, he told me, because his cousin was playing in regular street wear and a common T-shirt: "He's tripping around on those street shoes like some Azogueño!"[11] Later, he added, "If you're going to play, you better have the equipment. . . . [It's] a different game in Yoni."

After the game, pressures to consume usually did not end. A day in the park often included indulging in traditional Ecuadorian foods with friends. Along a designated section of the park, vendors sell roasted *cuy* with fried potato cakes *(llapingachos)*, a heaping plate of which can cost as much as $20. Some Ecuadorian journalists and scholars (e.g., Zambrano 1998) have triumphantly written about these food sales as an "Andeanization" of New York, but for many migrants these little touches of home were prohibitively expensive. If migrants I knew purchased food at all, they often split the cost and shared plates.

All told, whether migrants spent large amounts on personal consumption or conserved their earnings and took in only the cheapest of

---

11. Azogueños (residents of Azogues, the provincial capital of Cañar) are considered "Ecuador's Poles." Almost all Ecuadorians know a litany of jokes and humorous stories that highlight Azogueños' supposed ignorance, stupidity, and lack of street smarts.

amusements, they nonetheless collectively confronted a similar reality: their pursuits of the emblems of *iony* modernity and adventure often ran counter to their goal of saving money. Although no men I knew drew such an explicit connection between their desires and their obligations, the tension was no less palpable.

Genders and Spenders

If discretionary income and commodity consumption, however minor, allowed migrants to engage in "imagination as a social practice," to use Arjun Appadurai's words (1996, 31), the economic gymnastics required to make this practice possible often forced men to confront tensions between their pre- and postmigration identities. For example, claims to any kind of *iony* identity often came at the expense of denigrating the campesino life they left behind. Conversely, when men fell short of their expectations of *iony* accumulation, they invariably saw their failures to consume through the disparaging lens of *nuestro folklórico* and the critiques of consumption that often befell their fellow villagers back home. However, just as powerful were the gendered transformations that accompanied migrants' practices of spending and consumption. In their attempts to balance budgets and control spending, men I knew were inadvertently drawn into worlds of money management that in Ecuador would customarily be inhabited only by women. In important ways, adopting new money-management practices had real implications for gendered practice and identity formation *between* men. Nowhere was this result more evident to migrants I knew than in the consumption of alcohol in social situations.

Although couples in Andean communities typically pool their cash incomes, women are the designated *amas de la casa* (household managers) (Alberti 1986; Bourque and Warren 1981; Hamilton 1998, 174–78; McKee 1980; Nuñez del Prado Béjar 1975; Weismantel 1988; Weiss 1988, 7). In Jatundeleg, for instance, both sexes frequently told me that women were "smarter" with money and "más organizadas" (more organized and capable) to manage domestic finances, whereas men were naturally "untamable" *(rebeldes)* with respect to such matters.[12] As "proof," I was often encouraged to observe the female sellers in the market who, in the words of one man, "could add ten or more numbers without writing anything down." In turn, these beliefs structured a particular division of labor that I first glimpsed at work in numerous Jatundeleg households. My neighbor María Dolores Uruchima explained to me matter-of-factly how in her household she and her husband managed their finances:

> My husband works for the *cooperativa* [truck transport] and gets some money every day. It is always a different amount depending on how many customers he has and how far he drives. Sometimes he comes home with a lot, sometime almost nothing—I just have to trust him. I get a little money, too, from selling [milk] that I put in the same pool with his. He usually takes out a little bit of money for his spending, for a little drink [*tragitos*] and cigarettes, but it is not much. I take what is left and buy what we need each week, as well as pay the bills.

Although women's control of money signals a certain degree of female-held power, it is not a benefit without burdens (see, e.g., McKee 1980, 1997; Stølen 1987; Weiss 1988). Writing about gender relations in Quito's poor *barrios populares,* Weiss points out that "wives control the money allocated for consumption not for investment, and this control is delegated" (1988, 7). To be sure, men's ignorance of household finances could easily spark conflict in marriages, and wives grew easily frustrated with husbands who made large purchases irrespective of the domestic budget. For instance, a thirty-year-old woman laughed when I asked her if men helped with shopping. "They wouldn't know what to do!" she exclaimed. "The coste-ñas[13] would rip them off." Another barked, "I would trust my son to shop for me before my husband. My husband wouldn't know an onion from a

12. Paul Gelles provides another take on the essentialized notion of gendered money management from the Peruvian Andes, noting that "women have 'hot hands' *(q'uñi maki)* that hold on to maize and money, whereas men have 'wind hands' *(wayra maki)*" through which money and other goods flow too quickly (2000, 39).

13. *Costeñas,* women from the coastal areas of Ecuador, often come to market days in Azuay and Cañar to sell fruits, vegetables, and fish.

potato." For their part, men in Jatundeleg readily admitted to their lack of knowledge of "how to buy the week" *(comprar la semana),* referring to the totality of women's domestic spending. As men were aware, shopping in the weekly markets requires cunning and skill. Within a chronically unstable economy, women must relentlessly monitor price fluctuations on rice, cooking oil, and other staples so as to judge just the right time to make bulk purchases. Likewise, with unpredictable monthly incomes, women learn how and with which market vendors they can develop lines of credit *(fío).* Attending to these details not only ensures that family members are fed, but also strategically shields husbands from the ups and downs of the household budget, and women will go to great lengths to stretch their pocketbooks. If the truth be told, wives worry that husbands will feel humiliated that their contribution is not sufficient, become angry, and perhaps turn physically abusive (cf. McKee 1992; Weiss 1988, 7).

Among migrant men I knew in Queens, a lack of skills in managing finances—what men typically categorized as *trabajando para plata* (working for money)—surely impeded their ability to budget their money and save for remittances. As previously discussed, going from simply "making a living" *(ganarse la vida)* to working *para plata* required a indiscriminate reconfiguration of both the goals and strategies of earning and saving money. In New York, nowhere perhaps was this transformation more evident than in the times men spent drinking with other men. Here, men's premigration approaches to money management most clearly clashed with the necessities of migration economics.

To understand the importance of alcohol consumption for shaping men's money management as migrants first requires a brief exploration of the centrality of social drinking to men's lives in the Azuayo-Cañari region. Women in Jatundeleg threw up their arms at husbands who made large purchases spontaneously without respecting the domestic budget, but a more worrisome kind of spending included what villagers often glossed as *los vicios,* vices—alcohol, cigarettes, gambling, and, in rare cases, the purchase of prostitutes' services. After men turned over their earnings to their wives, they customarily demanded back a portion for *vicios.* A number of men explained to me that this was their special "reward" for working. Women could reward themselves for work by buying new things for the household, but men found their compensation in sharing alcohol with other men. How much money a man would demand and how often—in other words, how much he wished to reward himself—typically divided households where money spent on *vicios* represented little more than a nuisance from those where it had crippling effects on domestic life. In either case, however, villagers recognized the impact. As an elderly woman in Jatundeleg informed me, "It is women who 'compran la semana,' but it is men ultimately who have the power because they must feed their *vicios.*"

Although by no means causing serious problems for all households, alcohol consumption nonetheless significantly shaped the social lives of Azuayo-Cañari villagers. At Jatundeleg *mingas* and other communal work parties, for instance, women would lace through groups of workers of both sexes, pouring shots of warm *canelazos;* at fiestas, countless jugs of *chicha* animated traditional dances and games. Beyond these occasions, however, in more informal and sometimes less public settings, the form of alcohol consumption differed considerably. Most notably, informal social drinking was the preserve of men. Women rarely imbibed and never in front of children. In Jatundeleg, after wives and children had retired for the evening, otherwise silent nights would often be punctuated by raucous laughter and conversation as men drank in open *salas* and on *tienda* patios. The goal of drinking also changed in these informal contexts. Describing Andean drinking patterns, Penelope Harvey notes that although community drinking serves to "liven up" *(para animarse)* social settings, the goal of informal drinking is inebriation *(para emborracharse),* where "people are expected to drink until they lose consciousness, or are dragged away by a caring child or spouse" (1994, 214–15).[14]

On a number of occasions in Jatundeleg, I found myself partaking, at times unwittingly, in late-night drinking sessions consistent with the latter variety described by Harvey. Drinking typically began with little planning, instead emerging organically at the end of the workday wherever men happened to find themselves congregated. If men should congregate

14. Sánchez-Parga (1997) provides a useful overview of similar drinking patterns in the Ecuadorian Andes.

6.1. Jatundeleg men exchange bottles of Zhumir-brand *aguardiente* at a village festival. Photograph by the author.

at someone's home, drinking often began with a husband signaling to his wife to prepare a batch of *canelazos* or to fetch a bottle of *aguardiente* or a jug of *puro*.[15] Throughout the night, wives and children stayed in earshot of the festivities so as to heed a man's request for more alcohol. When the alcohol ran out, a child would be sent to a *tienda* for more. Hosts often shouldered the expense, although not without the exaggerated protest of guests waving money about, offering to pay. Beyond such gestures of generosity, the etiquette of male drinking in Jatundeleg is quite simple. Once one begins to drink, one should continue to drink as long as others stay the course or until drink mates lose the physical ability to drink more. Refusing a drink or trying to excuse oneself midsession contradicts the central purpose of drinking: to partake in an act of sharing through which community is created and social cohesion is expressed.

15. *Puro* is contraband sugarcane alcohol popular throughout Ecuador. It is considerably less expensive than *aguardiente* and other manufactured liquors and is often sold in used soda bottles and oil jugs.

6.2. *Puro* (sugarcane liquor) sales in a Cañar market. Photograph by the author.

Although it would be misleading to suggest that all Ecuadorian migrants conform to the pattern and purpose of drinking just described, it is reasonable to say that among men I knew in New York City the consumption of alcohol was an arena of meaningful practice, and especially a meaningful practice *between* men. To be sure, migrants I spent time with often mixed drinking with their socializing—after work, in parks, and even sometimes at work. Such instances, however, ultimately obscured the conflictive relationships some men developed with alcohol in an economy of working *para plata*. As Héctor Ayaguasa's answers to my questions on the subject suggest, the meanings of drinking remained the same as they did back in Ecuador, but men's ability to enact them in their new lives had changed.

"*¡Puhh!* Everyone drinks here!" he told me. "There is not much else to do."

"But what about you? Do you drink regularly?"

"When I first arrived, I drank so much. It was unbelievable![. . .]A *paisano* stole bottles of wine—super expensive wine—from the Italian restaurant where he worked. We would have little parties all the time. That was when I was working on the streets."

As Héctor later elaborated, working as an *esquinero* allowed him a degree of freedom to spend multiple days drinking. When he finally sobered up and returned to work, he paid his dues by taking extra shifts so as to save enough money still.

Héctor explained, "The reason I drank was because I was lonely. I didn't like it here, and I missed my family so. I had a long beard at the time, and I would think about how my wife would comb and stroke it. I would do it myself with my bottle in hand. I was so lonely, and there was nothing else for me to. . . . But I can't do that now."

"And now? You're not so lonely. Do you still drink much?"

"[Laughing] Sometimes yes. It's crazy, but you won't succeed. Sometimes, still, I will meet some friends, and we will be listening to some Ecuadorian music, and we'll have a few *tragitos* and that will be it. It has to be. I can't miss work. Yes, the life disciplines us [Sí, la vida nos castiga]."

Héctor's experiences with alcohol, including binges, drinking to combat depression, and eventually his almost complete abstinence from alcohol, were echoed in other migrants' stories of drinking. Others concluded that all-night sessions of imbibing with the express goal of getting drunk were quite simply costly affairs because each finished bottle called for a fresh one. Even the cheapest bottles of the alcohol could add up quickly in a night of drinking. In the United States, prices for Ecuadorian liquors—especially brands of poor-quality sugarcane *aguardiente* favored by campesinos, such as Zhumir and Cristal—were particularly high. (A Korean liquor store owner in Queens laughed all the way to the bank when I told him the price he charged for bottles of Zhumir represented a 100 percent markup from the cost in Ecuador.) Consequently, few men I queried continued to play host the way they may have back in their home village. One migrant even pointed out to me a New York State law that restricts the sale of single cigarettes. If he wished to drink and smoke, he told me, he had to buy a whole pack, then watch it be depleted by his fellow drinkers.[16] More costly than the money spent on alcohol, though, was the potential for missed work. As many migrants knew quite well, a long night of drinking could mean a long day of recovery, like falling ill. Even a single day without work could seriously derail scheduled remittances.

Not everyone, of course, shared Héctor's spendthrift approach. Rather, different drinking styles and priorities often placed migrants at odds with one another. Matthew Gutmann's description of drinking patterns in a working-class neighborhood of Mexico City fits the Ecuadorian Andes as well: "Coercion to drink among men is a standard element of drinking habits" (1996, 184). As was the case in Jatundeleg, men who attempted to cut out in the middle of drinking sessions in New York consistently found themselves embroiled in tense situations because they risked offending fellow drinkers. In particular, refusing a drink or making a gesture to leave a drinking session despite the cajoling to do otherwise could imply a lack of trust and a denial of mutual respect. Among migrants in New York whose social networks were typically small and tightly knit (often consisting of only roommates and fellow workers), and who perpetually brought the stresses of their undocumented lives into drinking sessions, the stakes were markedly high at times, and the likelihood of conflict frequent. My own interest in witnessing the intensity of these moments I heard so much about from migrant confidants was unfortunately never satisfied. Instead, the handful of participant-observation opportunities I had to drink with men were often stamped with an air of celebration where migrants temporarily suspended their restricted drinking behaviors to entertain (and I suppose be entertained by) the anthropologist.[17] Nonetheless, an incident

16. The sale of single cigarettes at *tiendas* in Jatundeleg is a critical component of male socializing. When a man arrives at a *tienda* where another male customer is already present, invariably one buys the other a cigarette.

17. This situation raises a crucial point. Not all drinking is informal. At times, migrants I knew attended festivities celebrating birthdays, holidays, and imminent departures *(despididas)* back to Ecuador. During such events, drinking patterns more closely resembled patterns back in Ecuador, with a clearly defined host. These kinds of events were the exception, however.

Miguel Quispe shared with me captures a familiar predicament that resonated with other migrants.

Miguel told me what happened when he began to restrict his drinking in an attempt to "better manage" *(mandar bien)* his finances and to save money *(guardar plata)*. Although he never stopped drinking altogether, a definitive change came after what he described as a month-long drinking binge *(borrachera)* in which he paid little attention to his finances. He could not pay a gas utility bill (presumably already past due), and his service was abruptly disconnected even though it was the middle of January. With minimal English-speaking abilities, Miguel did not understand the conditions of the shutoff and failed to get his service reinstated. "Usually I just pay the things when they come—I don't read what's written there. It's totally confusing. I didn't have heat for a month. I should have just paid it, but I couldn't. That was it."[18] Miguel's decision to curb his drinking became problematic one Sunday afternoon when he joined friends for beers on the patio of a friend's apartment after work. Miguel told himself he would share only a couple of beers with friends. When the other men in attendance decided to pool their money together for a bottle of rum, he plotted his exit strategy. "When they were planning to buy the rum, I said I had to go. I needed to make some calls. No one, though, believed me. They started saying I never spent any time with them. They wondered if I was really so busy or if I had just become stingy." Others migrants shared with me the less salutary remarks and hostility they received when they attempted to bow out of drinking sessions. A twenty-seven-year-old migrant from a village outside of Cuenca reenacted the response he slung back at a fellow migrant who called him a *mandarina* (sissy)[19] when he refused to keep drinking.

18. Miguel encountered a situation that undocumented migrants commonly face when dealing with utility companies. When he moved into his apartment, the utilities were already connected under a previous tenant's name. When the heat was shut off and Miguel went to reinstate it himself, he had to reapply. Yet because he did not possess previous housing and credit information, his application was initially denied. He ultimately was able to use his place of work and his employer as a reference to get the service reinstated.

19. See chap. 7 and note 2 in that chapter for a fuller discussion and definition of *mandarina*.

We were having a typical day, like any other, just drinking and having fun. Laughing and listening to music. Some guys were already drunk, as they always were. . . . They never worked it seemed, and they would be asking you for money. . . . You had to be careful. But with friends, it is different. You buy drinks for them, and they buy for you. Nobody is taking advantage of others [*no aprovechándose*].You just don't think about it. . . . Usually if I told myself I wasn't drinking, I would not drink—period. I know they wouldn't care, but I don't want them to think I'm taking advantage of them. There were a few guys, though, that would not leave me alone. One told me, "Come on, stay and have a few drinks." He was drunk and kept pushing me. He said, "Come on, *mandarina*," and then I got angry. . . . You can't imagine. I told him, "What about you? I have a family to feed and my kids back home. I'm not some macho, but I am not a *mandarina*." He has no kids, no wife. *He* is the one that has to be careful that he's not a *mandarina* or a *maricón* [homosexual].

More than just pragmatic concerns about saving money caused disagreements over alcohol. Selective abstinence also ran counter to a set of particularly male values that lay behind drinking styles and motivations. The conspicuous consumption of alcohol between men undoubtedly served as a "means to reputability" (Veblen 1953, 43), but status was not the only thing at play here. As other ethnographic explorations of male drinking hint, alcohol consumption, beyond defining relations between men, equally allows men to *become men* and to enact fundamental qualities of what it means to be a man (see Day, Papataxiarchis, and Stewart 1999, 13; Karp 1980). In a comparative framework, Ecuadorian patterns of alcohol use parallel Karp's portrayal of drinking by men among the Iteso (East Africa) insofar as drinking constitutes a "managed accomplishment [that] recapitulate[s] the social order of which [men] are a part" (1980, 113). The social order that Ecuadorian drinking has long recapitulated is fraught with uncertainty and potential instability. As men in both Jatundeleg and New York could attest, they drank together largely in mutual recognition of the uncertainties of life. Acknowledging that they could "make a living" and do their share to provide for their families, they often worried about their positions as breadwinners.

My ability to understand the tacit meanings behind male social drinking developed most clearly as I listened to men speak of the gendered division of labor between husbands and wives. As one man explained, "Yes, it is true men and women own the fields, and men and women work the fields. But if the fields don't produce and there is no harvest, families will blame the man. It is his responsibility. Although they [other people] may not say it, they certainly think it. So do the men. But what can you do? [Men's work] is uncertain. It's destiny [*destino*], a lottery [*una lotería*]." Similarly, a common expression I heard men use to describe their seemingly erratic behavior aptly captures the ethos that defined drinking among men: "Pan para hora y hambre para mañana" (Bread for today and hunger for tomorrow). The saying suggests that it is better to indulge in what you have now (bread being a luxury item) because you do not know what tomorrow will bring.

Among many migrants I knew in New York, especially those who had left wives and children in Ecuador, I ultimately noticed a different kind of perspective forming around the priorities of saving money and generating remittances. During conversations with migrants about their money-saving strategies, I grew accustomed to their critiques of some men whom they faulted for "squandering money" *(derrechondo la plata)* and for not being able to generate remittances. Borrowing the language of economics, migrants spoke triumphantly of their efforts to "make savings" *(hacer economías)* or "to hold on to money" *(guardar plata)*. In his discussion of changing gender roles in Mexico City, Matthew Gutmann introduces the term *degendering* to refer to the ways in which "activities become less (or more) gendered—less (or more) identified with women or men in particular" (1996, 151). In part, the taking hold of household finances represented for some migrant men a process of degendering because they did not necessarily identify their meticulous attention to finances as either men's or women's duties. However, a refined analysis of this transformation might also demonstrate a kind of *regendering*, a reassigning of the role of money manager to themselves in a particularly masculine form. Indeed, the economic shift of rural agri-artisan households to migration-based households often resulted in a reshuffling that positioned men as the primary breadwinners, especially as average monthly remittances could easily double a family's income and prompt households to discontinue previous money-generating work.

Migrant husbands and fathers abroad responded to their new breadwinner roles with a mixture of ambivalence, fear, and pride. As Miguel Quispe presented the situation to me, it was "simplemente la chulla vida," and there was little choice in the matter but to accept his position. As he described, "Everyone can work, that's simple. But for men who are fathers and have families back home it is different. You can't stop. You have to change your mentality. Men who do this are hombres más modernos y progresivos. They can't just drink and hope it will all work out. No, it's a different mentality." Miguel's construction of himself as a man "more modern and up-to-date" was echoed by others in both New York and Ecuador. Men drew upon comparisons with their own fathers as a foil to describe how they had become men "más moderno y progresivo." Although the comparison often hinged on criteria such as fathers who drank too much or never helped wives with domestic tasks, money management equally took center stage in these moments of identity construction. However, for many men in Miguel's position, the situation was hardly worth bragging about. Instead, being an "hombre más moderno y progresivo" entailed performing a juggling act with high stakes.

Most of the men I interviewed could tell me at least one story about a migrant who had failed in his pursuits to generate remittances. Likewise, migrants stayed abreast of the gossip that filtered back from their home villages telling of *chulqueros* who had usurped people's land and of families left hungry when husbands failed to wire remittances. Men in these situations often felt anxious and debilitated, at times in embodied ways, as one migrant father's testimony demonstrates:

> I had just counted my week's money and again and again. Very fast! [n.b.: Earlier we had discussed how he did not have enough money to send home yet.] I just shut my eyes and wished I could go back [to Ecuador]. I would farm and work my land. I didn't care. . . . But I knew I couldn't. I had to stay and work. I tried to calm my trembling heart down, but I couldn't. I knew it would be alright. I would be *tranquilo* again, but for

the moment I was struck with the *nervios.* I couldn't move, and there was a pain throughout my body.[20]

In addition to the pressures of unwittingly assuming the role of primary breadwinner, the challenge of being a man "más moderno y progresivo" also divorced migrants from the frequent and often ritualistic acts that enacted Ecuadorian manhood. To the extent to which drinking allowed men to identify their shared vulnerabilities with one another while simultaneously affording them an instant reward for hard work, doing away with that behavior in order to save money ultimately delayed these gratifications. Between these competing constructions of men's identities, migrants were often at pains to find new ways to define their sense of manhood. In their search, other forms of consumption often took central stage.

Consumption "Más Moderno y Progresivo": Shopping, Giving Gifts, and "Producing Locality"

If migrants I knew kept to a strict budget, they typically had some extra money to buy things for themselves, such as CDs, a pair of trendy jeans, or a nylon athletic jacket. However, few would say that their dreams of *iony* modernity had been fulfilled or even partially satisfied by this petty consumerism. At some point during their time abroad, many faced the reality that despite their attempts at urban adventure, such efforts were often mere pale reflections of the perceptions of life in the United States they had formed before migrating. In the same way that they accepted the fact that controlling spending on *vicios* was necessary to generate remittances, they also watched as money spent on new clothing, CDs, and the like gobbled up discretionary income that could be remitted back to Ecuador. In the face of such realities, the characterization of themselves as "hombres más modernos y progresivos" provided only partial reconciliation. Still, beyond sending remittances,

---

20. In the Ecuadorian Andes, *nervios* is a condition that typically afflicts only women (see, for example, Finerman 1989). The fact that this migrant claimed he fell victim to *nervios,* thus essentially assuming a feminized subject position, may suggest the strong degree to which he understood his failure to generate remittances as a gendered failure.

migrants did find opportunities, if only briefly, when they could bring into alignment their identities as husbands and fathers with their quest for *iony* modernity, creating a self-image that more closely approximated the construction of "hombres más modernos y progresivos." In particular, these moments were when migrants sent special gifts to their families, intended for specific recipients and often shipped at key times of the year (holidays, birthdays, confirmation parties, etc.). For undocumented migrants largely unable to find outlets for status in their transplanted communities, the act of remitting gifts—and the accompanying tasks of shopping, packaging gifts up with letters, and receiving family members' reactions to their purchases—helped men to look toward their home communities and produce a coherent identity of themselves as successful migrants, committed husbands, and attentive fathers.

A number of migration researchers have pointed out that, along with remittances and other essentials (medicines, for instance), gifts form a significant portion of the goods that travel along national and transnational flows (Cliggett 2005; Ghannam 1999; Levitt 1998; Mahler 1999; Parreñas 2001; Salih 2002). Among female transnational migrants who leave children back home, gifts have been shown to supplement and sometimes replace other forms of provisioning that constitute culturally specific definitions of mothering (Hondagneu-Sotelo and Avila 1997; Parreñas 2001). In some instances, gifts double as assets when migrants purchase and send home jewelry and other items that hold their value against unstable currencies (Gamburd 2000). In some Latin American contexts with long histories of transnational migration and where migrants shuttle with frequency between host and home communities, returning with gifts has been studied as an important component of how migrants successfully reenter into social relationships fraught with tensions (Fletcher 1999; Georges 1990; Levitt 1998). The Ecuadorian migrants I knew sent gifts for all of these reasons—to maintain status, enact parenthood, and generate assets. Without papers and financial resources, very few migrants could hope to accompany their gift sending with a visit home as in other migration contexts. Sending specific gifts therefore assumed an all-important role as one of the only acts men could perform from afar to stay connected to their home communities.

For men in Jatundeleg, aside from the exchanging of personal items in courtship, gift giving does not form an important part of the building and maintaining of affective relations with kin or friends and neighbors. In particular, few men in their capacity as fathers and husbands routinely give gifts to their immediate family. As usually described to me, men in their role as fathers provide generally for children, but do not make specific purchases. As one man in the village explained to me, "If he [my father] had, say, an apple or pear, he would split it into fourths so that every kid could have a portion. But that was it. He was tough, but he watched out for us and made sure we were provided for. The fathers today are más modernos y progresivos. They know what their kids want. They know better how to meet their needs." However, for migrants in New York, shopping and gift buying were more than ways to affirm their identities in their home communities. They were also welcomed activities against the backdrop of the rest of their lives. When I asked men about their leisure time, I was surprised to find them list among their limited choices *vitrinear* (window-shopping). This activity usually took place not in front of the famous Manhattan window displays, but rather in the more familiar surroundings of the migrants' own Queens neighborhoods.

Window-shopping was oftentimes purposeful as men worked to fulfill the requests of family members back home. When I first met Luís Uruchima, he was obsessed with getting his hands on anything that made reference to the Chicago Bulls or Michael Jordan for his seven-year-old son back in Jatundeleg. Unlicensed Michael Jordan paraphernalia could be easily and inexpensively purchased in almost any Azuayo-Cañari market, but the request from his son was for *cosas auténticas* (authentic goods). Discussing the mission before him, Luís emphasized his power of choice and the knowledge of his son's preferences rather than his mere ability to purchase goods for his family. Likewise, other migrants put almost as much care into the letters they wrote and packed along with the gifts. Inserted in cardboard boxes of otherwise impersonal gifts items, letters reading like laundry lists would outline what gift was for whom and sometimes why. Victor Saldañes agreed to be interviewed only if I would help him construct such a letter. We talked one afternoon as he sorted through a pile of gifts for his wife and children. Victor became adamant that each gift be labeled with its own proper English-language name. Like a linguistic anthropologist, he repeatedly asked me to clarify the names of the things he was sending—"What do you call this?" "What is another name for this?"—as he matched an authentic name with its *cosa auténtica*. Next to the name of each item, he also scribbled the name of the recipient.

Although men's consumption habits were shaped by their desires to fulfill family needs, shopping and commodity consumption everywhere is never a one-way street. Desires to shop must be created and sustained through persuasive advertising. As Arlene Dávila (2001) has shown, Latinos, especially recently arrived immigrants, are now squarely on Madison Avenue's radar. The content of much "Latino" advertising, whether it is for specific Latino products (Goya foods, for example) or clearly American brand names (McDonald's restaurants), is almost always the same: focused around an imagined solidarity of the "Latin American family" and nostalgia for Latin American homelands. In heavily immigrant-saturated regions such as Queens, this type of advertising is further localized and pitched to transnational audiences in particular.

For men I knew, the business that most captured their attention was Créditos Económicos, a binational department store specializing in household appliances whereby goods could be shopped for and purchased in New York, but delivered to their home communities from a warehouse in Ecuador. To keep costs down, many Créditos products were fully assembled in Ecuador. A range, for example, could be purchased for less than $80; refrigerators sold for less than $300. The men saved additional money because the goods did not have to be shipped from the United States, thus sidestepping the taxes collected on goods entering the country. Delivery was also free, and payment plans were available to make it possible even for the poorest of migrants to purchase their products.

The Queens branch of Créditos Económicos on Roosevelt Avenue was situated among an assortment of Ecuadorian money-wiring agencies, restaurants, and Latino music shops. However, in considerable contrast to these businesses, it always maintained an extremely clean exterior. It also had none of the long lines, complicated transactions, and general client frustrations that migrants associated with money-wiring and shipping services. In short, it offered a qualitatively different shopping experience from what most migrants were typically accustomed to having. To be sure, for many migrants, Créditos represented the opposite of the decidedly unglamorous world of thrift shops, where they would through unsorted bins of used clothing in search of *iony* styles. Créditos instead afforded poor migrants a shopping experience they closely associated with both middle-class Ecuadorians and Americans, complete with a helpful and courteous sales staff.

Romero, Luís Uruchima's roommate introduced earlier in this chapter, was one of the migrants who discussed his trip to Créditos with me. His story about purchasing a range for his wife and family back home centered on his shopping experience: "This woman—a beautiful *costeña*—came right up to help me. She was calling me 'sir' and acting polite. I was nervous since I didn't know what to do. I don't know about stoves and microwaves. . . . But she helped me. . . . I told her I couldn't pay for it all at once, and she directed me toward a payment plan." Romero's dark skin and "*cholo* boy" look (baggy sweatshirt and baseball cap pulled over his head) would surely have disadvantaged him if he had visited a department store in Cuenca.

6.3. Shops and services along Roosevelt Avenue in Queens. Photograph by the author.

During my many visits to Créditos, both alone and with migrant men on their shopping adventures, it was hard to miss the store's keen ability to target customers by playing on their desires to "produce locality" in their home communities. At any one time, the front windows of Créditos Económicos were decorated with dozens of three-by-five snapshots of the proud recipients of their products. The majority of pictures featured rural households of the Azuayo-Cañari region with campesinas in *pollera* skirts and their children standing next to refrigerators, ranges, and stereo systems. In some of the photos, children were shown literally hugging their new acquisitions within the confines of wattle-and-daub walls and dirt floors. In the front windows, pictures of *maíz* fields and *pollera*-clad campesinas became part of a seamless whole that includes elegantly dressed white Ecuadorian women working over shiny new stoves. Images of *nuestro folklórico* were nowhere to be found. As opposed to the case in Ecuador, the Créditos pastiche of "objects-in-motion"—mixing the traditional and modern, if commodified—was to be celebrated rather than denigrated (cf. Mankekar 2002).

6.4. Close-up of Créditos Económicos front-window display in Queens showing families in Ecuador next to their new appliances. Photograph by the author.

At Christmas time, Créditos launches into an aggressive sales mode, offering rock-bottom prices and guaranteeing holiday delivery in Ecuador, even with only a week's notice. The sign in the front window in December 2000 pronounced in bold letters, "Entregamos sus electro-domésticos a cualquier parte del Ecuador" (We ship your household appliances to any part of Ecuador). By combining symbols of rural Andean life with those of *iony* modernity, Créditos helps migrants temporarily to synthesize their own personal desires for a modern lifestyle with their obligations to family and their need to maintain status in their home communities.

Although the act of slipping a piece of jewelry into an envelope or mailing a box of baseball caps and athletic jerseys could go unnoticed by all those beyond the immediate recipients in their home communities, migrants took advantage of the particularly public reception that goods delivered by Créditos could offer. Foremost, they tried to coordinate the sending of gifts with special holidays. On a rainy Mother's Day in 1999, I witnessed the delivery of a new range to a migrant household in Ayaloma. The house was one of the village's oldest, and the new range look awkward situated next to an open fire pit. The event, as I recorded it in my field notes, unfolded as follows:

> Three women—a mother in her late thirties and her two sisters—rushed quickly out of doors to watch as the delivery truck chugged up the badly washed-out dirt road to their doorway. The women's children, five in total, followed up the rear screaming with excitement. The truck was easily recognizable as a Créditos delivery vehicle with its square box container emblazoned with the company's logo embedded in wavy folds of an American flag and shooting fireworks. As soon as the vehicle came to a halt and the driver set the brake, the children swarmed around the truck. The deliveryman stepped out and quickly went to unhitch and raise the back door, exposing a brand-new range. The loud crash from the door as it was being released caught the attention of other children playing across the way, and they quickly ran over to see what all the excitement was about. As the deliveryman removed the range from his dolly in the kitchen, he began to describe the features of the shiny chrome Ecuadorian-made Indurama *electro-doméstico,* complete with self-cleaning features and a selection of special racks. The children of the migrant wife

who was receiving the stove moved in closer, apparently to watch the overjoyed expression on their mother's face as the deliveryman demonstrated the oven's many uses, including a special rotisserie feature that he noted would "perfectly prepare *cuy.*" Handed a tumbler full of *trago*, I joined the three women and the deliveryman in a toast to Mother's Day, and then [in] another to the migrant husband in New York who had purchased the range. By this point, curious neighbors—men, women, and more children—came to ogle at the new range. The women's children pointed to a picture of their father that hung on the wall, explaining that he lived in New York but would be returning soon. After taking a couple more shots of *trago,* the deliveryman asked the wife and her children to pose for a picture in front of the new acquisition. The youngest child was given the responsibility of holding up a red cardboard sign with "Créditos Económicos" printed across the front. The deliveryman explained to me how the husband had placed the order in Queens with specific instructions to snap the photo. Already late in the afternoon on Mother's Day, he still had to deliver three more *electro-domésticos* to the wives of migrants, all of which were purchased in the same manner.

6.5. Créditos Económicos delivery truck. Photograph by the author.

Migrant Consumption

When the migrant husband who orchestrated the delivery of the new range to his family in Ayaloma received a copy of the photograph, he no doubt relished, in his relatively inexpensive act of sending, a far-reaching statement about migrant success, a claim to *iony* modernity, and a continued commitment to his family. But how best to analyze these practices and their results? Throughout this chapter, I have suggested different ways in which the practices of saving, budgeting, and consuming provide clues to the construction of men's identities as migrants. For undocumented Ecuadorians in New York City, consumption must be analyzed as more than simply a new "domain of choice" otherwise absent in their premigration lives. Daniel Miller proposes that consumption practices are perhaps better seen as scarce resources people appropriate as they seek to form and sustain affective relationships. "[I]ncreasingly people have *no choice*," Miller writes, "but to focus on consumption as the only remaining domain in which there are possibilities of sublation" (1987, 221, emphasis added). Indeed, for migrants physically separated from their families, increasingly divorced from other forms of meaningful exchange such as male drinking, and limited in their abilities to generate satisfying identities and statuses for themselves in U.S. society, transnational consumption arguably becomes one of the few avenues for them to create a sense of self and society in their lives.

As this chapter demonstrates, the consumption practices of migrants I knew were motivated by a variety of factors. At one level, consumption fulfilled purely instrumental goals. Sending gifts or orchestrating an *electrodoméstico* delivery by Créditos Económicos acted as an inexpensive means for migrants to create status for themselves in their home community and to maintain a respectful position in village affairs. Although it might take months to generate what most men would consider a sufficient remittance amount, a gift, even a new oven or range, could be delivered for much less. In some cases, the gifts often became representative of economic capital migrants did not otherwise have.

However, when migrants such as Miguel and Luís purchased gifts for their families, their actions reflected affective as well as instrumental purposes. Commodity consumption and the act of shopping also spoke to relationships between people—between the giver and receiver of the gift (Mauss 1967). As Miller proposes, the practice of shopping in complex societies mimics an act of sacrifice and therefore takes on the qualities of a devotional rite. Locating the essence of sacrifice in the activity of "construct[ing] the divine as a desiring subject," Miller promotes the seemingly mundane act of shopping to a purposeful one carried out "not so much to buy the things people want, but to strive to be in a relationship with subjects that want those things" (1998, 148). Among migrants who shared with me the dilemmas involved in saving, budgeting, and spending money, specific consumption decisions (saving money for remittances, buying a child a gift, or spending money on alcohol) often revealed important aspects of their relationships with others. But commodity consumption differs from the cementing of relationships in a gift economy. Miller argues that commodities have largely replaced the gift because relationships in modernity are no longer rooted in fixed social categories. In the range of choices of what kinds of gifts to purchase, modern shoppers can exploit selection in order to "negotiate the ambivalences and anxieties of relationships" (1998, 154). In this regard, migrants' simple acts of money management speak to more than just the need to balance their desires for *iony* modernity with the obligation to generate remittances. They also reveal the ways migrants seek to reconstitute transnational relationships, including conjugal relationships, as the next chapter explores.

7

Aprendemos a Convivir

Conjugal Relations, Coparenting, and Transnational Lives

convivir (v.): to live together; to coexist; to exist side by side
   —*The Oxford Spanish Dictionary*

Conecte tus sentimientos [Connect your sentiments].
      —Sprint billboard advertising international long
         distance, Cañar province, Ecuador, 1999

Help us to remain together despite the distance.
      —Prayer scrawled on the interior wall of the Sanctuary
         of the Señor de Andacocha, 2000

During my interviews with male Ecuadorian migrants working in Queens, as well as in their home communities in the Andes, discussions frequently moved to the topics of family, fatherhood, and the difficulty of maintaining the two during their long stints abroad. During one particular conversation with five migrant men who had recently returned to Jatundeleg, I asked the following question: "While you were abroad in the United States, what part of your life here was hardest to keep intact?"

Instantly, thirty-three-year-old Manuel Pañora blurted out a response: "Remaining a *matrimonio* [married couple], of course." By the looks on the others' faces and their affirmative nods, Manuel's fellow villagers appeared to agree with him and quickly followed up with their own comments.

"For me it was being able to keep my wife as my wife," added Roberto, a handsome twenty-six-year-old who spent four years in the United States.

245

"Living apart as husband and wife," Miguel Solano confirmed, commenting on his experiences of having spent both time alone and briefly with his wife in the United States.

From my early fieldwork experiences talking with villagers about cases of HIV/AIDS among returned migrants, I was familiar with stories concerning men's infidelities abroad. I decided to push the issue. "You mean staying faithful and not meeting other women? Is that what you mean?" The men laughed, some nervously, as a silent truth was spoken.

"Oh yeah. There is a lot of that," Luís Sinchi answered matter-of-factly. "Many guys—" but before he could finish, Miguel interjected with a clarification, lest the conversation do little more than recycle stereotypes of machismo.

"Well, maybe that too," he interrupted, "but it is something else. When I left, I had a good relationship with my wife, but in the United States, our relationship was not always so good. The distance is hard. You have to work at it on account that everything changes. The man changes; the woman changes. There is a whole change of mentality [*cambio de mentalidad*]. We learn to live in harmony with one another [Aprendemos a convivir conjuntos]."

In arguments regarding the deleterious effects of international migration, local critics, largely composed of Cuencan journalists, social scientists, and regional Catholic leaders, repeatedly point to rising incidences of spousal abandonment and divorce as among the primary casualties of high levels of male out-migration. Although actual figures of divorce in migrant-sending communities are difficult to substantiate and even more difficult to link concretely to out-migration, there is no denying the visible stresses and strains that migration places on marital relationships. Indeed, families I knew best in Jatundeleg would often acknowledge with considerable lament that as much as migration could help fulfill their dreams, it also could crush them when marriage unions could not withstand the separation. In Jatundeleg, Ayaloma, and Shullín, it seemed that nearly everyone could recite a story of how the pressures of migration had driven a wedge into a marriage. Some of the most painful cases involved women such as Gloria (see chapter 1), whose husband abandoned her to marry a female coworker he met in Queens, leaving

Gloria to raise their young child without the aid of remittances. Other unions ended with no explanation at all. Husbands simply stopped communicating with wives altogether, cut off ties to their home villages, and ceased to remit money. In New York City, a telling reminder of the strains migration placed on marriage were the handful of "multiserv" businesses along Queens' Roosevelt Avenue that helped migrants with rapid and affordable divorces from afar.

Although spousal abandonment, separation, and divorce are inevitable results of any migration situation, they alone cannot adequately explain how migration affects conjugal relationships. With respect to the Ecuadorian case, these negative outcomes are not even likely to tell the story of the majority of couples and families. Indeed, focusing too heavily on relationships that do not weather the trials of migration misses many of the nuances surrounding the ways in which men's mobility and women's reactions to it transform, reorient, and reprioritize conjugal relationships. Facile critiques by Cuencan experts regarding the disintegration of marriage have often led to laundry lists of the negative ramifications of migration on family life, with little ethnographic elaboration to explain them. For instance, with respect to failed marriages, few critics scrutinize the quality of a couple's premigration relationship and the possibility that migration may in fact help some women move out of untenable marital situations. Although my analysis acknowledges the positive benefits of this kind of separation, the more germane ethnographic issue tackled here concerns how *intact* couples work to redefine conjugal relationships and, in some cases, family life in transnational space.

As I argue, for many couples stretched between New York City and Ecuador's Azuayo-Cañari highlands, migration serves to reorient and question commonsensical and taken-for-granted gender roles and ideologies as both men and women work to fit their daily routines into the new rules and priorities of maintaining a transnational livelihood. In particular, two related processes occur. First, migration alters "traditional" roles, divisions of labor, and meaningful categories of gender construction. Simply put, male migrants now in charge of their own domestic lives come to assume many traditionally female roles, and women take on many of the tasks once carried out by their husbands. But, as Miguel Solano and others described to me, maintaining marriages transnationally requires more than simply accommodating to new roles. Beyond having to deal with the "degendering" of tasks assigned to men and women, couples must learn to work in tandem, to "learn to exist side by side" *(aprender a convivir)* in their conjugal relationships in order to meet their migration goals. What ultimately counts as "success" for many migrant households—minimally defined as a couple's ability to "get ahead" with remittances—depends as much or more on wives' ability to work with husbands to orchestrate household affairs and handle remittances as it does on husbands' labor abroad. The present discussion rejoins themes developed over the previous two chapters, focusing on the ways men's accommodations to lives as migrant laborers constitute gendered transformations. I follow this discussion with a similar kind of examination of the gendered experiences of women living without husbands in the migrant-sending villages of the Azuayo-Cañari highlands. Juxtaposing the experiences of husbands abroad and the experiences of their wives in Ecuador reveals subtle ways that couples negotiate the uncharted waters of maintaining a transnational relationship. The second half of the chapter moves from the general to the specific by returning to where this book began: a look into the migrant household headed up by Carmela Quispe and Miguel Pomaguiza. A close reading of their history together highlights the processual qualities of how husband and wife learn "to exist side by side" one another despite some of the challenges posed by migration.

Men's Domesticity in New York City

Among Carmela's collection of photos of her husband, Miguel, and his brothers in Queens, one picture stood out as her favorite. The photo shows Miguel standing in the tiny kitchen of his shared New York City apartment with his back to a sink of dirty dishes, his arms raised to accentuate a pair of yellow rubber gloves pulled over his hands. Carmela made it clear that the picture was contrived—that Miguel had staged it with some friends. This small fact, however, did little to blemish the meaning she found in the photo. Carmela treasured the picture because, to her, it was a commentary about the ways in which migration was changing men.

"The men here they don't do anything in the kitchen. There they do," she chuckled. "Look at him working like a dog!" Carmela, like other wives left behind, expressed delight at stories of their husbands experiencing the drudgery abroad that they themselves knew at home. The fact that the men remained "macho" made it all the better. Jatundeleg wives especially enjoyed sharing stories about their migrant spouses attending to their own laundry, cooking, and cleaning.

Matthew Gutmann has pointed out that "[just as] women's gender identities are constructed in the workplace as much as in the home . . . so conversely we must grasp that men's gender identities are developed and transformed in the home and not just in sites considered to be the typical male reserves, like factories, cantinas, and political forums" (1996, 147). In the Ecuadorian Andes, ethnographers have provided only brief glimpses of men helping with domestic tasks (Hamilton 1998; McKee 1980; Stølen 1987, 170). Men hold babies, watch children, and prepare meals, yet these tasks for them are often fleeting. Indeed, ethnographers often note that men help wives only when there is no other choice, such as in the period after wives have given birth. Men's hesitation to perform domestic tasks is closely associated with the public exercise of male power, as other scholars of gender in the Andes have discussed (Harvey 1994; McKee 1980; Weiss 1988). Ideally, men's relationships with wives and children are to be structured around the idiom of *respeto* (respect). Women and children are to obey husbands and fathers, allowing them to rule *(mandar)* as they wish as long as they provide for the household. A woman shows her respect and loyalty to her husband by bearing children and raising them. As one wife told me, "A man can beat his wife, be a drunk, and pay no attention to his children. But if he can provide for family and his family gives him respect, he is a considered a good man." To be seen by others performing domestic duties alone or alongside wives or children can send a message about the breakdown of *respeto* and the loss of a man's mandate to rule.[1] Men especially fear the biting remarks by male counterparts who are quick to affix the label *mandarina* (one who is controlled by another) to men who have

---

1. Men will also frequently shy away from displaying affection to wives and older children in public for the same reason.

lost respect.[2] Men I knew spoke convincingly of how being labeled a *mandarina,* in addition to applying the sting of ridicule, opened the door for other men to take advantage of them in local affairs and business dealings. Women could thus pay sorely for placing men in positions where they appear as *mandarinas,* with physical abuse *(maltrato)* being an all too common response (see Bourque and Warren 1981, 105; McKee 1991; Stølen 1987). Rosario Saldañes, who welcomed her elderly station in life when "men no longer care so much about their status," told me how in the past her husband would regularly beat her when he felt he was placed in a compromised position:

> I was a good wife. . . . But when I would leave to the *cerro* to feed the animals, I would worry what would happen. If the baby awakes and cries will he [my husband] grow angry? What will he do? So I would climb up the hill as quick as I could to do my work, wishing the whole time that he doesn't have to pick up and console the baby. If I could not get back soon, he would be angry and sometimes beat me. That is just how it was. But as an old man he is sweet and caring. He holds his grandchildren and thinks nothing of it.

Migrants I knew in Queens attended to their domestic tasks and errands *(quehaceres)* because they had no other choice. On their days off, they attended to tasks they could not accomplish within their busy workweek schedules. This day also typically constituted the only day I could schedule interviews with migrants, and my persistent questions served as welcomed distractions from the tedium accompanying cleaning floors, washing clothes, and cooking.

Men's attention to domestic duties that they associated with women in Ecuador ushered in a new level of awareness of the gendered nature of work that otherwise might be routinely understood as natural and unchanging.

2. Lauris McKee provides a layered etymology of the word *mandarina:* "[A] complex play on words that associates the name of a fruit (tangerine, also called a *mandarina*) with the verb *mandar* ('to command, to give orders') combined with a false 'feminine' ending *-ina.* The result can be loosely rendered as 'a fruit of a man who allows himself to be ordered by a bossy woman'" (1980, 59).

Their newfound roles as migrants brought out new appreciation, if not respect, for the work women perform in rural highlands households. One young migrant, a twenty-two-year-old husband and father, shared with me his experience washing his own clothes at a laundry:

> I take my clothes down there in the morning and put them all in [the machine] with some soap. I just throw them in. You know, it's so easy. When the women [back home] do the laundry, that's tough work. They carry the heavy bundles of clothes down to the river, and if the river is muddy, they can't do it. When they can, they are there all day . . . bam, bam, bam, beating the clothes clean on the rocks. Then you got to haul it all back and hang it up to dry. It's also frustrating work. If it rains, she has to run quickly and take the clothes off the line. She might do that two, three times a week before they get dry.

Similarly, cooking brought migrant men into the heart of women's working world. For men I knew in Queens, cooking offered none of the power associated with women's cooking practices in Ecuador (see Weismantel 1988) and represented little more than an onerous task. Because men took to producing large quantities of food for a week's time (usually rice dishes) that could be easily transported to work, they often complained of the time commitment involved in cooking. Without mechanized cookers, keeping watch over boiling pots of rice or beans gobbled up much of a migrant's only free day. In contrast to doing laundry or cleaning, cooking also required multiple skills and steps, including budgeting money for shopping trips and stocking ingredients. Women in Jatundeleg joked about their pathetic husbands calling for tips on how to cook a particular food and told stories of burned and overspiced dishes.

In addition to making explicit connections between domestic activities and gender identities, migrants also viewed these changes as part of a larger adherence to the discipline needed to be successful abroad. Many migrants described their time in the United States as a process of getting their lives *bien organizada* (well managed), of trying to develop stability and order in a context where they usually do not exist. This need for order extended to the domestic realm. When Ruben Cajamarca (see chapter 5) arrived in the United States, he took up residence with four other undocumented migrants in a cramped one-bedroom apartment. Two of the Ecuadorians were husband and wife and therefore occupied the bedroom alone. The other three (all men) shared the crowded main room, which barely accommodated three single mattresses and a television. For a time, the wife assumed the cooking and cleaning duties, yet stopped when she accepted a demanding job at a garment factory. As Ruben remembered, almost instantaneously the apartment fell into disarray, with dirty dishes and overflowing bags of trash plaguing the shared living spaces. Things changed only when the chaos began to affect his ability to work.

"*Puhh!* You couldn't believe the enormous mess! [Laughing] It was like out of a movie. . . . I used to work on a salad bar where I had to wear a uniform everyday—something like black slacks with a white shirt and a bow tie. One morning, I woke up late for work and was rushing around to get ready. There was so much garbage on the floor and the counters too that I couldn't find a thing. I needed my tie, and I couldn't find it. I also had to iron my shirt and couldn't find that either. I made it work, yes, but I nearly lost my job that day. So it had to change. Period [*punto*]."

"What had to change?" I asked.

"I told the other guys that we weren't going to live like goddamn pigs anymore. So I changed. I was cooking and cleaning. I even made a list of things I needed from the store. Now I am totally the *matrimonio* here. Man and woman in the same house."

For many Jatundeleg wives, however, delight in their husband's domesticity abroad could often be bittersweet. Migration almost certainly placed the men in situations where they had to carry out "women's work," but the detachment from family also served to exacerbate less desirable behaviors more closely associated with men's behavior in Jatundeleg. The temptations of extramarital sexual adventures were welcomed distractions to men who were out from under the watchful eye of relatives and neighbors and often overcome with loneliness. This blunt fact was not lost on the migrants' wives. During a focus-group session with a cohort of Jatundeleg migrant wives, one woman noted: "I know he has been with other women, but he would never tell me, and I would never ask." Another woman presented a more sober assessment: "Just as long as he sends remittances, I can't care what he does over there. I know he's my husband and he'll return to me."

The resignation some migrant wives were able to achieve with respect to the reality of men's extramarital relations abroad was only so strong, however. Undercutting their abilities to "accept" men's liaisons was a set of very real fears, including that of being abandoned by a husband who met another woman or of having a husband return infected with HIV/AIDS.

Migrant wives' claims of being "abandoned" *(abandonada)* require a semantic analysis. Some women defined "being abandoned" as not receiving remittances for two or more months, but others simply refused to use the label unless they heard explicitly from their husbands that they were leaving the marriage. In other cases, however, women cried abandonment only to later claim that their migrant husbands were back in their lives. In all cases, though, the fear of abandonment was real and direct. Accompanying the hurt and pain brought on by a spouse's rejection was the shame that could befall village women. Although invariably it was the extramarital actions of husbands that led to estrangement, abandoned wives were typically branded as victims of a *doble stigma*. Villager gossip would blame women first for "losing" their husbands—"Did she mismanage his money? Not take care to answer his letters?"—and second, when support from a husband abroad dried up, for the inability to care for her children properly. "Abandoned" women also found prospects for remarriage to be slim or nonexistent (cf. McKee 1980).

Despite the gossip built up around *esposas abandonadas,* I found the number of actual cases to be extremely low (only two instances in Jatundeleg and the neighbouring villages). Similarly, among men in New York, I questioned claims made by Jatundeleg women and migrant men that "most" migrants were engaged in extramarital relations. The experiences of my male informants in Queens closely paralleled those Gutmann (1996) discovered during his research in Mexico City. Like the supposed machos of the *colonia* Santa Domingo, migrants in Queens were apt to talk about taking lovers, buying prostitutes, and cheating on wives more often than they actually engaged in these practices. (The same was often true of drinking adventures.) The reasons for this difference are simple and pragmatic, again hinging on issues of time and money. Prostitutes were a luxury that few undocumented laborers could afford. Other types of noneconomic extramarital affairs were also difficult. Somewhat tongue-in-cheek, one young migrant described the "problem of getting sex this way." As he described, "It does not work that you just sleep with a woman anymore. They want a sign of commitment." Although extramarital relations most likely do occur, I met only two migrants over the course of my fieldwork who had engaged in affairs. One of them claimed his actions were purely functional: he hoped to marry a Mexican woman who had citizenship with whom he had been living. He planned to stay married to her just long enough to obtain legal status and later bring his original wife and children to the United States.

Solo
Intento
Dar
Amor ("I only intend to give love" AIDS [SIDA] graffiti, Ayaloma, 1999)

If women feared being abandoned when husbands left them to come north, AIDS is what they often feared when their husbands returned. Knowledge about HIV infection and measures of AIDS prevention was uneven in Jatundeleg, but most villagers had at least formed a clear association between the disease and migration. During my time in Jatundeleg, I attended three funerals for migrants who had died of AIDS complications.[3]

When women in Azuayo-Cañari communities did become infected with HIV, it was often as the unwitting sexual partners of HIV-positive husbands and lovers unaware of their own disease status.[4] Through the efforts of local NGOs and the media, women in Jatundeleg were aware of the risk, but often felt powerless to act. Studies by an NGO working in Cañar province found that although women used some form of contraception,

3. In two of the cases, the migrants returned in the advanced stages of the disease and died shortly thereafter. The third case should more accurately be called a memorial service because the migrant died in the United States, and his family in Jatundeleg could not afford to have the body flown back to Ecuador for burial. The deceased man's wife also had AIDS and was living in the United States. Her undocumented status and weakness from the disease also precluded her from returning.

4. On the link between returned male migrants and new HIV infections in women in Azuay and Cañar, see Urgilez, Ambrosi, and Flores 1996.

a condom was typically not one of them. Men, in particular, discourage condom use, often associating them with visits to prostitutes (HABITierra 1999, 6–7; Pájara Pinta 1996). Despite challenges, some women I knew in Jatundeleg did stand up to husbands upon their return. One woman told me, "When my husband returned, I demanded that he get a blood test to see that his blood was clean." When her husband refused, she did not let the issue drop and, as an act of protest, continued to live in her parents' house as she had during her husband's absence. Although rumors about a husband's infidelity abroad could cause little alarm or humiliation, accusations of harboring a feared and fatal disease like SIDA were not treated so lightly.[5] After his wife's protest had dragged on for a few weeks, the husband agreed to the test. In other instances, the fear of infection led some wives to prefer that their husbands not return at all and disrupt their lives.

"El Tiempo de las Mujeres" (The Time of Women)

When I first met Carmela Quispe in Jatundeleg in February 1999, she brimmed with a sense of confidence that hid the difficulties she had faced as the wife of a migrant.[6] Her home was impeccably clean and her *tienda* well stocked and orderly. Similarly, Jennifer and Valentino, her two children, seemed well adjusted to their father's absence. Both did well in school and were popular at village gatherings. However, Carmela's current situation masked the initial hardships many women go through when their

---

5. The scenario of the migrant's returning to his home village and infecting loved ones with HIV is commonly employed in HIV/AIDS education and local television productions. Pájara Pinta, a Cuenca-based NGO that carries out HIV/AIDS prevention and sexual education in the countryside, produced a popular *fotonovela* (comic book–style format using actual photographs) that chronicles the tribulations of a returned migrant who loses his family, friends, and honor when he returns to his home village infected with HIV. Another popular source of HIV information in Jatundeleg is gossip. One of the most well-circulated rumors regarded an HIV-positive migrant who upon his return to his home village knowingly tried to infect as many people as possible after learning of his wife's infidelities.

6. *Tiempo de las mujeres* is the name of a well-known documentary by Monica Vasquez (1988) about the lives of women in the migrant-sending community of Santa Rosa, Azuay province.

husbands leave for the United States. She described what happened to her: "The day after Miguel left I couldn't move. I was thrown into bed [*botada a la cama*] by the sadness and my *nervios*. I was sad and overwhelmed. I couldn't take care of these kids, and I didn't know what to do. You can imagine . . . I just kept saying, 'How could you leave me? What do you mean you went [to the United States] for us? I only know pain!'" Carmela's condition of "being thrown into bed" was common among Jatundeleg women, especially in situations where couples had already established an autonomous household and when children were present. In these cases, stress related to a husband's departure could be extremely acute. Another migrant wife shared the following experience with my research assistant:

> Before [my husband left], I thought that having a husband in the United States would be heaven, but then when he left it became an inferno. I feel for all the wives whose husbands have just left. It is terrible. For me, I would spend days in my bed with the windows blocking out the sun. Thanks to God, my sisters came and took care of my children. They made sure the kids were dressed and off to school and tended to the animals. I don't know what I would have done otherwise.[7]

Once women overcame the initial challenges of their husbands' departure, they faced a series of other hurdles both pragmatic and sociomoral. Wives already burdened with trying to balance the running of a household with farming activities had to reorganize their daily lives, incorporating their husband's tasks into their standard routines. As we saw in chapter 3, the relationship between agricultural production and migration is far from straightforward. Remittances reorganized household economies, so

---

7. Many women I spoke with mentioned experiencing embodied physical reactions to their husbands' departures, which they generally attributed to the psychological and physical conditions *pena* and *nervios* (also see Miles 1997, 66–68). Finerman (1989) and others have written about Andean women's health problems as mechanisms to cope with unbearable kinds of debilitating stress. By identifying their stresses as *pena* and *nervios,* women can take a legitimate "time out" from their work and can expect to receive ample help from extended family and neighbors. After a few days, the rest cures nerves, and women can return to their usual roles.

the individual decisions that couples had to make with respect to growing *maíz* and other crops rested as much on social and cultural considerations as they did on economic ones. However, during the early years after a husband's departure, growing crops remained critical to household survival. During this period, remittance behavior might be erratic as migrants adjusted to the demands of producing surplus cash. At the same time, debt obligations limited the amount of money allocated to meet a family's needs. In fact, as my household census revealed, few migrant families could continue their production activities without replacing a husband's labor. Many Jatundeleg wives found they spent considerable time securing workers to meet their labor needs. In some cases, this required oiling extended familial relationships with landless and land-poor relatives *(pobrecitos)* in need of a way to grow crops or contracting day laborers. In either case, attending to these new duties placed women in gendered positions once occupied only by husbands.

Although feminist scholars have long criticized the well-worn model of men/public sphere and women/private sphere (Rapp Reiter 1975a; Rosaldo 1980), versions of the dichotomy nonetheless live on as the ways in which people order their local worlds (e.g., Brusco 1995; see examples in Montoya, Frazier, and Hurtig 2002). Indeed, Jatundeleg villagers often iterated the common adage "El hombre es de la calle y la mujer de la casa" (Men are of the street and women of the house) to speak of gender relations. Some women identified a paradoxical reversal of roles in this model. As men migrated, women found their daily work taking them more centrally into the public world of *la calle,* while simultaneously their husbands abroad were increasingly forced into *la casa*—bound between their strict work schedules. Although surely not the most far-reaching of changes, perhaps the most visible was the presence of women behind the wheels of cars and trucks, a sight that only a few years before my fieldwork began would have been unheard of. As an elderly resident in Jatundeleg commented, "Women still won't get behind the power of a *yunta,* but now they drive big trucks." In migrant households especially, four-wheel-drive pickup trucks had become common purchases. Often hesitant at first, many women found driving a necessity in order to assume many of their husband's tasks. However, that women would drive alone or, worse yet, drive with men who were not their husbands was a source of much concern. The restriction occasionally led to awkward situations such as when I witnessed the wife of a migrant fret over how she would transport two male day laborers to work her family's fields six miles away from her home. Although she could competently drive her husband's pickup, she ended up uneasily allowing her elderly father-in-law to drive the truck despite serious misgivings about his driving abilities.

As the example of driving reveals, the absence of husbands at times caused a moral conundrum regarding gender roles and responsibilities. Although villagers tacitly accepted men's extramarital relations, both at home and abroad, women's infidelity was completely intolerable. Wives left behind typically found their comings and goings closely monitored by extended family. In-laws *(suegros),* in particular, often assumed as their chief role in the constitution of transnational households the safeguarding of respect for their sons by assuring the honor of their daughters-in-law. Even within the most amicable of family relationships, women often worried that in-laws might call their husbands abroad at the slightest sign of impropriety. Young couples did not always welcome their parents' vigilance, however, and many strove to achieve as much autonomy from their extended families as possible before a husband's departure. In some cases, the moral ambiguities associated with a young woman living without her husband were partially rectified when the couple had children and she could safely live alone with her children.

If men's exodus triggered an increased vigilance with respect to women's mobility and sociality, it also afforded women new freedoms, especially with regard to their relationships with other women. Men could become extremely jealous *(muy celo)* and feel threatened at the very hint that their wives were developing strong relationships with other women. Migration often alleviated this problem. In the absence of men, women were more apt to share meals with other women, to exchange resources between households, and to seek each other out for mutual support. This newfound freedom also spilled over into the assumption of leadership roles. Women occasionally assumed the public offices vacated by their migrant husbands, in addition to holding traditionally female roles that included coordinating children's catechism classes and leading hat-weaving cooperatives. Sandra

Pañora, who served as an activities coordinator at the Jatundeleg elementary school while her husband was in the United States and even after his return, told me assuredly that "women were advancing in this community." When I suggested migration was the catalyst, however, she looked at me in disbelief. "The men leaving helps," she noted. "But it is the women's natural strength [*fuerza*] that could not be held back. Women are gaining respect here on their own."

Sandra's reaction to my comment was an important reminder that not *all* changes experienced by women in the sending communities were the products of migration. Surely, women's empowerment was also the result of increases in the number of girls attending school, lower rates of illiteracy, and significant reverberations created by local and global women's organizing (Lind 2005). Nevertheless, migration and the development of the remittance economy had accelerated these historical changes and, in some cases, were channeling them in new directions. For women, these changes ushered in a mix of freedoms and burdens. Women in the sending communities found their new lives as the wives of migrants ambivalent transformations, much like men's gendered experiences, of which there were few models to follow. Nowhere perhaps were these changes greater than in the maintenance and development of their transnational conjugal relationships.

Learning to Live in Harmony: Miguel and Carmela

Men's migration to the United States and the attendant changes that accompany women's lives in the communities of the rural Andes together open up rich possibilities for new gendered conventions, conflicts, and challenges. Simultaneously celebrated and castigated, this reconfiguration of gender roles and practices presents men and women with, in Gutmann's words, "new stages on which to conduct their dramas" (1997a, 834). However, these changes do not take place irrespective of one another. To push Gutmann's metaphor further, although men occupy one stage in New York City and women another in the sending villages, they enact the same drama together. They share the same backdrop and the same plot lines, and they frequently interact with the same characters.

Yet each couple's drama that unfolds in the context of migration is specific; among other factors, it is a product of their relationship history, of
the role of their extended families, and of the goals they have set for themselves. In fact, some migrant households were simply more successful in labor migration than others for any number of possible reasons. However, in
all cases a critical aspect of their success as transnational families rested on
a couple's ability to integrate their separate gender dramas and to imagine
their lives as unfolding on the same stage. Men's transformations as labor
migrants in New York impacted women's gender roles and behaviors, and
the same was true in the reverse. As Gutmann argues, "whether women are
physically present or not, female identities often serve as the center point of
conscious and unconscious reference for men in the development, maintenance, and transformation of their own sense of what *ser hombre* (to be a
man) does and does not mean, and what it can and cannot mean" (1997a,
836). For instance, men I knew in Queens often resented their wives' ability
to move about their home villages effortlessly while they felt shackled to a
life of "from home to work and from work to home." But within the remittance economy, they understood and accepted, if reluctantly, the necessity of their wives' increased mobility for the smooth functioning of their
transnational household. Paying closer attention to the life story of Carmela Quispe and Miguel Pomaguiza, we can view some of the specifics of
this drama of learning to live together in transnational migration.

Beginnings

Carmela grew up in Ayaloma, the third child in a family of six. When her
parents married, they merged a little more than three hectares of land on
which they grew *maíz* and potatoes. Although they farmed a large landholding, the family struggled economically and often fell in debt to other
households in the community. To generate extra money, Carmela's father
and her two older brothers worked in construction in nearby towns. At
times, Carmela's mother would also send her to Cuenca to sell candy on
the streets with her younger sister. When Carmela turned thirteen, tragedy
struck when her father, Hipolito, was murdered on a construction site in
Guayaquil. He was asleep at the construction site when he awoke to a knife

at his neck and a demand for his money. Hipolito had just received his pay and was planning to return to Ayaloma with his money. Unwilling to have his plans spoiled, he resisted his robbers' demand and fought back. Outnumbered by his assailants, Hipolito took a number of gashes to the chest and later died from his wounds. For Carmela, her father's death coincided with a point in her adolescence when she was beginning to form judgments about the men in her life. As she described it, there were nothing but "chumados, vagos y mujeriegos" (drunks, vagrants, and womanizers). In the image of her father and the story of his death, she found both a martyr and a saint.

At age eighteen, Miguel Pomaguiza did not fit the saintly image Carmela had constructed for herself of the ideal husband, but, as she admitted, "El corazón no se manda" (You can't control your heart). In fact, Miguel seemed unfit to be the husband of even the least picky of women in the village. But, as their wedding photos attested, his good looks were infectious. Miguel was born into a relatively well-off Jatundeleg family. His father owned a significant amount of land (six hectares) and more than a dozen head of dairy cattle. As the eldest son, Miguel was coddled by his mother and allowed to do as he pleased, mostly drinking and smoking cigarettes with friends. When he began courting Carmela, though, his behavior quickly changed. He delighted in sharing walks up to the *cerro* with Carmela and spending time with her down by the river that divided Ayaloma from Shullín. Sealing their courtship was the overwhelming approval of their union by Carmela's mother and her uncle (who had assumed much of her dead father's parental duties). In early 1987, at age twenty-one and twenty, respectively, Carmela and Miguel married.

By the late 1980s, migration had become a prominent income-earning strategy among a majority of Jatundeleg families. Within Carmela and Miguel's families alone, at least four relatives had left for the United States. A number of migrants had also returned by this point, and many families were feeling the pressures of the increasingly "dollarized" economy. Soon after their marriage, Miguel and Carmela moved into a converted bodega attached to Miguel's parents' home and worked their families' land. Because the two of them hailed from large families, they predicted future bitter battles with their siblings over the inheritance of land. Neither expected to fare well in the process. With land prices rising, talk of migration began to creep up in their daily conversations and hopes for the future. In addition to the pressure to secure land, Carmela recalled how Miguel was slowly being seduced by the *iony* ways of returned migrants. Idle talk soon gave way to planning, and Miguel located a *chulquero* to start "bargain hunting" affordable illegal passage.

Carmela did not share Miguel's enthusiasm to migrate and begged him to postpone his plans. "¡Somos matrimonio! [We're a married couple!] You can't leave. This is crazy." Soon, however, Carmela became pregnant and gave birth to a daughter, Jennifer. Miguel put his plans on hold, recalling, "I couldn't go to the United States, so I gave my daughter an American name instead." A son, Valentino, followed two years later. Children proved a welcome distraction in a household that Carmela was beginning to realize was not the storybook scenario of which she had dreamed. Frustrated with unproductive farming, Miguel took to drinking and staying away from home. Although always careful not to present Miguel in a negative light, Carmela repeatedly told me, "I had my share of problems with Miguel, but he loved the children." As she recalled, Miguel lobbed every excuse possible at her when he could not live up to his end of the bargain in their relationship.

> Miguel wasn't the worst among them, but he drank. Oh, and he could tell me lies to get by! He would ask for a little bit of *plata* to go drink and smoke with friends. He told me it was his obligation. He said if we were ever to get ahead and help with our future, he needed to "play the game." The game lasted all night, and he would be in bed all day. . . . I'd say, "What about these kids? What am I supposed to do with them? They are your kids, too!"

When I interviewed Miguel, he elaborated:

> We couldn't always seem to get it together. I would drink too much. This is true, but that's because that village is full of nothing but *chumados* [drunks]! I love my wife and wanted something better for her and my kids. I promised if I went to the United States for a short while, things would get better. . . . But she didn't believe me. I understand. Men [back in Ecuador] can't always be trusted, "siempre a Dios y al diablo," as people

say ["always of God and the devil," meaning to seek the protection of something good and bad at the same time].

Despite Carmela's reservations about migration, she remained supportive. She also could not help sharing Miguel's dreams of success. Would they build a house? Own a cattle farm someday? Eventually move to the city? In 1995, Miguel accepted a cousin's help to get a dishwashing job in Queens. He paid $7,000 for his passage north, leaving Carmela to manage their payments to a *chulquero*. Rather than upset his children when he departed, he told them he had business in Guayaquil and would return within the week. In three weeks time, Miguel was in Queens.

Transnational Communication

In 1999, when I met Carmela in Jatundeleg and later Miguel in Queens, much had changed over the years in their abilities to communicate with one another across the thousands of miles of separation. When Miguel departed for the United States in 1995, few families in Jatundeleg, Ayaloma, or Shullín had telephones. (Many households had been on waiting lists of the state-owned telephone companies for five years or more.) To receive a call from Miguel in the early days of their separation required that Carmela walk a half-hour trip down to the EMETEL (state-run) phone office in Déleg. There, in a cramped booth with the muttered chatter of other talkers on either side, she would attend to her relationship. The couple kept their calls short and strained to hear each other through the poor connection. Sometimes, Carmela would altogether miss Miguel's calls, or Miguel would forget to call at their agreed time. For his part, Miguel had to battle with a pay phone each time he called, requiring that he feed it change every few minutes, often running out of coins before they were finished talking. Recalling these difficulties, Carmela retorted: "There are just so many problems that I told myself you just have to resign yourself to not living as a couple [hay que resignarse, adaptarse no más a vivir sin la pareja]."

By 1999, though, Carmela finally had a phone—a cordless model that allowed her to stroll about and talk to Miguel while she attended to her

children's needs and household chores (only an hour's time difference separated them). In Queens, Miguel was easily able to purchase discount phone
cards that afforded a crystal clear signal. As Carmela estimated, their calls
went from ten minutes on average when Miguel first migrated to more
than thirty when she got her own phone. The telephone and discount long-
distance rates were only part of the equation, however. In the nearly five
years Miguel had been in the United States, his ability to remit an average
of $200 per month had allowed the couple to purchase a vacant house in
the village. Carmela moved out of her in-laws' home and for the first time
had a modicum of privacy with respect to her marriage.

On occasion, Carmela and Miguel's communication took on a more
sophisticated face, such as around the time of Jennifer's first communion
party. As I describe later, Miguel was adamant that the party go according
to his plans, and he remitted extra money to ensure it. "If I can't be there, I
want her to know that I care," he told me. The party's complicated logistics
required that the couple stay in close contact with one another. For weeks,
Carmela, accompanied by her younger sister, frequently traveled to an Internet café in Cuenca, where they sent messages to and received messages
from Miguel (writing from a computer in his employer's office). Because
Carmela had less than a fourth-grade education, she relied on her sister
to type messages to Miguel as she dictated them. She also grew savvy in
her use of a "net-2-phone" service with which she and Miguel could talk
through an Internet connection at half the rate that Miguel paid in phone
card minutes.

Still, communication was never perfect. As other researchers who address "transnationalism from below" (at the familial and individual level)
have noted, transmigrant relationships are almost always uneven. Mahler
explains, "[T]he lived reality of [migrants themselves] is very focused on
the local and is punctuated by transnational activities. In contrast, for
the nonmigrant relatives and friends of these migrants, . . . transnational
ties are an inextricable feature of daily life" (2001, 110). To be sure, the
daily activities of migrants I knew in New York often revolved around
immediate concerns—getting to work on time, getting paid, finding time
to rest before another shift. In contrast, wives in the sending communities could easily spend much of their time tending to issues related to

their husbands' absences. They waited in anguish when remittances failed to arrive; weeks passed without telephone calls from husbands abroad. Sometimes these gaps were intentional. Some husbands I knew in New York admitted how occasionally they intimidated their wives with deliberate silences when they were upset or suspected that the women were not behaving "properly." If, through gossip coursing the transnational pipelines, a migrant heard that his wife had been unfaithful, he might skip his routine calls or delay sending his remittances, just long enough to exert his power. Although this unevenness typically worked to men's benefit, women also learned to exploit gaps in communication in order to create leverage in their relationships with their migrant husbands, especially in their roles as remittance managers.

Managing Remittances, Managing Relationships

Among the tasks Carmela attended to in her husband's absence, the one she considered the most important, was managing the remittances Miguel would send nearly every three weeks from a Delgado Travel on Roosevelt Avenue in Queens to a branch office in the dusty *centro* of Déleg. As she explained, "There are many things that we need that money for that I often feel it is already spent before I make it down actually to receive the letter. When Miguel first left, it seemed like all the money went to the *chulco*. There was nothing left to eat with [n.b.: Carmela and Miguel cancelled Miguel's smuggling debt in 1998]. Now we have more, but I have to be careful what to do. We have plans with our money, and if we are not careful there is nothing left. The money is, in reality, not so much. But we can still be moving forward."

I asked her, "Who decides how the money is spent?"

"We both do. Miguel tells me things we need, and I tell him things. Sometimes we fight and disagree. . . . We decide those things together."

In other Andean contexts, studies of migration collectively suggest that women fare poorly when men initiate migration (Collins 1988; Hamilton 1998; McKee 1997; Radcliffe 1986; Weismantel 1988). Drawing upon cases of internal migration, researchers point out that aspects of gender equality erode as cash flows back into sending communities, and women's nonremunerated work is devalued.[8] Given such strong evidence, what can be said to account for women's increased status in migrant-sending communities? In other words, why did women like Carmela feel they were "moving forward" *(adelantando)* even as their men were becoming primary breadwinners?

Part of the answer, as I have already suggested, lies in the qualitative difference between internal and transnational migration economies. In instances of internal migration, responsibility for both the generation and allocation of income generally rests solely in the hands of those, often men, who migrate. Transnational migration offers an alternative situation whereby wives often assume the role of what I term "remittance managers." Women in Jatundeleg ensured that remittances were received; they also cashed and banked checks and monitored exchange rates, deciding at which point to exchange money into the local currency (prior to the institution of dollarization). Some researchers have noted the onerous aspects of this job, including the long waits at money-wiring agencies and in bank lines to cash checks (see, e.g., Carpio Benalcázar 1992; Clearfield 1999; Miles 1997), but for many women I knew in Jatundeleg, managing remittances provided a critical component of their transnational conjugal relationships. In particular, the women acknowledged how men were forced to cede some of their decision-making power in order to see the productive use of remittances. Within the unevenness of communication, husbands often became dependent on wives to manage finances. At times, women would manipulate these situations to serve their own needs and consolidate money.

Carmela shared with me some of the creative measures she used to wrest power from Miguel in her role as a remittance manager. During the economic crisis of 1999 and 2000, the value of the sucre fluctuated tremendously against the dollar, requiring vigilant monitoring. Like many couples at the time, Carmela and Miguel stayed in closer-than-normal

8. These patterns are by no means exclusive to the Andean context and have been documented elsewhere with respect to a wide range of migration types (rural-urban, international, and transnational). See Hondagneu-Sotelo and Crawford 1999 and Nash 1999 for discussions of various non-Andean examples.

contact as they tried to coordinate Miguel's remittances with the best exchange rates. Although Miguel fretted over the sucre's persistent devaluation, the more he tried to micromanage the situation by demanding an accounting of the money he sent, the more Carmela selectively communicated with him. During a particularly rapid downturn of the sucre, Miguel insisted on knowing exactly where the money was going. Carmela did not return his calls. As she remembered, "He panicked, and I just let him panic for a few days. When he called back, I told him that I had received the money and had already exchanged it at the highest rate possible. Sure, he was angry that I had not spoken with him, but he was ultimately able to see that he needed me. He can't do it without me." Wives, for their part, also worried that their husbands might be holding back remittances and not sending all that they could, especially for household expenses. Nonetheless, women in their roles as remittance managers occupied a better position than nonmigrant wives to demand portions of their husband's earnings. Some migrant wives expressed how they could better stretch the lump sums husbands sent because men could scarcely demand back what they had already mailed. Especially within households that carried large amounts of debt, men feared they would lose everything if they did not remit all they could. As Carmela explained to me, "Miguelito doesn't know everything when he sends money. He knows I make the payments, but the rest is for me to decide."

For Carmela and other women, power *(el mando)* was gained not simply through men's dependency on them to manage their hard-earned wages competently; women's significant input in economic matters also often transferred to other realms of their relationships. Many women told me how their experiences of managing remittances allowed them more room to disagree actively with spouses and made their husbands become better listeners. "He still has the power, but at least we talk about things, and I have a say," one wife reported to me. In particular, remittance management invested women with an authoritative language through which to make better claims for household needs. The most successful transnational households were ones in which husbands abroad identified that managing remittances entailed not only consumption, but also production: the generation of more money. As migrant men realized that hard work and their own cost-saving measures alone could not ensure success, they were more apt to see the utility of learning to work in harmony with their wives back home.

Coparenting

When I interviewed Miguel in Queens, we often discussed his children. Miguel made it clear that he had "migrated for his children" (cf. Orellana et al. 2001). But like so many stock-in-trade narratives that frame the migration experience, Miguel's comment required an analytic teasing out of words from deeds. When Miguel left for the United States, he was spared his children's anxiety. Although Valentino and Jennifer did not succumb to the debilitating bouts of depression-like *nervios* that befell some Jatundeleg children when parents migrated (Pribilsky 2001b), they nonetheless did not understand why their father had left. Carmela, like many migrant wives, fell into a pattern of telling her children lies about their father to distract them from dwelling on his absence. "When they were very young," she laughed in disbelief, "I used to tell the children that their father had gone to look for special tires for the truck." The stories would only temporarily pacify the children's curiosity about their father. Carmela concluded, "In a few months I would have to tell them another."

In the Andean highlands, relationships between children and parents are strongly mediated by gender. Although buttressing the principle of *considerándoles* is the assumption that children will pay undue respect to parents, in actuality this means different things for each parent. In the survey I administered to junior high and high school students in Déleg, students defined their relationship with each parent using different terms. Mothers were typically described as fostering relationships of trust *(confianza)*, whereas fathers were defined as building relationships through *respeto* in much the same hierarchal fashion as traditional husband-and-wife relationships. A successful father, I was told numerous times in Jatundeleg, can raise his children "just by staring them down." Miguel, like many young migrants, had little idea of how to have a relationship with his children, let alone from abroad. His most immediate models—memories of his relationship with his own father—usually proved dissatisfying as a means of fostering bonds with children he barely knew. Indeed, commensurate with the relationship between life cycle and migration, most men traveled north when their children were very young and only dimly aware of their fathers; others left pregnant wives behind and at first came to "know" their children only through photographs and video recordings. In this context, men learned the sobering truth that if they wanted to have any relationship at all with their small children, they could not do it—literally or figuratively—by "staring their children down" from thousands of miles away.

The difficulty of fathering from abroad was real and direct and produced a variety of outcomes. Some men altogether avoided relationships with their children and hardly spoke of them during interviews. Others distanced themselves from their children and tried, usually with little success, to enforce relationships of *respeto*. Sometimes men returned to Jatundeleg to find they had no foundational relationship with their children at all, causing problems that festered throughout adolescence. However, enough fathers I met in both New York and as returnees in Jatundeleg assumed roles of parenting that challenged facile depictions of migrant fathers as being aloof or as having suspended their fathering role along with the rest of their gendered identity when they crossed borders (cf. Piore 1979).

Indeed, migration could produce surprising results with respect to parenting. Miguel told me point-blank that he felt like he was a better father because he had left. He based his self-assessment partially on his ability to provide more for his children and to make special gift purchases for them in ways he could not before. In an extended discussion in which he contrasted work and family relations, Miguel celebrated his ability to be a father in contrast to the undesirable aspects of his life in New York City.

> I have taken some really awful jobs in the United States—some downright dangerous! At times, I would think, man, I could be back in the *campo* [countryside] where the air is nice, with my family and friends close by, working my land, tending to my herds. But things would never change, I could never give them [his children] anything better. So I stayed. Fathers now can provide more for their kids. Fathers now take

more concern for their kids. They are not so macho [Ellos no tan machistas]. They do not father so strictly; there is more *cariño* [affection] between fathers and children.

For a number of migrant fathers I interviewed in New York, being able to develop relationships of *cariño* with children was a welcomed part of otherwise unsatisfying existences as undocumented migrants. Men consistently welcomed the freedom of developing relationships with children outside of the rigid strictures of *respeto* that defined the relationships they had with their fathers. Simply put, distance did make some hearts grow fonder. Yet the sources of men's desires to build alternative relationships with their children were difficult to tease out from the extreme importance placed on children and childhood within the production of locality and the judgment of status for migrant households. By embracing fathering practices "más modernas y progresivas," migrants could build relationships with children, but at the same time distance themselves from nonmigrant households who could not provide the same kinds of things for their children.

As we saw in chapter 3, children in migrant families had become an important index for gauging the success of migrant households. At the root of this development was the transformation of children's position within the village economy. As an increased reliance on remittances within migrant households triggered a move away from agricultural production, children were relieved of their obligations to the family farm economy. An increased emphasis on schooling was at the heart of this change. Rather than waking early to haul firewood or to help with the harvest, the children of migrants rushed to catch school buses, spending much of their day away from the household. Some parents also sent their kids to live with relatives in Cuenca to provide them with what they perceived to be a superior education. For transnational parenting, the transformation of children from economically worthless to emotionally priceless, to paraphrase Viviana Zelizer (1994), opened up new possibilities for the roles of both mother and father.

In Carmela and Miguel's case, as for other couples I interviewed, the new emphasis placed on children also moved women into a central role as the ones to foster and mediate migrant husband's relationships with their children. During their telephone conversations, Carmela would invariably field the same burdonsome questions from Miguel: "What do you tell them [the children] about me?" "What did they think of the gift I sent?" As the children aged and Miguel was able to develop his own telephone relationship with them, Carmela's job diminished, but only slightly. Miguel still relied on her to explain his absence to the children. Like in the situation of managing remittances, men were often thrust into a dependent position with respect to women's access to children. When a migrant "sent a sign" *(envio una seña)* to his family, for instance, he might wish to know how far that sign was noticed by others. As the repositories of tradition (as the only ones maintaining "indigenous dress" for instance), wives were called upon to mediate between their husbands' status claims of *iony* modernity, on the one hand, and the importance of family life and childhood, on the other.

In many cases, the receipt of gifts or the delivery of an *electro-doméstico* from Créditos Económicos were moments when wives shared in the status claims made by husbands abroad. Other times, however, these situations could be more taxing. Nowhere was this more evident than in the elaborate planning that accompanied children's parties to celebrate baptisms, first communions, and confirmations. Carmela, for instance, shared with me the details surrounding Jennifer's first communion. In describing Miguel's wishes, she said "He wanted a big party like everyone else." The party was expensive because it included hiring a disc jockey, ordering flowers and decorations, purchasing and preparing food, and buying special outfits for the children. At the party, the hard work and transnational negotiation and planning to which Miguel and Carmela had devoted so much time appeared seamless. Nevertheless, at one point during the planning, Carmela found herself in a shouting match with Miguel's mother, who accused Carmela of not spending the money on the party as Miguel had wished. Miguel had apparently contacted his parents to "check up" on Carmela to make sure the plans were coming along. When his parents mistook Carmela's difficulties in taking care of the party arrangements in a timely fashion for her own greediness, the situation temporarily exploded.

7.1. A confirmation party in Jatundeleg orchestrated by a father in New York City. Photograph by the author.

Convivir

Repeatedly, in their own way, numerous husbands and wives in migrant households told me that their relationships improved after migration. No couple escaped hardships altogether, but many adopted a language of process—how they had learned to live in harmony with one another over time. As the word *convivir* implies, though, harmony need not translate into perfection. Instead, couples often learned to accept one another and the roles each must assume to make migration successful. Men learned to listen to women and respect their decisions because they had to. Women accepted, albeit tacitly, men's infidelities and the burdens of representing men and their status in their home communities, but often not without also recognizing that husbands had become more attentive to household needs, sent money when asked, and paid attention to their children as best they could so many miles away.

8

Conclusion

Carmela Quispe and Miguel Pomaguiza's experiences represent common challenges and tensions many young couples of the Azuayo-Cañari region face as they work to form their own autonomous households in a context increasingly different from that of their parents and grandparents. Miguel, as an undocumented migrant, also represents thousands of young men whose labor in the United States has become absolutely crucial to the social reproduction of rural village life in Ecuador. At the same time, his work has been a critical element in the transformation of urban economies in the United States over the past three decades. The fact that young Ecuadorian men find few options beyond traveling thousands of miles to secure a livelihood in their home village additionally points to a host of political economic disparities between developed and undeveloped countries, but also within Ecuador itself. However, although young men's lives intersect with what Saskia Sassen (1991) calls the "new international division of labor," this intersection also brings them into critical engagement with local ideas of what being "modern" means. As much as or more than base economic considerations, these cultural struggles are responsible for propelling young Ecuadorians to the United States.

This book offers one perspective through which to situate the rapid socioeconomic changes that enveloped a corner of rural Ecuador as I observed them starting in the late 1990s, changes that have now quickly spread throughout the country.[1] This perspective is, of course, not the only way to look at these changes, and no doubt a different ethnographer in

1. See, e.g., the articles collected in two recent edited volumes on the changing face of Ecuadorian migration: Herrera, Carrillo, and Torres 2005 and Hidalgo 2004.

Jatundeleg or New York would have chosen to highlight different themes. Overall, my aim has been to place the people directly involved and affected by transnational migration in the center of the ethnography. As Smith and Guarnizo (1998) articulate this approach, it is an appeal for a "transnationalism from below." Early efforts to carve out a transnational perspective in the social sciences often fell prey to romantic and idealistic depictions of transnational migrants. Transnational activities were heralded for challenging the hegemony of state forces and for offering political and economic alternatives to those most powerless in state societies. The influence of borders and the consequences of crossing them for migrants and for those closest to them were largely overlooked in this celebratory moment.[2] In contrast, I have sought here to address how men and women from rural Ecuador have struggled to make sense of their experiences of change; I have also looked at the creative ways they compose lives based simultaneously in tradition and change.

Throughout this work, the expression "Así es la chulla vida" (as explained in the preface) has served as a useful way for me to think through the many nuances and contradictory experiences of migration. The idea of "only one life to live" or "one life with only one path to follow" was understood in different ways by the different individuals I met in both the rural Andes and New York City. For some, the *chulla vida* represented a welcomed and exciting destiny to fulfill dreams of becoming *iony*, whereas for others it delineated a life lacking in viable options. In many cases, people's use of the expression combined both perspectives. As we saw in chapters 5 and 6, young migrants are often attracted to the United States as a means to acquire the emblems of *iony* modernity and success potent in the lives of some returned migrants. The *chulla vida*, as destiny, presents itself as a means to quick enrichment. However, as many migrants learn, paying off debt, making ends meet in expensive New York, and generating remittances require a longer and more arduous stay than they first thought. In New York, young men often readjust their perspective to match the realities of life as undocumented migrants. Many find the transformation

---

2. For critiques of this early transnational literature, consult Guarnizo and Smith 1998; Mahler 1998.

they have undergone is not the dramatic adoption of *iony* status, but rather something more subtle and quotidian.

Although the central focuses of this work are migrants themselves and the families they leave behind in Ecuador, I began my discussion by grounding their experiences in the major historical and contemporary socioeconomic transformations of village life. The emergence of agri-artisan households placed rural producers in increasingly vulnerable positions vis-à-vis regional, national, and global economic structures. Two effects of this history are worth mentioning. First, new strategies for employment have tended to upset the traditional gendered division of labor. Where men's labor has become more critical to the wage economy, women's work has assumed a critical managerial role, ranging from the administration of remittances to the upkeep of agriculture. Second, with new forms of production have come new avenues for consumption and increased convenience in village life. In chapter 3, I explored how processes of economic change, in place since the Panama hat era, were amplified with the advent of international migration. In many instances, villagers successfully bypassed the state to bring new services to their community. Although migration has no doubt increased the gulf between rich and poor households in the community, the response to this development is anything but straightforward. Nonmigrant households fret over their ability to take advantage of the often costly new additions of convenience in village life, but simultaneously praise the progress and development that counters the disparaging image of them as *nuestro folklórico.*

Gender relations and family life were not the original intended foci of my research in Ecuador. Rather, the importance of gender as a category of difference and the meanings of family life closely attached to it initially emerged in my conversations with young men as they talked about their preoccupations with migration. As the remittance economy diminished the importance of agriculture and other local production activities, young men increasingly found themselves in the role of sole family breadwinner. Coupled with the unraveling of a long-standing tradition of inheritance as the basis to begin new households, young men faced tremendous pressures to migrate. Much of the discourse that surrounds migration decisions plays on ideas of proper manhood and stresses that the most eligible bachelors in the community are, paradoxically, the ones most likely to leave for the United States. This heightened sense of gender roles and expectations in the Azuayo-Cañari region makes for a fruitful examination of men's gender identities in a context where gender is often an unmarked category not always readily evident in the emic experience.

What it means to be a man *(ser hombre)* for men living as undocumented migrants in the United States, however, departs significantly from the gendered expectations of young men growing up in Jatundeleg. The Déleg mural of the Rambo-like migrant clasping hands with his Cañari *paisano* (discussed in chapter 5) often reminded me of the kinds of imagery imparted on young men destined to sojourn north. The image locates migrant masculinity in big muscles, defiance, and a manly fraternity with other men. But for migrants I knew, their marginal lives as undocumented migrants often placed them in what they considered to be traditionally female subject positions as they were forced to carry out acts they associated with their wives, mothers, and sisters back home. Moreover, the priorities of maintaining strict budgets and refraining from immediate forms of spending and consumption (especially of alcohol) often estranged men from one another, thus putting male sociality into conflict.

Social-science discussions regarding men's identities frequently employ the concept of "hegemonic masculinities." As interpreted by Robert Connell (see, e.g., 1996) and others, the concept refers to cultural ideologies that privilege some men by associating them with particular forms of power. In any given society, a regulated number of ways of being a man exert control over and define delegitimized forms of masculinity in subtle ways. In Queens, migrants found themselves in a liminal arena, no longer completely bound by the rigid definitions of maleness that pervade Ecuadorian society. Men who cooked, did their own laundry, and purposively avoided drinking parties did so at the risk of scorn and ridicule. At the same time, men encountered their desires for *iony* modernity in strikingly gendered forms. They saw images of men as fathers and husbands in television and other media that stressed the affective qualities of relationships shaped largely through consumption practices. They identified with images of men making special purchases for their children or pulling off the details of a birthday party. With what little disposable income they had available to them, men were able to rework, if only fleetingly, their identities as undocumented migrants into identities as men with *iony* status.

As this book explores, young men I knew—especially those who left to the United States as husbands and fathers—viewed their experiences abroad as causing significant transformations in their identities *as* men. Migrants were most often apt to see these changes as indicative of their becoming men "más modernos y progresivos" than their fathers and other men still in Ecuador. Thus, at times, they did not see learning to budget money, eschewing the temptations to go on drinking binges, and cooking and cleaning for themselves as the disciplinary necessities of making it as a migrant, but rather as personal transformations of identity that merged together their gendered expectations with their desires for *iony* modernity.

Still, men's desires to be "hombres más modernos y progresivos" often placed them on a tightrope, where they had to balance their limited options. Few men in actuality made the kinds of money needed to sustain the image of themselves they hoped to project back home. Most had to settle for small successes such as sending home a small amount of money or orchestrating the delivery of an *electro-doméstico* for all eyes to see. Many who achieved even partial success in the United States—for instance, earning enough money to buy land, build a home, and return to Ecuador—were in a few years' time after their return already contemplating heading back to the United States.

In the short term, though, male migrants and their wives invest in what is most important to them, their children. Viewing their children as "in development" rather than as potential labor, many parents consider themselves moderately successful if they can shield their children from dirty and frustrating agricultural work and keep them in school past the elementary years. By removing children from the family farm economy and the basic skills of agrarian life, however, these parents very likely do little more than groom children for lives as future migrants.

This study stresses the importance of paying close attention to men's identities in the migration experience. It is my hope that the results of this focus will suggest a number of areas for improving our understanding of the relationship between gender and migration. At a very basic level, bringing men's identities into the folds of migration research helps us to rethink long-held assumptions about *women's* roles in migration. In recent years, as women's experiences as transnational migrants are more heavily researched, scholars have grown increasingly comfortable talking about the proliferation of "transnational families" (see, e.g., Chamberlain and Leydesdorff 2004; Foner 1997a; Hirsch 2003). Especially in situations where female migrants leave children behind in home countries, scholars note how mothering practices are transformed to accommodate physical distance (Hondagneu-Sotelo and Avila 1997; Parreñas 2001). This recent interest, however, begs the question of the real newness of transnational families. Why is it that, for instance, researchers speak of transnational families only when looking at women's roles? What kind of importance should be attached to family when we are looking at men who leave and women who stay behind? For the most part, migration scholars have operated with limited assumptions about women as the ones performing "kin-work" (di Leonardo 1987). When men migrate, it is assumed, they tend to public matters; when women migrate, they tend to the domestic sphere. What has not received enough treatment are the examples of family formation in migration situations that do not have women at the center or that at least present a sharing of responsibilities.[3] Looking at male migrants and their practices of maintaining family ties from abroad helps to question these implicit assumptions.

If I stress the importance of looking at masculinity in migration contexts, I do so with a caveat. I do not wish to suggest that all migrants subscribe to one category of how to be a man, but rather that there is a plethora of emergent masculinities. The process of migration and the way it reorients taken-for-granted gender roles and practices pose challenges to the popular notions of what it means to be a man (or a woman) in Andean societies. Young men and women in the Azuayo-Cañari region are in the process of generating new definitions of what it means to "have gender" in ways unimaginable to previous generations. The results are far from seamless, and contradictions abound. As we have seen, for example, some men develop more equitable relationships with women in parenting

---

3. A notable exception is the work of the late Lionel Cantú (2003), which addresses the experiences of gay Mexican migrants and their creation of alternative family structures.

and budgeting money, even while they continue to have extramarital affairs. Other men stop spending money on alcohol, but burden wives with "producing their locality" (i.e., showing others that they are still part of the community) through the staging of elaborates parties and fiestas. Indeed, in stressing that men and women share common marital goals and unified ideas about parenting, I do not aim to downplay the dynamics of power that underlie all gender relations. Rather, by moving the analysis away from a narrowly defined masculine power in order to examine men's identities in all their facets, we can better discover those subtle instances where "what has changed is not male power as such, but its form, its presentation, its packaging" (Brittan 1989, 2).

While bringing men as gendered beings into clearer ethnographic focus, I have also been careful not merely to substitute one perspective on gender for another. As Gutmann's (1997a) pioneering work on masculinity makes clear, our efforts to investigate men's identities is profitable only when we do so in relation to women. In fact, as Gutmann stresses, it is often women who serve as the catalyst for changes in men's gendered identities and practices. In studies of migration, bringing men's perspectives into tandem with women's provides more than simply an expanded ethnographic record. As I suggested in chapter 7, it also helps to reframe some of the basic questions that have guided previous research on gender and migration. Many previous studies of migration that focus on gender fall prey to what I call a "balance sheet" approach. When the ways in which migration affects gender ideologies are examined, the tendency has been to ask, Who benefits and who loses? If men gain in status, what happens to women, and vice versa? Such questions, I think, seriously limit our understanding of the ways couples may work together toward common goals. In the case of the Ecuadorian couples I highlight here, it is important to keep in mind Carmela's statement (chapter 1) that "families had to change" to meet the goals and priorities of migration. Men I met did not become "modern fathers" who coparent with wives and take an interest in raising children simply because of exposure to "modern" forms of being a man. Instead, both men and women responded to the changing needs of work by reorganizing their gender roles as they did their labor roles.

Finally, this study also speaks to the enduring qualities of family in processes of migration. In the early 1990s, as men (and increasingly women)
from the Azuayo-Cañari countryside left for the United States, Ecuadorian migration researchers and journalists predicted that the countryside
would soon be afflicted with scores of "disrupted households" *(hogares
desorganizados)*. By contrast, in the late 1990s in Jatundeleg, Ayaloma,
and Shullín, I found the opposite: family continued to play an important
and perhaps even amplified role in facilitating and supporting transnational migration. As evidence of the breakdown of family, a number of
critics (see, e.g., Carpio Benalcázar 1992) bemoaned what they saw as an
increased "nuclearization" of households, whereby the extended family
ties appeared to be waning. Appealing to idyllic imagery of the mutually
dependent and extended Andean family, what researchers failed to notice
was the long process of nuclearization that had its roots in a premigration
era, when the decline of agricultural production and inheritances began
in the 1950s. By the time many of the young people I knew were reaching
adulthood in Jatundeleg, the nuclear family had already long been the
norm. I nevertheless observed countless instances where the importance
of extended family ties continued. Extended families were important for,
among other things, securing loans from *chulqueros,* providing childcare
(because sometimes both parents were abroad), and at times managing
remittances. In some cases, family ties were even extended in ways they
had not been in the past. Poor relatives were often given land-use rights
on property that absent migrants could not manage from afar. In short,
predictions about the ways that migration would disrupt family life are
anything but straightforward.

Family structures, though, do not merely stay in tact in the context of
migration; they also have become amplified, assuming a new importance.
In this book's introduction, I stressed the need to move our analyses of
family (especially within studies of migration) from narrow functional interpretations to interpretations with symbolic dimensions. Drawing from
the work of historian John Gillis, I pointed to different ways family in village life grew in significance while other kinds of bonds and affiliations
between community members waned. As the families that villagers lived
with became fraught with tensions and contradictions, the families that

villagers lived *by* assumed a new importance to smooth over the complex realities of migration.

One of the central areas of domestic life analyzed according to the symbolics of family concerns the placement of children in migrant households. In chapter 3, I discussed how during my fieldwork children's celebrations and parties had outpaced fiestas as the primary venue for solidifying community bonds and communicating status. Children also represented the key index by which villagers judged the success of migrant families. Child-related consumption and education joined the building of elaborate new homes and other forms of conspicuous consumption in signaling a migrant household's commitment to the community. Although this study only touches on the symbolic importance of children and childhood within a migrant-sending community and within transnational migration, it suggests new avenues of research on children's experiences in these contexts. A growing body of literature has begun to focus on the immigrant "second generation" (Portes and Rumbaut 2001), but the emphasis has been more on assessing the success of immigrants' progeny to the exclusion of the ideological dimensions that children hold in the motivations and priorities of migration.

The Rising Costs of *la Chulla Vida*

> Ante asunto tan tremendo
> en el mercado cambiario
> me siento un ente ordinario
> si el dólar sigue subiendo.
>
> ¿No es posible que se extriga
> este miedo a la inflación
> si asciende como un avión
> la vieja moneda gringa?
>
> Con esta gran "escalada"
> que deja vacías las manos
> nuestro sucre ecuatoriano
> queda reducido a . . . nada.

Con crisis en el estado
y en el costo de la vida,
con esta grave subida
ya estamos "dolarizados."

Venderé mi radio "Sony,"
mi casa y mi toro viejo
y si se rompe el espejo
¡mejor me voy a la "Yoni"!

In the face of matters so tremendous
in the changing market
I feel like an ordinary guy
if the dollar continues to go up

Isn't it possible to extinguish
this fear of inflation
if the old gringo money
goes up like an airplane?

With this great escalation
that leaves empty hands
our Ecuadorian sucre
is left reduced to . . . nothing

With the state in crisis
and in the cost of living,
with this grave increase
we're already "dollarized"

I will sell my Sony radio
my house and my old bull,
and if the mirror breaks
better I go to Yoni!
                    Don Epifanio, editorial page,
                    Extra, 26 September 1999

My fieldwork in Ecuador in 1999 coincided with the country's worst economic crisis in more than a century. Although economists writing in the nation's newspapers were apt to point out that the crisis had not reached textbook examples of "hyperinflation"—despite the fact that the rate of inflation had reached greater than 60 percent, the highest in Latin America at the time—it might as well have been for those struggling to hold on to their money. Conditions on the streets of Quito, Guayaquil, and Cuenca were starting to mirror notorious chapters of economic crisis in countries such as Brazil and Nicaragua a decade earlier. Prices for gasoline, cooking fuel, and basic food staples were skyrocketing. By the close of the millennium, the cost of drinking water had jumped 120 percent (Gerlach 2003:158). Like Brazilians and Nicaraguans, Ecuadorians quickly adopted the one sure strategy to combat devaluation: "Never go to sleep with a sucre in your pocket, lest it be worth nothing in the morning." Throughout much of 1999, Ecuadorians, both rural and urban, woke up each day wondering if they still had a job, a government, or their own currency. Then President Jamil Mahuad, amidst mounting criticism of his economic policies, announced on January 9, 2000, plans to dollarize the Ecuadorian economy. However, as don Epifanio, the cowboy poet featured daily in *Extra,* Ecuador's tabloidesque news daily, sang on September 26, 1999, as the sucre continued to lose its value, "We're already dollarized."

In Jatundeleg, villagers felt the effects of crisis in the violent fluctuations in prices on everything from cooking gas to the truckloads of green bananas people depended on to feed their pigs. My landlady felt the precipitous drop in the sucre's value each month I paid her. When I began my research, I paid the equivalent of $60 a month in sucres to rent a small house (a cost many told me was exorbitant). By the time I left, I was paying slightly less than $20.

The economic uncertainties of the crisis were paralleled by social unrest as well as organized and mostly peaceful protest from labor unions, sectors of the civil service, and indigenous groups. At times, Jatundeleg, as a somewhat remote location, could seem immune to the roadblocks, strikes, and occasional violent clashes that played out on the streets of Ecuador's major cities and rural highways. However, it would only take the punctuation of a week's routine with a new round of strikes by school-teachers and health workers or the blockading of roads and the suspension of transportation services to jar villagers' awareness. All Ecuadorians took immediate notice when, during the early morning hours of January 21, 2000, several thousand *indígena* under the leadership of the Confederación de Nacionalidades Indígenas del Ecuador (CONAIE, Confederation of Indigenous Nationalities of Ecuador) stormed the Legislative Palace and the Presidential House in Quito with tacit blessings from the country's military and police forces. Together, representatives from indigenous groups, the army, and the Supreme Court formed the Junta de Salvación Nacional (Junta of National Salvation) and forced President Mahuad out of office. After a brief wrestling of power, Vice President Gustavo Noboa Bejarano was sworn in as president to complete Mahuad's abbreviated term.[4]

Among the policy measures that survived Mahuad's administration was the plan to dollarize the economy. In March 2000, the Ecuadorian Congress passed legislation to substitute the use of dollars for sucres and mandated a six-month period (although it dragged on much longer) whereby citizens were to exchange their old currency at a rate of 25,000 sucres for every one dollar. Although it was still months before bus drivers, market vendors, and everyone else who had to make change on a regular basis would have to work in dollars officially, I was amazed to find on a return trip to Ecuador in July that so many people were already adeptly juggling the two currencies. Although the lack of numerals on U.S. coinage proved initially confusing (not to mention that the size of U.S. coins do not match their relative value), many were quick to catch on, aided by glossy newspaper inserts explaining *"nuestra moneda"* (our money). Television and radio campaigns helped to prepare people for the dollar, and street vendors were aggressively hawking sucre coins and bills encased in plastic as if they had already reached antiquity status.

4. A comprehensive history of the events leading up to and following the ouster of President Mahuad can be found in Gerlach 2003 (especially chaps. 7 and 8). See also Brian Selmeski's powerful documentary of the events as captured by Quito media outlets, *Imágenes impresionantes* (2000).

During my visit in summer 2000, I was especially interested to see how villagers in Jatundeleg and its neighboring communities were weathering the transition to dollarization. I wondered, in particular, how dollarization was affecting an economy in many respects already dollarized. My first stop was to see my elderly neighbor don Miguel Cusco at his Jatundeleg *tienda*. It was customary during my fieldwork for me to buy sodas and cigarettes for whoever might be loitering out front of the shop. This day was no exception, and I ended up making purchases for two elderly men I had met only once before. When it was time for me to leave, I motioned to don Miguel, and he began to total up my tab on a piece of brown scrap paper. Although I was paying with my U.S. currency, don Miguel tallied the cost in sucres and then converted it to dollars at the set 25,000-sucre rate. I called him on the practice: "Is this your way of protesting dollarization?" He laughed at my obviously ridiculous question and answered matter-of-factly, "No, those are just the numbers of my country." As a shopkeeper, don Miguel knew firsthand about price fluctuations as he tried to stock his shop with affordable goods and still turn a profit. For his part, he agreed with the dollarization plan, although, like many people his age, he did not believe that much would ultimately ever change.

Others in the community, in particular younger households, both migrant and nonmigrant, gave dollarization mixed reviews. For some, though, the change was profound. The plan was welcomed by members of most nonmigrant households who had long felt their community had become "dollarized" against their will with the actions of migrants setting prices in dollars. When migrant and nonmigrant households alike began operating in dollars, the playing field, if not actual resources, was beginning to level out. In the households deeply connected to the remittance economy, however, dollarization spelled the end to the tactic of stretching money through speculation. During my visits to the various households that had been critical to my study, a general apprehension rang through conversations that migration would no longer pay out as it once did. Nearly all households I visited during the trip reported receiving less in remittances in the months since dollarization had started to take hold. Similarly, the cacophony of pounding hammers and power saws that were formerly an all-too-familiar sonic background to my fieldwork had now quieted as fewer migrant households could afford to build new homes and improve old ones.

After leaving don Miguel's *tienda,* I hiked up to the *cerro* to look for Miguel Solano, whose morning routine included tending his twenty head of cattle. However, I had no idea if I would find him there or anywhere in the village that day. When I had left Jatundeleg earlier in the year, Miguel was strongly considering migrating to the United States again, this time with his sixteen-year-old son (see chapter 3). I was pleased (at least for my own sake) to find Miguel working away in the high, rolling pastureland, yelling obscenities at his cattle as he tried to herd them into a corral. After he completed his task, we sat in the *cerro*'s dry grass and talked about changes in the village and why he had not followed through with his plans to go to the United States. Although Miguel seemed happy to see me, his overall mood was sour and maudlin. He despised dollarization and felt it might mean he would never travel to the United States again. He also blamed his government for worrying more about pleasing the United States and less about its own people.[5] He elaborated: "We need some form of action, some power to get things done. We need some representation like the *taxistas* or the teachers. People who migrate need some help. We bring so much money here to this country. They need to realize this."

Miguel's comments presented a focus on migration I rarely heard articulated previously during fieldwork in Jatundeleg or in New York. Although I had over the course of my research listened to countless stories of the difficulties and vulnerabilities of migration, the responses to many hard luck stories were qualitatively different from Miguel's perspective that day. Specifically, when migrants I knew often told me about how they had failed to generate remittances or how they had been taken advantage of by employers, for instance, they invariably linked these incidences to personal shortcomings and inadequacies rather than to larger structural factors (such as immigration policy, corruption, or failed national development)

5. When Miguel criticized the United States, he was likely equating the country with the International Monetary Fund and the latest round of austerity measures it had mandated in Ecuador.

that impeded their success. Miguel, in contrast, located his discontent in factors that could be addressed, in his opinion, only with collective action. As others in the community I spoke with during this trip echoed a similar concern, I took note of a brewing consciousness that moved beyond the individual concerns of households and families.

I encountered a similar emerging discourse among migrants in the United States. In December 2001, just a few short months after the September 11 terrorist attacks, I was back in the New York City area working as a consultant for the Rockland County Department of Health on a project addressing high rates of tuberculosis among Ecuadorian migrants. In the village of Spring Valley, in a dilapidated apartment that reeked of guinea pigs being raised in a bathtub for a Christmas feast, I interviewed two male migrants, Roberto and Alejandro, both fathers with families back in Ecuador. As we began to speak about my project, Roberto interjected to ask me about the increased vigilance of the INS and whether or not the health department was now going to start reporting illegal migrants. September 11 and its aftermath were fresh in my informants' minds. As they told me, fewer and fewer of their friends and family had been able to make it safely across the border. Many others, fearful of the post-9/11 political climate, halted their plans altogether. Alejandro probed me to see what I knew about rumors he had heard of a guest-worker program for Latin Americans. He reminded me how on the morning of September 11, 2001, President George W. Bush and his Mexican counterpart Vicente Fox were to have met in Ohio to discuss the possibility of such a program, but that the meeting was called off for obvious reasons. He still wanted to know if I thought that Ecuadorians would be included in any such program in the future. I expressed my doubts, but he agreed and stressed the need for Ecuadorians to "organize like the Mexicans." Only with representation and help from the Ecuadorian government would things change, he thought.

Although my experiences in revisiting Jatundeleg to assess the early effects of dollarization on village households and in returning to New York City to evaluate the reverberations of September 11 for undocumented migrants were sobering moments that further exposed the increased difficulties for migrants and their families in getting ahead, they equally revealed glimmers of hope for a shifting mobilization. To the extent that the discussions at this time transferred concern and blame away from the individual level to the collective level, they signaled new strategies for survival for undocumented migrants. Even at the time of this publication, it is perhaps still premature to make a sound assessment of Ecuador's policy of dollarization or of the tighter U.S. immigration laws and border control efforts, but no doubt these developments will continue to place formidable challenges before transnational migrant households. They also, however, open up new avenues for change and reveal strategies to get ahead not yet tested. Since 2001, signs of a migrant mobilization have been evident. Two developments are worth mentioning. Migrants I knew well in Queens reported to me in early 2004 that efforts were under way to organize *esquineros* to fight for better wages and fair treatment by employers. The nascent group was working to set standards on daily wages, to identify unscrupulous employers (a list was kept, and migrants were warned of which potential bosses to avoid), and to protect workers from harassment. A second development, mobilized from Ecuador, strives to

8.1. MODEMI stages a migration awareness campaign in the Cuenca's main plaza, 1999. Photograph by the author.

lessen the effects of dollarization on remittances. Movimiento de Defensa de los Migrantes–Azuay (MODEMI) has established relationships with certain money-wiring agencies to help reduce the cost of fees for sending money to Ecuador. As migrants like those I knew in Jatundeleg and in Queens find it harder and harder to locate their *iony* dreams, such collective efforts may take on a new importance. How these actions will play out for men, women, and their families stretched between the United States and Ecuador awaits exploration.

Glossary

References

Index

Glossary

This glossary of terms used in the text reflects the mixture of Spanish, Quichua, English, and "Spanglish" in the language spoken by Azuayo-Cañari peasants and migrants. With only a few exceptions, all Quichua spellings and orthography are based on Luis Cordero's well-known 1895 Quichua-Spanish dictionary (Cordero 1992). (Cordero, who served as president of Ecuador from 1892 to 1895, was born only a few miles from Jatundeleg and grew up learning the local register of Quichua.) The abbreviations used in the entries are: A. = Aymara; Q. = Quichua; Sp. = Spanish; Spang. = Spanglish.

agotado/a (Sp.): exhausted person; frequently used to describe migrants who do nothing but work

aguardiente (Sp.): cane alcohol, typically commercially manufactured

ají (Sp.): hot pepper capsicum; also ubiquitous sauce condiment made from the peppers

ambulante (Sp.): street vendor without a fixed market site

bodega (Sp.): storage room or large closet space

cambiomanos (Sp.): literally "exchanging hands"; refers to reciprocal labor exchanges between households; same as *prestamanos*

camioneta (Sp.): pickup truck with seats in the bed used to transport people and goods between villages

campesino/a (Sp.): generic term for "peasant"; preferred term used by rural peoples to describe themselves

campo (Sp.): countryside

canelazo (Sp.): hot, spiced alcohol drink made with cane alcohol, herbs, and spices

cantón (Sp.): governmental geographic administration unit similar to a county

chacra (Q.): field or growing space (formerly *chacara*)

chala (Q.): corn stalks used as fodder; portion of a harvest

charla (Sp.): chat or group conversation

chicha (Q.): fermented maize beer

choclo (Q./Sp.): corn on the cob; term used to describe corn generally

chulco (Sp.?): loan made by a *chulquero/a*

chulquero/a (Sp.?): quasi-illegal money lender; "loan shark"; also referred to as *banqueros informales* (informal bankers); see also *prestamista*

chumado/a (Sp.): a drunk person

"comprar la semana" (Sp.): literally, "to buy the week"; refers to women's domestic spending

comuna (Sp.): common lands

comunero/a (Sp.): community member; village resident

convivir (Sp.): to live together; to coexist; to exist side by side

cooperativa (Sp.): cooperative of truck transport drivers

costa (Sp.): the coast

costeño/a (Sp.): person from the coast

Ekeko (A.): good-luck figurine depicting a portly merchant trader with a cigar

"enviar una seña" (Sp.): literally "to send the sign"; refers to the initial payment made on a *chulquero* loan

esquinero (Sp.): "street corner man"; migrant day laborer

familia (Sp.): family, typically connoting a household with children

fío (Sp.): loan

"ganarse la vida" (Sp.): literally "to earn one's self a living"; refers to men's subsistence economic practices

"hacer agosto" (Sp.): literally, "to make August"; refers to the time of the harvest when households are wealthiest; colloquially, *hacer agosto* means "to earn a lot of money"

herencia (Sp.): inheritance

indígena (Sp.): indigenous person

indio/a (Sp.): derogatory label for indigenous person

indocumentados/as (Sp.): migrants who have entered the United States illegally

invernadero (Sp.): greenhouse

iony (Spang.): term used to describe migrants and returned migrants who have adopted North American speech, fashion, and attitude (from the bumper-sticker and T-shirt catchphrase "I ♥ NY")

jornalero/a (Sp.): laborer, day laborer

ladrón (Sp.): thief or robber

longo (Q.): derogatory name for indigenous person

"llachapa vida" (Sp./Q.): "ragged life"

maíz (Sp.): generic term for corn in all its varieties

maizal (Sp.): cornfield

matrimonio (Sp.): matrimony; marriage; a married couple

media (Sp.): sharecropping agreement

migra (Spang.): generic colloquial term for U.S. Border Patrol or INS officials

migrante (Sp.): migrant

minga (Sp./Q.): communal work party

mitayo/a (Sp./Q.): in the colonial period, a term referring to a person who paid tribute *(mita)* to the Spanish; now a derogatory term referring to indigenous people

ñaño/a (Q.): son or daughter

ñaupa tiempos (Q./Sp.): *ñaupa* literally means "before" or "at another time"; refers to the past times or "in the olden days"

paisano/a (Sp.): "countryman/woman"

pampamesa (Sp./Q.): communal feast eaten on cloth laid on the ground

pandillas (Sp.): "street gangs"

"para plata" (Sp.): "for money"; refers to women's managing of finances

parva (Sp.): haystack made of cornstalks

pasador/a (Sp.): smuggler of migrants

plata (Sp.): money; silver

"por la pampa" (Sp.): "by land"; to travel illegally to the United States

prestamanos (Sp.): literally, "borrowed hands"; see *cambiomanos*

prestamista (Sp.): loan maker; see also *chulquero/a*

puro (Sp.): literally, "pure"; refers to bootleg cane alcohol

recuerdos (Sp.): objects often used in altar devotions to "remember"; also, small favors given at baptisms, first communions, and fiestas

sala (Sp.): living room or public space where guests are greeted in a home

seña (Sp.): sign

"sin papeles" (Sp.): literally "without papers"; undocumented immigration status

sombrero de paja (Sp.): straw hat or "Panama" hat

sucre (Sp.): Ecuadorian currency discontinued in 2001

suegra/o (Sp.): mother-in-law or father-in-law

tienda (Sp.): small store, usually built into the front of a home, selling grocery items, alcohol, and cigarettes

trago (Sp.): cane alcohol typically served in shot glasses; from *tragar,* "to swallow"

vicios (Sp.): "vices," including the consumption of alcohol and tobacco, gambling, and sex with prostitutes

Yoni (Spang.): New York City (adapted from the bumpersticker and T-shirt phrase "I ♥ New York")

yunta (Sp.): pair of oxen and yoke used for plowing fields

References

Abad, Andrés Merchan. 1997. "Coyotes: No pueden ser tan malvados." *Catedral Salvaje* (Cuenca, Ecuador) 138: 2–3.

Abdulrahim, Dima. 1993. "Defining Gender in a Second Exile: Palestinian Women in West Berlin." In *Migrant Women: Crossing Borders and Changing Identities,* edited by Gina Buijs, 55–82. Oxford: Berg.

Ahearn, Laura M. 2001. "Language and Agency." *Annual Review of Anthropology* 30: 109–37.

Alberti, Amalia M. 1986. "Gender, Ethnicity, and Resource Control in the Andean Highlands of Ecuador." Ph.D. diss., Department of Anthropology, Stanford Univ.

Albornoz, Victor Manuel. 1960. *Cuenca a traves de cuatro siglos.* Vol. 1. Cuenca, Ecuador: Dirección de Publicaciones Municipales.

Alicea, Marixsa. 1997. "A Chambered Nautilus: The Contradictory Nature of Puerto Rico Women's Role in the Social Construction of a Transnational Community." *Gender and Society* 11, no. 5: 597–626.

Allen, Catherine J. 2002. *The Hold Life Has: Coca and Cultural Identity in an Andean Community.* 2d ed. 1988. Washington, D.C.: Smithsonian Institution Press.

Alvarez, Robert R., Jr. 1987. *Familia: Migration and Adaptation in Baja and Alta California, 1800–1975.* Berkeley: Univ. of California Press.

Andrade, Xavier. 2000. "Apuntes etnográficos sobre masculinidad, cultura y poder." *Cuardernos de Antropología* 5: 51–85.

Andrade, Xavier, and Gioconda Herrera, eds. 2001. *Masculinidades en Ecuador.* Quito, Ecuador: FLACSO.

Andreas, Peter. 2000. *Border Games: Policing the U.S.–Mexico Divide.* Ithaca: Cornell Univ. Press.

Andrien, Kenneth J. 1995. *The Kingdom of Quito: The State and Regional Development.* Cambridge: Cambridge Univ. Press.

Appadurai, Arjun. 1996. *Modernity at Large: Cultural Dimensions of Globalization.* Minneapolis: Univ. of Minnesota Press.

Arízaga Rovalino, Irene, and Rosario Daquilema Miranda. 2001. "Migración conyugal y sus repercusiones en la salud de las mujeres: Comunidad Jatundeleg, Provincia de Cañar." Master's thesis, Univ. of Cuenca, Ecuador.

Artieda, Fernando. 1989. "Tierra de las mujeres solas." *Vistazo* 526 (20 July): 36–40.

Bailey, Thomas. 1985. "A Case Study of Immigrants in the Restaurant Industry." *Industrial Relations* 24: 205–21.

Balerezo, Susana P. 1984. "Tejedores de paja toquilla y reproducción campesina en Cañar." In *Mujer y transformaciones agrarias en la sierra ecuatoriana,* edited by Susana Balerezo et al., 147–244. Quito, Ecuador: Centro de Planificación y Estudios Sociales (CEPLAES), Corporación Editoria Nacional.

Basch, Linda, Nina Glick Schiller, and Cristina Szanton Blanc. 1994. *Nations Abound: Transnational Projects, Postcolonial Predicaments, and Deterritorialized Nation-States.* Langhorne, Pa.: Gordon and Breach.

Bauer, Brian S. 1996. "Legitimization of the State in Inca Myth and Ritual." *American Anthropologist* 98, no. 2: 327–37.

Bebbington, Anthony, and Graham Thiele, eds. 1993. *NGOs and the State in Latin America: Rethinking Roles in Sustainable Agricultural Development.* London: Routledge.

Belote, Jim, and Linda S. Belote. 1977. "The Limitation of Obligation in Saraguro Kinship." In *Andean Kinship and Marriage,* edited by Ralph Bolton and Enrique Mayer, 106–16. American Anthropological Association Special Publications no. 7. Washington, D.C.: American Anthropological Association.

Belote, Linda S., and Jim Belote. 1988. "Gender, Ethnicity, and Modernization: Saraguro Women in a Changing World." In *Multidisciplinary Studies in Andean Anthropology,* vol. 8, edited by Virginia J. Vitzthum, 101–17. Ann Arbor: Michigan Discussions in Anthropology.

Bender, Donald. 1967. "A Refinement of the Concept of Household: Families, Coresidence, and Domestic Functions." *American Anthropologist* 70: 309–20.

Benería, Lourdes, and Martha Roldán. 1987. *The Crossroads of Class and Gender: Industrial Housework, Subcontracting, and Household Dynamics in Mexico City.* Chicago: Univ. of Chicago Press.

Berdahl, Daphne. 1999. *Where the World Ended: Re-unification and Identity in the German Borderland.* Berkeley: Univ. of California Press.

Berger, John, and Jean Mohr. 1975. *Seventh Man: The Story of a Migrant Worker in Europe.* Harmondsworth, England: Penguin Books.

Berman, Marshall. 1982. *All That Is Solid Melts into Air: The Experience of Modernity.* New York: Penguin Books.

Bhabba, Homi K. 1990. "DissemiNation: Time, Narrative, and the Margins of the Modern Nation." In *Nation and Narration,* edited by Homi K. Bhabba, 291–322. New York: Routledge.

Bodnar, John, Roger Simon, and Michael P. Weber. 1982. *Lives of Their Own: Blacks, Italians, and Poles in Pittsburgh, 1900–1960.* Urbana: Univ. of Illinois Press.

Boisvert, Collette Callier. 1987. "Working-Class Portuguese Families in a French Provincial Town: Adaptive Strategies." In *Migrants in Europe: The Role of Family, Labor, and Politics,* edited by Hans C. Buechler and Judith-Maria Buechler, 61–77. New York: Greenwood Press.

Borrero, Ana Luz. 1991. "Las migraciones y recursos humanos: Situación reciente y tendencias." In *Cuenca y su futuro,* 93–172. Quito, Ecuador: Corporación de Estudios para el Desarrollo, Universidad de Azuay.

———. 2001. "Los costos de la migración en Cuenca y su región." *Cántaro* 9, no. 23: 38–42.

Borrero, Ana Luz, and Silvia Vega Ugalde. 1995. *Mujer y migración: Alcance de un fenómeno nacional y regional.* Quito, Ecuador: Ediciones Abya-Yala.

Bourdieu, Pierre. 1984. *Distinction: A Social Critique of the Judgment of Taste.* Cambridge, Mass.: Harvard Univ. Press.

Bourque, Nicole N. 1995. "Savages and Angels: The Spiritual, Social, and Physical Development of Individuals and Households in Andean Life-Cycle Festivals." *Ethnos* 60, nos. 1–2: 99–114.

Bourque, Susan C., and Kay Barbara Warren. 1981. *Women of the Andes: Patriarchy and Social Change in Two Peruvian Towns.* Ann Arbor: Univ. of Michigan Press.

Bourricaud, Francois. 1975. "Indian, Mestizo, and Cholo as Symbols in the Peruvian System of Stratification." In *Ethnicity: Theory and Experience,* edited by Nathan Glazer and Daniel Patrick Moynihan, 350–87. Cambridge: Cambridge Univ. Press.

Breckenridge, Carol, ed. 1995. *Consuming Modernity: Public Culture in a South Asian World.* Minneapolis: Univ. of Minnesota Press.

Brettell, Caroline B. 2000. "Theorizing Migration in Anthropology: The Social Construction of Networks, Identities, Communities, and Globalscapes." In *Migration Theory,* edited by Caroline B. Brettell and James F. Hollifield, 97–136. New York: Routledge.

Brittan, Arthur. 1989. *Masculinity and Power.* Oxford: Basil Blackwell.

Brownrigg, Leslie Ann. 1972. "The Nobles of Cuenca: The Agrarian Elite of Southern Ecuador." Ph.D. diss., Department of Political Science, Columbia Univ.

Brusco, Elizabeth E. 1995. *The Reformation of Machismo: Evangelical Conversion and Gender in Colombia.* Austin: Univ. of Texas Press.

Buechler, Hans C. 1987. "Spanish Galician Migration to Switzerland: Demographic Processes and Family Dynamics." In *Migrants in Europe: The Role of Family, Labor, and Politics,* edited by Hans C. Buechler and Judith-Maria Buechler, 221–64. New York: Greenwood Press.

Buechler, Hans, and Judith-Maria Buechler. 1971. *The Bolivian Aymara.* New York: Holt, Rinehart and Winston.

———. 1996. *The World of Sofia Velasquez: The Autobiography of a Bolivian Market Vendor.* New York: Columbia Univ. Press.

Buechler, Judith-Maria. 1976a. "Introduction." In *Women and Migration,* special issue of *Anthropological Quarterly* 49: 1–61.

———. 1976b. "Something Funny Happened on the Way to the Agora: A Comparison of Bolivian and Spanish Galician Migrants." *Anthropological Quarterly* 49: 62–69.

Burgos Guevara, Hugo. 2003. *La identidad del pueblo Cañari: De-construcción de una nación étnica.* Quito, Ecuador: Ediciones Abya-Yala.

Burke, Timothy. 1996. *Lifebuoy Men, Lux Women: Commodification, Consumption, and Cleanliness in Modern Zimbabwe.* Chicago: Univ. of Chicago Press.

Cabello de Balboa, Miguel. 1951. *Miscelánea Antártica: Una historia del Perú antiguo.* 1586. Lima, Peru: Instituto de Etnología, Facultad de Letras, Universidad Nacional Mayor de San Marcos.

Caillavet, Chantal. 1996. "Los grupos prehispánicos del sur del Ecuador según las fuentes etnohistoricas." In *Antropología del Ecuador,* edited by Segundo Moreno, 149–80. Quito, Ecuador: Ediciones Abya-Yala.

Cajamarca, Libia. 1991. "Mujer y migracíon internacional: Impactos de la migración internacional sobre roles y estatus de la mujer campesina. El caso de Jatunpampa." Master's thesis, Development Anthropology Program, Universidad de Azuay, Cuenca, Ecuador.

Calagione, John. 1992. "Working in Time: Music and Power on the Job in New York." In *Workers' Expressions: Beyond Accommodation and Resistance,* edited by John Calagione, Doris Francis, and Daniel Nugent, 12–28. Albany: State Univ. of New York Press.

Camacho, Gloria. 2004. "Feminización de las migraciones en Ecuador." In *Migraciones: Un juego con cartas marcadas,* edited by Francisco Hidalgo, 303–26. Quito, Ecuador: Ediciones Abya-Yala.

Cantú, Lionel. 2003. "A Place Called Home: A Queer Political Economy of Mexican Immigrant Men's Family Experiences." In *Perspectives on las Américas,* edited by Matthew C. Gutmann, Felix V. Matos Rodríguez, Lynn Stephen, and Patricia Zavella, 259–73. Malden, Mass.: Blackwell.

Carey, James W. 1987. "The Significance of Informal Social Support Networks for Rural Households in the Andes." In *Multidisciplinary Studies in Andean Anthropology,* vol. 8, edited by Virginia J. Vitzthum, 119–35. Ann Arbor: Michigan Discussions in Anthropology.

Carpio Benalcázar, Patricio. 1992. *Entre pueblos y metropolis: La migración internacional en comunidades austroandinas en el Ecuador.* Quito, Ecuador: Ediciones Abya-Yala.

Carrier, Joseph. 1990. *De los otros: Intimacy and Homosexuality among Mexican Men.* New York: Columbia Univ. Press.

Carrigan, Tim, Bob Connell, and John Lee. 1987. "Towards a New Sociology of Masculinity." In *The Making of Masculinities: New Men's Studies,* edited by Harry Brod, 551–603. Winchester, Mass.: Allen and Unwin.

Carter, William E. 1977. "Trial Marriage in the Andes?" In *Andean Kinship and Marriage,* edited by Ralph Bolton and Enrique Mayer, 217–39. American Anthropological Association Special Publications no. 7. Washington, D.C.: American Anthropological Association.

Castles, Stephen, and Mark J. Miller. 1993. *The Age of Migration: International Population Movements in the Modern World.* New York: Guilford Press.

Catedral Salvaje. 1989. Special issue on international migration. *El Mercurio* (Cuenca, Ecuador), Dec. 23.

Catholic Diocese of Azogues. 1997. "Results of Household Survey Conducted by the Pastoral Social de Migración, Azogues (Cañar)." Internal Document, Azogues, Ecuador.

Cevallos, Jorge. 1997. *The New York Labor Pool: Alucinaciones de un migrante.* New York: True North Press.

Chacón Zhapan, Juan. 1990. *Historia del corregimiento de Cuenca, 1557–1777.* Quito: Banco Central del Ecuador.

Chamberlain, Mary, and Selma Leydesdorff. 2004. "Transnational Families: Memories and Narratives." Introduction to *Transnational Families,* special issue of *Global Networks* 4, no. 3: 227–41.

Chavez, Leo R. 1991. "Outside the Imagined Community: Undocumented Settlers and Experiences of Incorporation." *American Ethnologist* 18, no. 2: 257–78.

———. 1992. *Shadowed Lives: Undocumented Immigrants in American Society.* Fort Worth, Tex.: Harcourt, Brace College.

Chin, Elizabeth. 2001. *Purchasing Power: Black Kids and American Consumer Culture.* Minneapolis: Univ. of Minnesota Press.

Chin, Margaret. 2001. "When Co-ethnic Assets Become Liabilities: Mexican, Ecuadorian, and Chinese Garment Workers in New York City." In *Migration, Transnationalization, and Race in a Changing New York City,* edited by Héctor R. Cordero-Guzmán, Robert C. Smith, and Ramón Grosfoguel, 279–300. Philadelphia: Temple Univ. Press.

Chiriboga, Manuel. 1988. "La reforma agraria ecuatoriana y los cambios en la distribución de la propiedad rural agrícola, 1974–1984." In *Transformaciones agrarias en el Ecuador,* edited by Pierre Gondard, Juan B. León, and Paola Sylva Ch., 39–57. Quito, Ecuador: Centro Ecuatoriano de Investigación Geográfia.

Cieza de León, Pedro. 1965. *La crónica de Perú.* 1553. Madrid: Espassa-Calpe.

Clark, A. Kim. 1998. *The Redemptive Work: Railway and Nation in Ecuador, 1895–1930.* Wilmington, Del.: Scholarly Resources.

———. 2001. "Género, raza y nación: La protección a la infancia en el Ecuador (1910–1945)." In *Estudios de género,* edited by Gioconda Herrera, 183–210. Quito, Ecuador: FLACSO-Ecuador, ILDIS.

Clearfield, Esha. 1999. *The Effects of Migration on Women and Children in Azuay and Cañar.* Final Report to the Fulbright Commission. Quito, Ecuador: n.p.

Cliggett, Lisa. 2005. "Remitting the Gift: Zambian Mobility and Anthropological Insights for Migration Studies." *Population, Space, and Place* 11: 35–49.

Collier, Jane Fishburne. 1997. *From Duty to Desire: Remaking Families in a Spanish Village.* Princeton, N.J.: Princeton Univ. Press.

Collier, Jane, Michelle Z. Rosaldo, and Sylvia Yanagisako. 1992. "Is There a Family? New Anthropological Views." In *Rethinking the Family: Some Feminist Questions,* edited by Barrie Thorne and Marilyn Yalom, 25–38. 1982. Reprint. New York: Longman.

Collins, Jane. 1988. *Unseasonable Migrations: The Effects of Rural Labor Scarcity in Peru.* Princeton, N.J.: Princeton Univ. Press.

Colloredo-Mansfield, Rudi. 1999. *The Native Leisure Class: Consumption and Cultural Creativity in the Andes.* Chicago: Univ. of Chicago Press.

———. 2002. "Don't Be Lazy, Don't Lie, Don't Steal: Community Justice in the Neoliberal Andes." *American Ethnologist* 29, no. 3: 637–62.

Comaroff, Jean, and John Comaroff, eds. 1993. *Modernity and Its Malcontents: Ritual and Power in Postcolonial Africa.* Chicago: Univ. of Chicago Press.

Confederación de Nacionalidades Indígenas del Ecuador (CONAIE). 1989. *Las nacionalidades indígenas en el Ecuador.* Quito, Ecuador: Ediciones Abya-Yala.

Connell, R. W. 1996. "New Directions in Gender Theory, Masculinity Research, and Gender Politics." *Ethnos* 61, nos. 3–4: 157–76.

Conover, Ted. 1987. *Coyotes: A Journey Through the Secret World of America's Illegal Aliens.* New York: Vintage Books.

Consejo Nacional de Universidades y Escuelas Politecnicas and Universidad de Azuay de Cuenca (CONUEP/UDA). 1995. "Cambios socio-culturales en comunidades campesinas de migración internacional en Azuay y Cañar." Unpublished research report, Cuenca, Ecuador.

"Construcción en la desocupación." 1999. *El Mercurio* (Cuenca, Ecuador), Nov. 23, 6A.

"Construcción incrementó en un 5, 32%." 1999. *El Mercurio* (Cuenca, Ecuador), Feb. 20, 5A.

Conway, Dennis, and Jeffrey H. Cohen. 1998. "Consequences of Migration and Remittances for Mexican Transnational Communities." *Economic Geography* 74, no. 1: 26–44.

Cooper, Barbara. 2001. "The Strength in the Song: Muslim Personhood, Audible Capital, and Hausa Women's Performance of the Haj." In *Gendered Modernities: Ethnographic Perspectives,* edited by Dorothy Hodgson, 79–104. New York: Palgrave.

Cordero, Luis. 1992. *Diccionario Quichua-Castellano y Castellano-Quichua.* 1895. Reprint. Quito, Ecuador: Corporación Editora Nacional.

Cordero de Espinosa, Susana. 1999. "El mestizaje en el habla Azuaya: El Quichua y el Cañari presentes en ella." In *Estudios, cronicas y relatos de nuestra tierra,* vol. 2, edited by María Rosa Crespo, 17–44. Cuenca, Ecuador: Casa de la Cultura.

Cornelius, Wayne A. 1982. "Interviewing Undocumented Immigrants: Methodological Reflections Based on Fieldwork in Mexico and the U.S." *International Migration Review* 16, no. 2: 378–404.

Cornwall, Andrea, and Nancy Lindisfarne, eds. 1994. *Dislocating Masculinity: Comparative Ethnographies.* New York: Routledge.

Corr, Rachel. 2002. "Reciprocity, Communion, and Sacrifice: Food in Andean Ritual and Social Life." *Food and Foodways* 10, no. 1: 1–25.

Coutin, Susan Bibler. 2005. "Being en Route." *American Anthropologist* 107, no. 2: 195–206.

Creed, Gerald W. 2000. "Family Values and Domestic Economies." *Annual Review of Anthropology* 29: 329–55.

Cuesta y Cuesta, Alfonso. 1963. *Los hijos.* Havana, Cuba: Casa de las Americas.

Cueva Malo, Rodrigo. 1991. "Campesinado, migración y desarrollo: Estudio de caso en la comunidad indígena El Rocío." Master's thesis, Development Anthropology Program, Universidad de Azuay, Cuenca, Ecuador.

D'Alisera, JoAnn. 2001. "I ♥ Islam: Popular Religious Commodities, Sites of Inscription, and Transnational Sierra Leonean Identity." *Journal of Material Culture* 6, no. 1: 89–108.

D'Altroy, Terrance N. 2002. *The Incas.* Malden, Mass.: Blackwell.

Dávila, Arlene M. 2001. *Latinos, Inc.: The Making and Marketing of a People.* Berkeley: Univ. of California Press.

Day, Sophie, Evthymios Papataxiarchis, and Michael Stewart, eds. 1999. *Lilies of the Field: Marginal People Who Live for the Moment.* Boulder, Colo.: Westview Press.

De la Cadena, Marisol. 2000. *Indigenous Mestizos: The Politics of Race and Culture in Cuzco, Peru, 1919–1991.* Durham, N.C.: Duke Univ. Press.

Diccionario económico juridico y político. N.d. Quito, Ecuador: Abya-Yala.

Di Leonardo, Micaela. 1987. "The Female World of Cards and Holidays: Women, Families, and the Work of Kinship." *Signs* 12, no. 3: 440–53.

———. 1991. "Introduction: Gender, Culture, and Political Economy: Feminist Anthropology in Historical Perspective." In *Gender at the Crossroads of Knowledge,* edited by Micaela di Leonardo, 1–50. Berkeley: Univ. of California Press.

Di Leonardo, Micaela, and Roger N. Lancaster. 1997. "Introduction: Embodied Meanings, Carnal Practices." In *The Gender/Sexuality Reader,* edited by Roger N. Lancaster and Micaela di Leonardo, 1–12. London: Routledge.

Diner, Hasia R. 1982. *Erin's Daughters in America: Irish Immigrant Women in the Nineteenth Century.* Baltimore: Johns Hopkins Univ. Press.

Dinerman, Ina R. 1982. *Migrants and Stay at Homes: A Comparative Study of Rural Migration from Mexico.* La Jolla, Calif.: Center for U.S.–Mexican Studies.

Domínguez, Miguel Ernesto. 1991. *El sombrero de paja toquilla: Historia y economía.* Cuenca: Ediciones del Banco Central del Ecuador.

Douglas, Mary, and Baron Isherwood. 1978. *The World of Goods: Towards an Anthropology of Consumption.* London: Routledge.

Durand, Jorge, and Douglas S. Massey. 1992. "Mexican Migration to the United States: A Critical Review." *Latin American Research Review* 27, no. 2: 3–42.

Durand, Jorge, Emilio A. Parrado, and Douglas S. Massey. 1996. "Migradollars and Development: A Reconsideration of the Mexican Case." *International Migration Review* 30, no. 2: 423–44.

Dwyer, Daisy, and Judith Bruce, eds. 1988. *A House Divided: Women and Income in the Third World.* Stanford, Calif.: Stanford Univ. Press.

Einzmann, Harald, and Napoleón Almeida. 1991. *La cultura popular en el Ecuador.* Vol. 6, *Cañar.* Cuenca, Ecuador: Centro Interamericano de Artesanías y Artes Populares.

Encalada Vazquez, Oswaldo. 1990. *Modismos Cuencanos.* Cuenca: Ediciones del Banco Central del Ecuador.

Engwall, Evan C. 1995. "Turbulent Relations Recast: The Mythohistory of the Cañaris and Inca Empire." *Journal of the Steward Anthropological Society* 23, nos. 1–2: 345–61.

Espinoza, Leonardo, and Lucas Achig. 1981. *Proceso de desarrollo de las provincias de Azuay, Cañar y Morona Santiago: Breve historia económica y social de la región Cañari.* Cuenca, Ecuador: CREA.

Fals-Borda, Orlando. 1962. *Peasant Society in the Colombian Andes: A Sociological Study of Saucío.* Gainesville: Univ. of Florida Press.

Fernández-Kelly, María Patricia. 1983. *For We Are Sold, I and My People: Women and Industry in Mexico's Frontier.* Albany: State Univ. of New York Press.

Fernández-Kelly, María Patricia, and Ana García. 1990. "Power Surrendered, Power Restored: The Politics of Home and Work among Hispanic Women in Southern California and Southern Florida." In *Women, Politics, and Change,* edited by Louise A. Tilly and Patricia Guerin, 130–49. New York: Russell Sage Foundation.

Fine, Gary Alan. 1996. *Kitchens: The Culture of Restaurant Work.* Berkeley: Univ. of California Press.

Finerman, Ruthbeth. 1989. "The Burden of Responsibility: Duty, Depression, and Nervios in Andean Ecuador." *Health Care for Women International* 19, nos. 2–3: 147–57.

Finn, Janet L. 1998. *Tracing the Veins: Of Copper, Culture, and Community from Butte to Chuquicamata.* Berkeley: Univ. of California Press.

Fletcher, Peri L. 1999. *La casa de mis sueños: Dreams of Home in a Transnational Mexican Community.* Boulder, Colo.: Westview Press.

Fock, Niels, and Eva Krener. 1978. "Los Cañaris del Ecuador y sus conceptos etno-históricos sobre los Incas." In *Amerikanistische Studien: Festschrift für Herman Trimborn,* edited by Roswith Hartmann and Udo Oberem, 170–81. St. Augustin, Germany: Haus Völker und Kulturen, Anthropos-Institut.

Foner, Nancy. 1978. *Jamaica Farewell.* Berkeley: Univ. of California Press.

———. 1997a. "The Immigrant Family: Cultural Legacies and Cultural Changes." *International Migration Review* 31, no. 4: 961–74.

———. 1997b. "What's New about Transnationalism? New York Immigrants Today and at the Turn of the Century." *Diaspora* 6, no. 3: 354–75.

Freeman, Carla. 2000. *High Tech and High Heels in the Global Economy: Women, Work, and Pink-Collar Identities in the Caribbean.* Durham, N.C.: Duke Univ. Press.

Gabaccia, Donna. 1994. *From the Other Side: Women, Gender, and Immigrant Life in the United States, 1820–1990.* Bloomington: Indiana Univ. Press.

Gailey, Christine Ward. 1992. "A Good Man Is Hard to Find: Overseas Migration and the Decentered Household in the Tongan Islands." *Critique of Anthropology* 12, no. 1: 47–74.

Galarza, Galo. 1987. "Viaje por el filo del mido." *Letras del Ecuador* 168–69 (May): 10–13.

Gamburd, Michele Ruth. 2000. *The Kitchen Spoon's Handle: Transnationalism and Sri Lanka's Migrant Housemaids.* Ithaca, N.Y.: Cornell Univ. Press.

Gamio, Manuel. 1930. *Mexican Immigration to the United States.* Chicago: Univ. of Chicago Press.

García Canclini, Néstor. 1995. *Hybrid Cultures: Strategies for Entering and Leaving Modernity.* Translated by Christopher L. Chiappari and Silvia L. López. Minneapolis: Univ. of Minnesota Press.

Gardner, Katy. 2002. *Age, Narrative, and Migration: The Life Course and Life Histories of Bengali Elders in London.* Oxford: Berg.

Gelles, Paul H. 2000. *Water and Power in Highland Peru: The Cultural Politics of Irrigation and Development.* New Brunswick, N.J.: Rutgers Univ. Press.

Georges, Eugenia. 1990. *The Making of a Transnational Community: Migration, Development, and Cultural Change in the Dominican Republic.* New York: Columbia Univ. Press.

Gerlach, Allen. 2003. *Indians, Oil, and Politics: A Recent History of Ecuador.* Wilmington, Del.: Scholarly Resources.

Ghannam, Farha. 1999. "Keeping Him Connected: Labor Migration and the Production of Locality in Cairo." *City and Society* 10, no. 1: 65–82.

Gillis, John R. 1997. *A World of Their Own Making: Myth, Ritual, and the Quest for Family Values.* Harvard, Mass.: Harvard Univ. Press.

Gilmore, David. 1990. *Manhood in the Making: Cultural Concepts of Masculinity.* New Haven, Conn.: Yale Univ. Press.

Glickman, Lawrence. 1997. *A Living Wage: American Workers and the Making of Consumer Society.* Ithaca, N.Y.: Cornell Univ. Press.

Glick Schiller, Nina, Linda Basch, and Cristina Szanton Blanc. 1995. "From Immigrant to Transmigrant: Theorizing Transnational Migration." *Anthropological Quarterly* 68, no. 1: 48–63.

González, Clementina. 1988. "Estrategias de reproducción en las familias campesinas de Cuenca: Un estudio exploratorio." *Revista del Insituto de Investigaciones Sociales de la Universidad de Cuenca* 19 (Nov.): 65–73.

González Aguirre, Iván, and Paciente Vásquez. 1982. "Movilizaciones campesinas en Azuay y Cañar durante el siglo XIX." In *Ensayos sobre historia regional: La región centro sur,* edited by Claudio Cordero, 179–232. Cuenca, Ecuador: Casa de la Cultura Ecuatoriana, Núcleo del Azuay, IDIS.

Grasmuck, Sherri, and Patricia P. Pessar. 1991. *Between Two Islands: Dominican International Migration.* Berkeley: Univ. of California Press.

Grünenfelder-Elliker, Barbara. 2001. "Exclusion to the Point of Attrition: Gendered Emigration from Ecuador at a Crossroads." Paper presented at the XXIII International Congress of the Latin American Studies Association, Washington, D.C., Sept. 6–8.

Guamán Poma de Ayalla, Felipe. 1936. *El nueva crónica y buen gobierno.* Ca. 1613. Paris: Istitut d'Ethnologie.

Guarnizo, Luis E. 1997. "Transnationalism from Below: Social Transformation and the Mirage of Return Migration among Dominican Transmigrants." *Identities* 4, no. 2: 281–322.

Guarnizo, Luis E., and Michael P. Smith. 1998. "The Locations of Transnationalism." In *Transnationalism from Below,* edited by Michael P. Smith and Luis E. Guarnizo, 3–30. New Brunswick, N.J.: Transaction.

Guayasamín Cruz, Soledad, and Miriam Moya Herrera. 2002. "'Ser de coyote' . . . Una condición para migrar como ilegales." In *Memórias de cuatro encuentro de universidades de la subregión Andina: Género y realidad Andina,* edited by C. Mendoza Eskola, 94–99. Cuenca, Ecuador: Univ. of Cuenca.

Gudeman, Stephen, and Alberto Rivera. 1990. *Conversations in Columbia: The Domestic Economy in Life and Text.* Cambridge: Cambridge Univ. Press.

Gupta, Akhil, and James Ferguson, eds. 1997. *Anthropological Locations: Boundaries and Grounds of a Field Science.* Berkeley: Univ. of California Press.

Gutmann, Matthew C. 1996. *The Meanings of Macho: Being a Man in Mexico City.* Berkeley: Univ. of California Press.

———. 1997a. "The Ethnographic (G)ambit: Women and the Negotiation of Masculinity in Mexico City." *American Ethnologist* 24, no. 4: 833–55.

———. 1997b. "Trafficking in Men: The Anthropology of Masculinity." *Annual Review of Anthropology* 26: 385–409.

———, ed. 2003. *Changing Men and Masculinities in Latin America.* Durham, N.C.: Duke Univ. Press.

Guyer, Jane. 1988. "Dynamic Approaches to Domestic Budgeting: Cases and Methods from Africa." In *A Home Divided,* edited by Daisy Dwyer and Judith Bruce, 155–72. Stanford, Calif.: Stanford Univ. Press.

HABITierra. 1999. *Diagnóstico sobre comportamientos de riesgo frente a enfermadades de transmission sexual, VIH y SIDA en mujeres de Cañar.* Internal report. Cuenca, Ecuador: HABITierra.

Hagan, Jacqueline M. 1994. *Deciding to Be Legal: A Mayan Community in Houston.* Philadelphia: Temple Univ. Press.

Hamilton, Sarah. 1998. *The Two-Headed Household: Gender and Rural Development in the Ecuadorean Andes.* Pittsburgh: Univ. of Pittsburgh Press.

Hannerz, Ulf. 1998. "Transnational Research." In *Handbook of Methods in Cultural Anthropology,* edited by H. Russell Bernard, 235–56. Walnut Creek, Calif.: AltaMira Press.

Harris, Olivia. 1978. "The Power of Signs: Gender, Culture, and the Wild in the Bolivian Andes." In *Nature, Culture, and Gender,* edited by Carol P. MacCormack and Marilyn Strathern, 70–94. Cambridge: Cambridge Univ. Press.

Harvey, Penelope. 1994. "Gender, Community, and Confrontation: Power Relations in Ocongate (Southern Peru)." In *Gender, Drink, and Drugs,* edited by Maryon McDonald, 209–33. Oxford: Berg.

Heald, Suzette. 1999. *Manhood and Morality: Sex, Violence, and Ritual in Gisu Society.* London: Routledge.

Heinze, Andrew R. 1990. *Adapting to Abundance: Jewish Immigrants, Mass Consumption, and the Search for American Identity.* New York: Columbia Univ. Press.

Herdt, Gilbert. 1994. *Guardians of the Flute.* Vol. 1, *Idioms of Masculinity.* Chicago: Univ. of Chicago Press.

Herrera, Gioconda, ed. 2001. *Estudios de género.* Quito: FLACSO-Ecuador, ILDIS.

Herrera, Gioconda, María Cristina Carrillo, and Alicia Torres, eds. 2005. *La migración ecuatoriana: Transnacionalismo, redes e identidades.* Quito, Ecuador: FLACSO, Ediciones Abya-Yala.

Heyman, Josiah McConnell. 1990. "The Emergence of the Waged Life Course on the United States–Mexico Border." *American Ethnologist* 17: 348–59.

Hidalgo, Francisco, ed. 2004. *Migraciones: Un juego con cartas marcadas.* Quito, Ecuador: Ediciones Abya-Yala.

Hirsch, Jennifer S. 2003. *A Courtship after Marriage: Sexuality and Love in Mexican Transnational Families.* Berkeley: Univ. of California Press.

Hirschkind, Lynn. 1980. "On Conforming in Cuenca." Ph.D. diss., Department of Anthropology, Univ. of Wisconsin, Madison.

———. 1995. "History of the Indian Population of Cañar." *Colonial Latin American Historical Review* 3 (summer): 311–42.

———. 1999. "Onomastics and the Ethnohistory of Population Replacement in the Southern Ecuadorian Highlands." Paper delivered at the Sixty-fourth Annual Society for American Archaeology Meeting, Chicago.

Hitchcox, Linda. 1993. "Vietnamese Refugees in Hong Kong: Behaviour and Control." In *Migrant Women: Crossing Borders and Changing Identities,* edited by Gina Buijs, 145–60. Oxford: Berg.

Hodgson, Dorothy L., ed. 2001a. *Gendered Modernities: Ethnographic Perspectives.* New York: Palgrave.

———. 2001b. *Once Intrepid Warriors: Gender, Ethnicity, and the Cultural Politics of Maasai Development.* Bloomington: Indiana Univ. Press.

Hondagneu-Sotelo, Pierrette. 1994. *Gendered Transitions: Mexican Experiences of Immigration.* Berkeley: Univ. of California Press.

———. 1999. "Gender and Contemporary Migration." *American Behavioral Scientist* 42, no. 4: 565–76.

———. 2001. *Doméstica: Immigrant Workers Cleaning and Caring in the Shadows of Affluence.* Berkeley: Univ. of California Press.

Hondagneu-Sotelo, Pierrette, and Ernestine Avila. 1997. "'I'm Here, but I'm There': The Meanings of Latina Transnational Motherhood." *Gender and Society* 11, no. 5: 548–71.

Hondagneu-Sotelo, Pierrette, and Cynthia Cranford. 1999. "Gender and Migration." In *Handbook of the Sociology of Gender,* edited by Janet Saltzman Chafetz, 105–26. New York: Kluwer Academic, Plenum.

Hyslop, John. 1984. *The Inka Road System.* Orlando, Fl.: Academic Press.

Idrovo Urigüen, Jaime. 1986. "Tomebamba: Primera fase de conquista en los Andes septentrionales." *Revista del Archivo Nacional de Historia, Sección del Azuay* 6: 49–70.

Immigration and Naturalization Service (INS). 1992. *Statistical Yearbook of the INS, 1990–1992.* Washington, D.C.: U.S. Government Printing Office.

———. 1997. *Statistical Yearbook of the INS, 1997.* Washington, D.C.: U.S. Government Printing Office.

Instituto Nacional de Estadística y Censos (INEC). 2001. *VI censo nacional de población y vivienda.* Quito, Ecuador: INEC.

International Monetary Fund (IMF). 2000. *Ecuador: Selected Issues and Statistical Annex.* Staff Country Report no. 00/125 (October). Washington, D.C.: IMF.

Isbell, Billie Jean. 1978. *To Defend Ourselves: Ecology and Ritual in an Andean Village.* Prospect Heights, Ill.: Waveland Press.

———. 1981. "La otra mitad esencial: Un estudio de complementaridad sexual Andina." *Estudios Andinos* 5, no. 1: 37–56.

Jamieson, Ross W. 2000. *Domestic Architecture and Power: The Historical Archaeology of Colonial Ecuador.* New York: Kluwer Academic and Plenum.

Jokisch, Brad D. 1998. "Landscapes of Remittances: Migration and Agricultural Change in the Highlands of South Central Ecuador." Ph.D. diss., Graduate School of Geography, Clark Univ., Worcester, Mass.

———. 2000. "From New York to Madrid: A Description of Recent Trends in Ecuadorian Emigration." Paper presented at XXIII International Congress of the Latin American Studies Association, Washington, D.C., Sept. 6–8.

———. 2002. "Migration and Agricultural Change: The Case of Smallholder Agriculture in Highland Ecuador." *Human Ecology* 30, no. 4: 523–50.

Jokisch, Brad and David Kyle. 2005. "Transformations in Ecuadorian Transnational Migration 1993–2003." In *Ecuadorian Migration: Transnationalism, Networks, and Identities,* edited by Gioconda Herrera, Maria Crisitina Carillo, and Alicia Torres, 57–70. Quito, Ecuador: FLACSO.

Jokisch, Brad D., and Jason Pribilsky. 2002. "The Panic to Leave: Economic Crisis and the 'New Emigration' from Ecuador." *International Migration* 40, no. 4: 75–101.

Jones-Correa, Michael. 1998. *Between Two Nations: The Political Predicament of Latinos in New York City.* Ithaca, N.Y.: Cornell Univ. Press.

Kanaaneh, Rhoda Ann. 2002. *Birthing the Nation: Strategies of Palestinian Women in Israel.* Berkeley: Univ. of California Press.

Karp, Ivan. 1980. "Beer Drinking and Social Experience in an African Community: An Essay in Experimental Sociology." In *Explorations in African Systems of Thought,* edited by Ivan Karp and Charles S. Bird, 100–120. Bloomington: Indiana Univ. Press.

Kasinitz, Phillip, and Judith Freidenberg-Herbstein. 1987. "The Puerto Rican Parade and West Indian Carnaval: Public Celebrations in New York City." In *Caribbean Life in New York City: Sociocultural Dimensions,* edited by Constance Sutton and Elsa M. Chaney, 327–50. Staten Island, N.Y.: Center for Migration Studies of New York.

Kearney, Michael. 1995. "The Local and the Global: The Anthropology of Globalization and Transnationalism." *Annual Review of Anthropology* 24: 547–65.

———. 1996. *Reconceptualizing the Peasantry: Anthropology in Global Perspective.* Boulder, Colo.: Westview Press.

Kibria, Nazli. 1993. *Family Tightrope: The Changing Lives of Vietnamese Americans.* Princeton, N.J.: Princeton Univ. Press.

Kim, Dae Young. 1999. "Beyond Co-ethnic Solidarity: Mexican and Ecuadorean Employment in Korean-Owned Businesses in New York City." *Ethnic and Racial Studies* 22, no. 3: 581–605.

Knapp, Gregory. 1987. *Geografía Quichua de la sierra del Ecuador.* 2d ed. Quito, Ecuador: Ediciones Abya-Yala.

Kottak, Conrad Phillip. 2003. *Mirror for Humanity: A Concise Introduction to Anthropology.* 3rd ed. Boston: McGraw-Hill.

Krüggeler, Thomas. 1997. "Changing Consumption Patterns and Everyday Life in Two Peruvian Regions: Food, Dress, and Housing in the Central and Southern Highlands (1820–1920)." In *The Allure of the Foreign: Imported Goods in Postcolonial Latin America,* edited by Benjamin Orlove, 31–66. Ann Arbor: Univ. of Michigan Press.

Kulick, Don. 1993. *Travesti: Sex, Gender, and Culture among Brazilian Transgendered Prostitutes.* Chicago: Univ. of Chicago Press.

Kyle, David Jane. 1996. "The Transnational Peasant: The Social Construction of International Economic Migration and Transcommunities from the Ecuadoran Andes." Ph.D. diss., Department of Sociology, Johns Hopkins Univ., Baltimore.

———. 2000. *Transnational Peasants: Migrations, Networks, and Ethnicity in Andean Ecuador.* Baltimore: Johns Hopkins Univ. Press.

Kyle, David, and John Dale. 2001. "Smuggling the State Back In: Agents of Human Smuggling Reconsidered." In *Global Human Smuggling: Comparative Perspectives,* edited by David Kyle and Rey Kosloski, 209–33. Baltimore: Johns Hopkins Univ. Press.

"Labor: Unemployment." 2001. *Migration News* 8, no. 11 (Nov.). Available at: http://migration.ucdavis.edu.

Lamphere, Louise, Filomena M. Silva, and John P. Sousa. 1980. "Kin Networks and Strategies of Working-Class Portuguese Families in a New England Town." In *The Versatility of Kinship: Essays Presented to Harry W. Basehart,* edited by Linda Cordell and Stephen Beckerman, 219–49. New York: Academic Press.

Lamphere, Louise, Helena Ragoné, and Patricia Zavella, eds. 1997. *Situated Lives: Gender and Culture in Everyday Life.* New York: Routledge.

Lancaster, Roger N. 1992. *Life Is Hard: Machismo, Danger, and the Intimacy of Power in Nicaragua.* Berkeley: Univ. of California Press.

Larrea, Carlos. 1998. "Structural Adjustment, Income Distribution, and Employment in Ecuador." In *Poverty, Economic Reform, and Income Distribution in Latin America,* edited by Albert Berry, 179–204. Boulder, Colo.: Lynne Rienner.

Larson, Brooke. 2004. *Trials of Nation Making: Liberalism, Race, and Ethnicity in the Andes, 1810–1910.* Cambridge: Cambridge Univ. Press.

Leacock, Eleanor, ed. 1980. *Women and Colonization.* New York: Praeger.

Lentz, Carola. 1991. *Buscando la vida: Trabajadores temporales en una plantación de azúcar.* Quito, Ecuador: Ediciones Abya-Yala.

———. 1997. *Migración e identidad etnica: La transformación histórica de una comunidad indígena en la sierra ecuatoriana.* Quito, Ecuador: Ediciones Abya-Yala.

León, Luis A., ed. 1983. *Compilación de crónicas, relatos y descripciones de Cuenca y su provincia.* Vol. 1. Cuenca: Ediciones del Banco Central del Ecuador.

León, Natalia. 1997. "Género, matrimonio y sociedad criolla en Cuenca durante la segunda mitad del siglo XVIII." *Procesos* 1, no. 1: 21–42.

Levinson, Bradley A. U. 2001. *We Are All Equal: Student Culture and Identity at a Mexican Secondary School, 1988–1998.* Durham, N.C.: Duke Univ. Press.

Levitt, Peggy. 1998. "Social Remittances: Migration-Driven, Local-Level Forms of Cultural Diffusion." *International Migration Review* 32, no. 4: 926–48.

———. 2001. *God, Ethnicity, and Country: An Approach to the Study of Transnational Religion.* Transnational Communities Programme Working Paper no. 01-13. Oxford: Transnational Communities Programme.

Lind, Amy. 2005. *Gendered Paradoxes: Women's Development, State Restructuring, and Global Development in Ecuador.* University Park: Pennsylvania State Univ. Press.

Logan, Jack R. 2001. *The New Latinos: Who They Are, Where They Are. Report on Metropolitan Racial and Ethnic Change—Census 2000.* Albany, N.Y.: Lewis

Mumford Center for Comparative Urban and Regional Research, Univ. of Albany.

Lomnitz, Larissa. 1977. *Networks and Marginality: Life in a Mexican Shantytown.* New York: Academic Press.

Love, Joseph L., and Nils Jacobsen, eds. 1988. *Guiding the Invisible Hand: Economic Liberalism and the State in Latin America.* New York: Praeger.

Lund Skar, Sarah. 1994. *Lives Together—Worlds Apart: Quechua Colonization in Jungle and City.* Oslo: Scandinavian Univ. Press.

Lutz, Catherine, and Jane L. Collins. 1993. *Reading* National Geographic. Chicago: Univ. of Chicago Press.

Mahler, Sarah. 1995. *American Dreaming: Immigrant Life on the Margins.* Princeton, N.J.: Princeton Univ. Press.

———. 1998. "Theoretical and Empirical Contributions toward a Research Agenda for Transnationalism." In *Transnationalism from Below,* vol. 6, *Comparative Urban and Community Research,* edited by Michael P. Smith and Luis E. Guarnizo, 64–102. New Brunswick, N.J.: Transaction Books.

———. 1999. "Engendering Transnational Migration: The Case of Salvadorans." *American Behavioral Scientist* 42, no. 4: 690–719.

———. 2001. "Suburban Transnational Migrants: Long Island's Salvadorans." In *Migration, Transnationalization, and Race in a Changing New York City,* edited by Héctor R. Cordero-Guzmán, Robert C. Smith, and Ramón Grosfoguel, 109–30. Philadelphia: Temple Univ. Press.

Mankekar, Purnima. 2002. "India Shopping: Indian Grocery Stores and Transnational Configurations of Belonging." *Ethnos* 67, no. 1: 75–98.

Marcus, George E. 1995. "Ethnography in/of the World System: The Emergence of Multi-sited Ethnography." *Annual Reviews of Anthropology* 24: 95–117.

———. 1998. *Ethnography Through Thick and Thin.* Princeton, N.J.: Princeton Univ. Press.

Margold, Jane A. 1995. "Narratives of Masculinity and Transnational Migration: Filipino Workers in the Middle East." In *Bewitching Women, Pious Men: Gender and Body Politics in Southeast Asia,* edited by Aihwa Ong and Michael G. Peletz, 274–98. Berkeley: Univ. of California Press.

Martínez, Luciano. 1984. "Pobreza y migración rural." In *El Ecuador agrario,* edited by Manuel Chiriboga, 105–34. Quito, Ecuador: Ediciones el Conejo.

Martínez Borrero, Juan, and Harald Einzmann. 1993. *La cultura popular en el Ecuador.* Vol. 1, *Azuay.* Cuenca, Ecuador: Centro Interamericano de Artesanías y Artes Populares.

Mauss, Marcel. 1967. *The Gift: The Form and Reason of Exchange in Archaic Societies*. 1950. Reprint. New York: W. W. Norton.

Mayer, Enrique. 2002. *The Articulated Peasant: Household Economies in the Andes*. Boulder, Colo.: Westview Press.

McCracken, Grant. 1988. *Culture and Consumption: New Approaches to the Symbolic Character of Consumer Goods and Activities*. Bloomington: Indiana Univ. Press.

McKee, Lauris. 1980. "Ideals and Actualities: The Socialization of Gender Appropriate Behavior in an Ecuadorian Village." Ph.D. diss., Department of Anthropology, Cornell Univ.

———. 1991. "Men's Rights/Women's Wrongs: Domestic Violence in Ecuador." In *Sanctions and Sanctuary: Cultural Perspectives on the Beating of Wives*, edited by Dorothy Counts, 139–56. Boulder, Colo.: Westview Press.

———. 1997. "Women's Work in Rural Ecuador: Multiple Resource Strategies and the Gendered Division of Labor." In *Women and Economic Change: Andean Perspectives*, edited by Ann Miles and Hans Buechler, 31–54. Society for Latin American Anthropology Publications series, vol. 14. Washington, D.C.: American Anthropological Association.

Mead, Margaret. 1935. *Sex and Temperament in Three Primitive Societies*. New York: William Morrow and Co.

Meisch, Lynn A. 1998. "Azuay Province." In *Costume and Identity in Highland Ecuador*, edited by Ann Pollard Rowe, 254–62. Seattle: Univ. of Washington Press.

Meisch, Lynn A., Laura Miller, and Lynn Hirschkind. 1998. "Cañar Province." In *Costume and Identity in Highland Ecuador*, edited by Ann Pollard Rowe, 230–53. Seattle: Univ. of Washington Press.

Merisalde y Santistéban, Joaquin. 1994. "Relación histórica, política y moral de la ciudad de Cuenca: Población y hermosura de su provincia." 1765. In *Relaciones histórico-geográficas de la Audencia de Quito (siglos XVI–XIX)*, vol. 2, edited by P. Ponce Leiva, 369–412. 1957. Reprint. Quito, Ecuador: Ediciones Abya-Yala.

"Migración equivale a desintegrar la familia." 1998. *El Mercurio* (Cuenca, Ecuador), Mar. 6, 4B.

Miles, Ann. 1991. "'Our Culture Depends on Yours': Poor Families and the Social Construction of Class and Gender Ideologies in Cuenca, Ecuador." Ph.D. diss., Department of Anthropology, Syracuse Univ., Syracuse, N.Y.

———. 1992. "Pride and Prejudice: The Urban Chola and the Transmission of Class and Gender Ideologies in Cuenca, Ecuador." In *Balancing Acts: Women and*

Process of Social Change, edited by Patricia Lyons Johnson, 120–39. Boulder, Colo.: Westview Press.

———. 1994. "Helping Out at Home: Gender Socialization, Moral Development, and Devil Stories in Cuenca, Ecuador." *Ethos* 22, no. 2: 132–57.

———. 1997. "The High Cost of Leaving: Illegal Emigration from Cuenca, Ecuador, and Family Separation." In *Women and Economic Change: Andean Perspectives,* edited by Ann Miles and Hans Buechler, 55–74. Society for Latin American Anthropology Publications series, vol. 14. Washington, D.C.: American Anthropological Association.

———. 2004. *From Cuenca to Queens: An Anthropological Story of Transnational Migration.* Austin: Univ. of Texas Press.

Miles, Ann, and Hans Buechler. 1997. "Introduction." In *Women and Economic Change: Andean Perspectives,* edited by Ann Miles and Hans Buechler, 1–12. Society for Latin American Anthropology Publications series, vol. 14. Washington, D.C.: American Anthropological Association.

Miller, Daniel. 1987. *Material Culture and Mass Consumption.* Oxford: Blackwell.

———. 1995. "Consumption Studies as the Transformation of Anthropology." In *Acknowledging Consumption: A Review of New Studies,* edited by Daniel Miller, 264–95. New York: Routledge.

———. 1998. *A Theory of Shopping.* Cambridge: Polity Press.

Miller, Tom. 1986. *The Panama Hat Trail: A Journey from South America.* New York: William Morrow and Co.

Millones, Luis, and Mary Louise Pratt. 1990. *Amor Brujo: Images of Culture and Love in the Andes.* Foreign and Comparative Studies, Latin American Studies series no. 10. Syracuse, N.Y.: Maxwell School of Citizenship and Public Affairs.

Mills, Mary Beth. 1999. *Thai Women in the Global Labor Force: Consuming Desires, Contested Selves.* New Brunswick, N.J.: Rutgers Univ. Press.

Monsalve Pozo, Luís. 1953. *El sombrero de paja toquilla.* Annales de la Universidad de Cuenca. 1944. Reprint. Cuenca, Ecuador: Universidad de Cuenca.

———. 1957. *Memorias de primer congreso de sociología ecuatoriana.* Vol. 1. Cuenca, Ecuador: Universidad de Cuenca.

Montaya, Rosario, Lessie Jo Frazier, and Janise Hurtig, eds. 2002. *Gender's Place: Feminist Anthropologies of Latin America.* New York: Palgrave.

Moodie, Dunbar (with V. Ndatshe). 1994. *Going for Gold: Men, Mines, and Migration.* Berkeley: Univ. of California Press.

Morokvasic, Mirjana. 1984. "Birds of Passage Are Also Women." *International Migration Review* 18, no. 4: 886–907.

Moser, Donald L. 1991. "Macho Men, Machismo, and Sexuality." *Annual Review of Sex Research* 2: 199–247.

Murra, John. 1946. "The Historic Tribes of Ecuador." In *Handbook of South American Indians*, vol. 2, edited by Julian H. Steward, 785–821. Washington, D.C.: Smithsonian Institution.

———. 1972. "El control vertical de un máximo de pisos ecológicos en la economía de las sociedades andinas." In *Iñigo Ortiz de Zúñiga, visita de la provincia de León de Huánuco en 1562*, vol. 2, edited by John V. Murra, 427–76. Huánuco, Peru: Universidad Nacional Hermilo Valdizán.

———. 1973. "Rite and Crop in the Inca State." In *Peoples and Cultures of Native South America*, edited by Daniel R. Gross, 393–407. New York: Natural History Press.

Nash, June. 1986. "A Decade of Research on Women in Latin America." In *Women and Change in Latin America*, edited by June Nash and Helen Safa, 3–21. South Hadley, Mass.: Bergin and Garvey.

———. 1999. "The Transformation of Gender Roles in Migration." *Latino(a) Research Review* 4, nos. 1–2: 2–15.

Netting, Robert M., Richard R. Wilk, and Eric J. Arnould, eds. 1984. *Households: Comparative and Historical Studies of the Domestic Group*. Berkeley: Univ. of California Press.

New York City Department of City Planning. 1999. *The Newest New Yorkers: A Report on New Immigrants in New York City, 1995–1996*. New York: New York City Department of City Planning.

North, Liisa L. 1999. "Austerity and Disorder in the Andes." *NACLA Report on the Americas* 33, no. 1: 6–9.

North, Liisa L., and John D. Cameron, eds. 2003. *Rural Progress, Rural Decay: Neoliberal Adjustment Policies and Local Initiatives*. Bloomfield, Conn.: Kumarian Press.

Nuñez del Prado Béjar, Daisy Irene. 1975. "El poder de decisión de la mujer quechua andina." *América Indígena* 35: 623–30.

Ochoa Ordóñez, Lenora. 1998. "Repercusiones psicológicas en los escolares de 6 a 12 años por abandono, debido a la migración de sus padres a los EE.UU: Sector del Portete-Azuay, 1997–1998." Master's thesis, Universidad de Azuay, Cuenca, Ecuador.

Ong, Aihwa. 1987. *Spirits of Resistance and Capitalist Discipline: Factory Women in Malaysia*. Albany: State Univ. of New York Press.

———. 1991. "Gender and the Labor Politics of Postmodernity." *Annual Review of Anthropology* 20: 279–309.

Orellana, Marjorie Faulstich, Barrie Thorne, Anna Chee, and Wan Shun Eva Lam. 2001. "Transnational Childhoods: The Participation of Children in Processes of Family Migration." *Social Problems* 48, no. 4: 572–91.

Orozco, Manuel. 2001. "Family Remittances to Latin America: The Marketplace and Its Changing Dynamics." Paper presented at the Inter-American Development Bank conference "Remittances as a Development Tool," Washington, D.C., May 17–18.

Ortner, Sherry. 1984. "Theory in Anthropology since the Sixties." *Comparative Studies in Society and History* 26, no. 1: 126–66.

Ortner, Sherry, and Harriet Whitehead, eds. 1981. *Sexual Meanings.* Cambridge: Cambridge Univ. Press.

Osella, Filippo, and Caroline Osella. 2000. "Migration, Money, and Masculinity." *Journal of the Royal Anthropological Institute* (n.s.) 6: 117–33.

Paerregaard, Karsten. 2001. *In the Footsteps of the Lord of Miracles: The Expatriation of Religious Icons in the Peruvian Diaspora.* Working Paper no. 01-02. Oxford: Transnational Communities Programme.

Pájara Pinta, comp. 1996. *El amor en el maíz: Migración, sexualidad y VIH-SIDA en comunidades rurales de Azuay y Cañar.* Cuenca, Ecuador: Pájara Pinta.

Palomeque, Silvia. 1982. "Histórica económica de Cuenca y sus relaciones regionales." In *Ensayos sobre historia regional en la región centro sur,* edited by Claudio Cordero, 117–40. Cuenca, Ecuador: Casa de la Cultura Ecuatoriana, Núcleo del Azuay, IDIS.

———. 1990. *Cuenca en el siglo XIX: La articulación de una region.* Quito, Ecuador: Ediciones Abya-Yala, FLACSO.

Parreñas, Rachel Salazar. 2001. *Servants of Globalization: Women, Migration, and Domestic Work.* Stanford: Stanford Univ. Press.

"Patron Saint Festival Creates Sense of Home for Ecuadoreans." 1999. *Westchester Journal News,* Dec. 10, 1B, 4B.

Peiss, Kathy. 1986. *Cheap Amusements: Working Women and Leisure in Turn-of-the-Century New York.* Philadelphia: Temple Univ. Press.

Peletz, Michael G. 1996. *Reason and Passion: Representations of Gender in a Malay Society.* Berkeley: Univ. of California Press.

Peña, Manuel. 1991. "Class, Gender, and Machismo: The 'Treacherous-Woman' Folklore of Mexican Male Workers." *Gender and Society* 5, no. 1: 30–46.

Pessar, Patricia R. 1982. "The Role of Households in International Migration and the Case of U.S. Bound Migration from the Dominican Republic." *International Migration Review* 16, no. 2: 342–63.

———. 1986. "The Role of Gender in Dominican Settlement in the United States." In *Women and Change in Latin America*, edited by June Nash and Helen Safa, 273–94. South Hadley, Mass.: Bergin and Garvey.

———. 1998. "The Role of Gender, Households, and Social Networks in the Migration Process: A Review and Appraisal." In *Becoming American/America Becoming*, edited by Josh DeWind, Charles Hirschman, and Philip Kasinitz, 53–70. New York: Russell Sage Foundation.

———. 1999. "Engendering Migration Studies: The Case of New Immigrants in the United States." *American Behavioral Scientist* 42, no. 4: 577–600.

Phelan, John Leddy. 1967. *The Kingdom of Quito in the Seventeenth Century: Bureaucratic Politics in the Spanish Empire*. Madison: Univ. of Wisconsin Press.

Pinos A., Guido, and Leonora Ochoa O. 1999. "Migración y salud." *Revista de la Facultud de Ciencias Medicas* (Cuenca, Ecuador) 23, no. 1: 7–17.

Piore, Michael J. 1979. *Birds of Passage: Migrant Labor and Industrial Societies*. London: Cambridge Univ. Press.

Portes, Alejandro, Luis E. Guarnizo, and Patricia Landolt. 1999. "The Study of Transnationalism: Pitfalls and Promise of an Emergent Research Field." *Ethnic and Racial Studies* 22, no. 2: 217–37.

Portes, Alejandro, and Rúben G. Rumbaut. 1996. *Immigrant America: A Portrait*. Berkeley: Univ. of California Press.

———. 2001. *Legacies: The Story of the Immigrant Second Generation*. Berkeley: Univ. of California Press.

Potter, David M. 1966. *People of Plenty: Economic Abundance and the American Character*. 1954. Reprint. Chicago: Univ. of Chicago Press.

Preston, David. 1974. *Emigration and Change: Experience in Southern Ecuador*. Working Paper no. 52. Leeds, England: Univ. of Leeds, January.

Pribilsky, Jason. 1999. "The Health of Transnational Populations: Ecuadorian Migrants and the Import/Export of Disease." *Anthropology News* 40: 69–71.

———. 2001a. *Indigenous Cañari Migrants in Suburban New York: Preliminary Ethnographic Assessment of Undocumented Labor, Health Status, and Transnational Ties*. Consultation report. New City, N.Y.: Rockland County Health Department.

———. 2001b. "Nervios and 'Modern' Childhood: Migration and Changing Contexts of Child Life in the Ecuadorian Andes." *Childhood* 8, no. 2: 251–73.

———. 2002. "Living the Chulla Vida." In *Personal Encounters: A Reader in Cultural Anthropology*, edited by Linda S. Walbridge and April K. Sievert, 74–79. Boston: McGraw-Hill.

Price, Richard. 1965. "Trial Marriage in the Andes." *Ethnology* 4, no. 3: 310–22.

Prieto, Mercedes. 2004. *Liberalismo y temor: Imaginando los sujetos indígenas en el Ecuador postcolonial, 1895–1950.* Quito, Ecuador: FLACSO, Ediciones Abya-Yala.

Radcliffe, Anne. 1986. "Gender Relations, Peasant Livelihood Strategies, and Migration: A Case Study from Cuzco, Peru." *Bulletin of Latin American Research* 5: 29–47.

Radcliffe, Sarah, and Sallie Westwood. 1996. *Remaking the Nation: Place, Identity, and Politics in Latin America.* London: Routledge.

Rahier, Jean Muteba. 1998. "Blackness, the 'Racial'/Spatial Order, Migrations, and Miss Ecuador 1995–1996." *American Anthropologist* 100, no. 2: 421–30.

Ramírez, Susan E. 1995. "Exchange and Markets in the Sixteenth Century: A View from the North." In *Ethnicity, Markets, and Migration in the Andes: At the Crossroads of History and Anthropology*, edited by Brooke Larson and Olivia Harris (with Enrique Tandeter), 135–64. Durham, N.C.: Duke Univ. Press.

———. 1996. *The World Upside Down: Cross-Cultural Contact and Conflict in Sixteenth-Century Peru.* Stanford, Calif.: Stanford Univ. Press.

Rapp Reiter, Rayna. 1975a. "Men and Women in the South of France: Public and Private Domains." In *Toward an Anthropology of Women*, edited by Rayna Rapp Reiter, 252–83. New York: Monthly Review Press.

———, ed. 1975b. *Toward an Anthropology of Women.* New York: Monthly Review Press.

——— [Rapp, Rayna]. 1979. "Examining Family History: Household and Family." *Feminist Studies* 5: 175–81.

"Los réditos escondidos de la migración de ecuatorianos." 2001. *Líderes* 3, no. 191: 7–9.

Reichart, Joshua S. 1981. "Migrant Syndrome: Seasonal U.S. Wage Labor and Rural Development in Central Mexico." *Human Organization* 40: 56–67.

Rodas, Hernán. 1985. "La migración campesina en el Azuay." *Ecuador Debate* 8 (April): 155–93.

Rosaldo, Michelle. 1980. "The Use and Abuse of Anthropology: Reflections on Feminism and Cross-Cultural Understanding." *Signs* 5, no. 3: 389–417.

Rosaldo, Michelle, and Louise Lamphere, eds. 1974. *Women, Culture, and Society.* Stanford, Calif.: Stanford Univ. Press.

Rostow, W. W. 1960. *The Stages of Growth: A Non-Communist Manifesto.* Cambridge: Cambridge Univ. Press.

Rothenberg, Jerome. 1977. "On the Microeconomics of Migration." In *Internal Migration: A Comparative Perspective,* edited by Alan A. Brown and Egon Neuberger, 183–205. New York: Academic Press.

Rouse, Roger. 1989. "Mexican Migration to the United States: Family Relations in the Development of a Transnational Migration Circuit." Ph.D. diss., Department of Anthropology, Stanford Univ.

———. 1990. "Men in Space: Power and the Appropriation of Urban Form among Mexican Migrants in the United States." Unpublished manuscript, Department of Anthropology, Univ. of California, Davis.

———. 1991. "Mexican Migration and the Social Space of Postmodernism." *Diaspora* 1, no. 1: 8–23.

Sachs, Susan. 2002. "Immigrants See Paths to Riches in Phone Cards." *New York Times,* Aug. 11, 1, 30.

Sackett, Theodore Alan. 1988. "Texturas, formas y lenguas." In *Jorge Icaza, el Chulla Romero y Flores,* edición crítica, edited by Richardo Descalzi and Renaud Richard, 299–315. Paris: Colección Archivos.

Safa, Helen. 1981. "The Differential Incorporation of Hispanic Women Migrants into the United States Labor Force." In *Female Immigrants to the United States,* edited by Delores M. Morlimer, 235–66. Washington, D.C.: Research Institute on Immigration and Ethnic Studies, Smithsonian Institution.

Salih, Ruba. 2002. "Shifting Meanings of 'Home': Consumption and Identity in Moroccan Women's Transnational Practices Between Italy and Morocco." In *New Approaches to Migration? Transnational Communities and the Transformation of Home,* edited by Nadje Al-Ali and Khalid Koser, 51–67. London: Routledge.

Salomon, Frank. 1987. "Ancestors, Grave Robbers, and the Possible Antecedents of Cañari 'Inca-ism.'" In *Natives and Neighbors in South America: Anthropological Essays,* edited by Harold O. Skar and Frank Salomon, 207–32. Etnologiska Studier, vol. 38. Gothenburg, Sweden: Etnografiska Museum.

———. 2004. *The Cord Keepers: Khipus and Cultural Life in a Peruvian Village.* Durham, N.C.: Duke Univ. Press.

Sánchez-Parga, José. 1997. *Antropo-lógicas andinas.* Quito, Ecuador: Ediciones Abya-Yala.

Sanjek, Roger. 1998. *The Future of Us All: Race and Neighborhood Politics in New York City.* Ithaca, N.Y.: Cornell Univ. Press.

Sassen, Saskia. 1984. "Notes on the Incorporation of Third World Women into Wage Labor Through Off-shore Production." *International Migration Review* 18, no. 4: 1144–167.

———. 1991. *The Global City: New York, London, Tokyo.* Princeton, N.J.: Princeton Univ. Press.

Sawyer, Susana. 2004. *Crude Chronicles: Indigenous Politics, Multinational Oil, and Neoliberalism in Ecuador.* Durham, N.C.: Duke Univ. Press.

Schodt, David W. 1987. *Ecuador: An Andean Enigma.* Boulder, Colo.: Westview Press.

Seligmann, Linda J. 1989. "To Be in Between: The Cholas as Market-Women." *Comparative Studies in Society and History* 31, no. 4: 696–721.

Selmeski, Brian R. 2000. *Imágenes impresionantes* (Remarkable Impressions) (documentary). New York: Latin American Video Archives.

Sempértegui M., Efrén. 1991. "La situación de la familia y su realidad frente al problema migratorio en la parroquia Déleg, provincia del Cañar, durante el año 1989." Master's thesis, Department of Political Science, Universidad de Cuenca, Azuay.

Setel, Phillip. 1999. *A Plague of Paradoxes: AIDS, Culture, and Demography in Northern Tanzania.* Chicago: Univ. of Chicago Press.

Silverblatt, Irene. 1987. *Moon, Sun, and Witches: Gender Ideologies and Class in Inca and Colonial Peru.* Princeton, N.J.: Princeton Univ. Press.

Singer, Merrill. 1999. "Studying Hidden Populations." In *Mapping Social Networks, Spatial Data, and Hidden Populations,* contributions by Jean J. Shensul, Margaret D. LeCompte, Robert T. Trotter II, Ellen K. Cromley, and Merrill Singer, 125–91. Walnut Creek, Calif.: AltiMira Press.

Smith, Joan, Immanuel Wallerstein, and Hans-Dieter Evers, eds. 1984. *Households and the World Economy.* Beverly Hills, Calif.: Sage.

Smith, Michael Peter, and Luis Eduardo Guarnizo, eds. 1998. *Transnationalism from Below.* Vol. 6, *Comparative Urban and Community Research.* New Brunswick, N.J.: Transaction Books.

Soja, Edward J. 1996. *Thirdspace: Journeys to Los Angeles and Other Real-and-Imagined Places.* Oxford: Blackwell.

Stack, Carol. 1974. *All Our Kin: Strategies for Survival in a Black Community.* New York: Basic Books.

Starn, Orin. 1999. *Nightwatch: The Politics of Protest in the Andes.* Durham, N.C.: Duke Univ. Press.

Statman, Mark. 1989. "La mayoría viene acá por el dinero." *Hoy* (Quito, Ecuador), Jan. 1, 10A.

Stavenhagen, Rodolfo, and Diego Iturralde, eds. 1993. *Entre la ley y la costumbre.* Mexico City: Instituto Indigenista Iberoamericano.

Stephenson, Marcia. 1999. *Gender and Modernity in Andean Bolivia.* Austin: Univ. of Texas Press.

Stølen, Kristi Ann. 1987. *A media voz: Relaciones de género en la sierra ecuatoriana.* Quito, Ecuador: CEPLAES.

———. 1991. "Gender, Sexuality, and Violence in Ecuador." *Ethnos* 58, no. 1: 82–100.

Stoller, Paul. 1997. "Globalizing Method." *Anthropology and Humanism* 17, no. 1: 81–95.

Striffler, Steve. 2002. *In the Shadows of State and Capital: The United Fruit Company, Popular Struggle, and Agrarian Restructuring in Ecuador, 1900–1995.* Durham, N.C.: Duke Univ. Press.

Sweetman, Caroline, ed. 1997. *Men and Masculinity.* Oxford: Oxfam.

Talwar, Jennifer Parker. 2002. *Fast Food, Fast Track: Immigrants, Big Business, and the American Dream.* Boulder, Colo.: Westview Press.

Thompson, E. P. 1967. "Time, Work-Discipline, and Industrial Capitalism." *Past and Present* 38: 56–97.

Tousignant, Michel. 1984. "Pena in the Ecuadorian Sierra: A Psychoanthropological Analysis of Sadness." *Culture, Medicine, and Psychiatry* 8: 381–98.

Turner, Victor. 1967. "Betwixt and Between: The Liminal Period in Rites de Passage." In *Forest of Symbols: Aspects of Ndembu Ritual,* by Victor Turner, 93–111. Ithaca, N.Y.: Cornell Univ. Press.

Urgilez, Hernán, Juan J. Ambrosi, and Carlos Flores (SOLSIDA). 1996. "La migración como un factor de riesgo para contraer VIH-SIDA en las provincias de Azuay y Cañar—1996." In *El amor en el maíz: Migración, sexualidad y VIH-SIDA en comunidades de Azuay y Cañar,* compiled by Pájara Pinta, 91–99. Cuenca, Ecuador: Pájara Pinta.

U.S. Bureau of the Census. 2000. *2000 Census of Population: Foreign-born Population in the United States.* Washington, D.C.: Government Printing Office.

Vale de Almeida, Miguel. 1996. *The Hegemonic Male: Masculinity in a Portuguese Town.* Providence, R.I.: Berghahn Books.

Valenzuela, Abel, Jr., and Edwin Meléndez. 2003. *Day Labor in New York: Findings from NYDL Survey.* Report. Los Angeles: Center for the Study of Urban

Poverty, Univ. of California, Los Angeles, and the Community Development Research Center, New School Univ.

Van Gennep, Arnold. 1960. *The Rites of Passage*. Chicago: Univ. of Chicago Press.

Vasquez, Monica. 1988. *Tiempo de las mujeres* (video). New York: Women Make Movies, Inc.

Veblen, Thorstien. 1953. *The Theory of the Leisure Class*. 1899. Reprint. New York: Mentor Books.

Vega, Felipe. 1996. "Una vista de ojos: al la historia de nuestra cultura sexual." In *El amor in el maíz: Migracion, sexualidad y VIH-SIDA en comunidades rurales de Azuay y Cañar*, compiled by Páraja Pinta, 29–46. Cuenca, Ecuador: Ediciones de Centro Cultural Pájara Pinta.

Vega Delgado, Gustavo. 1998. "El maíz: Un hilo conductor de la presencia andina en la Cuenca de hoy." In *Cuenca en los Andes*, edited by Rodrigo Aguilar Orejuela, 24–27. Cuenca, Ecuador: Monsalve Moreno.

Vintimilla, María. 1982. "Las formas de resistencia campesina en la sierra sur del Ecuador." In *Ensayos sobre historia regional: La región centro-sur*, edited by Claudio Cordero, 141–77. Cuenca, Ecuador: Casa de la Cultura Ecuatoriana, Núcleo del Azuay, IDIS.

Vizuete, Victor. 2000. *Cronología (21 de enero: La vorágine que acabó con Mahuad)*. Quito, Ecuador: El Comercio.

Weismantel, Mary J. 1988. *Food, Gender, and Poverty in the Ecuadorian Andes*. Philadelphia: Univ. of Pennsylvania Press.

———. 1989. "Making Breakfast and Raising Babies: The Zumbagua Household as Constituted Process." In *The Household Economy: Reconsidering the Domestic Mode of Production*, edited by Richard Wilk, 55–72. Boulder, Colo.: Westview Press.

———. 1991. "Maize Beer and Andean Social Transformations: Drunken Indians, Bread Babies, and Chosen Women." *Modern Language Notes* 106, no. 40: 861–79.

———. 1997a. "Corpus Christi: Masculinity, Ecology, and the Calendar in Andean Ecuador." *Journal of the Steward Anthropological Society* 25, nos. 1–2: 124–42.

———. 1997b. "Time, Work-Discipline, and Beans: Indigenous Self-Determination in the Northern Andes." In *Women and Economic Change: Andean Perspectives*, edited by Ann Miles and Hans Buechler, 31–54. Society for Latin American Anthropology Publications series, vol. 14. Washington, D.C.: American Anthropological Association.

———. 2001. *Cholas and Pishtacos: Stories of Race and Sex in the Andes*. Chicago: Univ. of Chicago Press.

Weiss, Wendy A. 1985. "The Social Organization of Property and Work: A Study of Migrants from the Rural Ecuadorian Sierra." *American Ethnologist* 12, no. 3: 468–88.

———. 1988. *The Structure of, and Contradictions in, Male Authority in Urban Households of Quito, Ecuador*. Michigan State Univ. Manuscript Series. Working Paper no. 163 (March). East Lansing: Michigan State University.

———. 1997. "Debt and Devaluation: The Burden of Ecuador's Popular Classes." *Latin American Perspectives* 24, no. 4: 9–33.

Weist, Raymond E. 1973. "Wage-Labor Migration and Households in Town." *Journal of Anthropological Research* 29, no. 3: 180–209.

Whitten, Norman, and Diego Quiroga (with P. Rafael Savoia). 1995. "Ecuador." In *No Longer Invisible: Afro-Latin Americans Today*, edited by Minority Rights Group, 287–317. London: Minority Rights Publications.

Wilk, Richard R., ed. 1989. *The Household Economy: Reconsidering the Domestic Mode of Production*. Boulder, Colo.: Westview Press.

Wilk, Richard, and Stephen Miller. 1997. "Some Methodological Issues in Counting Communities and Households." *Human Organization* 56, no. 1: 64–70.

Willis, Katie, and Brenda Yeoh. 2000. "Introduction." In *Gender and Migration*, edited by Katie Willis and Brenda Yeoh, xi–xxii. Cheltenham, England: Edward Elgar.

Winnik, Louis. 1990. *New People in Old Neighborhoods: The Role of Immigrants in Rejuvenating New York's Communities*. New York: Russell Sage.

Wolf, Diane L. 1991. "Does Father Know Best? A Feminist Critique of Household Strategy Research." *Research in Rural Sociology and Development* 5: 29–43.

———. 1992. *Factory Daughters: Gender, Household Dynamics, and Rural Industrialization in Java*. Berkeley: Univ. of California Press.

Wray, Alberto, ed. 1993. *Derecho, pueblos indígenas y reforma del estado*. Quito, Ecuador: Ediciones Abya-Yala.

Zambrano Castillo, Guido. 1998. *El sueño americano: Los inmigrantes ecuatorianos en New York*. Guayaquil, Ecuador: Corporación de Investigacion, Liderazgo, y Desarrollo Ecuatoriano.

Zelizer , Viviana A. 1994. *Pricing the Priceless Child: The Social Value of Children*. New York: Basic Books.

Zuidema, R. Tom. 1977. "The Inca Kinship System: A New Theoretical Overview." In *Andean Kinship and Marriage*, edited by Ralph Bolton and Enrique Mayer,

240–81. American Anthropological Association Special Publications no. 7. Washington, D.C.: American Anthropological Association.

Zukin, Sharon (with L. Amdur, J. Baus, P. Cho, D. Conley, S. Duncombe, H. Joseph, D. Kessler, J. Parker, and H. Song). 1995. "Artists and Immigrants in New York City Restaurants." In *The Cultures of Cities,* by Sharon Zukin, 153–86. Oxford: Blackwell.

Index

Migration: to coastal plantations, 54, 56, 63–64; Ecuadorians to the U.S., 7, 177–78; and effect on women's status, 265–66; organization for (Queens, N.Y.), 175; to Spain, 9; theories of, 10
Miles, Ann, 128
Miller, Daniel, 206, 243
Mills, Mary Beth, 208–9
Mingas, 90, 93; importance of alcohol at, 100, 226
Minifundio, 38, 49, 51, 52, 136; definition of, 51n. 12, effect of agrarian reform on, 65. *See also* Agriculture
Mining, 49
Mishquiri, Alfredo, 155–56
Mitamae, 48
Modernity, 12. *See also Iony*
Modernization, 41; and liberal revolution, 59
Money, 5, 29; and budgets, 211; difficulty distinguishing U.S., 284; frustrations over, 211; and migrant savings practices, 210–17, 233
Monsalve Pozo, Manuel, 61, 62n. 19, 63
Moodie, Dunbar, 18
Mother's Day, 215, 241
Movimiento de Defensa de los Migrantes-Azuay (MODEMI), 288-89
Multisited fieldwork, 30
Mural art, 170–71; depicting migrant resistance, 169
Murra, John V., 98

Nash, June, 14
National Geographic (magazine), 43n. 8
Ñaupa tiempos, 5, 68, 85, 89, 102, 109, 126

Neboa Bejarano, Gustavo (vice president), 284
Nervios, 235n. 20, 256, 268
New Latinos, 8
New York City, 1, 160, 171–75, 204; clothing factories in, 193–94; Ecuadorian community in, 177; idyllic images of, 217; link to Panama hat trade, 67, 117; number of Ecuadorians in, 173–74; as research site, 29–31; restaurant work in, 82, 175. *See also* Queens, N.Y.
NGO (nongovernmental organization), 25; in Jatundeleg, 89, 91
9/11, 30, 31n. 21, 287
Nobles, 41, 49; critique of migration, 114
Nuestro folklórico, 41, 44, 68, 97, 125–26; as challenged by conspicuous consumption, 72, 115
Nueva generación, 3, 81, 139, 141, 223

Obrajes, 48; collapse of, 52
Oil revenue, 9
Orozco, Manuel, 216n. 7

Packaged food, 86, 87
Palibriar (proposal of marriage), 146
Panama hats. *See Sombreros de Paja toquilla*
Pañora, Caesar, 162
Pañora, Manuel, 245
Pañora, Sandra, 81, 114
Pañora, Segundo, 106
Pasadores (coyotes), 162, 163, 165, 167–68
Passports: issuance in Ecuador, 9n. 11
Patrilocality, 141n. 6